Globalisation
and legal theory

Law in Context

Editors: William Twining (University College London) and
Christopher McCrudden (Lincoln College, Oxford)

Globalisation
and legal theory

William Twining
Research Professor of Law, University College London

Butterworths
London, Edinburgh, Dublin
2000

United Kingdom	Butterworths, a Division of Reed Elsevier (UK) Ltd, Halsbury House, 35 Chancery Lane, LONDON WC2A 1EL and 4 Hill Street, EDINBURGH EH2 3JZ
Australia	Butterworths, a Division of Reed International Books Australia Pty Ltd, CHATSWOOD, New South Wales
Canada	Butterworths Canada Ltd, MARKHAM, Ontario
Hong Kong	Butterworths Asia (Hong Kong), HONG KONG
India	Butterworths India, NEW DELHI
Ireland	Butterworth (Ireland) Ltd, DUBLIN
Malaysia	Malayan Law Journal Sdn Bhd, KUALA LUMPUR
New Zealand	Butterworths of New Zealand Ltd, WELLINGTON
Singapore	Butterworths Asia, SINGAPORE
South Africa	Butterworths Publishers (Pty) Ltd, DURBAN
USA	Lexis Law Publishing, CHARLOTTESVILLE, Virginia

A member of the Reed Elsevier plc group

A CIP Catalogue record for this book is available from the British Library.

ISBN 0 406 91359 5

Printed by Hobbs the Printers Ltd, Totton, Hampshire

Visit us at our website: http://www.butterworths.co.uk

To Terry Anderson

Acknowledgments

These essays were written over a period of nearly 10 years, during which I benefited from many kinds of help, advice and criticism from more people than I can list. Some of these debts were acknowledged when particular essays were first published. Thanks are due to librarians, especially the law librarians, at University College London, Boston College, Boston University, the University of Miami Law School, and the Center for Advanced Study in the Behavioral Sciences at Stanford. The author and publishers thank the following for their permission to reproduce copyright material: Ashgate publishers, Harcourt Brace, Oxford University Press, Routledge, SLS Legal Publications (Northern Ireland), and the editors of the Brooklyn Law Review, the Maastricht Journal for Europe and Comparative Law, and Tidsskrift for Rettsvitensdkap. Some material in chapter 3 was reproduced from 48 University of Miami Law Review 119 (1993) which holds copyright in the original article.

I am particularly grateful to students in seminars in Boston, Miami and London where many of my ideas were first tested out. Also to colleagues in Faculty seminars in Berkeley, Boston, Capetown, Cardozo Law School, Hong Kong, London, Maastricht, Miami, Tilburg and Warwick for many helpful suggestions and questions. I owe a general debt to Terry Anderson, Susan Haack, Michael Likovsky and Joseph Perkovitch. My wife, as ever, provided constant support, encouragement, and practical help.

This book was completed while I was a Fellow at the Center for Advanced Study in the Behavioral Sciences at Stanford. I am especially grateful for the marvellous support provided by the Center and its staff.

WLT

Stanford, *December 1999*

Contents

Chapter 4

Jeremy Bentham and general jurisprudence   91

Chapter 5

Other people's power: the bad man and English positivism, 1897–1997   108

Table of abbreviations

Some of the points and themes in the text are treated at greater length in other writings by the author. The following abbreviations are used in the notes:

ALLP   'Academic Law and Legal Philosophy: the Significance of Herbert Hart' 95 LQR 557 (1979)

ANALYSIS   *Analysis of Evidence* (with Terence Anderson, London and Chicago, 1991, 1998)

CCC   'Constitutions, Constitutionalism and Constitution-mongering' in Irwin P Stotzky, *Transition to Democracy in Latin America: The Role of the Judiciary* (Boulder, 1993), ch 25

HTDTWR   *How to Do Things With Rules* (with David Miers, 4th ed, London, 1999)

JJM   'The Job of Juristic Method: A Tribute to Karl Llewellyn' 48 *University of Miami Law Review* 601 (1993)

KLRM   *Karl Llewellyn and the Realist Movement* (London and Oklahoma, 1973, 1985)

LIC   *Law in Context: Enlarging a Discipline* (Oxford, 1997)

LTCL   *Legal Theory and Common Law* (ed, Oxford, 1986)

OPP   'Other People's Power: The Bad Man and English Positivism 1897-1997' 63 Brooklyn L Rev 189 (1997)

RB   'Reading Bentham' Maccabean Lectures, 75 *Proceedings of the British Academy* (1989), at 97-141

RE   *Rethinking Evidence* (Oxford, 1990; Chicago and London, 1994)

TAR   'Talk about Realism' 60 *New York University Law Review* 329 (1985)

Chapter 1

Introduction

1 A NEW WORLD?

One way of introducing students to the study of law is to ask them to read every word in a daily newspaper and to mark all the passages that they think deal with law or are 'law-related'.[1] They nearly always have difficulty in deciding what to include and what to leave unmarked. Even those who adopt a narrow conception of law find it on every page: on the sports pages bodies such as football clubs, national tennis associations, or international sporting bodies (IOC, FIFA, etc) issue decrees, negotiate, litigate, or are even accused of corruption. Professional players deal with sponsors, sack their agents, or are 'bought' and 'sold', disciplined, charged with drug abuse, or involved in labour disputes. On the arts pages pornography, copyright, defamation, and other issues relating to freedom of expression arise along with licensing, charities law, taxation, and the ubiquitous contract. The advertisements are permeated with legal words and phrases. And so on through the paper.

Students quickly recognise that law is pervasive in society and in many aspects of their lives and that, far from being new to them, they have experienced it directly from birth as bearers of children's rights, contractees, trespassers, consumers, debtors, copyright violators, internet surfers, protesters, criminals, and victims. This newspaper exercise illustrates how law is pervasive, dynamic, important, complex, and interesting. It also brings home that it is not only domestic law that features in their newspapers. Public and private international law, human rights, religious law, and many kinds of 'foreign law' bear directly on the

1 The newspaper exercise is discussed in detail in *BT*, pp 4-11 and *LIC*, pp 210-213. For the key to abbreviations used in the footnotes see p xi above.

news, in the financial, sports, features, and other sections as well as on the pages dealing with foreign or international news.

A variant on this exercise is to ask of a newspaper or magazine: how many of the events, processes, and transactions that are reported or discussed involve relations that cross geographical boundaries, such as those of the local district, a county or other administrative unit, a state or province, a nation state, a regional grouping (such as the European Union), and so on. It would not be surprising to find a cosmopolitan publication, such as the *Economist*, or *Newsweek*, *The Wall Street Journal* or *The Manchester Guardian Weekly*, regularly and persistently moving between and across local, national, inter-communal, transnational, international, regional, and global relations, and even extending into outer space. What may be more surprising is to look at one's local paper in this way. It is not nearly as parochial as one might expect. As I write this, I glance at the latest edition of the local newspaper, the *Palo Alto Weekly*. I find items not only about local crime, by-elections, and parish pump issues, but also about foreign films, 'ethnic' restaurants, jet-setting artists and lecturers, Japanese cars, immigration, world cruises, multiculturalism, Islamophobia, cosmopolitan TV programmes, and, of course, e-mail, CNN, and the World Wide Web. Palo Alto may be unusually cosmopolitan; look at your own local paper through these lenses. How 'local' is it?

Trying to sort out this flood of messages from all over the world is part of our daily experience. It is also part of understanding law. So, one may ask, how well equipped are we to deal with all this? And to what extent is this a radically new situation? Changes in communications technology have often been heralded as 'revolutionary'. Consider, for example, the impact of the introduction of printing, the penny post, the telegraph, radio, television, the telefax, e-mail and the Internet – to say nothing of what we may expect in ten or twenty years' time. Closely linked to these developments in complex ways are topics that are part of the daily news – wars, genocide, famines, refugee camps, floods, the status of children and of women, global warming, endangered species, currency fluctuations, and market booms and busts. But are there not also continuities that are as least as important? And where is this all heading? In the last two decades such matters have often been discussed under the loose and possibly rhetorical label of 'globalisation'. Each of us has to try to make sense of these bewildering messages in our own way. As a jurist, my special interest has been in the rather esoteric subject of Anglo-American legal theory. In the early 1990s I decided that I should try to get to grips with the implications of this changing situation for my special subject and, a bit more broadly, for the study of law. I decided to start on familiar ground. The project is not finished – how could it be? – but after nearly ten years, at the cusp of a new millennium, it seems appropriate at least to provide an interim report. Hence this book.

After some preliminary forays, in the spring of 1995 I tapped the keywords 'global' and 'globalisation' into a computerised union library catalogue in Boston.[2] I gave up after I had scanned entries for some 250 books in which one or other of these words featured in the title. The vast majority of these works had been published in the previous 12 to 15 years. They included books on economics, international relations, business studies, sociology, anthropology, political theory, cultural studies, Islamic and African history, development studies, and world history. Almost none of them were specifically focused on law, although there were, of course, large bodies of specialised literature relating to such fields as public international law, the environment, regulation, and human rights. For a brief period, I seemed for once to be ahead of fashion. But this intellectual lag, if such it was, proved to be short-lived. One only has to look at the titles of articles, books, conferences and new journals to see that by the late 1990s words like 'global', 'globalisation', and 'globalism' were as much in vogue in law as in other disciplines.

My project represented the convergence of three persistent strands in my interests and concerns: a specialised interest in the Anglo-American tradition of jurisprudence, especially the ideas of Jeremy Bentham, Karl Llewellyn and Herbert Hart; a life-long personal involvement with Eastern Africa – a region that includes Sudan, Uganda, Tanzania, Kenya, and Rwanda; and a continuing, but intermittent, set of professional concerns about law and development, legal anthropology, North-South relations, and the political, economic, and humanitarian problems of poorer countries.

The immediate impetus behind this project can be succinctly stated. By the mid-1990s the discipline of law in the United Kingdom and, to a lesser extent, the United States was becoming increasingly cosmopolitan, but its theoretical branch, jurisprudence, seemed to have lagged behind. In the English-speaking world traditional positivism, normative legal philosophy, critical legal studies, post-modernism, and even economic analysis of law appeared to have been going through a somewhat parochial or inward-looking phase, although there were some notable exceptions. It seemed that the time was ripe for a revival of a more general jurisprudence. However, what this might involve was far from clear. It seemed a daunting task. So I decided to begin with a series of preliminary forays, starting with that part of our heritage of juristic ideas with which

---

2   In fact I used both 'globalization' and 'globalisation'. In the text, I have followed the publisher's spelling convention of using -'ise' rather than -'ize' except where the latter is used in quotations.

I was most familiar, viz Anglo-American jurisprudence from 1750 to the present day.

The essays included here are largely the result of these preliminary explorations. They focus on selected phases of our intellectual heritage of Anglo-American jurisprudence and comparative law in the light of changes associated with the complex processes that are loosely referred to as 'globalisation'. Partly historical, partly critical, they explore how far what has been institutionalised as belonging to the 'mainstream' in Anglo-American jurisprudence and comparative law is relevant and useful in trying to make sense of law in the modern world from a cosmopolitan perspective. Before introducing them, it is necessary to outline my views on globalisation and on jurisprudence and its role within the discipline of law.

2 GLOBALISATION

We are now living in a global neighbourhood, which is not yet a global village.[3] In the present context the term 'globalisation' refers to those processes which tend to create and consolidate a unified world economy, a single ecological system, and a complex network of communications that covers the whole globe, even if it does not penetrate to every part of it. Anthony Giddens characterises the process as 'the intensification of world-wide social relations which link distant localities in such a way that local happenings are shaped by events occurring many miles away and vice versa'.[4]

Roland Robertson breathlessly evokes some indicators of an historical process that my generation has experienced, at least vicariously through the media:

'Inclusion of the Third World and heightening of global consciousness in the late 1960s. Moon landing. Accentuation of "post-materialist" values. End of Cold War and spread of nuclear weapons. Number of institutions and movements greatly increases. Societies increasingly face problems of multiculturality and polyethnicity. Conceptions of individuals rendered more complex by gender, ethnic and racial considerations. Civil rights. International system more fluid – end of polarity. Concern for humankind as a species community greatly enhanced. Interest in

3   Eg *Our Global Neighbourhood*, The Report of the Commission on Global Governance (Ingvar Carlsson and Shridath Ramphal, Co-Chairmen) (1995).
4   A Giddens, *The Consequences of Modernity* (1990) at p 64; cf his *Sociology* (1990), Ch 16.

world civil society and world citizenship. Consolidation of global media system.'[5]

These processes tend to make the world more interdependent, but this does not mean that we are moving inexorably towards a single world government nor does it mean the end of nation-states as the most important actors. Indeed, while the processes of globalisation inevitably change the significance of national boundaries, the impact is not always in the direction of centralisation or the creation of larger units or even of homogenisation.[6] The post-modern mood stresses cultural relativism. At the same time as the European Union grows in size, we are also witnessing the revival or growth of smaller nationalisms and local identities. It by no means only the Balkans that are becoming balkanised.

The global does not exclude the local, but rather they interact in very complex, sometimes contradictory ways. As Boaventura de Sousa Santos puts it, one needs to distinguish between 'globalized localism' and 'localized globalism': in the former some local phenomenon is successfully globalised – examples include the spread of the English language or Coca Cola or American copyright laws; 'localized globalism' occurs when local conditions, structures and practices change in response to transnational influences, such as the impact of tourism on local crafts or wildlife, ecological dumping, or the adaptation of local commercial law to deal with transnational transactions,[7] or deforestation to pay for foreign debt. In Santos's analysis 'the core countries specialize in globalized localisms, while upon the peripheral countries is imposed the choice of localized globalisms'.[8] These concepts map two extremes of North-South relations in a context in which other more complex interactions occur at many levels.

It is difficult to interpret these trends and it is easy to underestimate them; but it is also easy to exaggerate the extent and the speed of the process, to oversimplify its dynamics, to foreshorten history by treating

5   R Robertson, 'Mapping the Global Condition: Globalization as the Central Concept' in M Featherstone (ed) *Global Culture: Nationalism, Globalization and Modernity* (1990) at p 16.

6   R Robertson in Mike Featherstone, Scott Lash, and Roland Robertson (eds) *Global Modernities* (1995) at p 34.

7   For example, the National Law School of India University in Bangalore, in collaboration with the Government of India and UNDP has embarked on a major programme of research into the implications for policy in respect of (local) economic laws in the context of the globalisation of the economy (Project LARGE, 1993-); see, for example, N R Madhava Menon and Bibek Debroy (eds) *Legal Dimensions of Economic Reforms* (New Delhi, 1995).

8   Boaventura de Santos, *Toward a New Common Sense: Law, Science and Politics in Paradigmatic Transition* (1995) at, p 263. Santos contrasts the ideas of localised globalism and globalised localism with two 'counter-hegemonic' trends, cosmopolitanism and the common heritage of mankind, see below, Ch 8.4.

a story that stretches over several centuries as if it is a recent development, to assume some inevitable, teleological progress in a single direction, and to ignore the countervailing processes of fragmentation and localisation.[9]

Recognition of these processes has stimulated a new academic industry, 'globalisation theory'. In most disciplines in the humanities, social sciences and physical sciences the implications of globalisation are firmly on the agenda. A fairly typical summary reads as follows:

> '[I]n social science there are as many conceptualizations of globalization as there are disciplines. In economics globalization refers to economic internationalisation and the spread of capitalist market relations ... . In international relations, the focus is on the increasing density of interstate relations and the development of global politics. In sociology, the concern is with increasing world-wide social densities and the emergence of "world society". In cultural studies, the focus is on global communications and world-wide standardization, as in CocaColonization and McDonaldization, and on the post-colonial culture. In history, the concern is with conceptualizing 'global history' ... '[10]

There has already been a series of debates, some familiar, some relatively new – for example, about the relative significance of the nation-state as an actor on the world stage or how to explain the collapse of communism or the significance of Islamic fundamentalism.[11] It is not necessary for present purposes to enter here into the debates between strong globalisers, such as Benjamin Barber, Boaventura de Sousa Santos, and Anthony Giddens[12] and sceptics who, like Paul Hirst, claim that 'globalizing

9   See generally, Fred Halliday, *Rethinking International Relations* (1994).
10 Jan Nederveen Pieterse 'Globalization as Hybridization' in M Featherstone, S Lash and R Robertson, *Global Modernities* (1995). Equally typically, there is no mention of law.
11 Within international relations as a discipline, Halliday identifies at least four major perspectives that have advanced 'solutions' to the challenges presented to the subject by the accelerated globalisation: traditional empiricism or the 'English School', of whom Martin Wight and Hedley Bull were leading examples; 'Scientific Empiricism or Behaviouralism', an American tendency, which proclaimed a quantitative, ahistorical, and rigorously social scientific approach to the study of international politics; the neo-realism of Kenneth Waltz, which applied a version of systems theory to international relations; and post-modernism. Halliday, adopting a modified Marxian perspective, criticises all four for being 'unanchored in historical explanation'. Fred Halliday, *Rethinking International Relations* (1994), Ch 2.
12 Benjamin R Barber, *Jihad vs. McWorld: How the Planet is Both Falling Apart and Coming Together and What This Means for Democracy* (1995); Santos (1995), op cit; on the much more complex views on globalisation of Giddens, see David Held

rhetoric' can be dangerously overblown.[13] Indeed, it serves my purpose to keep strong globalisers and moderate sceptics in counterpoint. On some issues I am frankly agnostic; on a few I am quite close to the sceptics. However, I believe that the world is increasingly interdependent, that the significance of national boundaries and of nation states is changing rapidly, and that one cannot understand even local law by adopting a purely parochial perspective.

Attention to globalisation has stimulated quite fundamental rethinking in a number of disciplines. There is, of course, no consensus. There are, however, some relatively clear themes that are directly relevant to my thesis.

First, it is widely agreed that the processes of globalisation are not entirely new. In some respects they antedate the rise of the modern nation state and can be traced back at least until the 16th century. As Halliday puts it:

> 'One can indeed argue that far from the "international" arising from the national, and from a gradual expansion of links between discrete entities, the real process has been the other way around: the history of the modern system is both of the internationalisation and the breakdown of pre-existing flows of peoples, religion, trade into separate entities: the precondition for the formation of the modern nation-state was the development of an international economy and culture within which these distinct states then coalesced.'[14]

What has changed recently is the pace and complexity of the processes, especially in the area of communications.

Secondly, there has been a good deal of self-criticism within disciplines about the extent to which they have over-emphasised the importance of boundaries and have treated societies, states, and 'tribes' as self-contained, decontextualised units. In the mid-1980s, I attended a week-long seminar at Bellagio which was notable for the fact that a collection of distinguished anthropologists confessed to having erred in treating small-scale societies in which they had done their fieldwork as if they were timeless, self-contained units, isolated from the outside world. Their fault had been that they had ignored the wider contexts of time and space. They reaffirmed the idea that the core *focus* of

---

and John B. Thompson (eds) *Social theory of modern societies: Anthony Giddens and his critics* (1989).

13 Paul Hirst and Grahame Thompson, *Globalization in Question* (1996), cf 'Globalisation: Ten Frequently Asked Questions and Some Surprising Answers', 4 Soundings 47 (Issue on The Public Good, 1996).

14 Halliday, op cit, at p 2; cf p 20.

anthropology must still be small societies and communities, but in future the study of the local must be seen in the context of history and of ever-widening geographical spheres – relations with neighbours, colonial boundaries, Western colonisation generally, and the world economy.[15] Since then most work in anthropology has shifted in this direction.[16] Similarly, Anthony Giddens and others have criticised orthodox sociology for giving far too much weight to the idea of 'society' as a bounded system.[17] Again, moral philosophers have been criticised for failing to face up to the ethical implications of interdependence. Nowhere is this more apparent than in the criticisms of the treatment of international relations in John Rawls' *A Theory of Justice* and its assumption that any theory of justice today can treat a society as a 'hypothetically closed and self-sufficient' unit.[18] To which his friendly critic, Thomas Pogge replies:

> 'In the modern world there are no self-contained national societies; a closed background system exists only at the global level. The question, therefore, is whether Rawls's conception, if it applies at all, applies to open national societies (as Rawls seems to prefer) or to the closed social system of humanity at large … .'[19]

The general theme is clear across disciplines: the processes of globalisation are fundamentally changing the significance of national and societal boundaries and generally, but not inevitably, making them less important. This presents a challenge to all 'black box theories' which treat nation states or geographically bounded 'societies' or legal systems as discrete entities that can be studied in isolation either internally or at the international level.

A third theme, on which there is broad agreement, is that one needs to distinguish between different patterns and levels of relations. It is now widely accepted that international relations, which traditionally focused

15 See Jane Collier and June Starr (eds), *History and Power in the Study of Law* (1989); cf Gulliver's later work on Ireland: Marilyn Silverman and P H Gulliver (eds), *Approaching the Past: Historical Anthropology Through Irish Case-studies* (1992).

16 For example, three book-length works advancing different interpretations of globalisation as it bears on anthropology were published in 1996: Arjun Appadurai, *Modernity at Large: Cultural Dimensions of Globalization*; Ulf Hannerz, *Transnational Connections*; and Michael Kearney, *Reconceptualizing the Peasantry: Anthropology in Global Perspective* . I am grateful to Anna Tsing for these references see A Tsing, 'The Global Situation' (forthcoming).

17 Giddens, op cit, above.

18 J Rawls, 'The Law of Peoples', in Stephen Shute and Susan Hurley (eds.), *On Human Rights* (Oxford Amnesty Lectures, 1993) at p 44, discussed below at Ch 3.4.

19 Thomas W Pogge, *Realizing Rawls* (1989) at pp 7-8. Cf Halliday, op cit, pp 78-81.

on relations between nation states, have expanded to include non-state relations across frontiers (transnational relations) and the operation of the global system as a whole (global relations).[20] But, of course, the web of relations is very much more complicated than that. Consider, for example, the internal and external relations of such groupings as major religions (the Islamic world, the Catholic Church, Judaism), the Commonwealth, the Irish Diaspora, OPEC, the European Union, NATO, international drugs networks – all of which cut across simple geographical divisions. This raises a number of conceptual questions about the relations between such notions as sovereign states, governments, peoples, nations, societies, communities, and classes.[1]

A fourth theme from the inter-disciplinary literature on globalisation is the variety of significant actors who are relevant to analysis of patterns of legal and law-related relations in the modern world:[2]

'A wide range of actors may be involved in any one area of governance. To cite just one example, those with a role in bringing order to international trade in sugar and sweeteners include transnational firms, national and international authorities in charge of competition policy, a global group (The International Sugar Council) with specific responsibility for trade, and a host of smaller private associations, including plantation workers, beet farmers, and dieticians. An international organization may easily develop an interest in a local issue, as when the World Bank finances an agricultural project in a country. A local voluntary association may just as easily become a participant in an international regime.'[3]

Despite disagreements about the relative importance of particular kinds of actor and their long-term prospects – for example, about the long-term political significance of multi-national corporations, the United Nations and small states – it seems reasonable to assume that nation states will continue to be among the most powerful kind of actors for a long time to come, and that some major powers will be more equal than others. Conversely, anything approaching world government is not likely to be on the agenda for the foreseeable future. However, in analysing the contemporary world, it is not enough to focus on the traditional small cast of actors: sovereign states, official international organisations, and

20 Halliday, Ch 1.
1   See below, Ch 3.5 and 7.2.
2   Ingrid Detter usefully distinguishes between actors, subjects and creators within public international law, but rather less plausibly suggests that nation states are the only formal creators of legal rules: *The International Legal Order* (1994) at pp 176-178.
3   *Our Global Neighbourhood*, op cit, n 1, at p 3.

individuals. Can one, for example, give an adequate account of law in the modern world which does not give some attention to the significance of transnational non-governmental organisations (Amnesty International, Greenpeace, the Catholic Church, transnational women's networks, international trade union organisations), to peoples that are nations without states (the Maoris, the Welsh, gypsies, the native peoples of North America and Australia), to organised crime, liberation movements, multi-national companies, transnational law firms, and significant classes such as the vast herds of displaced persons (both refugees and the internally displaced)?[4] The concept of legal personality, an old favourite in Austinian analytical jurisprudence, may be ripe for a revival in a global context.[5]

Finally, the processes of globalisation change the agenda of issues with which any field of study is concerned: it revives and recasts old issues such as those surrounding sovereignty and war; it makes familiar problems more urgent, such as environmental control and the regulation of multi-national corporations; and it creates new ones such as those connected with developments in technology and communication, for example, Internet and CNN World News. What are problems, what should be the agenda, what are priorities depend on a whole raft of ideological and other assumptions. But it is clear that if legal theory is to engage seriously with globalisation and its consequences a critical re-examination of its agenda, its heritage of ideas, and its conceptual tools is called for.

3   JURISPRUDENCE AND LAW AS A DISCIPLINE

Globalisation, I have suggested, seemingly offers fundamental challenges to contemporary legal theory. In order to clarify what this

---

4   The sharp distinction between international refugees and internally displaced persons (an even more numerous category) is rapidly breaking down, F M Deng, *Protecting the Dispossessed: A Challenge to the International Community* (1993).

5   I remember reading Dennis Lloyd's *The Law of Unincorporated Associations* (1938) as part of the study of the concept of legal personality in analytical jurisprudence over forty years ago. Remarkably little has happened in legal theory on the subject since Lloyd wrote about it (a notable exception is S Stoljar, *Groups and Entities* (1973)). The concept of legal personality is no longer a standard topic in taught jurisprudence. Yet, if our discipline is to take the implications of globalisation seriously, both the formal conceptions of legal personality and the sociological concepts of significant legal actors and, more generally, of agency are in need of re-examination. On the dearth of recent literature in England, see Roger Rideout, 'The Limited Liability of Unincorporated Associations' (1996) 49 CLP 187, n 1. This article gives a graphic account of the continuing vagueness of the treatment accorded by both legal theory and English courts to unincorporated bodies.

means, it is necessary to restate my conception of the nature and role of jurisprudence within the discipline of law. I have elaborated this view at length elsewhere, so I can be quite brief.[6]

The primary mission of the institutionalised discipline of law is to advance and disseminate understanding of the subject-matter of law. Academic lawyers perform other functions, such as organising information, providing primary training, recommending reform, providing advice and so on – but all of these activities are dependent upon the basic function of advancing understanding.

One way of looking at jurisprudence is as the theoretical part of law as a discipline.[7] A theoretical question is one posed at a relatively high level of generality. In this view, jurisprudence is that part of the institutionalised study of law that is concerned with more or less general questions. As such it is one part of the enterprise of understanding law. Theory and practice is a false dichotomy: for there is no necessary correlation between generality and practical utility. Some general ideas are extremely useful, even in the short term; others have no discernible applications.

Within that enterprise theory can perform a variety of functions. By standing back one can survey the field, or some sector of it, as a whole and see how different parts are related to each other: one might call this the mapping or synthesising function. Theorising can help us to construct and clarify conceptual frameworks, models, ideal types, and other thinking tools – this might be called the conceptual or analytical function. Constructing general concepts, principles, taxonomies, and hypotheses can also save repetition and be economical – one might call this the simplifying function.

The division of intellectual labour into more or less self-contained institutionalised specialisms tends to create artificial boundaries between disciplines and discourses; these boundaries tend to disappear or fade as one moves up ladders of abstraction. Theories of justice, for example, are as much the concern of lawyers, economists, and political theorists as they are of moral philosophers. Similarly, basic problems of evidence and inference in legal contexts are to a greater or lesser extent shared with historians, social scientists, physical scientists, statisticians, and logicians – as David Schum has recently demonstrated.[8] This

6   On the discipline of law in England see *BT*. On jurisprudence, see 'Some Jobs for Jurisprudence', (1974) 1 *British Journal of Law and Society* 157; 'Theory in the Law Curriculum', (with Neil MacCormick) in *LTCL*, reprinted in *LIC*, Ch 7.
7   The terms 'jurisprudence' and 'legal theory' are synonyms in this context: *LIC*, pp 110-114.
8   David Schum, *Evidential Foundations of Probabilistic Reasoning* (1994); Iain Hampsher-Monk and William Twining (eds), *Evidence and Inference in History and Law* (forthcoming, 2000).

transcending of boundaries between institutionalised fields of learning might be called the cross-disciplinary function. Jurisprudence is also involved in other tasks, such as the history of legal thought, the construction of working theories for participants (for example, prescriptive theories of legislation, adjudication, mediation, or advocacy) and, as I have suggested elsewhere, in the development of legal technology – that is the invention or creation of concepts, devices, institutions, and procedures as solutions to practical problems.[9]

However, the most important theoretical function of all is the sustained teasing out, articulation, and critical examination of the general assumptions and presuppositions underlying the discourse of any discipline or praxis at a given moment in history. In this view, one of the main jobs of jurisprudence is the critical exploration and evaluation of prevailing assumptions underlying legal discourse – both law talk and talk about law. On this view, jurisprudence is not a subject apart. Rather it has some specific tasks to perform in keeping the discipline of law in a healthy state. If things are going well, jurisprudence both feeds off and feeds into more specialised areas.

One can consider jurisprudence, so conceived, from at least three different perspectives – as a heritage, as ideology, and as an activity. Each of these is relevant to my project. First, one can conceive of jurisprudence as a *heritage* of texts and ideas; this heritage is so vast that, as teachers and scholars, at any given time we are forced to select a minute proportion of the whole for study or as a resource. Such selections are susceptible to the vagaries of fashion and what are considered to be the pressing issues of the age. When they become institutionalised we can talk of a 'canon', a list of authors or texts that has been recognised officially or by convention as being standard or important. Secondly, one can view jurisprudence as *ideology*, either in the Marxian sense of a body of beliefs fashioned and often distorted by self-interest which is typically used to mystify, justify or legitimate an existing legal regime or order, or one can use 'ideology' as a more neutral term to refer to a general system of beliefs, roughly equivalent to a *weltanschauung*. In either usage, one's beliefs about law are intimately related to one's more general beliefs about ethics, politics, society, and the nature of the world in which we live. Thirdly, one can view legal theorising as an *activity* directed to the posing, reposing, answering, and arguing about general questions relating to law. I am concerned with all three perspectives in considering to what extent our contemporary jurisprudence is adequate to respond to the challenges of globalisation.

A distinction is sometimes drawn between particular and general jurisprudence: particular jurisprudence focuses on the general aspects

9   JJM.

of a single legal system or order and its constituent phenomena, for example, American constitutional theory or the basic concepts of English law. General jurisprudence focuses on legal phenomena in more than one jurisdiction – ie several, many, or all legal systems or orders. Generality is a relative matter; general jurisprudence stretches from the relatively local (two or more orders within one region) to the fairly broad (eg the common law world or state legal systems in industrialised societies) to the universality claimed by classical natural law theory, Bentham's universal science of legislation, Kelsen's general theory of law and state, Llewellyn's law jobs theory, or macro-theoretical social theories of law. As these last examples illustrate, general jurisprudence can address empirical, analytical, normative and other questions or combinations of them.

This is, in short, a pluralistic vision of legal theory which includes a variety of perspectives and a multiplicity of levels of generality. A central argument of this book is that in this era of globalisation there is a pressing need for a revival of general jurisprudence, but that it is important to distinguish between the ideas of looking at law from a global perspective and 'general jurisprudence', which may be more restricted in its geographical scope.

4 OVERVIEW

The essays in this book are presented mainly in the order in which they were written. They have been pruned and slightly reorganised to reduce repetition. The sections on globalisation, jurisprudence, and pluralism have been consolidated, but otherwise, apart from a few changes and additions, they are published largely in their original form. Each can be read on its own, but they represent a sequence which also sketches the path of my own evolving ideas.

The essays fall into three main groups. Chapters 2-5 concentrate on ideas of a few individual jurists who are treated as canonical in our tradition – in particular, Bentham, Austin, Holmes, Llewellyn, Hart, Dworkin and Rawls.[10] The next two chapters (6-7) venture farther afield into areas most often associated with mainstream comparative law.

10 During the 1990s I was invited to participate in a series of celebrations of the work of Karl Llewellyn (1893-93), Oliver Wendell Holmes' 'The Path of the Law' (1897-97), Jeremy Bentham (1748-1998), and Torstein Eckhoff (the first Eckhoff Lecture, 1998). On each of these occasions I dealt with topics relevant to this book, usually as part of a broader theme. A shortened adaptation of the relevant part of the lectures on Llewellyn has been added to Chapter 3. Chapters 4 and 5 are abbreviated versions of essays on Bentham and Holmes given on these celebratory occasions.

Chapter 8 focuses on a recent book, which deserves the attention of anyone interested in globalisation and law. Boaventura de Santos's *Toward a New Common Sense* [11] is an important work of social theory in its own right. It also serves as a useful sounding-board for addressing contemporary concerns about post-modernism, globalisation and pluralism in relation to law. The epilogue (Chapter 9) considers the main lessons from these explorations, and puts forward some provocative propositions for discussion. These may also serve as a starting-point and possible agenda for reviving general jurisprudence as part of the institutionalised discipline of law at the start of the new millennium. The appendix contains some suggestions for law teachers based on my experience of teaching about globalisation and law, mainly in the United States.

This book, then, is mainly a stock-taking of some salient aspects of our intellectual heritage in a rapidly changing situation as a preliminary to rethinking jurisprudence and comparative law as sub-disciplines from a cosmopolitan perspective. By concentrating mainly on a selection of well-known texts and jurists, I have deliberately adopted a strategy that may seem rather cautious and conservative. I have found that starting with the familiar and the mainstream has been helpful to me in trying to get to grips with issues that are bewildering in their range, complexity, and pace of change. These essays are presented here in the hope that they may also ease the way for students and others who are interested in following a similar path.

11   Santos, (1995) op cit, n 8.

Chapter 2

General and particular jurisprudence: three chapters in a story[*]

I INTRODUCTION

This essay is the first of a series exploring the implications for legal theory and the discipline of law of globalisation and globalisation theory. It deals with one narrow topic: three distinct phases of the history of the distinction between 'general' and 'particular' jurisprudence within the tradition of English legal positivism: first, the place and significance of the distinction in the thought of Jeremy Bentham and John Austin; secondly, the fifty-year long debate surrounding Professor T E Holland's idea of a 'formal science of law' and his denial of the possibility of 'particular jurisprudence'; and, thirdly, the recent revival of the distinction as a basis for arguing that H L A Hart and Ronald Dworkin were involved in quite different enterprises, rather than disagreeing: Hart doing general jurisprudence, Dworkin confining himself to a particular, participatory theory of adjudication. The essay concludes with a brief consideration of the implications of this story for reflecting on globalisation and law.

2 JEREMY BENTHAM AND JOHN AUSTIN

(a) Bentham

'J.B.'s frame of mind.
    J.B. the most ambitious of the ambitious. His empire – the empire he aspires to – extending to, and comprehending the whole

---

[*]   This is a revised version of an essay first published in Stephen Guest (ed), *Positivism Today* (1996) and later in *LIC*, Ch 8.

human race, in all places. – in all habitable places of the earth, at all future time.

J.B. the most philanthropic of the philanthropic; philanthropy the end and instrument of his ambition.

Limits it has no other than those of the earth.'[1]

Bentham wrote this in his Memorandum-book the day after his 83rd birthday. This was not just an old man's private musings. From *A Fragment on Government* and other early writings until the end of his life Bentham often explicitly adopted the standpoint of a (or the) 'citizen of the world'.[2] This standpoint was based on utility as a universal principle which extended to humankind in general, sometimes going further to include all sentient beings. It formed the cornerstone of his jurisprudence, which was in key respects truly global.[3]

As is well known, Bentham's project was to extend the experimental method of reasoning from the physical sciences to the moral sciences, especially legislation:

'What Bacon was to the physical world, Helvetius was to the moral. The moral world has had its Bacon, but its Newton is yet to come.'[4]

Underpinning Bentham's perspective was a quite elaborate series of distinctions, which have been succinctly summarised by Philip Schofield:

'... Bentham's conception of jurisprudence had two branches: the first, expository, the second censorial, or the art of legislation. "To the province of the *Expositor* it belongs to explain to us what, as he supposes, the Law *is*: to that of the *Censor*, to observe what he thinks it *ought to be*."[5] He divided jurisprudence into authoritative, when it was the product of the legislator himself, and unauthoritative, the work of any other person. He then made a

---

1   *Works*, vol xi, p 72.
2   *A Fragment on Government* (eds J H Burns and H L A Hart, 1977) (hereafter *Fragment*) pp 397-398; cf *Introduction to the Principles of Morals and Legislation* (eds Burns and Hart, 1970) (hereafter, *IPML*), pp 294-295.
3   See further, RB, p 129 ff. Bentham claimed to be doing *universal* jurisprudence, Austin *'general'*, Buckland and Gray favoured *'particular'* and *'comparative'*, and Bentham allowed for *'local'* (ie sub-national). This point should be distinguished from the issue of whether Bentham's utilitarianism was 'parochial' or 'universal', on which see, eg, David Lyons, *In the Interests of the Governed* (1973, rev edn, 1993) and F Rosen, *Jeremy Bentham and Representative Democracy* (1983) at pp 203-206. On 'extent', see below Ch 3.4(b).
4   *Jeremy Bentham's Economic Writings*, ed W Stark, (London, 1952-54)) vol 1, pp 100-101.
5   *Fragment*, op cit, at p 397.

further distinction between local jurisprudence, concerned with the laws of one nation or a particular group of nations, and universal jurisprudence, concerned with laws of all nations. Though in substance no two nations had exactly the same laws, while others possibly had none in common, there were certain words corresponding to concepts, for instance power, right, obligation, liberty, which could be found in all.[6] It followed that universal expository jurisprudence had very narrow limits: it could not apply to the substance of laws, but "must confine itself to terminology". Censorial jurisprudence on the other hand, considering both substance and terminology, was much wider in scope: there were "leading points"[7] which it would be advantageous for all nations to introduce into their laws.'[8]

Here, three points deserve emphasis: first, the distinction between general (or universal) and local (or internal) jurisprudence was subordinate to the more fundamental distinction between expository and censorial jurisprudence. 'The expositor was to be the servant of the censor, who in turn would be the adviser of the legislator.'[9] Bentham distinguished the is and the ought for the sake of the ought.[10]

Secondly, the distinction between universal and local jurisprudence is not co-extensive with the distinction between the censor and the expositor. In *A Fragment on Government*, it is suggested that 'the *Expositor* … is always the citizen of this or that particular country: the *Censor* is, or ought to be the citizen of the world'.[11] Elsewhere, Bentham modified this by including analysis of some fundamental concepts as part of

6   In *IPML*, p 295. Bentham ends this list of examples with the significant words 'and many others'. Earlier, in the same work, he talked of 'the short list of terms, the exposition of which contains all that can be said with propriety to belong to the head of *universal jurisprudence*'. He listed as examples 'obligation, right, power, possession, title, exemption, immunity, franchise, privilege, nullity, validity, and the like'. Ibid at p 6; cf *Works*, iii, p 217.

7   'Points' here refers to the substance of laws: *IPML*, pp 293-295.

8   Philip Schofield, 'Jeremy Bentham and Nineteenth-Century English Jurisprudence', (1991) 12 *Journal of Legal History* 58 at 59.

9   Ibid at 61. Bentham was quite explicit about his lack of interest in simple exposition: 'The business of simple exposition is a harvest in which there seemed no likelihood of there being any want of labourers: and into which therefore I had little ambition to thrust my sickle.' *Fragment*, Preface, p 404. The context of this statement is a passage in which he justifies his attack on Blackstone in the character of Expositor, because 'the imbecility' of his treatment of the censorial infected his exposition of English Law.

10   Oren Ben Dor has pointed out to me that the is/ought distinction for Bentham operates at different levels. Here I am concerned with the distinction between law as it is and law as it ought to be.

11   *Fragment*, p 398.

universal expository jurisprudence, but as Schofield notes, this was very limited in scope.[12] However, this became the starting-point of Austin's conception of general jurisprudence.

Thirdly, Bentham coined the term international jurisprudence to apply to relations between sovereigns and contrasted it with internal jurisprudence, which he sub-divided into national, provincial, and local. The latter term applied to small districts, such as towns, parishes, and manors, which he acknowledged could have laws of their own.[13] He observed that: 'It is evident enough, that international jurisprudence may, as well as internal, be censorial as well as expository, unauthoritative as well as authoritative'.[14] Thus Bentham at least made provision for jurisprudence to operate at a number of different levels from the global to the very local, but he restricted the term 'international' to relations between sovereigns.

Bentham's distinction between universal and local was in part developed in connection with his critiques of Blackstone. However, it was more important in connection with his constructive project for a pannomion – a comprehensive body of codes. He was a forerunner of the modern constitution-monger and legal 'expert' who offer their services to foreign governments.[15] Anyone involved in this trade has a vested interest in claiming that their expertise is of general application. Bentham was no exception. He was acutely aware that there was a tension between the claims of universality of the Censor and the need to be sensitive to local exigencies. He returned to this theme again and again.

At first sight Bentham did not appear to maintain an entirely consistent stance on the extent to which the censor needed to take account of local circumstances in proposing legislation. In some passages he appears to assume that the pannomion would have wide applicability in respect of substance as well as form. In *A Fragment on Government* he suggested:

12   'To be susceptible of an universal application, all that a book of an expository kind can have to treat of, is the import of words: to be, strictly speaking universal, it must confine itself to terminology.' *IPML*, p 295.
13   *IPML*, pp 296-297. He suggested that 'particular' might be substituted for local, but in the present context I shall confine the term particular jurisprudence to what he called 'internal' in this passage, but which he referred to at different times as 'local' and 'national'. He criticised Blackstone's use of 'municipal' to apply to national law and the term 'law of nations' to apply to international jurisprudence rather than internal laws of nations. The terminology is unimportant; but Bentham's willingness to recognise a multiplicity of levels is significant.
14   Ibid.
15   Eg, J Bentham, *Constitutional Writings for Greece and Tripoli*, ed P Schofield (1990) and below, n 17. See further, W Twining, 'Some Aspects of Reception' (1957) *Sudan Law Journal and Reports* 229 and CCC. A less sceptical view, closer to Bentham's position on the transferability of laws, is developed by Alan Watson in *Legal Transplants* (1974).

'That which is Law, is, in different countries, widely different, while that which ought to be, is in all countries to a great degree the same.'[16]

Similarly, in offering his services as a codifier to James Madison, the President of the United States, he played down the amount to which his draft codes would need to be adjusted to local conditions in respect of either form or substance.[17] This could be read as an example of sustained special pleading, but it is consistent with his general position. The central argument is that only in a few areas would the preparatory work he had already done (on penal law, civil law, judicial establishment, procedure, evidence, and constitutional law) require extensive amendment to fit local conditions. For example:

'Thus in the case of Penal Law. Of the *genera* of Offences, as distinguished or distinguishable by their generic names – Murder, Defamation, Theft, Robbery and so forth – definitions for the most part are the same all the world over. But for particular species, occasion may be afforded, by particular local circumstances: and so in regard to causes of aggravation, extenuation, justification, or exemption, with demand for corresponding varieties in respect of *satisfaction* or punishment. And so in regard to *contracts*.'[18]

Bentham even went so far as to suggest:

'… that, upon a closer scrutiny, the points, which present a demand for local knowledge, would not, it is supposed be found to cover, in the field of law, so great an extent, nor yet to be so difficult to discriminate beforehand, as upon a transient glance, general notions might lead any person to imagine.'[19]

This general statement needs to be read in context: Bentham was making the case for employing an Englishman as legislative adviser to a political leader whose legal system was historically and culturally closely related to English Law, but who had to be wary of local nationalist sentiment. Bentham was careful to show his familiarity with American legal developments and to pronounce them to represent 'prodigious

---

16 *Fragment*, pp 397-398; cf *IPML*, p 295.
17 Letter to Madison, 30 October 1811, 8 *Correspondence* 182-215 (ed S Conway, 1988). A version of this long letter was published as part of *Papers Relative to Codification and Public Instruction* (1817) and was partly reprinted in the Bowring edition, *Works*, vol iv, pp 453-467.
18 Ibid, p 203.
19 Ibid, p 202.

improvements' on English Law.[20] Local knowledge could be supplied by locals, who in any event would have the final say.

On the other hand, Bentham usually maintained a sharp distinction between form (especially terminology) which should in most respects be universal,[1] and substance in which he was often rather cautious in recommending change. In considering directly the influence of time and place in matters of legislation, he was prepared to give some weight to local customs and circumstances. And, as Michael Lobban has suggested, he acknowledged that even the common law was a rich source of raw materials for the censor, that his objections to it related much more to form than to substance, and that he was in respect of reform of substantive law surprisingly cautious.[2]

Although there are differences of emphasis, Bentham's general position can be interpreted as being quite consistent: existing laws of different nations vary considerably in respect of both form and substance.[3] However, the principle of utility and the form of laws in the pannomion are of universal application; but caution needs to be exercised in legislating for a particular country in case expectations based on local customs and circumstances should be disappointed – for the non-disappointment principle is an important principle subordinate to utility.

Thus Bentham's project was to develop a science of legislation which was both 'censorial' and universal; the *construction* of precise conceptual tools – what Mary Mack called 'a legislative dictionary'[4] – was one narrow, subordinate, but important, part of the science or art of legislation.

20   Ibid, p 211.
1   Eg *Of Laws in General*, (ed H L A Hart, 1970), pp 233-234, discussed by Hart in his *Essays on Bentham* (1982) Ch 5, especially p 125.
2   See M Lobban, *The Common Law and English Jurisprudence 1760-1850* (1991), pp 179-184 which contains a useful discussion based on a variety of published works and unpublished manuscripts from different periods.
3   Eg *IPML*, p 295. The distinction between form and substance in the thought of Bentham and other writers discussed below deserves further exploration. Professor Robert Summers is currently working on a major project on 'the formal character of law', which, *inter alia*, reminds us that the description of the form and structure of legal systems and of laws is not solely a matter of elucidation of concepts. For preliminary reports see Summers, 'The Formal Character of Law', (1992) 51 *Cambridge Law Journl.* 242 and 'The Formal Character of Law III', (1994) 25 *Rechtstheorie* 125.
4   Mary Mack, *Jeremy Bentham: An Odyssey of Ideas 1748-1792* (1962); cf Douglas Long, 'Censorial Jurisprudence and Political Radicalism: A Reconsideration of the Early Bentham', (1988) 12 *The Bentham Newsletter* 4, arguing that 'Bentham was a radical *about* political terms'.

(b) Austin

John Austin is the prototype of a disciple who subverts his master. Recent scholarship has convincingly shown that Bentham had a broader vision, a more subtle and flexible mind, and a much more radical programme than his tortured follower. Austin did follow his master in three important respects that are relevant to this essay: the sharp distinction between law as it is and law as it ought to be; a subordinate distinction between the study of one particular legal system and legal systems or law(s) in general; and the identification of analysis of concepts that transcend particular legal systems as a distinct field of study. However, Austin's enterprise was quite different from Bentham's and he used these distinctions, and to some extent altered them, for his own purposes.

Bentham's objective was to develop a politically radical science of legislation. Austin's enterprise was to establish the study of positive law as an autonomous scientific discipline quite separate from censorial jurisprudence or the science of legislation. Bentham distinguished the is and the ought for the sake of the ought; Austin made the same distinction for the sake of isolating law as it is for detached study.

Both thinkers are subject to multiple interpretations. There may be several Benthams and at least two Austins.[5] However, in the present context some points are reasonably clear. The most important is that Austin confined jurisprudence to the analysis and description of positive law. The science or philosophy of legislation[6] was not part of jurisprudence, but constituted a separate discipline. This was no mere semantic point: Austin wished his science to be apolitical; although he himself treated the philosophy of legislation to be important, his distinction paved the way for a conception and practice of the discipline of law that were avowedly uncritical.[7] This was very far from the spirit of Bentham.

Like Bentham, Austin distinguished between general and particular jurisprudence and explicitly concentrated on the former. Both treated the laws of individual sovereign states as the main subject of particular jurisprudence and state legal systems as the primary units of law; both emphasised the importance of studying basic legal concepts that

5   Lobban, op cit, p 256.
6   In several places Austin used the terms 'science' and 'philosophy' interchangeably, eg J Austin, 'The Uses of the Study of Jurisprudence' (1863, ed Hart, 1954), p 365 (hereafter *Uses*).
7   Austin included Legislation among the subjects that should be studied as a preparation for legal practice or politics: *Uses*, pp 387-388. He stressed the need for law to be based on ethics, but his interpretation of utility was more conservative than Bentham's.

transcended particular legal systems. Following Hobbes, Austin declared that his aim was 'to show, *not what is law here or there, but what is law*'.[8]

Austin devoted much more space than Bentham to the distinction between general and particular jurisprudence.[9] In an important passage he specified the scope of general jurisprudence:

'I mean then by "General Jurisprudence", the science concerned with the principles, notions, and distinctions which are common to systems of law: understanding by systems of law, the ampler and maturer systems which, by reason of their amplitude and maturity, are pre-eminently pregnant with instruction.

Of the principles, notions and distinctions which are the subjects of general jurisprudence, some may be esteemed necessary. For we cannot imagine coherently a system of law (or a system of law evolved in a refined community), without conceiving them as constituent parts of it.

… Of the principles, notions, and distinctions which are the subjects of General Jurisprudence, others are not necessary (in the sense which I have given the expression). We may imagine coherently an expanded system of law, without conceiving them as constituent parts of it. But as they rest upon grounds of utility which extend through all communities, they in fact occur very generally in matured systems of law; and therefore may be ranked properly with the general principles which are the subjects of general jurisprudence.'[10]

---

8   *Lectures on Jurisprudence*, p 32 (Austin's italics). Rumble has pointed out that Austin slightly misquoted Hobbes: W Rumble, Introduction to Austin, *The Province of Jurisprudence Determined* (1995).

9   At least in print. Bentham's early manuscripts, on which Douglas Long has done pioneering work, contain some further discussions of the distinction.

10   *Uses*, pp 367-369. This passage is almost identical to a passage in Lecture XI of *LJ*, which contains a longer analysis of the distinction between general and particular jurisprudence. This is one of the passages which has led to controversy about the interpretation of Austin. Did his reference to utility here and his lengthy treatment of it in his lectures undermine his positivism? Indeed, some later critics suggested that he was a closet natural lawyer. And was Austin's conception of General Jurisprudence 'formal' (as Moles and Lobban suggest) or 'empirical', as is argued by W L Morison, *John Austin* (1982)? My own view is that there are passages in which Austin's references to utility did threaten to undermine his strict positivism; it seems to me to be clear that he considered concepts to be *tools for empirical description*, that these were to some extent constructed from real life examples, but that his general jurisprudence did not claim to be empirical in the sense that it could be falsified by evidence, and so in that sense it was analytical or formal. See further, Lobban at pp 223-227. On Hart's claim to be describing 'the form, structure and content' of legal systems in general see below at p 38 n 14.

Austin's list of examples of necessary notions is quite long. It includes the notions of Duty, Right, Liberty, Injury, Punishment, Redress; Law; Sovereignty, and Independent Political Society; the distinctions between written and unwritten law; rights in rem and rights in personam; obligations arising from contracts, injuries, and 'quasi ex contractu'; and so on. It is a longer list than Bentham's and it is not entirely clear what he meant by 'necessary' in this context.[11] By including additional 'common' concepts and by focusing mainly on shared features of 'maturer' systems he may have extended the scope of his concept of general jurisprudence a bit beyond Bentham's universal expository jurisprudence, but overall his conception of law and of its study is much narrower than Bentham's.

Austin emphasised the distinction between general and particular jurisprudence because he wished to lay a foundation for an autonomous discipline distinct from the Science of Legislation and from historical and empirical enquiries. General jurisprudence was anterior to and the necessary foundation for the systematic study of both particular jurisprudence and the science of legislation.[12] It was the theoretical part of law as a discipline.

Austin did not advocate the study of jurisprudence for its own sake. In his lecture on 'The Uses of the Study of Jurisprudence' he emphasised its pedagogical value as the basis for the 'theoretico-practical' study of English law. By providing a map of the whole and making clear the rationale of law in general and of its practice, it would contribute to more efficient vocational training for legal practice and public life. It would also be of value in understanding foreign legal systems, in daily legal practice, in adjudication, in law reform, and in the development of 'a juridical literature worthy of the English Bar'.[13] Austin's vision was of an institutionalised, autonomous discipline of law which would at once be as systematic as that of Prussia, but without the 'secluded habits' of German Professors. 'In England, theory would be moulded to practice.'[14] Significantly, he asserted: 'The only practical jurisprudence is particular'.[15]

David Sugarman and Philip Schofield have sketched the story of the rise of analytical jurisprudence (not Austin's term) and 'the expository

---

11 If it means 'logically necessary', Austin's list should have been confined to a few meta-concepts, such as sovereign, command, sanction and a very small number of legal concepts, of which duty or obligation and legal persons may be almost the only ones. In theory, one could envisage a legal system which prescribed only absolute duties, backed by sanctions that did not include punishments. If, as seems more plausible, by 'necessary' Austin meant important or basic or salient, then the distinction between necessary and common is vague and not very significant.
12 Eg *Uses*, p 372.
13 *Uses*, p 390.
14 Ibid, p 372.
15 Ibid.

tradition' of academic law in the late nineteenth century.[16] The outlines
are familiar: Austin sterilised and narrowed Bentham's jurisprudence;
the followers of Austin further narrowed down Austin, by excluding his
discussions of utility and by shifting the focus to particular jurisprudence.
Bentham was rendered impotent by a combination of misunderstanding,
misinterpretation and neglect. It was claimed that Bentham was essentially
a destructive thinker, whereas Austin was constructive and that Austin's
theory of law was an improvement on Bentham's.[17] Such claims are
specious. A more plausible interpretation is that the pioneering full-
time academic lawyers were concerned to establish their credentials
with both the practising profession and the scholarly community.
Bentham's radicalism and antipathy to the common law would antagonise
the former; Austin's rigorously 'scientific' approach might persuade the
latter of the intellectual respectability of this new discipline. This story
is broadly correct. But, in the present context, it requires to be modified
in at least two respects. Austin was never accepted uncritically even
within English positivism and, as we shall see in the next section, the
distinction between general and particular jurisprudence was the focus
for a long-running and rather sterile debate that was symptomatic of a
wider unease about the development of academic law.

Poor John Austin! A public and a private failure in his lifetime, after
his death he was elevated to the status of 'Father of English Jurisprudence'
to be used for purposes quite different from what he had intended and to
serve as a whipping-boy until he was decently buried by Herbert Hart. It
was Austinian jurisprudence that was said to stink in the nostrils of the
practising barrister.[18] Austin provided the main target for attack by Henry
Maine, James Bryce and other proponents of historical jurisprudence.
Some of his closest disciples, Clark, Holland, and Salmond, carped and
criticised him. By 1945 Buckland could say: 'He was a religion; to-day
he seems to be regarded rather as a disease'.[19] In recent years scholars
have usually treated Austin as a lesser figure than Bentham. In 1961,
Herbert Hart secured his own reputation by destroying Austin's, only
for a series of well-intentioned scholars to disinter him – in one case to
use him as a launching-pad for a virulent and largely irrelevant attack on
Hart.[20] These 'debates' can mostly be read as a series of family squabbles

16   D Sugarman, 'Legal Theory, the Common Law Mind, and the Making of the
     Textbook Tradition', in *LTCL* at p 26; Schofield, op cit.
17   J S Mill, 'Austin on Jurisprudence', (1863) cxviii *The Edinburgh Review*, 439-441,
     discussed by Schofield, op cit, pp 70-71.
18   The phrase is attributed to Dicey; cf W W Buckland, *Some Reflections on
     Jurisprudence* (1945).
19   Buckland, op cit (1945), p 2.
20   Robert Moles, *Definition and Rule in Legal Theory: A Reassessment of H L A Hart
     and the Positivist Tradition* (1987). Moles makes some interesting points, but his

with strong Oedipal overtones within English legal positivism. Since World War II the most persistent attacks on analytical jurisprudence have been from without: on the one hand, the attack on the alleged amoralism of positivism exemplified by the criticisms of Hart by Devlin, Fuller and Dworkin – a line of criticism that largely ignores the significance of Bentham's distinction between expository and censorial jurisprudence; on the other hand, the broader critique of formalism and the expository tradition, most recently exemplified by Morton Horwitz's categorisation of the English analytical tradition as being unhistorical, unempirical, uncritical, and based on an outdated hermeneutics.[1]

It was Austin's intention to develop and disseminate Bentham's ideas, not to dethrone him. He can hardly be blamed for the uses to which he was put after his death. His originality as a thinker and his influence have often been greatly exaggerated, except perhaps in his role as someone to react against.[2] A charitable interpretation suggests that he struggled valiantly, but unsuccessfully, with some intractable problems; a less kind view is that he was hopelessly confused. He deserves to be reburied and allowed to rest in peace.

3   HOLLAND AND HIS CRITICS

From 1863, when Austin's lectures first became available, until the 1890s there is a case for saying that his doctrines 'dominated the teaching of Jurisprudence in England and the Commonwealth'.[3] Several factors explain this: Austin's positivism and his antipathy to Natural Law; the apolitical and 'scientific' nature of his analytical jurisprudence; his relative sympathy with the common law tradition compared to Bentham; and, above all, the absence of rivals.[4]

However, such claims to Austin's 'dominance' should be taken with a large pinch of salt. First, university legal education in this period was

---

criticism of Hart rests on the secondary, and by no means uncontroversial, claim that Hart misread Austin; Moles eccentrically pays almost no attention to Austin's relationship to Bentham.

1   Morton J Horwitz, 'Why is Anglo-American Jurisprudence Unhistorical?', (H L A Hart Memorial Lecture, May 1995) (1997) 17 OJLS 551.

2   Apart from Bentham, the influence of Hobbes on later English positivists, such as Pollock, is often underestimated.

3   H L A Hart, 'John Austin' in A W B Simpson, *Biographical Dictionary of the Common Law* (1984), p 23.

4   The first generation of university law teachers believed that the production of students' works was a high priority in the struggle to establish law as an academic discipline. Works by Foster, Amos and Markby did not meet the felt need for an accessible text on jurisprudence; nor did the full version of Austin's lectures, but students' works based on them, such as those by Campbell (1874) and Clark (1883) were produced to fill the gap. See further Schofield, op cit, at pp 72-73.

new and very small in scale. Secondly it took some time for jurisprudence to become firmly established in the curriculum. In London, Austin's successors in the Chair in the subject were more notable for their rapid turnover, their lack of students and their interest in other subjects than for their productivity – the major exception being Sheldon Amos.[5] In the older universities for a long time jurisprudence was almost 'unheard of'.[6] Furthermore, Austin was the subject of persistent criticism after the publication of his lectures, and for a time the Historical School, led by Sir Henry Maine, threatened to become a serious rival.[7]

In the 1880s jurisprudence began to be recognised as an important element in legal education, even by the Inns of Court.[8] But it was felt that there was no satisfactory student text on the subject. Thomas Erskine Holland decided to fill the gap.[9] His *The Elements of Jurisprudence* was first published in 1880. At one level it was a success; it went through 13 editions in his lifetime, and was reprinted several times after his death in 1926; it was pirated in the United States and for almost 50 years it was the most widely used textbook on jurisprudence in England – but again one should bear in mind the relatively small scale of academic law throughout that period.[10]

Holland was a quite suitable person to follow in Austin's footsteps. He was a strong positivist, a lucid writer and 'the whole bent of his mind was towards orderliness and simplification'.[11] He was impervious to criticism, precise to the point of pedantry, and well read in Roman Law

5   Ibid, p 69.
6   Ibid.
7   It is significant that most of the leading pioneers of English university law teaching in this period, Bryce, Maitland, Dicey, to a lesser extent Pollock, and later Vinogradoff, distanced themselves from analytical jurisprudence. The main exception was Holland. However, nearly all went out of their way to stress the potential compatibility of what they saw as distinct enterprises.
8   Pollock, *Essays on Jurisprudence and Ethics* (1882), p 1.
9   Sir T E Holland (1835-1926) was Chichele Professor of International Law at Oxford from 1874 to 1910. The page citations used here are from the 10th edition (1906). Holland had earlier published *Essays on the Forms of Law* (1870). This was concerned with legislation and codification in England and could, ironically, be interpreted as a contribution to particular jurisprudence.
10 Holland's *Jurisprudence* was seen as the main vehicle of Austinian analytical jurisprudence. It was more systematic and more readable than Austin. By and large, it was treated with respect in Holland's lifetime, but it did not stand the test of time. In later writings in the tradition it was almost never cited with approval and it was used as a target for criticism by Kocourek, Stone, Dias and others. It has been almost completely ignored by writers as diverse as Friedmann, Hart and Dworkin. Today, it seems seriously flawed in respect of both conception and execution – an elementary textbook on a subject not suited to textbook treatment. Cf W Twining, 'Is your textbook really necessary?' (1970) XI *JSPTL (NS)* 81.
11 J L Brierley, Obituary (1926) 42 *LQR* 475.

and English Law as well as International Law and History. Above all he was a good expositor. As Pollock said, compared to Austin's work, 'Professor Holland's is concise without abruptness, flowing without tediousness, and distinct without wearisome repetitions'.[12]

Holland considered himself to be a pioneer. Bentham and Austin had helped to highlight the need for a formal science, but Bentham had muddied the waters by his distinctions between expository and censorial, and between authoritative and unauthoritative jurisprudence. Censorial jurisprudence, Bentham's main interest, referred to the Art of Legislation rather than the Science of Law; 'authoritative' jurisprudence is nothing more than a body of law; 'unauthoritative local jurisprudence' is mere commentary; only 'unauthoritative general jurisprudence' is scientific and Bentham contributed little to this.[13] Austin made a significant contribution, presenting, in Holland's words, 'the spectacle of a powerful and conscientious mind struggling with an intractable and rarely handled material'.[14] Unfortunately, 'the defects of the work are even more widely recognized than its merits'.[15] Austin's work was fragmentary, repetitive, neglecting large tracts of his subject, while devoting too much space 'to digressions upon questions such as the psychology of the will, codification and utilitarianism'.[16] Holland found little in modern civil law scholarship, except among pandectists, that bore directly on analytical jurisprudence as he conceived it.[17]

The way was therefore open for the first systematic work on the formal science of law. Holland followed Austin and Clark in concentrating on general analytical jurisprudence. However, he went one step further in refusing to recognise particular jurisprudence as a serious or even a proper pursuit. For him, the issue was not just one of semantics, a loose extension of the term 'jurisprudence' to the study of particular municipal legal systems. Jurisprudence is 'the formal science of positive law'[18] and science must be general. 'Particular jurisprudence' might mean either of two things: it might be a general science derived from observation of the laws of one country, in which case the particularity applies to the sources from which the science is derived, rather than to the science. Thus, one might start to build up a science of geology by observing strata in England,

---

12 F Pollock, op cit (1882), p 9.
13 This is a misjudgement based on ignorance of some of Bentham's less well-known published writings as well as his unpublished work.
14 Preface, Holland, *Jurisprudence*, p vii.
15 Ibid.
16 Ibid.
17 Holland suggests that this is because 'continental jurists find in Roman law a ready-made terminology and a typical method, upon which they are little inclined to innovate' (Preface, p viii).
18 Ibid, p 13.

but the outcome would not be 'English geology', for the findings would only be scientific if the generalisations would hold good everywhere, 'insofar as the same substances and forces are everywhere present.'[19] Alternatively, particular jurisprudence may mean acquaintance with the laws of a particular people; 'but it is improper to apply the term "science" to such merely practical and empirical knowledge'.[20]

Holland argued that a better analogy was with Grammar – 'the science of those ideas of relation which, in greater or less perfection, and often in most dissimilar ways, are expressed in all the languages of mankind.'[1] There is a fundamental difference between learning a particular language and studying the scientific principles of grammar. The formal science of law is concerned with 'those few and simple ideas which underlie the infinite variety of legal rules' (in all systems).

Holland sought to explain his idea of a 'formal science' by an example. If a scholar accumulated knowledge of every European system of law and found each to be entirely unlike the rest, there would be no basis for constructing a science. There would just be a heterogeneous body of information:

> 'Suppose however, *as is the case*, that the laws of every country contain a common element; that they have been constructed in order to effect similar objects, and involve the assumption of similar moral phenomena as everywhere existing; then such a person might proceed to frame out of his accumulated materials a scheme of the purposes, methods, and ideas common to every system of law. Such a scheme would be a formal science of law; presenting many analogies to Grammar ...'[2]

This passage is vulnerable to criticism on several grounds: first, what Holland describes is an empirical rather than a formal science; secondly, he lacked the evidence to support his assertion that the laws of every country contain a common element; he merely asserted what his science set out to prove; third, he includes purposes, assumed moral phenomena, and methods as well as ideas. But elsewhere his formal science is presented as dealing only with analysis of concepts.

Here we are only concerned with Holland's idea of a formal science of positive law. Holland was a rigid positivist and a severe formalist and, as such, open to attack by critics of such positions. But his conception of

19   Ibid, pp 10-11; cf Maine's use of the analogy with geology in *Ancient Law* (1861), Ch 1.
20   Ibid, p 11.
1   Ibid, p 7. On the link between Bentham's Universal Jurisprudence and his idea of a Universal Grammar see D Long, op cit, pp 16-18.
2   Holland, *Jurisprudence*, p 7 (italics added).

analytical jurisprudence was also criticised from within legal positivism by Pollock, Buckland and Gray among others. Holland stood his ground and only made passing reference to his critics.

Frederick Pollock was the first critic of consequence. In a review article on 'some recent contributions to Legal Science',[3] he criticised Holland's conception of a formal science on educational grounds. The analogy with Grammar was 'felicitous, and only too felicitous', for there is little demand for books on the science of grammar. One learns grammar through learning one concrete language and not *vice versa*. The saving grace of Holland's book is that the author, while denying its possibility, in fact practises particular jurisprudence concisely and intelligibly. However, jurisprudence of this abstract kind is doomed to vacillate between two unsatisfactory alternatives: a pure theory of legal classification ('a catalogue of blank forms') or partial exposition of a particular system. An institutional work on English Law, a successor to Blackstone's *Commentaries* or analogous to the German *Pandekten* would serve the needs of students and practitioners better than a purely abstract study of legal ideas.[4]

John Chipman Gray of Harvard challenged Holland's conception of jurisprudence, also mainly on grounds of practicality. There are three kinds of jurisprudence: Particular; Comparative; and General. All are scientific, in the sense that they involve systematic study. Particular Jurisprudence is more than the particular law of a particular people – 'It means the scientific knowledge of the law of a particular people'. Particular Jurisprudence is of much more utility to intending practitioners than Comparative or General Jurisprudence.[5]

One particularly harsh critic, Albert Kocourek, criticised Holland for not staying loyal to his conception of an abstract science.[6] But Kocourek's own contribution to abstract jurisprudence was ignored or dismissed as being totally impractical and useless. This supports the hypothesis that Holland's *Jurisprudence* survived in spite of rather than because of his commitment to a formal science.[7]

The most interesting criticism of Holland's 'formal science' came from W W Buckland of Cambridge. This took the form of one of the longest-running non-debates in the history of Anglo-American

3   F Pollock, op cit (1882).
4   Pollock, in his *First Book of Jurisprudence* (1896) Preface, explicitly distanced himself from the analytical school.
5   J C Gray, *The Nature and Sources of Law* (1909) Ch 7.
6   A Kocourek, *Jural Relations* (1928).
7   F H Lawson wrote of Holland's *Elements of Jurisprudence* that it resembled Markby's *Elements of Law* 'in containing quite a good deal of what is not so much jurisprudence as law', and quoted Lord Birkenhead as saying that it was 'one of a number of books which appeared in Oxford in the eighties which made sense of English law'. *The Oxford Law School, 1850-1965* (1968) at p 75.

jurisprudence. In 1890, Buckland published an article in *The Law Quarterly Review* on 'The Difficulties of Abstract Jurisprudence', in which he attacked Holland's conception of general jurisprudence as misconceived.[8] Whereas Holland had denied the possibility of particular jurisprudence, Buckland doubted the feasibility of general jurisprudence. Holland, who was not one to change his mind, ignored the criticism in successive editions. Fifty-five years later, Buckland renewed the attack in almost identical terms, claiming that he saw nothing to alter in what he had said.[9]

Buckland followed Pollock in doubting the utility of abstract jurisprudence, while praising Holland for improving on Austin in respect of his exposition and arrangement. But he launched a more substantial attack on his conception of the subject. Holland defined jurisprudence as 'the formal science of those relations of mankind which are generally recognised as having consequences'. This assumes that there are legal concepts that are widely shared among systems of law: to what extent that is true, even of Western systems, is an empirical question to be determined by detailed comparative study of actual bodies of law.

If jurisprudence is a formal science like grammar, it is of very limited utility. If it is an empirical science, the analogy with geology is inappropriate: one may start to build up a picture of geological strata because they are subject to physical laws which are everywhere the same; but law is dependent on its social context. The extent to which there are shared legal concepts is an empirical question requiring proof by comparative study of many systems. But where is the evidence? Holland either assumes what he set out to prove or else was relying on *a priori* axioms reminiscent of German transcendentalism; in that case, like John Austin, he may be suspected of being a closet natural lawyer.[10] In fact, Buckland as a comparatist and Roman lawyer, knows of some evidence which suggests that there are a few common notions, such as duty, but their bulk is not great and a 'science' based on these alone would be meagre at best.[11] The fundamental notions of law are not everywhere the same, for law is 'to a great degree the product of the milieu in which it has developed'.[12] Holland's analogy with grammar might be apt, but it suggests at most the limited scope and utility of such a science; on the other hand, the analogy with geology was misleading because geology is subject to universal physical laws, whereas law is culturally relative.

8   W W Buckland, 'Difficulties of Abstract Jurisprudence' (1890) 24 *LQR* 436.
9   W W Buckland, *Some Reflections on Jurisprudence*, op cit, Ch VI, at p 68. This work is fairly typical of Buckland's style: succinct, perceptive, astringent, and strongly positivist.
10 Eg *Reflections*, p 68.
11 Ibid, p 70.
12 *Reflections*, p 69.

For Buckland, general jurisprudence is either empirical and speculative or else it is formal, in which case it is both narrow and useless. On the other hand, particular jurisprudence, as the study of the underlying notions of one system of law is both feasible and useful. The method is scientific, but the subject is empirical. Its aim, to show 'the underlying principles and broadest generalisations' of a given system as a foundation for the study of domestic law.

In several respects the differences between Holland and his critics were not very great. First, Holland, Pollock and Buckland, and in different ways, Gray and Kocourek, were all committed legal positivists who maintained a sharp distinction between law and morals and sought to establish the study of positive law as a distinct discipline, separate from politics, ethics and sociology. Holland, Pollock and Buckland all criticised Austin for treating utilitarianism as part of jurisprudence.[13] For example, Pollock referred to it as 'irrelevant and mostly bad moral philosophy'[14] – a far cry from Bentham. Buckland insisted that jurisprudence was 'Austin's real subject. This was the analysis of legal concepts.'[15]

Secondly, they shared a conception of law that treated municipal legal systems as the primary subject of the study of law. Each was sympathetic to the idea of viewing Public International Law as analogous to municipal law; and they treated it as dealing almost entirely with relations between sovereign states.[16] In short, they all held similar, strong versions of a 'black box' theory of law.

Thirdly, Holland and Buckland wished to confine jurisprudence to the analysis of concepts; Pollock was more circumspect. All placed the study of legal doctrine at the centre of legal education. The fact that all three fought hard for this admittedly narrow enterprise does not mean that they were narrow-minded as men or as scholars. Pollock is well-known for the breadth of his interests. Buckland was a Roman lawyer and linguist who was familiar with German and French legal literature. Holland wrote extensively on the history of International Law and, largely through frequent letters to *the Times*, participated in many contemporary public debates, while maintaining a rigidly positivistic stance on the interpretation and application of principles of International Law.

Fourthly, Pollock doubted whether discussions of uses of the word 'law' and the theory of sovereignty – the subject of the first two chapters of Holland's *Elements* – were properly within the scope of jurisprudence,

13 Eg Holland at p vii; Buckland, *Reflections*, pp 2 and 42-43.
14 F Pollock, *Introduction to the History of the Science of Politics* (1890), p 67.
15 *Reflections*, p 2.
16 Eg Holland, Ch xvii; Pollock (1896); Buckland, *Reflections*, Ch 2. Holland referred to International law as 'law by courtesy' (*Jurisprudence*, p 127) and its study as 'the vanishing point of jurisprudence' (ibid, p 380).

but rather should be treated as prolegomena. Buckland agreed, but took a stronger line:

> 'Jurisprudence has no independent existence. Its formulae are meaningless except in relation to concrete legal rules. It is a part of the law. That the same jurisprudence is a part of all law is a point to be proven not assumed.'[17]

This was a crucial part of his argument that analytical jurisprudence is in first instance particular. Its primary task is analysis of the basic legal concepts of a single municipal legal system. It is an empirical question to what extent, if at all, even advanced legal systems have common concepts. This is a matter for comparative legal research. Buckland, on the basis of his knowledge of Roman Law and some contemporary civilian systems, was inclined to scepticism. He suspected that the universalism of Bentham, Austin and even Holland undermined the distinction between the is and the ought and opened the way for natural law to re-enter by the back door. Buckland it seems was a relativist in respect of both ethics and culture. However, he was as committed as any to the systematic study of legal doctrine.

What was at stake in these debates? It was not merely or mainly a semantic question about the meaning of the term 'Jurisprudence'. The main concerns were pedagogical: the search for a suitable underpinning for the detailed study of English Law. It is striking that Buckland's article of 1890 begins with reference to the attitude of 'disgust and scarcely veiled contempt' of practical lawyers towards jurisprudence as a subject. In the context 'abstract' is used pejoratively. The article assumes that most undergraduate law students are intending barristers. This fits the thesis, convincingly developed by David Sugarman, that the establishment of a narrow expository orthodoxy by legal scholars, who were themselves far from narrow-minded, represents a compromise aimed at establishing the study of English Law in universities as being at once scientific and of clear practical value. In the present context the primary reference group was the practising Bar. This required that jurisprudence should be simultaneously rigorous, uncritical and in tune with the legal culture of the common law. This in turn necessitated a

---

17 (1890) at p 438; cf *Reflections* at p 3: 'Law and sovereignty are not legal conceptions; they are presuppositions...'. This is reminiscent of Thayer's treatment of 'relevance' as being a presupposition of the law of evidence, rather than part of it. (J B Thayer, *A Preliminary Treatise on Evidence at Common Law* (1898), pp 264-265). For both Buckland and Thayer the distinction between presuppositions and legal rules was logically, but not pedagogically, important. Buckland acknowledged that his *Some Reflections on Jurisprudence* was a misnomer as much of it dealt with what he considered to be prolegomena to Jurisprudence (Preface).

distinct shift of emphasis from general jurisprudence to a form of particular jurisprudence that was closely integrated with the study of substantive doctrine – the basic concepts of common law talk rather than of talk about law.

On revisiting these largely forgotten texts, one is struck by the modesty of their intellectual ambitions. Unlike Bentham, Austin and Maine, who were serious theorists, Pollock, Holland and Buckland were competent legal scholars who were suspicious of philosophy. The debate between universalists and particularists took place in the context of the preparation of elementary student texts by lawyers, for whom jurisprudence was an avocation. Over time the particularists won the day and by 1945 Buckland could write: 'Most English writers deal with Particular Jurisprudence'.[18] Bentham was ignored, Austin was bowdlerised, and Maine was marginalised. Holland was at first treated as a particularist *malgré soi* and was in due course superseded.

4 HART AND DWORKIN[19]

I began my study of law in Oxford in 1952, the year in which Herbert Hart was elected to the Corpus Chair of Jurisprudence in succession to A L Goodhart. So when I embarked on the study of jurisprudence towards the end of my second year, I found myself at the cusp of two traditions of English legal positivism. I experienced both versions.

By the early 1950s taught jurisprudence had become rather eclectic, exemplified by the main textbooks – Paton and Salmond. Some cursory attention was paid to 'schools', such as Natural Law, the Historical School, and Sociological Jurisprudence. More emphasis was placed on particular analytical jurisprudence, which fell into two parts: the sources of English Law as they were treated, for example, in C K Allen's *Law in the Making*, and analysis of concepts, including law, sovereignty, legal personality, ownership, possession, *ratio decidendi*, rights, and duties. A typical essay topic was: 'Does English Law have a theory of possession? Does it need one?' One approached such questions by reading a mixture of cases and secondary writings. These were interpreted as 'Numquestions', that is questions expecting the answer 'No'. So in dealing with possession one compared the use of the term in cases on larceny, bailment, sale of goods, trespass to land and goods and concluded that it had a slightly different definition in each context, thereby confirming 'the pragmatism' and distrust of abstraction of English legal culture.

18 *Reflections* at p 71.
19 Except where it is indicated otherwise, this section focuses on two texts: Hart's *The Concept of Law* (2nd edn, 1994), including his posthumous Postscript, and Ronald Dworkin's *Law's Empire* (1986) (hereafter, *LE*).

Such exercises were particularistic in two ways: the focus was on concepts of English law and they were studied at a relatively low level of generality. However, the approach was not entirely parochial. One might read (or read about) Savigny on possession, German theories of corporate personality, and American writers on rights. One made regular comparisons with Roman Private Law, possibly referring to Buckland and McNair.[20] Buckland's argument about the possibility and value of particular analytical jurisprudence was fully vindicated. It was clearly relevant to other subjects that we were studying; it served to break down the artificial boundaries between fields of law and to make a number of connections; and it helped one to see the common law – especially private law – as a whole, if not quite as a system.[1] For the degree I took two papers in Roman Law (having also done Roman Law for the preliminary examination, 'Mods') and one in Legal History. When I revised for my Finals, I studied the English and Roman law of contract, the history of English contract doctrine, and Hohfeld's analysis of rights simultaneously. It made a lot of sense. This kind of 'particular analytical jurisprudence' has virtually disappeared. From an educational point of view, something of real value was lost as these exercises in applied jurisprudence were replaced by more abstract enquiries.

Of course, this kind of study had distinct limitations. It was narrowly focused; it was somewhat uncritical;[2] it bore little relationship to law in action in society; and it was strikingly atheoretical, especially in respect of method. The subject, as Buckland had suggested, was part of English law; one *did* it as one did any other subject: one read secondary writings and some cases and one wrote an essay.

In his inaugural lecture on 'Definition and Theory in Jurisprudence', Hart seized on the methodological weaknesses of traditional or classical jurisprudence.[3] Questions framed in such terms as 'What is law?', 'What

---

20 W W Buckland and A D McNair, *Roman Law and Common Law* (1936).
1   The standard justification for studying Roman law was that it enabled one to study a legal system as a whole. In fact, one focused almost entirely on the rules and concepts of Roman Private Law.
2   Horwitz, op cit, characterises English Analytical Jurisprudence as ahistorical, unempirical, apolitical, and uncritical. This is only partly correct in respect of the version I encountered as an undergraduate at Oxford: everything one studied was suffused with history, albeit of a rather narrow kind – the tracing of the development of doctrines of English private law largely through the cases. The predominating approach was doctrinal-empirical rather than social-empirical. We were not discouraged from criticism (*de lege ferenda*), but we were not equipped to do this in an intellectual way. The predominant approach was apolitical, except that some of us drew inspiration from the writings of Wolfgang Friedmann.
3   H L A Hart, *Definition and Theory in Jurisprudence* (reprinted in (1953) 70 *LQR* 37).

is a right?', 'What is a legal person?' were misposed. They invited answers in the form of definitions of single words *per genus et differentiam*; this was inappropriate for elucidating familiar abstract terms and it failed to dissolve the puzzlements underlying the questions. While theory in law was welcome, the growth of theory on the back of definition was not. In one seminal lecture Hart re-established links with philosophy and provided some powerful tools of analysis of potentially wide application. Significantly, he explicitly gave the credit to Bentham for the main tool, paraphrasis, by implication dismissing the methods of all of the intervening jurists in the analytical tradition, including Austin.

In his lectures, which culminated in *The Concept of Law* in 1961, Hart focused mainly on those concepts which particularists like Pollock and Buckland treated as prolegomena to jurisprudence – law, legal system, command, rule, sovereignty, sanction and the like. However, he drew no sharp distinction between general and particular jurisprudence and some of his best later work – on causation, intention, responsibility and rights – could reasonably be interpreted as contributions to particular jurisprudence. For much of his life, such categorisations were unimportant.

The main challengers to Hart, such as Fuller, Dworkin, and Devlin, and defenders, such as Raz and MacCormick, have generally concentrated on issues relating to his positivism and modified utilitarianism. The approach has been philosophical and the debates have normally taken place at a rather abstract level, often quite far removed from the particularities of English law.[4] There has, of course, been criticism from a variety of other perspectives. In considering the distinction between general and particular jurisprudence it is worth referring briefly to two of these. First, Brian Simpson, drawing on his deep knowledge of English legal history, has argued that Hart's concept of a legal system just does not fit the 'muddle' of the English common law.[5] This can be interpreted as turning on its head Bentham's argument that the common law is not law.[6] Simpson's argument is that a theory of law which excludes the common law must be defective. Subsequently, Charles Sampford has argued at a more general level that it is fundamentally misleading to think of law anywhere as 'systematic'.[7] His picture of law as being part of a 'social mêlée' at both national and international levels is very much in

---

4   The problem of building bridges between abstract theorising and the study of specialised fields of law is explored in *LTCL*, the central theme of which is that, for purposes of legal education and legal scholarship, 'Jurisprudence should not be a subject apart'.

5   A W B Simpson, 'The Common Law and Legal Theory' in Simpson (ed), *Oxford Essays in Jurisprudence*, 2nd series (1973); reprinted in *LTCL*, Ch 2.

6   Eg *OLIG*, Ch xvi.

7   Charles Sampford, *The Disorder of Law* (1989).

tune with the thrust of those aspects of globalisation theory, and of legal pluralism, which challenge all 'black box' conceptions of law. At first sight Simpson's thesis looks particularistic, Sampford's general. But both represent important challenges to theories of law that treat legal systems as self-contained and 'systematic' in a strong sense. As such they are contributions to general rather than particular jurisprudence, if the distinction has any value.

A second challenge to Hart took the position that his kind of analytical jurisprudence, by focusing on lawyers' talk, divorced law from its social context and diverted attention from sociological enquiries that are essential to understanding legal phenomena. One of the first versions of this line of criticism, by Edgar Bodenheimer, was made before the publication of *The Concept of Law*.[8] It provoked an immediate response from Hart, who argued that his form of conceptual elucidation was as important for sociology as for law and that sociologists could do well to put their own house in order. For jurists clarity begins at home. It may be that the exchange with Bodenheimer was behind the famous claim in the Preface that *The Concept of Law* 'may also be regarded as an essay in descriptive sociology'. This statement has provoked hoots of derision from the sociologically inclined, but little analysis.

My own view, as one who is committed to developing broader approaches to law, has been that Hart 'won' the battle with Bodenheimer, but by not following through in making the case for the importance of conceptual elucidation in *any* approach to the understanding of law, he missed an opportunity to extend the scope of analytical jurisprudence. In short, he exposed the naiveté of traditional analytical jurisprudence in respect of *method* (Bentham excepted), but accepted uncritically its *agenda*.[9] One implication of this argument is that, if legal theory is to respond adequately to the challenges of 'globalisation', it needs, *inter alia*, to develop a sophisticated conceptual apparatus for the task. This will be a

---

8   Edgar Bodenheimer, 'Modern Analytical Jurisprudence and the Limits of its Usefulness', (1955-56) 104 *University of Pennsylvania Law Review* 1680; H L A Hart, 'Analytical Jurisprudence at Mid-Twentieth Century: A Reply to Professor Bodenheimer', (1957) 105 *University of Pennsylvania Law Review* 953.

9   '... Hart has not in a systematic way attempted to proceed beyond the confines of Bentham's expository and censorial jurisprudence into the kind of broader perspective that is encompassed by phrases such as "sociology of law". He has not, for example, devoted sustained attention to analysis of key terms in the vocabulary of sociological theories about law such as society, group, class, function, process, dispute, social problem, institution or decision. He has clarified concepts, such as rule, habit, and sanction, which are important in social theory as well as analytical jurisprudence; but he has, on the whole, been content to reformulate and refine issues posed by a fairly narrow tradition of academic law, rather than to raise in a sustained way the kinds of questions which a broader social perspective is likely to treat as central or significant' ALLP at pp 578-579.

central task for a revived general jurisprudence. Here, however, it is pertinent to note that the generalists as well as the particularists in the analytical tradition are equally open to the charge of 'narrowness', insofar as they concentrated almost exclusively on legal concepts (with a few 'prolegomena'), that is on 'law talk' to the almost total exclusion of 'talk about law'.

It is sometimes suggested that Hart's *The Concept of Law* is solely concerned with 'linguistic analysis' and in this sense is semantic. Buckland, as we have seen, equated analytical jurisprudence with 'analysis of legal concepts'. However, Hart's conception of a descriptive jurisprudence goes far beyond this: it includes both elucidating concepts and *using* them;[10] Concepts and models (such as the model of law as a system of rules) are tools of description. *The Concept of Law*, and general descriptive jurisprudence, go beyond conceptual clarification to describing common features of the form, structure and content of legal systems.[11]

The distinction between general and particular jurisprudence was for a long time treated as of little significance and the debates surrounding it were usually treated as trivial logomachy. However, the distinction was revived in a symposium based on a conference in Jerusalem held in honour of Hart. Commenting on some draft chapters of Dworkin's *Law's Empire*, shortly before it was published, Ruth Gavison wrote:

'Dworkin's analysis of law as an interpretive concept, under his own model of interpretation, makes classical legal theory impossible. In other words, Dworkin is challenging here the possibility and the value of 'general jurisprudence', the attempt to analyse societies at their most general (like the attempt to analyse human nature) and identify those features common to all social organizations which might lead to the need for similar institutions and practices. Law is one such social institution found in all societies and exhibiting a core of similar features.'[12]

---

10 Eg Postscript at p 240: 'As a means of carrying out this descriptive enterprise my book makes repeated use of a number of concepts...'.

11 See the passage quoted below at n 14.

12 Ruth Gavison, Comment in Gavison (ed), *Issues in Contemporary Legal Philosophy: The Influence of H L A Hart* (Oxford, 1987) p 28. Later Gavison continues: '... I shall risk being called a "semantic scholar" and say that for these comparative lessons to be drawn we need some universal conceptual scheme, in terms of such basic legal functions such as dispute resolution, which may help us both to understand the similarities and highlight the differences between societies.' (p 29).

Hart made a similar point in the same volume, but developed it much further in his Postscript to *The Concept of Law*, which was published posthumously in 1994. Here he defended his views largely in terms of two propositions: that Dworkin has misrepresented his position on a number of key issues and that he and Dworkin were involved in two different, not necessarily incompatible, enterprises, the one general, the other particular.

Hart claimed that he and Dworkin have very different conceptions of legal theory. Hart's is *general* 'in the sense that it is not tied to any particular legal system or legal culture';[13] and it is *descriptive* 'in that it is morally neutral and has no justificatory aims'.[14] Dworkin's jurisprudence is in large part evaluative and justificatory and 'is addressed to a particular legal culture', which is typically the theorist's own.[15] Dworkin is concerned to interpret the settled law and legal practices of a particular system and to provide the best moral justification for them.[16] Hart considers that these two enterprises are so different as not to involve any substantial joinder of issue that need constitute a disagreement.

The Concept of Law deals with the nature of law in general rather than the law of a given society. Hart's work is clearly in the tradition of general jurisprudence, occasionally concretised by particular applications to English or to Anglo-American law. But can we say that Dworkin is doing particular jurisprudence? At first sight it looks absurd to confine Dworkin's ideas in this way. For example, the idea that interpretation of

13   *The Concept of Law*, Postscript, p 239.
14   Ibid, p 240. In his response to Dworkin in the Jerusalem symposium, Hart states: '... there is a standing need for a form of legal theory or jurisprudence that is descriptive or general in scope, the perspective of which is not that of a judge deciding "what the law is", that is, what the law requires in particular cases ... but is that of an external observer of a form of social institution with a normative aspect, which in its recurrence in different societies and periods exhibits many common features of form, structure, and content'. 'Legal Theory and the Problem of Sense', in Ruth Gavison (ed), op cit, at p 36. Hart goes on to state that descriptive analytical jurisprudence is preliminary to the articulation of a justificatory theory of a community's legal practices ... (p 37). I am grateful to Robert Summers for reminding me of this important passage. The main point of difference between Hart and Dworkin here is that Dworkin does not accept that description can be neutral nor that it is preliminary to interpretation (eg *LE*, pp 13-14). It is not clear why Hart excludes the interpretation that Dworkin may be offering a general prescriptive theory of adjudication (including legal reasoning) or that his justificatory theory need not be limited to a particular community rather than, as with Rawls's theory of justice, any constitutional democracy or 'decent' society. On the claim that descriptive general jurisprudence can describe the content of legal systems, compare Buckland's cautionary admonitions (above) and the 'jurisprudential relativism' of Atiyah and Summers (below).
15   Ibid, citing *LE*, p 102.
16   Ibid, p 241.

a social practice involves 'showing it in its best light'[17] or the distinction between semantic and interpretative theories are not ideas that are linked to any given legal system. Are not Dworkin's ideas on democracy, equality and liberty founded on some idea of universalisability? His model judge, Hercules, clearly has roots in American legal tradition. He may not be a citizen of the world, but does he not provide one model for judging in any liberal democracy both in respect of his conception of his role and his method of interpretation? Does not Dworkin advance a prescriptive theory of adjudication that is general, if not universal? And, surely, Dworkin's criticisms of legal positivism are not confined to England and the United States.

One possible interpretation of the claim that Hart and Dworkin are involved in significantly different enterprises is that they are addressing different questions. Jurisprudence is a wasteland of false polemics and one way of disposing of such squabbles is to show that the best interpretation of two apparently conflicting positions is that they provide answers to different questions rather than rival answers to shared questions. Prima facie this looks attractive in the present context. In *The Concept of Law* Hart's explicit agenda was to consider three recurrent issues: (1) How does law differ from and how is it related to orders backed by threats? (2) How does legal obligation differ from and how is it related to moral obligation? (3) What are rules and to what extent is law an affair of rules?[18] Dworkin claims that *Law's Empire* is centrally concerned with the problem of sense, that is the truth conditions for correct interpretation of propositions of law. Here, one needs to distinguish between a general theory of legal interpretation or of legal reasoning and what constitutes the best interpretation of a particular rule in a given system. One might render this in the form: 'Under what conditions is it true to say that "rule X means this" or that "this is the correct interpretation of rule X" '? This is a different question from those listed by Hart, but it is in similar form at the same level of generality as Hart-type questions, such as: 'Under what conditions is it true to say that a legal system exists?' or 'Under what conditions is it true to say that X has a right?' *All* of these questions are general in that they are not confined to or derived from a single legal system and they can be asked of many, if not all, legal systems. Similarly, for both Dworkin and Hart, questions such as 'Is this the best interpretation of rule X?' or 'Does Y have a right to delivery of goods from the seller?' require local knowledge of a particular legal system as well as a general theory guiding the answer. Here, the distinction between general and particular jurisprudence

17 *LE*; p 90.
18 *CL*, p 13; cf Postscript, p 240.

provides no basis for distinguishing between the theories of Dworkin and Hart.

It is also doubtful whether the technique of attributing different questions to different positions will take us very far. Hart and Dworkin have different, but overlapping agendas. For example, Dworkin is interested in Hart's questions (2) and (3) and Hart acknowledges that his theory has implications for adjudication and interpretation. He also acknowledges that they do have some substantial differences of view.[19] There are some grey areas, for example where Hart claims that Dworkin has misinterpreted or caricatured his position, but insofar as Dworkin does not accept this, they are disagreeing about the best interpretation of Hart.[20] What is significant in the present context is that Dworkin's criticisms of Hart and Hart's reply are almost without exception pitched at a higher level of generality than any particular legal system. Neither is claiming that they are solely or even mainly arguing about English law or some American jurisdiction or even the common law family. So, again the distinction between general and particular jurisprudence explains almost nothing about the exchanges between Hart and Dworkin.

However, it is Dworkin who insists that: 'interpretive theories are by their nature addressed to a particular legal culture, generally the culture to which their authors belong'.[1] In the same passage he draws a distinction between 'the very detailed and concrete legal theories lawyers and judges construct for a particular jurisdiction' and the abstract conceptions of law that philosophers build, which are not so confined.[2] He argues that an abstract philosophical conception of law, still less a justificatory theory for a given system (or, semble, a family of systems belonging to one legal culture), will probably not fit 'foreign legal systems developing in and reflecting political ideologies of a sharply different character'. His main point is that one can only determine whether a given proposition of law is true for a given system by participating in that system, because this activity involves interpreting and choosing between contested meanings and that necessitates taking sides. For Dworkin there is no such thing as neutral interpretation.[3] However, in making these *caveats*, Dworkin may be being unduly cautious about the general significance of his theory.

---

19 Eg Postscript, pp 248, 261, 264-267.
20 Eg, Ibid, pp 244-248; at the time of writing Dworkin has not yet replied in print to Hart's Postscript.
1   *LE*, p 102. cf. Rawls, discussed below Ch 3.4(c).
2   Ibid, pp 102-103.
3   Dworkin agrees with Hart that one can report a debate about the meaning of a legal rule or the content of the rule of recognition from the outside, but as soon as one purports to say what any law means one is involved in interpretation and hence is participating and, in any actual or potential contest, taking sides.

A charitable interpretation of Dworkin's emphasis on the particularity of interpretation may include two points which we have already encountered. He may draw almost exclusively on Anglo-American materials and he may leave open the scope of the applicability of his ideas to civilian and other systems on the grounds of limited expertise, but so did Austin, Maine and Holland, all of whom claimed to be doing general jurisprudence. This seems rather like Holland's example of a geologist who has only studied English strata and who is cautious about generalising beyond his data base.[4]

Secondly, in emphasising the importance of local knowledge, Dworkin seems to be making a similar point to that made by Buckland in his critique of Holland. If general jurisprudence is confined to describing the features that are common to all or nearly all legal systems, the description will almost certainly be rather thin because in fact legal systems are quite diverse and the interest of a legal system lies typically in its detail. General jurisprudence on its own will be too abstract to be useful or interesting. In so far as Dworkin is concerned with interpretation, argumentation and justification by legal practitioners and judges, he would agree with Austin that jurisprudence to be practical has to be local and particular. But that does not mean that the core elements in his theory only apply to one system.

Moreover, only by studying all legal systems in detail can one identify which features are universal or common. Dworkin's variant on this argument is that general jurisprudence cannot deal with the problem of sense, that is the attribution of truth values to propositions of law.[5] This seems to conflate a general theory of adjudication or legal interpretation with its application in a local context. The former may be lean, but that does not mean that it is not important. *Law's Empire* advances a general theory of law, or at least of adjudication; it contains very few concrete examples of interpretation and those are mainly illustrative; some of Dworkin's other writings are more local, but these can be interpreted as applications of his general approach.[6]

---

4   This is analogous to Raz writing about Rawls: 'The writer's theory must, to be successful, apply to his society at the time of writing, but there is no general answer as to which societies and what other times it applies to. The applicability of the theory to different societies must be examined on a case-by-case basis'. Joseph Raz, *Ethics in the Public Domain* (1994) 63n.

5   Dworkin concedes that there are other questions for general legal theory – historical, sociological etc which may produce illuminating propositions *about* law – but maintains that such enquiries have to build on interpretive theories about the meaning of propositions *of* law: *LE*, pp 13-14.

6   Eg 'How to Read the Civil Rights Act', *New York Review of Books*, 20, December 1979, 37.

A less charitable interpretation of Hart and Dworkin is suggested by Atiyah and Summers, who advocate 'jurisprudential relativism' in the interpretation of legal cultures:

> 'In our view, then, the primary subject-matter of jurisprudence is not a single universal subject matter, abstracted from the variant phenomena of law in all societies. It should, rather, consist of relevant features of the phenomena of law in one or more particular societies.'[7]

Atiyah and Summers were comparing and contrasting the legal cultures of England and the United States which are closely related by history, language, and continuing links. Interestingly they suggest that the two cultures even have different conceptions of some concepts which are usually allocated to the meta-language of general jurisprudence, such as 'law' and 'rule' and 'legal validity'. In their view, both Hart and Dworkin are best interpreted as contributing to, or as being most useful at the level of, particular jurisprudence. Dworkin's theory is both derived from American intellectual tradition and fits American culture better than English. Conversely Hart is recognisably English in respect of the derivation of his ideas and their application. For example, the ideal role for judges and legislators is dependent on context, for political institutions are fashioned by history, tradition and culture:

> 'What is the practical utility of a theory which postulates how Hercules J. ought to behave on the bench, if appointing authorities insist on nominating judges who do not even want to emulate Hercules?'[8]

This ethnographic perspective raises many intriguing questions that cannot be pursued here. Atiyah and Summers acknowledge that it may be possible to identify some features and concepts which are common to the phenomena of law in all societies, but the list is likely to be short and its explanatory value meagre. This is very like Buckland's view that law is culturally relative and that jurisprudence must in the main be particular. I have some sympathy with this position, but I do not think that this is an interpretation that makes Hart's and Dworkin's theories the best they can be. I would rather suggest that both theories largely stand or fall on an assessment of their value as contributions to general jurisprudence.

7   P S Atiyah and R S Summers, *Form and Substance in Anglo-American Law* (1987), p 418.
8   Ibid, p 420, cf pp 264-266.

Dworkin is not a strong cultural relativist.[9] It is one thing to claim that a thick description of any society or culture or social practice must depend on local knowledge and hence be particular; it is another to claim that a society or culture or practice can only be described, interpreted or explained solely in its own terms. Most writing by historians and social anthropologists is particular and local, because they tend to study events and phenomena that are unique in important respects; but those writings are based on theories, methods and concepts that have some claim to generality – and some may be unknown locally. Conversely, it is a truism, accepted by both Hart and Dworkin, that to give an adequate account of a particular social practice or legal system typically involves taking into account the internal point of view of participants in that practice or system, including their concepts and language. One cannot give a 'thick' account of English or Tiv or Barotse law either solely in terms of some foreign or meta-language, which does not capture the ways of thought of the participants, nor solely in terms of the folk concepts of the participants themselves.[10] Hart is not committed to ignoring or discounting the internal point of view; Dworkin is not committed to treating local concepts as exclusive for purposes of justification or description. For example, in the standard example of a foreign anthropologist describing and interpreting a rain-making ceremony, the external observer needs to take into account the beliefs of some or all participants that it does indeed make rain, but s/he could explain and possibly justify the practice in terms of social solidarity: 'Whether or not it makes rain, it serves a useful purpose for them'.

9   Gavison comes close to accusing Dworkin of this: she asserts that Dworkin's theory challenges the possibility and the value of 'general jurisprudence' (above). She argues that one implication of Dworkin's subversion of the distinction between law and a theory of law is that a theory of law is no more than the general assumptions about law in a given community, 'ie theories of law are time- and community-dependent' (pp 26-27). My own view is that Dworkin need not be so confined: he may be right in maintaining that to give a precise meaning to a particular provision of the US Constitution or some aspect of English doctrine is participatory, but what is interesting about Dworkin is his general perspective and approach which has wide potential application, whether right or wrong.

10 Cf the debate in legal anthropology between Gluckman and Bohannan about the relative importance of 'folk concepts' and meta-language for giving an account of customary law, Max Gluckman, *The Judicial Process among the Barotse of Northern Rhodesia* (1957); Paul Bohannan, *Justice and Judgment among the Tiv of Nigeria* (1957). This reflected a wider debate about 'emics' and 'etics' in social anthropology, on which see Ward Goodenough, *Description and Comparison in Social Anthropology* (1970), Thomas Headland, Kenneth L Pike, and Marvin Harris (eds), *Emics and Etics: The Insider/ Outsider Debate* (1990). It is now widely accepted that both 'folk concepts' and meta-languages are necessary tools, but that meta-languages are themselves culturally located social constructs.

What colour is Hercules's passport? He may be of American origin, have a slight American accent, and possibly some deep-rooted American cultural biases.[11] But clearly he is offered, and deserves, attention as a possible role model for judges in many systems – certainly the common law family, almost certainly Western civilian systems, possibly the European Union and judges of international tribunals, perhaps even the judiciary in an Islamic state. The reason for this is obvious: the basic ideas underlying Hercules's approach are not derived from nor confined to any one legal system or culture: law as integrity; interpretation as making a system the best it can be; reasoning by the two stage process of fit and justification; justification in terms of institutionally embedded principles of political morality. All of these concepts are not system-specific. Hercules has strong claims to be a citizen at least of the West, and possibly of the World.

Let us consider some possible objections to this. First, it might be argued that these ideas are not sufficient conditions for appointing Hercules as a judge in any jurisdiction. Of course, that is correct. In order to be able to perform the role of a judge well one needs a number of other qualifications, including a good deal of local knowledge about, for example, the general prescriptions of the legal system concerning authoritative sources of law, including any rules of priority and interpretation; and about other factors subsumed under the idea of 'fit'.[12] Similarly in interpreting the law in a hard case, Hercules' duty is to resolve difficulties by reference to fundamental principles of political morality which give *this* system integrity. These will typically be contested, but in Dworkin's theory this does not mean that Hercules should merely resort to his personal opinions; rather he should seek for the 'best' solution in the system's own terms. Such justificatory principles are not purely local, but form part of a coherent theory of political morality which, one assumes, makes some claim to generality. Dworkin makes clear his commitment to a particular version of liberal democratic theory of wide application, but he recognises that Hercules may serve in a system based on a different moral theory. Presumably that moral theory is basically compatible with Hercules's own values, for he could not

---

11 Atiyah and Summers, pp 264-266.
12 The amount of 'local knowledge' required of some judges may not be very great. For example, the British Colonial Legal Service, whose members could be posted and transferred relatively freely from jurisdiction to jurisdiction, was an example of how a legal culture can operate relatively detached from local social contexts. Whether many judges in that tradition emulated Hercules is another question.

otherwise in good conscience have taken the judicial oath.[13] Hercules's characteristics are not sufficient conditions for judicial appointment; they are presented as desirable, ideal, perhaps even necessary, standards for good judging.

A second objection, suggested by Atiyah and Summers, is that Hercules just does not fit most actual legal systems. If he were a candidate for judicial appointment in England, he would probably not be appointed. Dworkin has two possible answers to that: first, if a system does not subscribe to his aspirational standards for judging, more's the pity. His is 'the best theory' prescribing an ideal. Secondly, Dworkin – more controversially – claims that his theory describes good practice in the Anglo-American system. In this view, Atiyah and Summers misrepresent English practice.

A third objection is that Dworkin advances a general theory of adjudication, but courts and judges are institutionalised in different ways in different societies and so have different roles, methods and so on. Even in modern Western societies third party adjudication is only one of several modes of dispute-processing and, in terms of frequency and accessibility, it is often one of the least important in practice. What precisely is the role of courts in a given society varies considerably according to time and place. This argument can be extended in two ways: first, as any comparative lawyer knows, even terms like 'court', 'judge', 'lawyer', 'case' and 'trial' are culture-specific. Secondly, some societies do not have any institutionalised third-party adjudication at all.[14]

This is a powerful argument that needs to be taken into account by any legal theory that claims to be even minimally sensitive to 'social realities'. It is particularly pertinent in considering globalisation, given the relative unimportance of 'courts' in international, transnational and other global relations. Here I think that Dworkin may have done himself a disservice by claiming to advance a theory of adjudication. What he is really advancing is a theory of correct interpretation of legal norms. Hercules is not just a role model for actual judges; rather he is a symbol for the Upright Interpreter, who is loyal to the system – that is for anyone who is concerned to reach the correct or 'best' or 'right' interpretation of the law.[15] This includes upright officials, good citizens, and other

13 My personal view is that Dworkin's theory is at its most persuasive when applied to the judicial oath (and all that it symbolises), for this represents an undertaking to be loyal to the system and to try to make it 'the best it can be'. For a more sceptical view of his idea of 'interpretation' in other contexts, see *HTDTWR*, pp 375-379.

14 Eg P Gulliver, *Social Control in an African Society* (1963) (an account of the Arusha of Northern Tanzania).

15 On other kinds of interpreters, see *HTDTWR*, *passim*, especially pp 68-76, 168-175.

participants who wish to make decisions based at least in part on clear understandings of what the law prescribes. One doubts whether labelling Dworkin's theory as 'a theory of adjudication' is making it the best it can be. It has a much wider reach than that.

Finally, Atiyah and Summers draw a distinction between their 'jurisprudential relativism' and moral (or ethical) relativism, which they reject. They also express scepticism about Utopian universalism in the field of law and, as we have seen, dismiss Hercules as representing an Utopian ideal with regard to the role of judges. It seems that they are more sympathetic to Hart's concern to develop a descriptive theory that fits the facts of actual legal phenomena, but they place more emphasis on cultural or local specificity than Hart does.[16] Here, there is a more fundamental difference with Dworkin; for although he makes some allowance for cultural diversity, he considers that law and its interpretation are a moral and an argumentative enterprise, founded on a moral theory that is a general theory of political morality and a theory of rationality that is similarly based on general principles of valid reasoning. Thus, at its core, Dworkin's seemingly particularistic theory is at least as general as its positivistic rivals.

Hart's Postscript and the mutual courtesies of the two friendly protagonists suggest that the differences between them can easily be exaggerated. They come from a shared philosophical tradition, but from somewhat different legal cultures. Neither has drawn much inspiration from anthropology, sociology or history. They both present a picture of law in terms of monistic unity: law as a system of rules and law as integrity treat the laws of independent nation states as units of analysis in ways that approximate to the ideal type of 'black box' theories. Even at what many consider to be the key point of differentiation between positivist and anti-positivist positions, one can argue that they may not be very different. On the one hand, some would interpret Dworkin as a 'positivist' in that Hercules must look for underlying principles that are institutionally embedded in an existing system; conversely, Hart's insistence on a sharp distinction between the is and the ought has sometimes been interpreted as a conservative attempt to legitimate legal systems – conservatism masquerading as neutrality. A more plausible reading is that for Hart, as for Bentham and Holmes, separating the 'is' and the 'ought' serves clarity of thought, which in turn is based on a moral concern: one needs a vocabulary for depicting actual legal institutions and systems in terms that can depict the true awfulness of many such exercises of power – like *The Bonfire of the Vanities* writ large. I am personally more sympathetic to this last interpretation, but in the

16 Atiyah and Summers, as well as Hart, are interested in 'ideal interpretive method', but as a distinct enterprise.

present context the main point is that the distinction between general and particular jurisprudence does little or nothing to illuminate the similarities and differences between Hart and Dworkin.

5   CONCLUDING OBSERVATIONS

This essay suggests that sharp distinctions between general and particular jurisprudence are of limited value. Its starting-point was the suggestion that some Anglo-American jurisprudence seems to have been going through a somewhat parochial phase and continues to be dominated by theories which treat societies, nation states and legal systems as largely self-contained units. In this context, 'parochialism' can relate to focus, or to sources, or to perspectives.[17] Jurisprudence, can be inward-looking in respect of its agenda, ethnocentric in respect of its perspective, or limited in respect of its sources and inspiration. Globalisation brings to the fore a wide range of issues at transnational, international and global levels and is rapidly changing the significance of national boundaries. As such it challenges 'black box theories', it is inimical to ethnocentric perspectives on transnational issues, but it does not minimise the importance of the local. 'The citizen of the world' may still be a rooted cosmopolitan, in Bruce Ackerman's phrase,[18] setting the study of local issues and phenomena in a broad geographical context.

This preliminary study of one aspect of the vast heritage of jurisprudence suggests that the English positivist tradition has tended to emphasise general more than particular jurisprudence; it has been quite cosmopolitan in outlook, but over time it increasingly narrowed its focus to a relatively narrow range of concepts and issues relating mainly, but not exclusively, to English or Anglo-American legal doctrine. Of the individuals considered here, Bentham was the one who was most consistently committed to the viewpoint of 'the citizen of the world' and, although he did not develop his ideas very far in this respect, he was more sensitive than most of his successors to the limitations of 'black box' theories of national or municipal legal systems.[19]

It is worth commenting briefly on each of these points. First, English legal positivism since Bentham has usually placed more emphasis on general than on particular jurisprudence. Bentham, Austin, Maine, Holland, Hart, and Raz all fit this category, as do many others. Holland's English critics, such as Pollock and Buckland, were not being parochial or ethnocentric in respect of perspective. They were mainly concerned

17   See below, Ch 5.
18   Bruce Ackerman, 'Rooted Cosmopolitanism' (1994) 104 *Ethics* 516.
19   RB, pp 134-136.

that an over-abstract approach to the teaching of jurisprudence would be less useful than the systematic study of the basic concepts and principles of English Law and would reinforce the resistance of the practising profession to the academic study of law and especially to legal theory. I have argued that the differences between Hart and Dworkin cannot be usefully explained in terms of a distinction between general and particular jurisprudence and that Dworkin's central ideas, both explicitly and implicitly have general, if not universal, significance.

Secondly, the English tradition of academic law has generally been quite cosmopolitan. Historically, the study of Roman Law, Canon Law, Public International Law, and to a lesser extent, Comparative Law have been an important part of our intellectual tradition. The British Empire, the Commonwealth, the European Union, and the strong networks within the extended family of common law jurisdictions have usually kept in check any tendencies to confine legal studies to English domestic law. Even the advocates of particular jurisprudence such as Buckland and Pollock were hardly Little Englanders. They were familiar with Roman Law and contemporary European legal thought. Like them, generalists such as Austin and Maine, drew most of their examples from Roman and English Law. The recent decline in the study of Romanist systems, the confining of 'core subjects' to domestic law, and the general parochialism of modern professional examinations, will almost certainly prove to have been a relatively short historical phase. The European Union, the transnationalisation of much legal practice, and the broader processes of globalisation will ensure that.

Thirdly, analytical positivism was, however, narrow in a different sense. The sharp distinction between the is and the ought, and between law and other disciplines, supported a tendency to confine the study of law to the exposition and analysis of legal doctrine. The expository tradition tended to become ahistorical, decontextualised and uncritical.[20] Despite a series of challenges it remains the dominant force in our academic legal culture.[1] This is clearly illustrated in the work of our most influential modern jurist, Herbert Hart: his method was of potentially very wide application, his commitment was to general jurisprudence, but his focus and agenda for jurisprudence were quite narrow. Conceptual clarification and formal description are as important for broader approaches to law as for legal dogmatics, but Hart neither applied his great analytical skills to the basic concepts needed for such approaches nor did he encourage others to do so. Similarly, Ronald Dworkin's agenda for Legal Philosophy is really quite narrow. Insofar as his main interest is adjudication, he confines his focus to questions of

20   ALLP; cf Horwitz, op cit, p 25 n 1.
1   See *BT*, Ch 6.

law in hard cases, ignoring almost entirely the whole range of problems of interpretation and justification involved in other important decisions in legal contexts.[2]

Another limitation of the tradition has been to treat societies and municipal legal systems as self-contained units and to pay scant attention to transnational and global relations and to legal pluralism. Even in respect of traditional Public International Law, theorists as different as Hart, Rawls and Dworkin share the tendency to treat 'legal systems' as isolated and self-contained phenomena, and as a result they tend to be at their least convincing at the international and transnational levels. How far their central ideas can be rescued from such criticism requires further exploration.[3]

Finally, the distinction between general and particular jurisprudence has a function, but it has been and is likely to be of limited value in setting an agenda for the discipline of law and for jurisprudence as its theoretical part. I, for one, benefited as a student from exposure to particular analytical jurisprudence and regret its passing. But 'general' and 'particular' are relative matters and the distinction cannot bear much weight. In considering the implications of globalisation for legal theory, it will be necessary to be concerned with a wide range of questions at different levels of generality. We need jurisprudence that can transcend jurisdictions and cultures, so far as that is feasible and appropriate, and which can address issues about law from a global and transnational perspective. However, 'thick description' of local particulars set in broad geographical contexts will be as important as ever in the development of a healthy discipline of law in a more integrated world.

2   This theme is developed in *LIC*, Ch 17.
3   Below Ch 3.

Chapter 3

Globalisation and legal theory: some local implications*

I GLOBALISATION: THREE CHALLENGES TO LEGAL THEORY

Jeremy Bentham sometimes referred to himself as a citizen of the world. In his later writings he recognised the tension between his universal ethics and his theory of sovereignty, and he wrestled with it not very successfully.[1] I was born in Uganda of an English father and a mother of Welsh-Huguenot descent. I had a colonial childhood, an anti-colonial adolescence, a neo-colonial start to my career, and a post-colonial middle age. I married an Irish wife. My daughter was born in Khartoum and my son in Dublin. I have just returned from India. I seem to have far better credentials than Bentham to claim to be a citizen of the world. Yet in style, residence, outlook, accent and prejudices, I am irredeemably English. At best I am, in Bruce Ackerman's phrase, a rooted cosmopolitan.[2] And it is as a cosmopolitan, rooted in London and Oxford, that I want to share with you some thoughts about the local implications of globalisation for jurisprudence as a subject and for the institutionalised discipline of law in this country.[3]

Globalisation has stimulated major rethinkings in several fields. I propose to argue that jurisprudence has so far responded only patchily to these challenges, but that the prospects for a sustained response are better than might appear on the surface. The processes of globalisation are extremely complex and their impact is already pervasive. Here I

---

* This is an expanded version of a lecture delivered at University College London and published in 49 (1996) CLP No 21. The relevant parts are reproduced here by kind permission of the Delegates of Oxford University Press.
1 RB at pp 133-138.
2 Bruce Ackerman, 'Rooted Cosmopolitanism', (1994) 104 *Ethics* 516.
3 On globalisation and my views on legal theory, see Ch 1 above.

shall focus on three themes which seemingly present fundamental challenges to legal theory.

First, globalisation and interdependence challenge 'black box theories' that treat nation states or societies or legal systems as discrete, impervious entities that can be studied in isolation either internally or externally. This challenge operates in two main ways: municipal law can no longer be treated in isolation from outside influences, legal or otherwise. To take a familiar example, consider the daily impact of European Law, the European Convention on Human Rights, GATT, and transnational religious laws on our internal legal relations between local citizens, the state and other legal persons.[4] Conversely, the twin doctrines of national sovereignty and non-interference in internal affairs of independent states is being steadily challenged, most prominently, but not exclusively, by international humanitarian and human rights law and regional legal orders, such as the EU.[5] In so far as our stock of theories of law assumes that municipal legal systems are self-contained or that public international law is concerned solely with external relations between states, such theories just do not fit the modern facts.

Secondly, mainstream Anglo-American legal theory has traditionally focused on only two types of legal order: municipal state law and public international law. Today, a picture of law in the world must deal with a much more complex picture involving established, resurgent, developing, nascent and potential forms of legal ordering. At the global level, there is a need for new orderings, especially in respect of communications, the environment, and natural resources on this and other planets. What are the prospects for a genuine *ius humanitatis* dealing with the common heritage of mankind?[6] And what will be its philosophical or political base? Can public international law, as traditionally conceived, cope adequately with such problems as environment, international crime, and basic human needs or rights at the global level? At the transnational level, are we seeing the development of a new *lex mercatoria* – a system of largely private regulation within the capitalist world economy with institutions such as international arbitration playing an increasingly significant role? Also at the transnational level, what is general jurisprudence to make of, for example, the revival of Islamic Law in which the theological-juridical schools transcend national boundaries and in many countries are part of the opposition to the government of the day? Even in officially Islamic states, those in power may represent only one point of view in ongoing juristic debates.[7]

4   *HTDTWR*, pp 141-143.
5   Neil MacCormick, 'Beyond the Sovereign State' (1993) 56 *MLR* 1.
6   Boaventura Santos, *Toward a New Common Sense* (1995) at pp 365-373.
7   Eg Abdullahi An-na'im, *Toward an Islamic Reformation* (1990).

At the regional level, new legal orders are developing rapidly. The European Union is the most salient from our vantage-point, but it is not the only one. Only relatively recently have fundamental questions begun to be asked in a sustained way about the juridical nature of EU Law.[8] Does it fit any of our standard stock of theories of law and, conversely, which, if any, of the theories can provide any useful guidance to its development? Public International Law, I have suggested, has expanded and diversified in so many ways that it no longer fits old simple models of external relations between states. But further questions arise as to whether Public International Law, in which the nation state still plays by far the dominant role, provides a suitable framework for conceptualising transnational relations, both in obvious areas such as humanitarian and human rights law, but also in less obvious ones such as labour and domestic relations. One clear example of an uneasy fit is the artificial distinction between problems of international refugees, which fall largely under public international law, and the problems of internally displaced persons (now a more numerous group) who by and large are treated as the responsibility of their own states, which are often at least partly the cause of the problem.[9]

One theme that links the emergence or re-emergence of these new kinds of legal order is the disengagement of law and state.[10] A *ius humanitatis*, a transnational *lex mercatoria*, Islamic law, transnational humanitarian and human rights law, and, in a different way, some new regional orderings, and even parts of public international law itself are all arguably more or less clear examples of the amorphous category 'non-state law'. I shall return to this idea when I consider normative and legal pluralism, but it is worth noting here that an account of the phenomenon of law in the contemporary world would for most purposes be incomplete if it did not treat of legal families and legal cultures. Nation states have, of course, played a major role in the diffusion and imposition of law in modern times, but so have immigration, informal networking and the globalisation of communication. One suspects, for example, that most of the younger generation in Continental Europe have obtained their picture of courts and trials and lawyers from American

---

8   A useful appraisal is Ian Ward, *A Critical Introduction to European Law* (1996) Ch 5. Cf F Snyder, ' "Out on the Weekend": Reflections on European Law in Context', in G P Wilson (ed) *Frontiers of Legal Scholarship* (1995), Ch 9. See generally the writings of Joseph Weiler, eg 'The Transformation of Europe' (1991) 100 Yale Law Journal 2403.

9   Deng, op cit.

10   This is a central theme of writings on legal pluralism, eg Santos, op cit; J Griffiths, 'What is Legal Pluralism?', (1986) *Journal of Legal Pluralism* 24 and works cited below, section 5.

films and soap operas and, recently, from such live dramas as the O J Simpson case on CNN. One suspects also that orthodox accounts of reception and diffusion of law, at least in modern times, have been unduly influenced by formalist, state-oriented conceptions of law, which tend to downplay or overlook the other, often more elusive, elements that go to make up a legal culture.[11]

The third challenge of globalisation to legal theory that I wish to highlight is rather less fashionable. This is the matter of conceptual clarification, more particularly the construction of a conceptual framework and a meta-language of legal theory that can transcend legal cultures. During the nineteenth century this was a central concern of both analytical and historical jurists. Bentham aspired to construct a universal legislative dictionary.[12] The focus of Austin's jurisprudence was on those 'principles, notions and distinctions' which were either necessary or commonly to be found in more mature systems.[13] Austin and Bentham were mainly concerned with the fundamental legal conceptions either used in or presupposed by legal rules (the concepts of law talk) – such as sovereign, law, sanction, legal person, duty, and injury. This was a very limited list, as they clearly recognised, because laws tend to be expressed differently in different legal cultures and systems. Sociologically oriented jurists, such as Maine, Tonnies[14] and Vinogradoff, also started to develop a meta-language for comparing legal systems and cultures from the outside in terms of stages of development and forms of law. For Maine, for example, such concepts as contract, status, fictions, equity, legislation, and corporation were part of a meta-language for cross-cultural study of law in general.[15] During the period 1870-1950 English analytical jurisprudence became increasingly particular, focusing mainly on the elucidation of fundamental conceptions of English law, including peculiar ideas such as trust and seisin as well as ownership, possession and contract.[16]

When Herbert Hart revived the study of jurisprudence in the 1950s, he shifted the emphasis back from particular to general jurisprudence; he radically changed the methods of conceptual analysis, but he did not significantly alter the agenda: the list of concepts that he treated as central to general descriptive jurisprudence was not greatly different from the

---

11 A useful discussion of the concept of 'legal culture' is John Bell, 'English Law and French Law – Not So different?' (1995) 48 *C L P.* 63.

12 Mary Mack, *Jeremy Bentham: An Odyssey of Ideas 1748-92* (1962).

13 John Austin, 'The Uses of the Study of Jurisprudence' (1863, edn Hart, 1954), at pp 367-369.

14 On the significance of Tonnies, see Edward Shils in Alan Diamond (ed) *Sir Henry Maine: A Centennial Appraisal* (1991), Ch 8.

15 On Maine's concepts, see *ibid*, esp. Chs 6-10.

16 Ibid, Ch 3.

attenuated lists of Austin and Bentham.[17] He did not, for example, apply his methods to important sociological concepts such as dispute, process, system, institution, function, and group. This was particularly unfortunate given that historical jurisprudence had faded away and the sociology of law, under American influence, had become both particular and ethnocentric. Over a long period of time, mainstream legal theory had generally failed to address problems of cultural pluralism, at least transnationally.

Similar considerations apply to the sociology of law. For example, the sociology of legal professions, having made great strides at local levels, especially in the United States, has foundered on the absence of a meta-language for even the most elementary description of legal functionaries and personnel. It is obvious that words like 'lawyer', 'private practitioner', 'notary', or 'advocate' mean significantly different things, both formally and functionally, in different legal systems, even within the common law family. To date the comparative sociology of legal professions has barely begun to develop a conceptual framework for making valid comparisons.[18] The problem of how far law as a phenomenon is so culture-specific as to defy detailed comparison between legal systems and cultures is itself a central, and somewhat underworked problem of legal theory. Meanwhile, Austinian analytical jurisprudence that emphasised conceptual elucidation has largely been replaced by substantive political philosophy.

2   LEGAL STUDIES IN LONDON IN THE MID-1990s

Jurisprudence is not a subject apart. It has some specific tasks to perform in keeping the discipline of law in a healthy state. If things are going well, it both feeds off and feeds into more specialised areas. In considering these challenges of globalisation to the discipline of law, and to jurisprudence as its general part, I shall adopt the standpoint of a London-based jurist as a licensed subversive, considering the health of his discipline and his subject in a particular place at a particular time. Let me begin then, by briefly considering some aspects of the situation in London.

---

17 Hart did, however, make important contributions to the analysis of a few concepts, such as causation, responsibility and powers. Surprisingly, as he himself admitted at the end of his life, his analysis of the concept of 'rule' was seriously incomplete (Postscript at pp 259-263).

18 See the valiant, but in my view largely unsuccessful, attempts to grapple with these issues in Richard Abel and Philip Lewis (eds) *Lawyers in Society: Comparative Theories* (1989).

The study of law in the University of London, and at University College in particular, has a strong cosmopolitan tradition. Let me remind you of a few points. First, Public International Law and the study of legal systems and ideas in the Romanist tradition have been an important part of our enterprise for most of our history. It is true that there was a time when Roman Law first ceased to be a compulsory subject and then became somewhat marginalised as a minority option within the LLB. It has not even been offered at postgraduate level in recent years. This process coincided with the period in which the so-called 'core' subjects were limited to domestic law and the professional examinations were similarly parochial.[19] Membership of the European Community and Union has already changed that. European Union Law has been made a core subject for purposes of professional exemption and, more important, European Union Law, the European Convention on Human Rights (in the run up to the implementation of the Human Rights Act) and the study of contemporary civilian systems are now a crucial part of our activities. Whether the study of Roman Law can be revived on the back of these developments remains to be seen.[20]

Our academic culture has always been part of an extraordinarily strong network in the common law world, embracing both the United States and the Commonwealth. We recruit New Zealanders as well as South Africans; we export teachers and postgraduates to other common law countries; and, until recently, when we jet-setted, it was nearly always to anglophone countries. It is an entrenched part of our tradition that the study and teaching of English domestic law has always been informed by legal developments and ideas in other parts of the common law world. Again, academic law in England is open to criticism that it has been almost exclusively concerned with Western law and has tended to neglect other legal cultures. If we are to take globalisation seriously, we shall in future have to pay more attention to non-Western law and other traditions of legal thought. However, it can be said in defence of London that it has been the headquarters of nearly all British attempts, however modest, to pioneer the local study of Islamic, Chinese, Hindu, African, Soviet or Socialist and, most recently, Japanese Law.

Furthermore, at the postgraduate level our practice is truly cosmopolitan. A very rough analysis of the syllabuses for the London LLM degree for internal students in 1994 showed that out of nearly 130

19 Andrew Lewis suggests that a major factor in the decline of Roman Law teaching in English universities was its ceasing to be a compulsory subject in the Bar Examinations in the early 1960s. Roman Law ceased to be offered as an option in the London LLM after 1983 for lack of suitable candidates.

20 On a recent controversy about Roman Law teaching in Continental Europe, see Reinhard Zimmerman, 'Roman Law and Comparative Law: The European Perspective' (1995) 16 *Journal of Legal History* 21.

courses listed, only 31 purported to concentrate on some aspect of English (or United Kingdom) law and most of these made explicit reference to developments abroad or in the EU. In a further 14 or so the syllabus could be said to have been roughly divided between a focus on local laws and institutions and explicit treatment of comparative or international topics. Over 80 courses, more than two-thirds of the total, dealt mainly with international, transnational, foreign or comparative subjects. The geographical reach of the LLM is truly remarkable. The question remains to what extent has this fed into and been assisted by legal theory?

Finally, and as important, our student population is marvellously cosmopolitan. One of the great pleasures of teaching in London is the international spread of our student body, not only at postgraduate level. What we give them may be distinctively English; what they give us in hundreds of ways are constant reminders of a wider world.

Why, you may ask, this purple passage in praise of our cosmopolitanism? Not, I can assure you, to soothe you into complacency. My central argument is that we need some quite fundamental rethinking at the level of theory, if we are to respond coherently and sensibly to the challenges of globalisation. Law schools in London are rather well equipped by tradition, resources and outlook to make an adequate response to the challenge.

The syllabus for the LLM, which grew like Topsy, suggests that our practice may have outrun our theory. By this I mean that what we teach and write about as 'mainstream jurisprudence' may be a good deal more parochial than what we study elsewhere in the curriculum, especially at postgraduate level. Conversely, one senses that our main cosmopolitan areas, such as public international law, comparative law, European law and the study of foreign legal systems have not been particularly well-served by legal theory in recent years.

3   THE LOCAL JURISTIC CANON

My immediate purpose is modest. I propose to look critically at a few examples of that part of our heritage of Anglo-American jurisprudence that is currently treated as canonical at UCL – and more generally in the United Kingdom – and ask how far it can be defended against charges of excessive parochialism and irrelevance to problems of globalisation.

Academic law in England today is characterised by an extraordinary pluralism.[1] Recently, as we shall see, legal theory has diversified to a comparable extent. However, if one looks at standard student works,

---

1   *BT*, Chs 6 and 7.

syllabuses for courses on jurisprudence, and articles in law journals, there are sufficiently stable patterns for one to be able to talk quite confidently about 'mainstream jurisprudence' or even a contemporary juristic canon.[2] In a 1994 survey of taught jurisprudence by Hilaire Barnett[3] five jurists featured as being studied 'in depth' in more than 50% of undergraduate courses on the subject in the United Kingdom in 1993-94. These were in order of frequency: Hart, Dworkin, Rawls, Finnis and Austin, with Bentham, Kelsen and Llewellyn coming equal sixth on 47%-48%.

These eight figures seem to me to be reasonably representative of the current 'canon' in taught jurisprudence, subject to a few *caveats*. For example, Barnett would be the first to acknowledge that too much weight should not be attached to the figures in this popularity poll.[4] However, the survey does suggest a slow but steady trend towards studying selected jurists in the original rather than having superficial and inaccurate Cook's tours of 'schools' and 'isms'. Barnett's list reflects the coverage of most standard student works – although Lloyd and Freeman ranges much more widely[5] – and all of the top eight names feature in Part A of our own LLB Jurisprudence course.

2   Recently the idea of a canon has become controversial. For example: 'Originally the Canon meant the choice of books in our teaching institutions, and despite the recent politics of multiculturalism, the Canon's true question remains: What shall the individual who still desires to read attempt to read, this late in history? The Biblical three-score years and ten no longer suffice to read more than a selection of the great writers in what can be called the Western tradition, let alone in all the world's traditions.' Harold Bloom, *The Western Canon* (1994) at p 15. The idea of a canon is used here merely as a convenient way of referring to jurists and texts that are treated as part of 'the mainstream' in a given time and place. The jurisprudential 'canon' includes not only texts treated as standard in taught jurisprudence, but also theoretical works that are influential in particular fields. For example, Grotius and Lasswell and McDougal are still influential on thinking about public international law, but they are not studied regularly in most British courses on jurisprudence. Canons both exclude and include: cf Santos: 'As there is a literary canon that establishes what is and what is not literature, there is also a legal canon that establishes what is and what is not law' (op cit 1995) at p 473.

3   Hilaire Barnett, 'The province of jurisprudence determined – again!' (1995) 15 *Legal Studies* 88. This is the third in a sequence covering a period of 20 years: cf Barnett and Yach (1985) 5 *Legal Studies* 151 and R Cotterrell and J Woodliffe [1974] *JSPTL* (NS) 73. The 1994 survey was expanded to cover Australian and Canadian (Common Law) universities and includes an analysis of trends in taught jurisprudence over the 20-year period.

4   For example, it stretches belief that in nearly half of undergraduate jurisprudence courses the ideas of Jeremy Bentham are studied 'in depth', bearing in mind that only about half of his work is yet available in reliable editions and that *The Collected Works*, when completed, will run to an estimated 68-70 substantial volumes.

5   Dennis Lloyd's *Introduction to Jurisprudence* (6th edn, M D A Freeman, 1994).

Barnett notes that over the past twenty years taught jurisprudence has diversified and changed quite substantially. There are some continuities at the top of her tables, but in the middle and lower reaches the most striking trend is diversification. This new pluralism in legal theory is nowhere more apparent than in London. When I came to UCL in 1983, I was the only holder of a Chair in Law in the University of London who professed legal theory as his main interest. In 1996 at least 13 professors of law in the University could make such a claim, and there were many other colleagues with a strong interest in the subject. The diversity of interests and perspectives is striking. Traditional positivism, liberalism, natural law, Marxism, realism, sociology and anthropology of law, Bentham studies, and law and economics are all represented; so are feminism, critical legal studies, deconstruction, psychoanalytic theory, legal pluralism, various forms of post-modernism, law and literature, law and development, and systems theory. A profusion of flowers has bloomed, along with some weeds, chaff, and wild oats. Workshops and series of seminars have been organised on Psychoanalysis and the Law, Law and the Senses, Law and the Passions, Law and Literature, Law and Religion, and Medicine, Ethics and Law – to mention just a few.[6]

Legal theory in London, and in the common law world generally, has diversified considerably and shows signs of a confusing, sometimes confused, intellectual ferment. But very little of this seems to be directly related to globalisation, let alone to be a response to it. The two most obviously relevant approaches, law and development and legal pluralism have been quite marginal in London and elsewhere in the United Kingdom in recent years. So, too, has historical jurisprudence. Indeed, some of the most fashionable pursuits could be accused of being quite parochial.

The pattern is even clearer across the Atlantic. For example, during the last twenty or so years two movements have captured the foreground in the United States: economic analysis of law and critical legal studies. If one looks at two books that were fairly representative of the genre up to the early 1990s, Posner's *Economic Analysis of Law* and Kelman's *Critical Legal Studies*, what is striking about them is that they are almost exclusively American in focus, sources and cultural assumptions.[7] It is, perhaps, not remarkable that micro-economic analysis should have been particular in its orientation, although this is not a necessary characteristic.

6   Compare the diversity of appoaches represented in the symposium on 'Legal Theory at the end of the Millennium' (1998) 51 CLP, Preface by Michael Freeman.

7   Mark Kelman, *A Guide to Critical Legal Studies* (1987); Richard Posner, *Economic Analysis of Law* (4th edn, 1992). Since this was written economic analysis of law has considerably broadened its geographical focus; cf the work of Ugo Mattei on economic analysis in comparative law.

The story of American critical legal studies is perhaps more surprising. In the course of its rise and decline, critical legal studies in the United States could have been treated as an example of American isolationism. In the early years in particular, critical legal studies focused almost exclusively on American law, American ideas, American institutions (especially courts and law schools) and local American hang-ups – such as constitutional interpretation in the United States and the peculiar, tragic histories of local race relations.[8] Even R/realism was treated as an American exclusive, although one would have thought that what is involved in being realistic about legal institutions and the law in action is a concern of all legal cultures.[9]

Latterly, American critical legal studies have fragmented and parts, notably feminist legal theory, have belatedly begun to come to grips with more fundamental problems of cross-cultural theorising, such as those involved with the place and role of women in traditional societies.[10] Both economic analysts of law and even some former critical scholars have been spotted constitution-mongering and advising on such matters as privatisation in Eastern Europe and Latin America. Much of this smacks more of exporting American ideas – globalising a particular localism – than of a sustained engagement with issues of globalisation and interdependence.[11] And, one senses that, from the perspective of

8   It is true that the early critical theorists drew some of their inspiration from Continental Europe, using contemporary French and German critical theory to castigate, *inter alia*, versions of liberalism based on the ideas of 'dead white European males'. The one major exception, the Brazilian Roberto Unger, seemed to me to be associated with American Critical Legal Studies almost by accident and that there was an uneasy mismatch between his macro-theoretical perspective, which clearly has global implications, and the much more parochial and inward-looking concerns of left-wing American academic lawyers. Significantly, Kelman distances Unger from the Critical Legal Studies Movement.

9   When I attended the 1982 critical legal studies conference at Harvard ('in the belly of the whale'), I stayed on for the conventional breast-beating session at the end. 'What did we do wrong?', asked Duncan Kennedy, the organiser. A woman got up: 'Half the population, that is women, were under-represented', she said. Kennedy acknowledged this and promised to do better next time: 'What else did we do wrong?' Someone got up, I think that it may have been the same person: 'Ethnic minorities were under-represented'. Again Kennedy did penance. 'What else did we do wrong?' asked Kennedy. I got up and pointed out that although it was odd for me to claim to represent the rest of humankind, I was apparently the only foreigner in the room and one of only a handful at the whole conference. Subsequently, critical legal studies conferences gave much more attention to issues of gender and race, but to an outsider they appeared to continue to be strikingly inward-looking.

10 See, for example, Rebecca J Cook, *Human Rights of Women: National and International Perspectives* (1994); Martha Nussbaum, *Women, Culture and Development* (1996). The work of David Kennedy on public international law also can be treated as an exception.

11 See CCC.

Khartoum or Kigali or Sarajevo, some of the more frolicsome aspects of critical legal studies, post modernism, law and literature, and other current fashions look rather like irresponsible rich playboys and girls fiddling while Rome burns.[12] When foreigners with little or no local knowledge come as 'experts' to advise on practical issues of policy, it may often seem to the locals that it would be less harmful if they continued to fiddle at home.

If we take the top eight jurists in Barnett's survey as representing the mainstream of taught jurisprudence, it is worth asking to what extent either explicitly or by implication they are relevant to issues of legal ordering in a period of rapidly changing significance of national boundaries. At first sight the list looks quite strikingly parochial. With the exception of Kelsen, all the thinkers on it belong to a single broad intellectual tradition that can be characterised as post-Enlightenment Anglo-American liberalism. All eight belong to the period of the hegemony of the modern nation state. In so far as they have been involved in debates and disagreements, these have been debates within this tradition, mainly about positivism, legal reasoning, and liberal democratic theories of justice, rights, and utility.

However, in some important respects their work has not been parochial. For, all of them can be interpreted as making contributions to general as opposed just to particular jurisprudence. Bentham advanced utility as a universal principle; he presented a theory of laws in general; and he specifically claimed to be trying to develop a *universal* science of legislation. As we have seen, Austin, somewhat more guardedly, claimed that his General Jurisprudence was concerned with the principles, notions, and distinctions common to 'the ampler and maturer systems'. This in effect meant Roman Law and nineteenth century Western nation states.[13] But he was emphatic that his aim was 'to show not what law is here or there, but what is law'. Herbert Hart in *The Concept of Law* was similarly concerned to provide a general descriptive theory of legal systems in general.[14]

There is room for debate about the geographical reach of Dworkin's main ideas, but they must surely be interpreted as transcending American or Anglo-American law, and applying to any modern society, at least one based on a liberal democratic ideology. As such they are a contribution to general jurisprudence. John Finnis is the leading modern local

---

12 See below, Ch 8.3(b)
13 Op cit. Austin drew heavily on Roman Law, which is hardly a clear example of 'state law'; he denied that International Law was law properly so called.
14 In his recently published Postscript to *The Concept of Law* (2nd edn, 1994) Hart attempted to reconcile his differences with Ronald Dworkin by confining the latter's ideas to particular jurisprudence. On why this is unconvincing, see above, Ch 2.

proponent of classical Natural Law, a tradition which has claimed universality for its principles and which significantly antedates the rise of the nation-state. Hans Kelsen's pure science of law was also explicitly about law in general, rather than the laws of any particular legal system or legal culture. And Kelsen was an international lawyer who struggled gamely, if unconvincingly, with the place of public international law in his general theory. Rawls' theory of justice claims to be a theory relating to the institutions and culture of a liberal or at least 'decent' society,[15] but he has disappointingly retreated towards a more parochial stance in his recent writings.[16] Karl Llewellyn does not fit the pattern quite so easily: Legal Realism has been generally treated by commentators as an American exclusive, limited moreover, to a particular period in United States history. Llewellyn's last major work, *The Common Law Tradition*, was explicitly concerned with American state appellate courts and his writings on commercial law, although informed by his knowledge of German law, were almost entirely particular to the United States. However, his general sociological theory, the law jobs theory, explicitly encompassed all human groups from a two person family to nation states to the world community. I shall suggest that it can be treated as transcending national boundaries and as being applicable to orders that are more or less detached from a nation state.[17]

Thus all eight of the jurists in our orthodox local canon can be interpreted as having made contributions to general jurisprudence. With the exception of Llewellyn, and in a different way Finnis, they tended to assume that a theory of law is only concerned with two types of law, viz municipal state law and public international law. For the most part, their theories of law do not purport to give an account of non-state law, of legal families (such as the common law), of legal cultures, of religious laws independent of any particular state, nor of such possible emerging forms of legal ordering as a new transnational *lex mercatoria* or a putative *ius humanitatis*.

Some of the issues traditionally treated as central in relation to domestic law are clearly also relevant to international, transnational, and global legal orders. For example, positivism and anti-positivism; utility and rights; universalism versus relativism; and, within liberalism, the relationship between liberty and equality, and between free market, welfare and related ideologies. Such issues resurface in these other contexts; but questions will also arise about the extent to which the agenda of issues and our stock of ideas and theories developed in relation

15 J Rawls, *Political Liberalism* (1993) at pp 11-15; 'The Law of Peoples', in Stephen Shute and Susan Hurley (eds) (1993), op cit, at pp 220-221.
16 See generally T Pogge, *Realizing Rawls* (1992), discussed below at section 4(c). See also Rawls, *The Law of Peoples* (1999).
17 See below, section 4(d).

to municipal legal systems are transferable, with or without modification, to global and transnational contexts.

Underlying the construction of a canon is a judgement about the quality of mind of those selected. I personally have no reservation in acknowledging that this somewhat arbitrary list includes several of the best minds in the heritage of modern Anglo-American legal thought. So far as this is so, one should be cautious about jettisoning a thinker as démodé solely because the context has changed. In the case of at least half of the canonical eight, the potential *relevance* of their ideas to developing a genuinely globalised legal theory is fairly obvious.

So, John Finnis's ideas on natural law are clearly directly relevant to questions about humanitarian law, human rights and related matters at global, transnational and other levels.[18]

John Austin's aspiration was to develop a general science of positive law. In my view his general theory of law and his treatment of public international law deserve a decent burial. However, as was suggested above, the time may be ripe for a revival of general analytical jurisprudence in the Bentham-Austin tradition, but with modern tools of conceptual elucidation and construction extended to a much broader range of concepts.

The relevance of Kelsen, as we have seen, can also be taken for granted, if only as a worthy opponent. Those of us who are sceptical of the systematic nature of law in any strong sense, or who doubt that legal knowledge can be either autonomous or pure, have to confront this most tenacious and subtle of analysts. Kelsen suggested that the only way to make sense of the confused mêlée of overlapping orderings in the modern world is to take refuge in picturing all state legal systems (and possibly other legal orders) as being subsumed under international law in a single monist system.[19] Hart, has convincingly shown that this position is neither logically tenable nor a realistic account of relations between state law and public international law.[20] But refutation of the monistic view may be one of the most powerful strategies for building up a case for maintaining that a global jurisprudence needs to depict the phenomena of law in the modern world as to a large extent disorderly, unsystematic and serendipitous.[1] Here it is sufficient to note the relevance of Kelsen as once again representing an illuminatingly misguided position.

18 This essay does not attempt to do justice to Finnis's work nor to the potential contribution of recent natural theory to the study of problems of globalisation and law nor to the ideas of other contemporary jurists as varied as Neil MacCormick, Joseph Raz, Gunther Teubner, or Roberto Unger.
19 Eg H Kelsen, *General Theory of Law and State* (1946) p 398. For an incisive, though brief, discussion, see Lloyd and Freeman, op cit, at pp 288-289.
20 H L A Hart, *Essays in Jurisprudence and Philosophy* (1983), Ch 15.
1   Charles Sampford, *The Disorder of Law* (1988), discussed above pp 35-36.

I have discussed Hart at some length in Chapter Two. So I shall deal with him briefly here. I agree with the view that he is one of the best minds to have graced legal theory in this century. Indeed, I think that it is a tragedy that he did not bring his outstanding combination of clarity, rigour and good sense to bear on a richer agenda of issues. I have already suggested that we need something like Hart's method of conceptual clarification in order to develop an adequate language for cross-cultural and global legal studies. Our current conceptual framework is clearly inadequate for the task. Hart's treatment of public international law and of so-called 'primitive law' now seems rather simplistic and old-fashioned, but he is nevertheless still worth reading on some of the traditional issues. There are some interesting questions to be asked about how far Hart's picture of a legal system, his conception of law, can be detached from the idea of state law on the one hand and geographically defined national boundaries on the other, so that some of his key ideas, such as the union of primary and secondary rules, can be applied to other legal orderings, for example transnational non-state law. The main limitation in my view is that the idea of law or a legal order as a system of rules does not come anywhere near to catching in today's world the richness, complexity, elusiveness and variety of the phenomena of law which it is the task of our discipline to try to understand, describe and explain. Hart's descriptive sociology is not an adequate tool of even thin description, let alone of explanation or prescription.[2] However, Hart has consistently claimed to be doing general jurisprudence and he remains an important reference point in the present context.

While the relevance to a globalised jurisprudence of Finnis, Austin, Kelsen and Hart is relatively clear, the significance of the remaining members of the 'canon' needs rather more explication. Let us then look in rather more detail at one aspect of Dworkin, Bentham, Rawls and Llewellyn.

4   FOUR CANONICAL JURISTS

(a)   Dworkin's Geographical Reach

It has been suggested that the views of Hart and Dworkin can be reconciled by resort to the distinction between general and particular jurisprudence: Hart's *The Concept of Law* is a contribution to general jurisprudence, whereas Dworkin's theory is a theory of adjudication that is particular, because what he calls the problem of sense (assigning a truth value to propositions of law) can only be resolved within a particular

2   For more extensive discussions of Hart, see Ch 2 above and ALLP.

legal system.[3] Correct adjudication is local, so Dworkin's theory is particular. In Chapter 2 I argued that this attempt at reconciliation does not work, mainly because Dworkin is also contributing to general jurisprudence. That is, most of his basic ideas transcend any particular legal system and have potentially far-reaching implications and applications. I shall not repeat my argument here, but I shall elaborate on one point.

Dworkin claims that he is advancing a theory of adjudication, but his core ideas can be equally well characterised as a theory of interpretation and argumentation. His central question is: what constitutes a valid and cogent argument on a question of law in a hard case? Viewed thus, this question and Dworkin's answer can be separated off from our special English and American conceptions of courts and judges. The result is much wider than a theory of common law adjudication for at least three reasons: first, within any legal system, judges are not the only actors involved in interpretation.[4] Officials, good citizens, and expositors, for example, are typically concerned with the best interpretation of law and not just to second-guess judges.

Secondly, concepts like 'judge' and 'court' are quite culture-specific. One does not have to spend very long in a civil law jurisdiction, such as the Netherlands, to realise that 'trials', 'appeals', 'judges', and 'courts' mean significantly different things in our respective jurisdictions. But ideas about correct interpretation of legal rules can, to some extent at least, transcend particular cultures. Santos points out that Kantorowicz usefully characterised law at a very general level in terms of justiciability: 'a rule is justiciable if it is considered to be fit to be applied by a judicial organ by some definite procedure'.[5] In short, third party 'justiciation' of disputes is a much wider concept than Anglo-Saxon conceptions of adjudication.[6]

Finally, as Dworkin has acknowledged in conversation, his ideas about interpretation and argumentation could possibly apply in societies that have no third party adjudication, such as the Arusha of Northern Tanzania as described by Gulliver.[7]

3   Essays by Ruth Gavison and H L A Hart in R Gavison (ed) *Issues in Contemporary Legal Philosophy: The Influence of HLA Hart* (1987) and Hart's Postscript to *The Concept of Law*, op cit.
4   See *HTDTWR*, *passim*.
5   H Kantorowicz, *The Definition of Law* (1958), cited by Santos at pp 126-128.
6   In this context, judicial organ was used in a very, broad cross-cultural sense to include 'state judges, jurors, headmen, chieftains, human gods, magicians, priests, sages, doomsmen, councils of tribal elders, kinship tribunals, military societies, parliaments, international institutions, areopagi, sports umpires, arbitrators, church courts, *censores*, courts of love, courts of honour, *Bierrichter*, and eventually gang leaders'. Santos, op cit, p 126.
7   Seminar at University College, May 1994; cf P Gulliver, *Social Control in an African Society* (1963).

Dworkin is sensibly cautious about the potential implications of his ideas for societies and legal cultures that he has not studied, but it is no surprise that attempts have begun to be made to apply these ideas to civil law systems, international tribunals, and the European Court of Justice.[8] There is no reason in principle why the possible application of his most general ideas should not be tested, through interpretation, rational reconstruction or ethnographic analysis, in respect of non-Western cultures and discourses. There are, no doubt, many problems, methodological and interpretative, in considering the potential cross-cultural application of a set of ideas like Dworkin's. Similarly, there are unresolved puzzles to be untangled about the implications of his monistic vision of law as integrity when applied to 'semi-autonomous social fields'. To date, Ronald Dworkin has been too modest about the geographical reach of his more general ideas.

(b)   Bentham on Extent[9]

Ambivalence about Bentham as a resource is characteristic of Bentham scholarship. On the one hand, his breadth, depth and incisiveness have regularly been underestimated, and his popular image as a crude, pedantic, Gradgrind of early nineteenth century utilitarianism is a travesty. Modern Bentham scholarship is rapidly destroying that caricature. Indeed, at first sight Bentham is more in tune with the idea of a global jurisprudence than any subsequent English thinker. His aspiration was to develop a universal jurisprudence; he recognised the existence of law at multiple levels from the very local to the world as a whole – including something that looks remarkably like non-state law; his criticisms of the very idea of non-legal rights still have to be taken seriously by contemporary theories of human rights, even if his arguments are not as dispositive as some may have thought;[10] he anticipated issues about divided and incomplete sovereignty;[11] the originality and depth of his theories of democracy and constitutionalism are only just beginning to be appreciated;[12] as we have seen, he at least

8   Eg, J Bengoetxea, *The Legal Reasoning of the European Court of Justice* (1993), at pp 270-274.
9   Chapter 4 contains a more detailed general discussion of Bentham's jurisprudence.
10   The best discussion is J Waldron, *Nonsense Upon Stilts* (1987); see also W Twining, 'The Contemporary Significance of Bentham's Anarchical Fallacies' (1975) XLI *ARSP* 315; and G Postema, 'In Defence of "French Nonsense": Fundamental Rights in Constitutional Jurisprudence', in Neil MacCormick and Zenon Bankowski (eds) *Enlightenment, Rights and Revolution* (1989), p 107.
11   J H Burns, 'Bentham on Sovereignty: an Exploration', in M James (ed.) *Bentham and Legal Theory* (1973), p 133.
12   Below, Ch 4.2(d).

posed sharp questions that still bite about the duty of representatives of a nation state when the interests of their own subjects clash with the general welfare, globally or regionally. And, of course, he claimed to be a citizen of the world.

That is a formidable, but incomplete, list of claims to continuing attention in the present context. It is always worth checking on what Bentham had to say on a particular issue, but one needs to be careful about over-selling the greatest of British jurists as a resource for tackling contemporary issues. He was, after all, a person of his time. The world has changed since he wrote, law has changed, the agenda of issues for legal theory has changed, and in some key areas his ideas have been developed, refined, discredited, or superseded by others. We must be careful to distinguish between the historical importance of a thinker and his or her immediate utility as a resource in tackling current issues.

There is one point, however, where the ideas of Bentham and his modern disciples are directly relevant to my present theme. That is the question: 'Who is my neighbour in an interdependent world?' This issue affects all moral agents, including governments, corporations, non-governmental organisations and individuals. The question is now recognised to be central to the fast developing field of international ethics. The classic Benthamite offers an answer that poses a sharp challenge to conventional or complacent views in uncompromising, stark Benthamic terms.

Bentham's version of the utilitarian calculus includes the dimension of *extent* – the number of persons to be taken into account in determining the general welfare. This has been much discussed in relation to future generations and animals, but rather less in respect of the needs and interests of strangers. The utilitarian concept of extent can be expressed in terms very similar to Lord Atkin's neighbour principle in *Donoghue v Stevenson*, except that in the eyes of many the reply to the question: 'Who is my neighbour?' in today's world receives an extensive reply: 'Anyone who one can foresee is likely to be directly or indirectly affected by my act'. Utility as a guide to decision uses reasonable foresight as the main test; for *ex post facto* evaluation it looks to actual consequences. Everyone counts for one and ultimately the happiness of my child or colleague or friend counts for no more in the calculus than a stranger in a far country. From this viewpoint, considerations such as family ties, nationality, loyalty, reciprocity, friendship, or dependency are at best secondary. So too are national boundaries. Such considerations are not totally irrelevant to the felicific calculus for three main reasons: first, many of our choices and actions do not have far-reaching consequences; second, it is often less easy to calculate consequences that are remote in time or place – in which case the dimensions of certainty and propinquity have a bearing on the calculation; and, third, institutions and associations, such as the family, local community organisations, and the nation state may be judged to be normally conducive to the general welfare. Utilitarianism is not committed to ignoring loyalty or locality, but such factors are contingent and secondary. In the present context, the crucial point is that territorial boundaries often do not define the limits of social and moral obligation.

Many forms of rights theories lead to similar conclusions. But the rhetoric of rights is sometimes weak or unclear about the allocation of duties and responsibilities. One of the challenges thrown down by Bentham to some rights statements was that many assertions of non-legal rights are at best incomplete, because 'rights' are words of relation. In the modern analysis, developed by Hohfeld and others on the backs of Bentham and Austin, a claim-right implies a correlative duty in some identifiable person, and a privilege-right merely implies no-duty owed to another. Take, for example, in a famine situation a statement of the kind: 'X has a right to food'. If this means no more than X *needs* food, it merely states a problem in rather obscure language, without offering any suggestion of a solution. As Bentham said: '[W]ant is not supply – hunger is not bread'.[13] If the statement means no more than that X may have food (a liberty/ privilege) this both trivialises and obfuscates the problem. If, on the other hand, the statement means that X has a claim to food, the statement is incomplete because it fails to state who has the correlative duty. In the case of famine the statement begs the crucial question of allocation of responsibility. Whose responsibility is it to avert and mitigate famine situations? In many contexts, says the Benthamite, such loose talk may be positively harmful, because it lets the world off the hook. It is akin to saying: 'Yes, we shall formally recognise your right to food, but it is not our responsibility to do anything about it'.[14]

This is an area in which Bentham's ideas have, in a sense, been updated. We are fortunate in having in Peter Singer a formidable philosopher who can be treated as a modern representative of Benthamite utilitarianism. In his extensive writings on practical ethics Singer has explored the implications of a simple set of utilitarian premises for such pressing contemporary issues as abortion, euthanasia, animal liberation, famine and world poverty.[15] He has done this with clarity, rigour, and passion.

---

13   J Bentham, *Anarchical Fallacies* , 2 *Works* (J Bowring, ed, 1838-43) at p 501.
14   The 1959 Declaration on The Rights of the Child includes in the Preamble the phrase: 'Whereas mankind owes to the child the best it has to give', but expresses the principles in terms of rights. The 1989 Convention on the Rights of the Child is mainly expressed in terms of the duties of states parties.
15   Peter Singer, *Practical Ethics* (2nd edn, 1993); *The Expanding Circle* (1981).

Singer has graphically spelled out the implications of Bentham's idea of extent in respect of famine. Building on empirical evidence that nearly all modern famines have been avoidable,[16] Singer argues that in an interdependent world utility imposes an obligation on all moral actors to take measures to prevent famines: 'If it is in our power to prevent something bad from happening, without sacrificing anything of comparable moral importance, we ought morally to do it'.[17] This is a matter of duty not charity. Famines are preventable and all involved moral agents have a duty to prevent them without regard to national boundaries, proximity or distance. In an interdependent world almost everyone is involved. Singer acknowledges that the principle as formulated 'does seem to require reducing ourselves to the level of marginal utility'.[18] While he personally favours this strong version, he points out that more moderate versions which require less heroic sacrifices nevertheless would result in 'a great change in our way of life'.[19]

Singer has dealt extensively with a number of objections to his thesis.[20] For example, it has been argued that it is unrealistic because it sets too high a standard, requiring sacrifices that the better off will not in practice be prepared to make.[1] A second objection is that there are 'spheres of justice' or limits to our moral concern that justify drawing quite sharp distinctions between our duties to members of our own community and those who are close to us and our duties to outsiders, especially unidentified and distant strangers.[2] And, thirdly, Singer's thesis is based on premises that are open to many of the standard criticisms of utilitarianism.

It is not possible to do justice to these complex issues here. Singer rightly dismisses the first objection as not being a moral argument.[3] The

---

16   The *locus classicus* is Amartya Sen, *Poverty and Famines: An Essay on Entitlement and Deprivation* (1981); see also, Robin Attfield and Barry Wilkins (eds) *International Justice and the Third World* (1992). There have attempts, not entirely convincing, to treat 'the right to food' as a social right ('a fundamental social objective that must not be abandoned'), discussed in Henry J Steiner and Philip Alston, *International Human Rights in Context* (1996), pp 166-176. This does not engage with the issue of allocation of responsibility.

17   Peter Singer, 'Famine, Affluence and Morality' in Charles Beitz et al (eds) *International Ethics: A Philosophy and Public Affairs Reader* (1985) at p 249, a useful anthology on which I have drawn heavily in this section.

18   Ibid at pp 258-259.

19   Ibid.

20   Ibid and 'Reconsidering the famine relief argument', in Peter Brown and Henry Shue (eds) *Food Policy* (1977).

1   Beitz et al, op cit.

2   The *locus classicus* is Michael Walzer, *Spheres of Justice* (1983); see the debate between Luban and Walzer in Beitz et al, op cit, Part II.

3   The fact that people will in practice be unwilling or reluctant to give up what they have when it is right to do so, does not affect the extent of their obligations.

second objection, that needs to be taken more seriously, will be considered below in relation to Rawls' theory of justice.

The third objection has been confronted by Onora O'Neill who, in her deservedly well-known essay 'Lifeboat Earth', develops a non-utilitarian position that both by-passes criticisms of simple utilitarianism and meets the point that theories of rights tend to beg questions of allocating responsibility for realising rights.[4] Although she in fact agrees with many of Singer's arguments, she constructs a moral position for global responsibility for extreme evils (her main example is deaths from famine) that transcends different ethical theories. The argument goes as follows: 'any non-bizarre ethical theory which has any room for a notion of rights' will include a right not to be killed.[5] This right has a correlative obligation on everyone not to be involved in the killing of another without justification.[6] In brief, she lays the responsibility on any body who is involved in the world economy, which in effect means all of us – as individuals, as citizens and as participants in associations or corporate bodies, for example as shareholders, managers, or directors of large business enterprises.

Three factors are combining to make this kind of thesis seem less utopian than it might have done even ten years ago: the rapid increase in interdependence; the immediacy of extreme problems such as famine, civil war, and genocide; and the increasing scope of an overlapping consensus at world level about what constitutes intolerable situations in other countries.

(c)   Reorienting Rawls

John Rawls' *Theory of Justice* is widely regarded as the most important theory of its kind in modern times.[7] It led to a revival of theorising on a

---

And, it has been pointed out, that many of the more extreme versions of human suffering in the modern world could be prevented or drastically reduced if, for example, individuals in rich countries gave a small part of their income to appropriate 'charities' or causes and all governments met the United Nations targets, modest and arbitrary as they are, for foreign aid.

4   In Beitz et al, op cit, at pp 262-281.

5   Ibid at p 268, n 2.

6   This duty applies 'even though we (a) do not kill single-handedly those who die of famine; (b) do not kill instantaneously those who die of famine; (c) do not know the individuals who will die as result of the pre-famine and famine policies we support (unless we support something like a genocidal famine policy); (d) do not intend any famine deaths' Beitz et al, at 277.

7   John Rawls, *A Theory of Justice* (1971) (hereafter '*TJ*'); the theory has been defended, modified and extended subsequently in a series of essays, the most important of which are: 'The Basic Structure as Subject' (1977) 14 *American Philosophical Qtrly* 159 (BSS); 'Kantian Constructivism in Moral Theory', (1980)

grand scale in political philosophy and it has provided both a starting-point and a benchmark for discussions of justice in ethics, political theory and jurisprudence for over 20 years. It is a clear example of 'a black box theory'.[8] It can accordingly serve as an example of both the challenges presented by globalisation to such theories and possible ways in which they might respond to such challenges.

Rawls has modified and developed his position in response to numerous criticisms, but the core of the theory has remained fairly constant. The outlines are well-known, but it may be helpful to remind you of the basic ideas in Rawls' own words:

'My aim is to present a conception of justice which generalizes and carries to a higher level of abstraction the familiar theory of the social contract as found, say, in Locke, Rousseau and Kant. In order to do this we are not to think of the original contract as one to enter a particular society or to think up a particular form of government. Rather, the guiding idea is that the principles of justice for the basic structure of society are the object of the original agreement. They are the principles that free and rational persons concerned to further their own interests would accept in an initial position of equality as defining the fundamental terms of their association. These principles are to regulate all further agreements; they specify the kinds of social co-operation that can be entered into and the forms of government that can be established. This way of regarding the principles I shall call justice as fairness.'[9]

The people in the original position would choose the following two principles:

---

77 *Journal of Philosophy* 515 (KCMT); 'Justice as Fairness: Political not Metaphysical' (1985) 14 *Philosophy and Public Affairs*, 223-251 (JFPM); 'The Idea of an Overlapping Consensus' (1987) 7 *OJLS* 1 (IOC); 'The Law of Peoples', in Stephen Shute and Susan Hurley (eds), *On Human Rights*, (1993) op cit, (LP). See also, *Political Liberalism*, op cit, (1993) (PL). See now J Rawls, *The Law of Peoples* (1999).

8   Rawls's theory satisfies the conditions of a 'black box theory' in that: (i) it treats the political society of a nation state as a more-or-less self-contained unit; (ii) society is a union of social unions; associations such as churches, universities, families and corporations are treated as sub-units within these national boundaries; (iii) international relations are treated as almost entirely concerned with relations between sovereign nation-states which are themselves treated as self-contained units that are representative of states or of the persons within that society. (*TJ* p 378).

9   *TJ*, p 1.

'*First principle*: "Each person is to have an equal right to the most extensive total system of equal basic liberties compatible with a similar system of liberty for all."

'*Second principle*: "Social and economic inequalities are to be arranged so that they are both:
(a) to the greatest benefit of the least advantaged, consistent with the just savings principle, and
(b) attached to offices and positions open to all under conditions of fair equality of opportunity.' "[10]

In his later writings, Rawls has emphasised a number of points that are relevant here: first, he claims that his is not a metaphysical or epistemological theory dealing with universal moral conceptions;[11] rather it is a practical theory aimed at providing a moral foundation for political, social and economic institutions in a particular kind of society – a modern constitutional democracy.[12] Secondly, the primary subject of the theory is the basic structure of political, economic, and social institutions in such a society.[13] Thirdly, the theory is particularly concerned with the fact of pluralism in respect of values; its aim is to provide a basis for co-operation in conditions where there are 'opposing religious, philosophical, and moral convictions';[14] this basis is to be found in the idea of an overlapping consensus.[15] Fourthly, this theory of justice is not co-extensive with morality: it is a theory of political justice and it is independent of 'any particular comprehensive religious, philosophical or moral doctrine'.[16] Fifthly, the theory attempts to articulate certain fundamental ideas implicit in the public political culture of a liberal society.[17] Finally, this kind of political culture is historically specific and

---

10 *TJ*, p 302.
11 *JFPM*
12 *JF*, p 226. Cf Joseph Raz: 'Four themes have to be distinguished, all of which are captured by the slogan "Justice as Fairness: Political not Metaphysical". First the theory is of *limited applicability*; second, it has *shallow foundations*; third, it is *autonomous*; finally, it is based on *epistemic abstinence*': 'Facing diversity: The case of epistemic abstinence', in *Ethics in the Public Domain* (1994), Ch 4 at p 62. Raz's important paper targets the element of epistemic abstinence in 'Rawls's modest conception of political theory' and suggests how the theory can be re-interpreted and adjusted to meet this line of criticism. Here I am concerned with a different issue: the implications of the change in significance of national boundaries and of territoriality for a theory of justice.
13 *BSS*.
14 *KCMT*, p 542.
15 *IOC*.
16 *LP*, pp 220-221, n 2.
17 Ibid.

exists within the borders of a nation-state which is viewed as a more or less complete and self-sufficient scheme of co-operation.

All of these points are controversial, but here we are only concerned with the last. Rawls is quite explicit about the domain of his theory. It is restricted to a society which is 'a self-contained national community',[18] 'more or less self-sufficient',[19] 'a closed system isolated from other societies'.[20] A theory of justice between nations or peoples is an extension of the theory which requires modification in this different context.

There are several possible explanations for Rawls' express limitation. First, he was following tradition in treating a theory of justice as being directed to a single society. Domestic justice had normally been distinguished from global and international justice and had usually attracted the most attention. More important, perhaps, Rawls envisages global justice as being built up on foundations of local justice; a just world would be a world of internally just societies. In one of the weakest sections of *A Theory of Justice*, he envisages a second session of parties in the original position considering principles for a just international order and concludes that they would by and large confirm existing principles of international as expounded in the 1963 edition of Brierley's *Law of Nations*.[1]

Rawls's treatment of justice at the international, transnational and global levels has attracted a good deal of criticism: that his picture of international law is both outdated and naive; that by concentrating on domestic affairs, he fails to confront some of the most pressing problems of injustice of our age to do with North-South relations, or political inequalities in dealing with supranational issues, such as those of the environment, nuclear proliferation, war, displacement of populations, or international trade; that he hardly deals at all with transnational

18   *TJ*, p 457.
19   Ibid, p 4.
20   Ibid, p 8. Cf *LP* at pp 44, 46, 48, 56-57.
1   On the ambiguity of Rawls's formulation here as to whether parties in the second session of the original position represent states or individual persons, see Pogge, *Realizing Rawls* (1989), op cit, at pp 242-244. In his later writings Rawls emphasises that his project is to develop a criterion of justice that would appeal to the common sense of reflective Americans because they are embedded in '*our* history and the traditions of *our* public life'. (*KCMT*, pp 518-519, italics added). In one paper he begins: 'The aims of political philosophy depend on the society it addresses' (*IOC*, p 1). Although this may not have been intended, this self-limitation has given succour to those like Walzer and Fishkin who wish to set robust limits to the sphere of justice. Rawls's limitation may be symptomatic of a more general conservative retreat, on which see Pogge at pp 4, 9-11, 254, and *passim*. This section is based on *Realizing Rawls*. Since then Pogge has developed his ideas in a series of stimulating articles, including 'An Egalitarian Law of Peoples' (1994) 23 *Philosophy and Public Affairs* 195, and 'A Global Resources Dividend' in David Crocker (ed) *The Ethics of Consumption and Stewardsip* (1997).

relations and the global system as a 'system';[2] that he gives an unjustified moral importance to arbitrarily or artificially determined borders. As Thomas Pogge puts it: 'In our world national borders function as welcome blinders to our moral sensibilities'.[3]

More fundamental is the criticism that a theory of domestic justice is dependent upon a broader theory of international or global justice, a point made by Kant:

'The problem of establishing a perfect civic constitution is dependent upon the problem of a lawful external relation among states, and cannot be solved without a solution to the latter problem.'[4]

This is the line taken by Pogge in his interesting attempt to defend and develop Rawls's basic ideas at the global level. Pogge's argument is lengthy and complex, but the gist of it can perhaps be rendered as follows: there are no self-contained national societies in the modern world, nor are there likely to be. The only closed social system is humanity at large.[5] A theory of justice for any other kind of association, including the nation state, is dependent on background principles or 'ground rules' formulated at the global level. Rawls's core ideas for a practical theory aimed at providing a criterion of justice for basic institutions can be applied to the global system with a few adjustments along the following lines: we live in an interdependent world, in which all are involved and

2   See Pogge, Ch 5. Pogge treats humankind as a society; whether it is more appropriately treated as a class, group, community or agglomeration depends on context. Elucidation of such concepts is crucial for any theory of law, such as those of Llewellyn and Honoré (*Making Law Bind*, Chs 2 and 3 (1987), that treat human groups as their starting-point.

3   T Pogge, op cit, at p 254.

4   Quoted by Pogge from Kant's *Political Writings* (ed H Reiss, 1970). Rawls follows Kant (*Perpetual Peace* (1795)) in rejecting a centralised regime of world government on the grounds that it would either be a global despotism or else an unstable and fragile empire torn by civil strife. *LP* at pp 54-55. This is a quite different point from the argument that any domestic political order needs to be set in a wider, transnational or global context.

5   Although Pogge talks of 'the global system' as if it were the ultimate black box, not much would be changed by substituting some looser term, such as humankind, for the term 'global system'. Pogge himself seems to envisage an extension of the Rawlsian model of a hierarchy of associations acting as systems within systems, whereas the picture that I have suggested is a much more complex one of overlapping and cross-cutting semi-autonomous social spheres operating in a global context which is itself very complex. However, Pogge's theory can be interpreted as one which suggests that any theory of justice, including highly localised ones within families, societies, regional groupings, transnational associations and so on, has to be set in a much broader context which prescribes background rules and constraints for more localised spheres of justice.

from which 'we cannot just drop out'; this is a world of widespread deprivations and disadvantages, many of which have been promoted by existing institutions; one test of basic institutions is the benefits and burdens they engender; and the position of the least advantaged is one important measure of just institutions; it is highly probable that improved global institutions would help to alleviate at least some of the existing deprivations and disadvantages of the worst off. Rawls's two principles (perhaps extended to give more weight to social and economic needs) and some of his basic ideas, such as the search for an overlapping consensus, the individual as the ultimate unit of justice,[6] and the basic structure are more coherently applicable to 'the global system' than to artificially bounded societies or states, not least because 'all institutional matters, including the ideal extent of national sovereignty, are now systematically addressed within a single framework'.[7]

Pogge's argument shifts a fairly comfortable theory of domestic justice into one that provides the basis for a potentially radical critique of existing arrangements in the world as a whole:

> 'It is not easy to convince oneself that our global order, assessed from a Rawlsian perspective, is moderately just despite the widespread and extreme deprivations and disadvantages it engenders. Even if we limit our vision to our advanced Western society, it is hardly obvious that the basic institutions we participate in are just or nearly just. In any case, a somewhat unobvious but massive threat to the moral quality of our lives is the danger that we will have lived as advantaged participants in unjust institutions, collaborating in their perpetuation and benefiting from their injustice.'[8]

Pogge concludes, on the basis of this neo-Rawlsian approach, that 'our current global institutional scheme is unjust, and as advantaged participants in this order we share a collective responsibility for its injustice'.[9]

I am not here concerned with the details of Pogge's argument. He himself acknowledges that it leaves open a number of important issues and that the practical work of designing feasible institutions guided by this theory would be a multi-disciplinary enterprise involving contributions from economists, jurists, politicians and others. It is

6   Pogge, op cit, Ch 2, defends Rawls against charges of atomism – that is of treating individuals as if they are socially and politically isolated and self-suffcent; but Rawls does treat the individual human being as the ultimate moral unit.
7   Pogge, op cit, p 258.
8   Ibid at p 36.
9   Ibid, p 277.

interesting here as an example of an attempt to extrapolate some core ideas from a well-known 'black box theory' and to apply them at the global level. It is especially interesting because as Rawls has retreated towards a more conservative position, one of his disciples has adapted his theory in a way which is calculated to undermine any moral complacency about the justice of our world order.

(d)   Beyond Llewellyn's Law-Jobs Theory[10]

Karl Llewellyn's law-jobs theory was developed and restated over a period of more than 30 years. The theory was stimulated by his work with Hoebel on the Plains Indians in the 1930s that culminated in *The Cheyenne Way*.[11] It received its fullest statement in an article in the *Yale Law Journal*, published in 1940.[12] For present purposes one can isolate five rather different concerns that fed into the 1940-41 version.

First, from an early stage Llewellyn was keen to construct a general framework for his ideas, what he called a 'working Whole View'. He chose to root this in social theory. A second underlying concern was with inter-disciplinary co-operation, and in particular with developing a picture of law and a theoretical vocabulary which might bridge the divide between law and other social sciences, especially sociology and anthropology. A third concern was with the law-in-action and hence with 'realistic' jurisprudence. Fourthly, throughout his life Llewellyn was fascinated, some might say obsessed, by method.[13] *The Cheyenne*

---

10 This section is based on parts of lectures given in Chicago and Leipzig in 1993 to commemorate the centenary of the birth of Karl Llewellyn. Slightly different versions were published as 'Karl Llewellyn's Unfinished Agenda: Law in Society and the Job of Juristic Method' (Chicago Papers in Legal History, 1993), and with variations in (1993) 48 *University of Miami Law Review* 119 (*JJM*) and in Ulrich Drobnig and Manfred Rehbinder (eds) *Rechtsrealismus, Multikulturelle Gesellschaft und Handelsrecht* (1994). These versions contain more detailed references and extended discussions of particular topics. I am grateful to the Editors of the University of Miami Law Review for permission to reproduce copyright material.

11 K N Llewellyn and E Adamson Hoebel, *The Cheyenne Way* (1941).

12 The Normative, the Legal and the Law-Jobs: The Problem of Juristic Method', (1940) 49 *Yale Law Journal* 1355. The theory was restated in summary form in a number of other essays, and lectures, published and unpublished, up to his death in 1962. Aspects of the theory were developed further in his course materials on 'Law in Our Society', which he was planning to make the basis for a book, a project that he did not live to complete.

13 Llewellyn's earliest formulations of his general sociology of law emphasise that 'science' (*Wissenschaft*) develops out of useful real world practices (*praktische Lebenskunst*) and institutionalised group responses to problems (*Handlungsgefüge*) and that a primary notion of 'law' encompasses a variety of crafts and skills.

Way is about Cheyenne *law-ways*, in particular *how* they resolved the
eternal tension between established form and felt justice, the same tension
that he later claimed is resolved by the Grand Style of appellate judging
and advocacy.[14] Llewellyn was a pioneer in the movement for the direct
teaching of professional legal skills.[15] His most important published
version of the law-jobs theory is subtitled 'The Problem of Juristic
Method'. His work is shot through with 'how' questions. Llewellyn is
par excellence the jurist of the How.

A fifth concern was more immediate. Hoebel's account of his first
meeting with Llewellyn in 1933 illustrates how a quite specific problem
generated a solution that in time suggested answers to questions of much
wider significance.[16] In 1933 Hoebel was a graduate student in the
anthropology department at Columbia that was adorned by Franz Boas,
Ruth Benedict, and Margaret Mead. Hoebel's proposal that he should
study the law of the Plains Indians was met by extreme scepticism on two
main grounds. First, the Plains Indians had no courts, no sovereign and
no centralised sanctions and hence no law 'properly so called' – a revealing
example of the disastrous influence of Austinian analytical jurisprudence.
Secondly, the Plains Indians were perceived as unable or unwilling to
articulate their 'customary' rules or norms in general terms. When asked
about what would happen in particular hypothetical situations, the
standard reply was: 'It all depends'. Whether this was an accurate
perception is neither here nor there. This combination of a particular
conception of law with a perception of the Plains Indians as informants
was considered to be a fatal bar to Hoebel's project. Fortunately Franz
Boas was sufficiently open-minded to suggest that there was someone in
the law school who might hold a different view.

According to Hoebel, Llewellyn solved his problem at their first
meeting in June 1933. The solution was simple: all societies and groups
have disputes and the need to prevent and settle them. One can find out
how a given group deals with these needs or 'jobs', not by asking general
questions which in any case invite misleading answers, but by asking
detailed questions about particular cases and how they were dealt with
by whom in what arenas with what results and how far these ways of
solving problems of order were institutionalised. Llewellyn recognised
that myths and stories were almost as useful in getting at institutions and
law-ways as historically accurate accounts. Thus, according to this
version of history, the case-method was introduced into anthropology
and Llewellyn, well aware that method is dependent on theory, was
stimulated to develop a rounded statement of the law-jobs theory.

14 *The Common Law Tradition: Deciding Appeals* (1960).
15 See *LIC*, Ch 10.
16 This account is based largely on interviews with Hoebel. See generally the
    symposium in his honour in (1964) 18 *Rutgers Law Review* (1964).

The bare bones of the law-jobs theory can be restated as follows: All of us are members of groups, such as a family, a club, a teenage gang, a sports team, a school, a commercial organisation, a trade union, a political party, a nation, a nation state, an international NGO, the world community. In order to survive and to achieve its aims, in so far as it has aims, *any* human group has to meet certain needs or ensure that certain jobs are done. For purposes of convenient study, these can be broken down into five or six rough categories.

First, and the most unmistakably 'legal', is adjustment of the trouble-case (dispute, grievance, offence).[17] When conflict or other trouble arises, it has to be resolved or, at least kept to a tolerably low level, or else the group will disintegrate or its objectives will be frustrated or impaired. The second, and perhaps the most important, job is the preventive channelling of conduct and expectations to avoid trouble. Thirdly, as needs, conditions, and relations change, so the conduct and expectations of the group have to be re-channelled. Fourthly, there is the job of 'Arranging for the Say and the Manner of its Saying', that is, the advance allocation of authority and the regulation of authoritative procedure for decision. This job is prototypically the primary function of a 'constitution' of a club, or organisation or a nation state. Where power and authority diverge, as any realist knows, there tends to be a gap between what in fact happens and what is meant to happen. Giving a realistic account of a constitution as a kind of institution is accordingly problematic.[18] Fifthly, there is the job of 'providing Net Positive drive: Integration, Direction, Incentive for the whole'. Llewellyn, like Bentham, explicitly linked positive and negative sanctions (rewards as well as punishments, for example) within his conception of law-government.

Finally, in any group but especially in complex groups, techniques, skills, devices, practices, procedures and traditions need to be developed, institutionalised and adjusted if the first five needs or jobs are to be dealt with adequately or well. This is what Llewellyn called the Job of Juristic Method. It is the most original part of 'the law-jobs theory' and deserves a brief excursus.[19]

17 Llewellyn's choice of 'trouble' is a good example of his use of deliberately vague terms in some contexts to avoid definitional problems. 'Dispute' is a concept that has given rise to difficulty in legal anthropology and in discussions of 'alternative dispute resolution' because there is pressure to extend the term to include such diverse phenomena as welfare claims, criminal prosecutions, and clashes of interest of which one or more of the parties may not be aware. The broader 'trouble' avoids these difficulties and points to links with the idea of 'problem solving'. See further 'Alternative to What?' (1993) 56 *M L R* 380.

18 K N Llewellyn (1934) 34 *Columbia Law Review* 1; a shortened version was reprinted in Llewellyn's *Jurisprudence: Realism in Theory and Practise* (1962), pp 233-262. See further, *CCC*.

19 For more extended treatment of 'juristic method', see the original versions of this paper (*JJM*).

The concept of juristic method in this context is very broad indeed. It is not confined to the skills and techniques of individual specialists (the crafts of the lawyer, styles of judges, the skills of different kinds of negotiator). It includes craft-traditions (for example, the organisation and ways of work of English Chancery barristers in Dickens' time or in 1999); legal inventions (such as the trust, the letter of credit, legal fictions, Mareva injunctions, the ombudsman);[20] institutional design (different models of constitution, different architectural styles of code, types of procedural system, or more specific institutions, such as modern alternative dispute resolution devices like 'rent-a-judge' or the mini-trial); and any kind of machinery or institutionalised way of doing any of the law jobs. Juristic method is 'the *ways* of handling "legal" tools to law-job ends and of the ongoing upkeep and improvement of both ways and tools'.[1]

The term 'juristic method' can easily be confused with 'legal method', a much narrower category in ordinary legal usage, that is typically confined to that narrow range of skills relating to interpreting and arguing about questions of law – what is commonly referred to by that justly criticised phrase 'thinking like a lawyer'.[2] Llewellyn was among those who have emphasised that such rule-handling skills represent only one phase of the skills of the lawyer, but because he had a special interest in the crafts of judging and legal practice, his idea of 'juristic method' can easily be interpreted too narrowly. Just as the concept of 'law-jobs' is very much wider than 'lawyer-jobs', so 'juristic method' is very much wider than 'lawyer-crafts', a term which transcends individual skills to include craft traditions, practices and settled ways of thought. Furthermore, 'the theory of crafts' is not confined to 'lawyers', but extends to all participants in legal action.[3] 'Juristic method' encompasses all

20   *LIC*, pp 341-343.
1   Llewellyn (1940) op cit, p 1392. The breadth of the general conception of legal technology is illustrated in *LIS*, which contains sketches for a series of sub-theories linked to the idea of Juristic Method: a general theory of law-crafts, with a sub-theory of lawyer-crafts; theories of problem-solution in general; of dogmatics in general and legal dogmatics; of legal aesthetics; and working theories on appellate judging, appellate advocacy, and counseling, and promises of chapters on legislation and codification, viewed from this perspective.
2   See below, p 183.
3   The concept of 'lawyer' is context-dependent and quite unsatisfactory as a tool for cross-cultural study. Abel and Lewis's major comparative study of *Lawyers in Society* (3 vols, 1988-89) recognised the problem (eg Vol II at pp 2-5) but never resolved it satisfactorily. Llewellyn's 'theory of crafts' is suggestive in linking 'the law-crafts' to a general sociology of law and in identifying certain tasks that 'center on eternal human needs, in all human groups: spokesmanship, decision, advice: trouble-shooting, generally, in regard to the team-work of people' (*KLRM*, p 510; *LIS*, p 18). Legal personnel, or Llewellyn's rather loose term 'law's people', may suit comparative needs better, but such concepts are in need of

aspects of institutional machinery which, said Llewellyn, includes 'ways *and* personnel *and* ideology about both'.[4]

The main claims for the value of the law-jobs theory may be restated as follows:

1. It roots a general theory of law-government in an established and rich tradition of social theory.[5]
2. It is general in that it claims to apply to all human groups.
3. It can be interpreted and used as a flexible perspective and set of concepts for asking open questions about any human group. It is open-ended in that it makes almost no universal empirical assumptions about human nature or methods of group ordering beyond the proposition that all groups are susceptible to internal conflict and to changing conditions which may give rise to conflict.
4. Unlike some functionalist theories, it makes no necessary normative or empirical assumption that conflict and dispute are inherently bad nor that there are uniform or universal ways of doing the law jobs.
5. It is holistic or contextual in that it provides a lens for looking at particular institutions, devices, traditions, events, and other phenomena in the context of a total picture or whole view of an entirety; it makes no assumption that any entirety is self-contained nor that a group or entirety is necessarily to be equated with a 'system'.
6. It can easily accommodate notions of normative and legal pluralism, non-state law, and different levels of global, transnational, and local relations and so can provide a basis for dealing with issues raised by globalisation and interdependence.
7. It draws the semantic sting of obsession with definitions of law and related concepts. By emphasising focus without artificial drawing of conceptual boundaries, Llewellyn neatly sidestepped definitional problems at the most general level, emphasising the continuities between legal and other social phenomena.[6]

---

refinement. One task for general jurisprudence is to develop a more precise meta-language and conceptual framework for the comparative sociology of legal professions (or legal work generally).

4   Llewellyn (1940) at p 1392.
5   Llewellyn was a legal positivist of a kind, but a rather weak one. In the much-quoted statement of a positivist starting-point for legal realism, he includes two qualifiers, one in italics: 'The *temporary* divorce of Is and Ought for purposes of study' (*Jurisprudence* (1962) at pp 55-57). His later statements of a legal positivist position are even more guarded. Llewellyn was never as unequivocal a positivist as Bentham or Holmes or Hart. But it is fair to say that he belongs to that tradition.
6   On the issues surrounding Llewellyn's aversion to precise general definitions see *KLRM*, pp 177-179 and Ch 8.4(b) below.

8. By focusing on actual events, disputes, practices etc, it provides a basis for giving concrete, particularised accounts of the relationships between what is meant to happen (aspiration, official views, the law in books) and what happens in fact ('empirical reality', interposed norms and practices, actual consequences and effects, the law in action).

9. It is entirely compatible with the axioms of interpretive sociology that (i) descriptions and explanations are constructed by interpreters with different standpoints and perspectives; and (ii) that such interpretations have to include both an external interpretive conceptual scheme (etics) and the internal concepts and ways of thought of actors (emics).[7]

10. It provides for change and for the consideration of dynamic processes, with participants, choices, contingencies, institutions, traditions viewed over time, and it allows scope for questions about 'the social functions of conflict' in such processes.

11. It gives a place to rules and other norms (and principles and discourses and concepts) as an important element in legal phenomena without making them paramount; it is always an open question: to what extent are the law-jobs in fact being done by rules or other norms (paper or real) and/or by other means?

12. It takes 'how' questions seriously and these have often been neglected in legal theory; it links legal sociology with general rationalistic ideas about problem-solving, on the one hand, and unconscious, or semi-conscious patterns of behaviour and ways of thought within a general concept of group culture, including legal culture.

13. It is easily understood and applied in a wide variety of contexts.

The simplicity and generality are, in my view, a source of strength. It is easily grasped and extremely flexible. One reason for the broad reach and flexibility of the law jobs theory is that it is almost devoid of empirical or normative content. The theory can claim to be applicable to all human groups because it has no, or almost no empirical, content in what Llewellyn called 'its bare bones' aspect. On one interpretation the sole claim is that all groups need orderly prevention and settlement of 'trouble' in order to survive and flourish.[8] On another interpretation it is a tautology. When Llewellyn says 'the jobs get done always – or the group simply is no more',[9] what this means depends on the meaning of 'group' in this context. If the term is defined in terms of co-operation and absence of conflict, then by definition if the level of conflict rises to a certain level there is no longer a 'group'. 'Vague, vacuous and possibly

---

7   Above, p 43, n 10.
8   For a more explicit formulation of this interpretation see *KLRM* at p 175 ff.
9   (1940) 49 *Yale Law Journal* 1355 at 1382.

tautological – what on earth is the use?', one might ask. A simple answer
is that this provides a framework of concepts for asking intelligent open-
ended questions about the ordering of any human group, with minimal
commitment to empirical or normative assumptions.

The law-jobs theory and some ideas associated with it have been
influential in areas as varied as legal anthropology, archives policy, the
study of Soviet law, and the skills movement in legal education and
training.[10] Llewellyn and Mentschikoff used it in some later studies,
most of which were not completed. Llewellyn conspicuously failed to
use it in *The Common Law Tradition: Deciding Appeals*.[11] The record is
uneven and rather disappointing. One feels that the theory has not realised
its potential for providing as a simple, broad, interdisciplinary framework
for enquiry in a wide range of contexts. There are several reasons for this
of which two are immediately relevant. First, while the 'bare bones' of
the theory are quite well known, less attention has been paid to Llewellyn's
later development of particular ideas, such as his 'theory of crafts' and
his models for systems of dispute settlement. He died before he had
completed work on a comprehensive formulation of his most general
theory. A second reason is that it has been subjected to several lines of
criticism that deserve to be addressed, in particular that it is vulnerable
to standard criticisms of functionalism; that it does not deal sufficiently
with differences between groups in respect of such matters as size,
structure and organisation; and that it places insufficient emphasis on
power relations, discourse, and meaning. While some of these criticisms
are unjust (it is *not* an example of crude functionalism), it is fair to say
that some of the basic ideas could be refined and extended and that there
is a need for some more sharply honed conceptual tools in specific
contexts. It is, in my view, in need of elaboration and refinement.

At first sight the law-jobs theory looks like a simple version of 1930s
functionalism and, interpreted as such, it could easily be dismissed as
outdated or even discredited. I have argued elsewere that Llewellyn's
theory can be interpreted in a way which rescues it from most, if not all,
of the charges that have been levelled against 'extreme functionalism'.[12]

Nevertheless, some aspects are in need of further development. One
can readily concede that in Llewellyn's formulations rather little attention
was paid to questions about power, structure, change, discourse and
meaning. It is, indeed, a rather simple and unsophisticated theory. How
far it can be fruitfully developed within Llewellyn's own framework is
too large a question for me to address here. Suffice to say that I would
defend the view that a sound understanding of law as a social phenomenon

10 For details see *JJM*, *LIC*, Ch 10, and *BT*, pp 18-21.
11 *KLRM*, pp 148-150.
12 *JJM*.

needs to be rooted in a sound sociology and social theory. As part of such understanding, concepts such as group, order, need, norm, conflict, problems, process, institution, tradition, and even function, are as fundamental and as much in need of elucidation as 'fundamental legal conceptions' such as right, obligation, principles, sanction, state, sovereignty and law. One advantage of theorising about law in these terms provides direct links with a rich body of literature that deals with conceptual and other issues relating to such abstractions. There is no need to start from scratch.

The vocabulary of social theory is as necessary to legal theory as the vocabulary of analytical jurisprudence and political philosophy. The tradition of sociology within which Llewellyn worked has been enriched and refined by Merton, Goffman, Giddens, Geertz and Turner, among others. In constructing a sophisticated sociology of law as part of a general jurisprudence for an inter-dependent world, one would need to draw on ideas from many, quite diverse thinkers within a broad intellectual tradition. It is my contention that Llewellyn's law-jobs theory still has something of unique value to offer to that enterprise and that a large part of this is inherent in his idea of juristic method.

5   NORMATIVE AND LEGAL PLURALISM[13]

This essay explores the potential relevance of some of the ideas of our mainstream jurists to issues of globalisation. The central theme is that they are more relevant than they may seem, but we need both to reinterpret them in this new context and to use them differently, in some cases perhaps focusing on different texts by the same authors. We also need to revise and extend the canon, in the sense of reviewing our heritage of texts and thinkers to identify those that may be the most useful. For example, there is a rich tradition of theorising about international law that is directly relevant – from Hugo Grotius, to Myres MacDougal, Philip Allott and contemporary theorists of international human rights. This is a theme for another occasion. However, there is one body of work that is so obviously relevant that I must at least touch on it – that is the literature about legal pluralism.[14]

---

13   This section has been transferred and adapted from the original text of Chapter 7 below, so some of the references, eg to the *Pinochet* case, refer to more recent events than the rest of this chapter.

14   The literature up to 1988 is usefully surveyed in Sally Engle Merry, 'Legal Pluralism' (1988) 22 *Law and Society Review* 869. Important early writings include J Gilissen (ed) *Le Pluralisme Juridique* (1971); J Vanderlinden in ibid; Leopold Pospisil, *Anthropology of Law: A Comparative Theory* (1971); Barry Hooker, *Legal Pluralism* (1975). The starting-point of recent work is John Griffiths, 'What is

The terms normative pluralism and legal pluralism refer to certain social facts rather than to a school of thought. We all experience normative pluralism – that is to say the coexistence of different bodies of norms within the same social space – every day of our lives. As I wrote this passage, I thought about the kinds of norms that I had directly encountered during the previous twenty-four hours. These included the rules of table tennis, the house rules of the place I was staying, the rules of logic and grammar, of English and American spelling, good manners of several cultures, a vast range of institutional rules, relations and conventions (any law school has an extremely complex normative order), Florida road traffic law and conventions (or lack of them), the various legal orders involved in the *Pinochet* case before the House of Lords, a variety of municipal, transnational, and international legal norms associated with my teaching, and the normative background to other interesting items in that day's newspaper.[15] That is just a sample. Think about your experiences during the past week and then tell me you do not believe in normative pluralism as a fact of life.

Legal pluralism is a species of normative pluralism. The concept, in broad terms, refers to legal systems, networks or orders co-existing in the same geographical space; but over time different conceptions have developed. Initially, the term designated state legal pluralism. For example, Tanzania in the 1960s was said to have a plural legal system which involved local legislation, Islamic, Hindu, and 'customary' law. English common law and 'statutes of general application' served as a residual law under a standard 'reception clause'. All of these bodies of law were recognised by the state and so formed part of a single national legal system. In this view, Tanzanian law was 'plural' only in the sense that the state recognised different rules for specific categories of person, especially in such matters as inheritance, family and some aspects of land tenure. There were in theory many possibilities for conflicts of laws, but in practice courts rarely dealt with these explicitly as such. Instead judges and magistrates tended to apply the law they knew.[16]

Even in the typical colonial and post-colonial situation of the 1950s and 1960s, anthropologists realised that a great deal of social ordering

Legal Pluralism?' (1986) 24 *Journal of Legal Pluralism* 1. Sally Falk Moore, *Law as Process: An Anthropological Approach* (1978); *Social Facts and Fabrications* (1981). Hanne Petersen and Henrik Zahle, *Legal Polycentricity: Consequences of Pluralism in Law* (1995). See G Woodman, 'Ideological Combat and Social Observation: Recent Debate About Legal Pluralism' (1998) 42 *Journal of Legal Pluralism* 21; G Teubner (ed) *Global Law Without a State* (1997).

15 I regularly set students exercises involving reading whole newspapers in order, *inter alia*, to illustrate the pervasiveness of law and the multiple levels of normative pluralism: see *HTDTWR*, at pp 7-8, 141-143, 381. See below, p 259.

16 W Twining, *The Place of Customary Law in The National Legal Systems of East Africa* (1964) pp 24-25, 55-56, n 1, On Sudan, see below, Ch 6.4(a).

and conflict resolution took place under traditional norms and processes which were not officially recognised as 'law' and which sometimes were in conflict with national or state law.[17]

In time, the equation of legal pluralism with state law was challenged either on the grounds that it is too narrow or else that it is misconceived.[18] The challenge was in part theoretical, but also involved a political attack on 'state centralism' – the idea that the state has a monopoly of lawful power within its own territory. Instead, it was suggested, all societies have a diversity of legal orders, of which 'official' state law is only one, and not necessarily the most powerful. This broader conception of legal pluralism shifts the main standpoint from the judge, who typically has to take a monistic view of a legal order, to external observers or to the individual or other legal subject who typically finds himself or herself governed by a variety of regulatory orders, which overlap, interact and often conflict.[19] It is a commonplace of everyday life that individuals find themselves subject to a variety of regimes,[20] but the attack on state centralism was controversial. As Merry pointed out:

'The new legal pluralism moves away from questions about the effect of law on society or even the effect of society on law toward conceptualizing a more complex and interactive relationship between official and unofficial forms of ordering. Instead of mutual

---

17 Lloyd Fallers, *Law Without Precedent*, (1969). Cf P Gulliver, *Social Control in an African Society* (1963).

18 One leading commentator has suggested that 'the idea of a pluralistic legal system is impossible'. Jacques Vanderlinden 'Return to Legal Pluralism: Twenty Years Later', (1989) *Journal of Legal Pluralism* 149, at p 154.

19 Vanderlinden, op cit.

20 This phenomenon is, of course, not confined to twentieth century colonial society and the contemporary world. It is just part of the human condition. For example, Patrick O'Brian sums up the situation of seamen in Nelson's time as follows:

' "it seems to me that the great mass of confusion and distress must arise from these less evident divergencies – the moral law, the civil, military, common laws, the code of honour, custom, the rules of practical life, of amorous conversation, gallantry, to say nothing of Christianity, for those that practise it. All sometimes, indeed generally, at variance; none ever in an entirely harmonious relation to the rest; and a man is perpetually required to choose one rather than another, perhaps (in his particular case) its contrary. It is as though our strings were each tuned according to a completely separate system – it is as though the poor ass were surrounded by four and twenty mangers."

"You are an anti-nomian," said Jack.

"I am a pragmatist", said Stephen.'

Patrick O'Brian, *Master and Commander* (1971) at p 319.

influences between separate entities, this perspective sees plural forms of ordering as participating in the same social field.'[1]

In this view, pluralistic state legal systems (like those of Tanzania and the United Kingdom) are a sub-species of legal pluralism. This broader conception of 'legal pluralism' has an obvious appeal in the present context. The idea of 'semi-autonomous social fields' is substituted for closed societies or communities[2] and is not confined by national boundaries.[3] It paves the way for recognising that local, national, transnational, regional and global orders can all apply to the same situation. Clearly, a global jurisprudence has to come to terms with the phenomena of legal plurality in this broad sense. There are, however, a number of difficulties.

First, conceptual problems arise in various contexts about when, where and how to draw distinctions between legal and non-legal phenomena and between legal orders, systems, traditions and cultures. These are all puzzling and slippery concepts. To acknowledge such conceptual and other theoretical difficulties does not involve denying the basic facts of the co-existence of multiple normative and legal orders.

Secondly, very few orders or systems of norms are complete, self-contained or impervious. Many normative orders do not have discrete boundaries, they tend to be dynamic rather than static, and the relations between them are extremely complex. We owe a debt to Sally Falk Moore for popularising the term 'semi-autonomous social fields', which nicely catches the imprecisions and porosity of the social contexts of most normative orders.[4] But even this is too simple, for autonomy, precision (of boundaries), interdependence and even identity are all matters of degree. Such factors add to the difficulties of doing comparative work in law. Often one is not comparing tangible, static, individuated entities.

Thirdly, co-existing normative and legal orders interact in complex ways. Sometimes they compete or conflict, sometimes they sustain or reinforce each other; often they influence each other through interaction, imposition, imitation, and transplantation. Often such influence is reciprocal; sometimes the traffic is largely one-way, or at least seems to

1   Merry, op cit, at p 873.
2   Moore (1978, 1981).
3   Woodman (1998) notes that some of the pioneers of the study of legal pluralism, including Ehrlich, Vanderlinden and Pospisil, tried to confine it within a bounded notion of society ('au sein d'une société determinée', Vanderlinden, 1971). This is problematic and inconsistent with the perspective adopted here.
4   Moore (1978, 1981).

be.[5] Santos refers to these complex relations as 'interlegality', a concept that is well worth developing.[6]

Fourthly, Santos points out that there is a tendency to romanticise pluralism, especially in the context of reactions against codification, centralisation and claims to monopoly of state power. I agree with him that 'there is nothing inherently good, progressive, or emancipatory about "legal pluralism". Indeed, there are instances of legal pluralism that are quite reactionary.'[7]

Fifthly, one should not conflate 'normative pluralism', as a term referring to co-existing orders or bodies of rules or norms, with the idea of a pluralistic approach to or the bringing of multiple perspectives to bear on a phenomenon. It is one thing to say that many different cultures and even more normative orders co-exist in Belfast; it is quite another to say that one could quite easily give fifty-five or hundreds of different accounts of Belfast as a city.[8]

Finally, it is sometimes suggested that legal pluralism is the concern of anthropologists and sociologists rather than lawyers. If this means that few lawyers have been involved in its study this is false. Lawyers have played a leading role in studying the phenomenon and in institutionalising its study in the *Journal of Legal Pluralism*, the Commission on Folk Law and Legal Pluralism (IUAES) and so on. If this means that legal pluralism is only marginally relevant to the concerns of practising lawyers – that it is 'academic' rather than 'practical' – this is an increasingly dangerous attitude. All lawyers working in European Union countries or involved with transnational transactions or 'alternative dispute resolution' are operating in contexts of normative pluralism that typically involve non-state law as well as 'official law'. With growing consciousness of problems of multi-culturalism, regional orders, the law of indigenous peoples, and issues surrounding displaced persons and refugees, lawyers are increasingly involved in complex problems of 'interlegality'.[9]

5   See, for example, Martin Chanock's account of 'customary law' as a result of reciprocal interaction between coloniser and colonised, *Law, Custom and Social Order* (1985).

6   See below, Ch 8.4(b).

7   Santos (1995) at p 114. Santos wishes to substitute 'plurality of legal orders' for legal pluralism, but in the process appears to conflate the phenomenon (which is best seen as a species of normative pluralism) and the conceptual difficulties associated with differentiating legal orders from other forms of social control. Santos, more generally, seems to conflate epistemology and ontology, a point that is discussed below, Ch 8.3(a).

8   The theme of the analogy between depicting cities and legal orders and of the possibilities of multiple depictions is explored below in Ch 6.6.

9   Santos (1995), Ch 4 provides a useful overview.

There is a widespread feeling among commentators that there is something deeply unsatisfactory about the literature on legal pluralism.[10] In an important article Gunther Teubner identifies a central weakness in the current literature:

'Postmodern jurists love legal pluralism … The crucial question of how to reconstruct, in postmodern architecture, the connections between the social and the legal fields finds a highly vague answer: interpenetrating, intertwined, integral, superposed, mutually constitutive, dialectical… we are left with ambiguity and confusion. After all, this is the very charm of postmodernism.'[11]

Teubner's solution is to subject the concept of legal pluralism to autopoietic analysis.[12] I am inclined to agree with his diagnosis, but to be wary of his prescription. If I understand him right, he treats even the ordering of 'semi-autonomous social fields' as being bounded by autonomous, self-contained discourses. This seems to me to be paradoxical. Furthermore, he treats as the distinguishing characteristic of the 'legal' the binary dichotomy legal/illegal; valid/invalid; liable/not liable and so on. While I would concede that most adjudication is binary, the processes of non-state law and unofficial forms of dispute-resolution which are genuinely alternative to those managed by the state are characterised by compromise, polycentricity and other non-dichotomous outcomes. To confine the idea of 'legal orders' and 'legal processes' to those that are governed by binary codes is to narrow and formalise the conception of the 'legal' at the very point that concepts like legal pluralism open the door to a broader conception of law. The arguments are too complex to pursue here, but this opens up a promising area of dialogue with proponents of modern systems theory.

Much of the debate has centred around the defects of 'legal pluralism' as a 'scientific concept'.[13] There may indeed be room for conceptual

10 See especially Griffiths (1986); Merry (1988); Santos (1995) passim, esp pp 114–117; Brian Tamanaha, 'The Folly of the Concept of Scientific Pluralism' (1993) 20 *Journal Law and Society* 192; Gunther Teubner, 'The Two Faces of Janus: Rethinking Legal Pluralism' (1992) 13 *Cardozo Law Review* 1443; Gordon Woodman, review of Petersen and Zahle (eds) (1995), in (1997) 39 *Journal of Legal Pluralism* 155.

11 Teubner,(1992) at pp 1443-1444. For a rather different critique, see Santos, op cit, at pp 114-118, 234-243.

12 Autopoiesis is a form of systems theory, developed by Niklas Luhmannn and Gunther Teubner, that treats legal systems as self-reflexive systems of communication, that are characterised by binary distinctions (guilty/not guilty, liable/not liable etc). See G Teubner (ed), *Autopoietic Law: A New Approach to Law and Society* (1988).

13 See generally, Tamanaha (1993), Woodman (1998).

elucidation and development, but I suspect that the main difficulties are not conceptual or semantic. Rather they lie in the sheer complexity and elusiveness of the phenomena themselves. These are phenomena that both general jurisprudence and comparative law have to deal with.[14]

6   CONCLUSION

This essay reports on work in progress. Globalisation is, in more senses than one, a big subject. So is legal theory. In order to make my subject manageable, I have adopted the standpoint of a rooted cosmopolitan who is concerned about the state of the institutionalised discipline of law in his own locality and of the role of his own subject within it. I have further narrowed the focus by considering the potential relevance to some challenges of globalisation of a small selection of the texts and jurists that currently are reasonably representative of mainstream or orthodox jurisprudence – what I have called the local juristic canon.[15]

(i)   A healthy global general jurisprudence should be able to give a total picture (descriptive/explanatory/normative/analytical) of the phenomena of law in the modern world. Such accounts can be constructed from multiple perspectives. For most purposes, they need to include not only municipal legal systems and traditional public international law, but also global, regional, transnational, and local orderings that deserve to be treated as 'legal' for given purposes and the relations between them. This will involve addressing the phenomena of legal pluralism, both within and beyond municipal legal systems and different cultures and traditions.

(ii)   The facts of interdependence cast doubt on any 'black box' descriptive or normative theories which treat legal or other normative orders as self-contained and in particular those which purport to limit the sphere of their application to notionally self-contained nation states, societies or other impervious units. For few, if any, such units exist.

14 See further below, Ch 8.4(b).
15 Some colleagues may challenge my interpretation of the canon as being dated. Of course, the canon is changing and my list is merely illustrative. The selection is deliberately conservative, partly because there is evidence that these are the jurists who are most studied in our law schools, partly as a reaction against current tendencies to be over-responsive to fashion (a new paradigm every month) and to be intolerant or dismissive of some of the best minds in our intellectual heritage as démodé, but mainly because I believe that these mainstream jurists still represent an invaluable resource in dealing with pressing issues for legal theory in the modern world.

(iii) If the task of the discipline of law is to advance the understanding of law in the modern world, the facts of globalisation and interdependence, although open to multiple interpretations, dictate that even the most local phenomenon needs to be viewed in ever-widening contexts, up to and including the world and humankind in general.

(iv) Globalisation does not imply homogenisation. One of the key challenges to contemporary jurisprudence is to accommodate the implications of globalisation with the facts of ethical and cultural pluralism.

(v) General jurisprudence needs an adequate conceptual framework and a meta-language that can transcend particular legal cultures.

(vi) At first sight the main writings of the eight jurists selected here as representative of our contemporary local juristic canon do not seem to be a particularly promising resource for confronting the challenges of globalisation. Few addressed globalisation directly; most have tended to focus on two types of legal order – municipal law of nation states and public international law; nearly all can be fairly categorised as 'black box' theorists; and the English analytical jurists who emphasised the importance of conceptual elucidation, notably Bentham, Austin and Hart, envisaged an extremely short list of 'fundamental legal conceptions' as belonging to general jurisprudence; they focused almost entirely on basic doctrinal concepts (the concepts and presuppositions of 'law talk') and neglected the equally important and much wider range of concepts that might form a cross-cultural meta-language for inter-disciplinary 'talk about law', such as the concepts of historical, anthropological, sociological or political jurisprudence.

(vii) Despite these limitations these eight jurists represent an invaluable part of our intellectual heritage viewed as a resource for tackling a revised agenda of questions. Speaking personally, I think that Llewellyn can be refined and adapted to a global perspective; whether Rawls can be rescued or realised, as Pogge suggests, is an open, but important question; I would drop Austin from my team, but I would argue for a revival of general analytical jurisprudence in a greatly extended form drawing on the techniques of conceptual elucidation of Hart and others; the potential geographical reach and the cross-cultural fit of the ideas of Dworkin and Finnis need to be explored; at the very least, Bentham, Kelsen, and the contemporary spokespersons for systems theory deserve to be treated as sounding-boards or as worthy opponents; and the time for legal pluralism has come. Of course, the development of a localised globalism in jurisprudence will require both reinterpretation of texts within the existing canon (for example, I have only recently begun to explore the implications of Bentham's idea of 'extent') and, more important, a revision of the canon, not least in respect of other legal cultures – can we, for example, continue to ignore Islamic legal theory?

(viii) So much for our heritage of theoretical texts. But jurisprudence, I have suggested, needs to feed off as well as feed into more specialised fields of legal study. In this paper, I am all too aware that I have trespassed on specialist fields of which I am largely ignorant: international law (both public and private), European Union law, foreign and comparative law, transnational commercial law, media law, to mention but a few. That is my job: the jurist is a licensed dilettante as well as a hired subversive. And after sampling some of the standard works in these fields, I have come away with a sense of strong unease at the level of theory. Public international lawyers have been engaged in theoretical debates for years;[16] recently the theoretical underpinnings of comparative law[17] and European Union law[18] have come under sharp critical scrutiny; few can claim to make sense of the communications revolution. In all of these fields I sense that, echoing Holmes, there is too little theory rather than too much. But jurists, as the generalists of legal scholarship, and legal specialists need each other: And, I suspect, the most fruitful way forward in developing a global jurisprudence will be to subject to critical scrutiny the discourses, concepts and agendas of different specialisms within law, both scholarly and activist, as a joint enterprise.

---

16   Useful recent discussions include Sol Picciotto, 'International Law in a Changing World', in G P Wilson (ed) (1995), op cit, and Philip Allott et al, *Theory and International Law: An Introduction* (1991).

17   On internal critics, such as Legrand and Ewald, see below, Ch 7.4.

18   Ian Ward, op cit, citing *inter alios*, J Derrida, *The Other Heading* (1992).

Chapter 4

Jeremy Bentham and general jurisprudence*

I CELEBRATING BENTHAM

In 1998 we are celebrating two great jurists who were also remarkable human beings. This is the first Eckhoff lecture; 1998 is the 250th anniversary of the birth of Jeremy Bentham. Their ideas and their personalities were both quite different, but I shall try to point out some hidden affinities. My lecture is mainly about Jeremy Bentham. Let me start with a few simple facts. Jeremy Bentham was born in 1748, educated at Westminster and Queen's College, Oxford, and called to the Bar at Lincoln's Inn. He abandoned practice at the bar in disgust and devoted the rest of his life to the criticism and reform of legal, political, and social institutions on the basis of the Principle of Utility or 'The Greatest Happiness Principle'. When he died he had probably written more than any other English jurist before or since. Although he died in 1832 he still sits in a corridor in University College London, dressed in his own clothes, with a benign, but possibly bored expression, as if he were listening to one of the dry lectures of his disciple, John Austin. The

---

* This is a shortened version of the text of the first Torstein Eckhoff Lecture, delivered at the University of Oslo on 16 September 1998 and published in *Tidsskrift for Rettsvitenskap* (1999). This in turn was based in part on a lecture entitled 'Imagining Bentham' delivered at University College London in December 1997 as a prelude to Bentham 250, the year-long celebrations of Bentham's birth. The full text is published in (1998) 51 Current Legal Problems 1. The overlapping passages are reproduced by kind permission of the Delegates of Oxford University Press and the editors of *Tidsskrift for Rettsvitenskap*. The other version contains a more extended treatment of Bentham's relationship to University College and of his constitutional theory. This lecture deals at greater length with the topic of general jurisprudence.

'auto-icon', as it is known, is an ambiguous object that symbolises some of the underlying ambiguities and tensions in Bentham's thought.[1]

February 1998 was the 250th anniversary of the birth of Jeremy Bentham. It was felt that a birthday party at The Jeremy Bentham public house would not itself be a sufficient celebration. So we decided to treat the whole of 1998 as 'Bentham 250' and to organise a series of other events in London during the year. Other celebrations have taken place in the United States, Russia and Japan, including a bizarre tele-conference between nearly 50 Bentham scholars meeting in Austin, Texas and Mr Bentham himself, sitting in his cupboard in London.

It is natural to ask: 'Why the fuss?' What aspects of Bentham's life and works are still worth celebrating in 1998? So far as lawyers and law students are concerned, is he not a figure of merely historical interest? In so far as he had good ideas, they have been adopted and taken further by others; in so far as he was wrong, or merely eccentric, or hopelessly Utopian, is he worth remembering? Does he have any contemporary significance in Norway, or more generally? Why Bentham? Why bother?

Outside specialist circles, Bentham is mainly remembered today for three rather uncomplimentary images: the auto-icon or skeleton in the cupboard; the Panopticon, Bentham's design for prisons, asylums, and other institutions, in which everyone in the building would be subject to surveillance;[2] and Charles Dickens' Mr Gradgrind in his novel, *Hard Times*.[3] These images are dangerously misleading. If Bentham is worth sustained celebration, it must be for other reasons. The auto-icon is an entertaining, possibly instructive, diversion; the panopticon is an embarrassment; and the Gradgrind image is a caricature. So how should we imagine Bentham when we celebrate him? His significance is almost entirely in his thought.

Bentham deserves attention at many levels and in respect of an astounding array of topics. In this lecture I shall focus on his idea of 'General Jurisprudence', a topic which deserves our attention in an era which is notable for globalisation on the one hand and for a tendency to particularisation and localisation of legal theory on the other. However, we must first set this in the context of his work as a whole.

1   On 'Benthamic ambiguity' see RB, pp 110-111.
2   See the powerful critique by Michel Foucault, *Discipline and Punish* (trs A Sheridan, 1977) treating this as a symbol of repressive authoritarian control, and the partial defence by Janet Semple in *Bentham's Prison* (1993) pointing out, *inter alia*, that transparency was intended to control those with power as well as those subject to it. See the discussion in (1998) 51 CLP 1 at 3-5.
3   Especially: 'All I want is Facts. Teach these boys and girls nothing but Facts, Facts alone are wanted in life. Plant nothing else, and root out everything else', Charles Dickens, *Hard Times* (1854) Bk 1.1. This is a travesty of Bentham's own views, see (1996) 51 CLP, at 6-7.

It has been estimated that over 20 million words of Bentham's writings still survive; yet only a small proportion of these were published during his lifetime and a substantial amount of his writings, including some that are very significant, are still available only in manuscript. The Bentham Project at University College London is charged with producing a definitive edition of his *Collected Works*. Twenty-one out of a projected 68 volumes have appeared so far and several more are in the pipeline. Until the project is completed it will be difficult to make a fully informed assessment of England's greatest jurist. Nevertheless, the general outlines of his many achievements can be sketched. These have been succinctly summarised by a former General Editor of the *Collected Works*, the late John Dinwiddy:

'His writings are remarkable for their range, originality and influence. He was one of the greatest reformers, perhaps the greatest, in the history of English law. He was a legal philosopher of major importance, being one of the founders of legal positivism. In ethics he provided the classic exposition of the utilitarian theory which has been a major strand in moral philosophy since the eighteenth century. In political thought he was important both as a critic of established doctrines such as that of natural law, and as the originator of one of the main theoretical justifications for democracy. In the fields of public administration and social policy, he arguably had more influence than any other thinker on the process of administrative and social reform in Victorian Britain. In economic thought, his ideas about the measurement of utility lie at the root of modern theories of cost-benefit analysis and welfare economics. He has been recognised, too, as a pioneer in other fields ranging from international law and the birth control movement to motivational psychology and deontic logic. He has been described by C. K. Ogden as "the greatest social engineer in history" and by A. J. P. Taylor as "the most formidable reasoner who ever applied his gifts to the practical questions of administration and politics." '[4]

Bentham should be viewed above all as a jurist: his legal writings constitute the great bulk of his work; one of his first published works was his attack on Blackstone's Lectures on English Law;[5] among his last was *Constitutional Code* Vol. I.[6] Jurisprudence is the most extensive, the most

---

4   John Dinwiddy, unpublished note on the Bentham Project (undated). Dinwiddy's *Bentham* (1989) is the best modern general introduction.

5   *A Fragment on Government* (1776)

6   *Constitutional Code* Vol I (1830).

original and the most neglected part of Bentham's legacy. Yet he is better known as a philosopher, political theorist and social reformer.

Bentham's contributions to legal thought are generally under-rated – both historically and in terms of contemporary significance. Here, I shall use just one issue to illustrate the point: his conception of and his agenda for Jurisprudence. My thesis is, first, that Bentham's conception of legal theory is at once wider, richer and more coherent than nearly all contemporary conceptions; and, secondly, that such a conception, revised and updated, is badly needed in an era of globalisation.

Bentham explicitly aspired to be to Jurisprudence what Luther was to Christianity or Newton was to Science.[7] The extent of his ambition has often been remarked; but the nature of his vision of Jurisprudence has only been dimly perceived. The intellectual climate in England in the twentieth century has generally been quite hostile to grand theory[8] and Bentham's more expansive vision has been dismissed as grandiose rather than treated as grand.

What was that vision? I suggest that it is based on five main pillars: the principle of utility; the theory of fictions; his positivist command theory of law; the idea of a universal science of legislation; and, as a late, but crucial, addition, his democratic theory. The first three pillars have been the subject of an extensive, but uneven, secondary literature. The last two are generally less familiar. These five elements fit together in a single ambitious conception of the nature, agenda and uses of Jurisprudence. Each warrants a brief comment.

2   THE FIVE PILLARS OF BENTHAM'S JURISPRUDENCE

(a)   Utility

The starting-point of all Bentham's thought was the principle of utility. Out of the massive secondary literature we can extract a few central themes. Bentham refined his ideas on utility over time. The key texts are not the compressed early version in *Introduction to the Principles of Morals and Legislation*, but the much more sophisticated versions set out in general terms in the *Deontology* and some still unpublished manuscripts.[9] The more general aspects of utilitarianism were not new, although Bentham developed them in some significant respects; the originality and interest lie more in his applications of the basic ideas. For example,

---

7   *Works*, vii (Bowring ed) 270n, Ross Harrison, *Bentham* (1983) at p 141.
8   See eg Iris Murdoch, *Under the Net* (1954) at pp 65-66.
9   F Rosen, Introduction to *Introduction to the Principles of Morals and Legislation* (1996) at li-lix.

it is the principle of utility that gives coherence and bite to his very detailed treatment of evidence, the classification of crimes, the rationalisation of punishment and numerous other specific topics. He used utility as a weapon. One does not need to agree with Bentham's utilitarianism to find him continually challenging. As Herbert Hart put it: '… where Bentham fails to persuade, he still forces us to think'.[10]

Benthamic ambiguity begins at the very root of his thought: Does pleasure refer to satisfaction or to preference? Was he a direct or an indirect utilitarian? Does Bentham's utilitarian actor maximise his own pleasure or is every human choice, in individual morality and collective decision-making, to be judged by its tendency to maximise the general welfare? How far does the concept of 'extent' extend? In other words, does the general welfare always include all humankind and all sentient beings (including animals) or is the primary concern of the sovereign, his subordinates, and individuals rightly confined to one's own community, subject to certain exceptions?[11] Bentham's ideas developed and deepened over time and he was not always entirely consistent.[12] Some excellent work has been done on aspects of his utilitarianism,[13] but we cannot have a comprehensive reconstruction of the core ideas of Bentham as utilitarian until the whole range of texts in which he purported to *apply* the utilitarian calculus in particular contexts is made available.

Nevertheless, some aspects of Bentham's position are tolerably clear. Of particular importance is the point that utility is a principle of both individual ethics and social and political morality, of morals and legislation.[14] In Jurisprudence we are mainly concerned with utility as a principle of 'legislation' broadly interpreted. It is the basic principle to be used both in guiding practical social decision-making and in evaluating the actual consequences of such choices. At the core of Bentham's jurisprudence is the idea of design: design of institutions,

---

10 H L A Hart, op cit (1982), p 39.
11 My own view is that the most coherent rational reconstruction of Bentham's views makes him a preference-utilitarian and an act-utilitarian, concerned with the general welfare of humankind (and generally of all sentient beings) at the level of both individual morality and social philosophy. This does not fit all the texts, but neither does any other rational reconstruction.
12 For example, in many places Bentham often restricted the application of utility to a single, impliedly enclosed community; but there are indications, especially in his later work, that he was concerned about the question whether any community could properly be treated as self-contained for this purpose – an issue of considerable importance as the world becomes more interdependent. On extent, see above, Ch 3.4.
13 The best recent works are, Rosen, op cit, (1996); Paul Kelly, *Utilitarianism and Distributive Justice* (1990); Gerald Postema, *Bentham and the Common Law Tradition* (1986).
14 A J Ayer, 'The Principle of Utility' in *Philosophical Essays* (1963).

constitutions, codes, procedures, practices and particular laws. Bentham's legal theory is not solely a design theory, because he is also concerned with such matters as interpretation, application, implementation, enforcement, and impact.

It is no coincidence that the most important modern grand theory in political philosophy, John Rawls' theory of justice, is also pre-eminently concerned with the design of institutions and their basic structure.[15] It is, of course, regularly interpreted as a rival to classical utilitarianism. Rawls's and Bentham's enterprises overlap substantially. But their situations and agendas as well as their ideas were not the same. One difference is that most of Bentham's energies were directed to applying the principle of utility rather than to establishing or elucidating it.[16] Bentham did not attempt a proof of utility; his refinements largely took the form of afterthoughts; he used utility as a weapon for dealing with specific practical problems in what he considered, not always realistically, to be a realistic fashion. Like Marx he was more concerned to change the world than to understand it. Of our contemporaries, Peter Singer is closer to Bentham in spirit than is Rawls, focusing on the detailed application of utility to contemporary practical problems more than considering in depth its philosophical foundations.[17] The fact that Bentham is still taken quite seriously as a moral philosopher, even in respect of individual ethics, can be as much a diversion as a compliment. Most of his jurisprudence is an application of utility as a principle of legislation rather than of morals.

(b)   The Theory of Fictions

Bentham's theory of logic and language anticipated in important respects key developments in English analytical philosophy over a century later. The theory of fictions contains Bentham's basic ontology and epistemology and logic as they developed over a number of years. Much of the key material has just recently been made accessible in English and French, based on a text established by Philip Schofield.[18] It is essentially a theory about language. It is impossible to do justice to it here. But it is worth emphasising two key points.

First, Bentham's theory of fictions is a constructivist epistemology based on utility: we construct our knowledge of the world through the

15 Above, Ch 3.4.
16 On Rawls' own 'epistemic abstinence' see Joseph Raz, *Ethics in the Public Domain* (1994), Ch 4.
17 See, for example, Peter Singer, *Practical Ethics* (1993); *Animal Liberation* (1975).
18 Jeremy Bentham, *De l'ontologie et autres textes sur les fictions* (eds J-P Cléro and C Laval; trs P Schofield, 1997).

lens of language, itself a human construct, which is both necessary and dangerous: language is necessary, because it is our window on the world; it is dangerous because it is a distorting lens. But it is the best tool we have for knowledge and understanding. Bentham's theory arguably has affinities with pragmatism, the sociology of knowledge, and even some of the milder kinds of post-modernism. His conception of 'facts' is worlds away from that of Gradgrind.

Secondly, both construction and elucidation of abstract concepts is essential to jurisprudence and the science of legislation. Concepts are the basic tools both for expressing and expounding law ('law talk') and for talking about law. For almost a century an impoverished version of conceptual analysis, under the name of analytical jurisprudence, dominated legal theory in Britain.[19] In the 1960s and 1970s a reaction set in, both as part of the general reaction against the excessive claims of so-called linguistic or 'Oxford' philosophy, in part because it was perceived that legal theory should address a much wider range of issues than elucidation of concepts. I am personally sympathetic to these concerns: like Torstein Eckhoff, I have devoted much of my career to arguing for a contextual, socially sensitive conception of law. But in retrospect one may concede that there was an over-reaction against rigorous conceptual analysis and the balance needs to be adjusted. Bentham was quite right in treating the construction and elucidation of concepts as one of the main jobs of jurisprudence.

(c) Legal Positivism and the Command Theory

Bentham's general positivist theory of law is probably that aspect of his jurisprudence that is most vulnerable to criticism. The notions of sovereign, command, and habit of obedience have all taken a hammering, especially in the Austinian version. Positivism versus anti-positivism is still treated by many Anglo-American jurists as the main battleground of jurisprudence. A modern Benthamite would need to re-conceptualise the basic phenomena of law within the framework of Bentham's general vision. And a sharp distinction between is and ought cannot be maintained across different contexts. In short a case can be made for concluding that strong legal positivism is the weakest of the five pillars of Bentham's science of legislation.[20]

However, even here, we should not be too dismissive. For example, for his time Bentham was extraordinarily percipient about the conceptual problems of the notion of 'sovereignty' in respect of divisibility,

---

19 Above, Ch 2.
20 On 'strong positivism' see below, p 106, n 10 and Ch 5.2.

limitability, and omnicompetence.[1] Professor Neil MacCormick, a well-known Scottish nationalist as well as jurist, has expressed doubt as to whether there are any sovereign states in Europe.[2] Bentham might have agreed, at least in respect of members of the European Union. Towards the end of his life he posed acute questions about the extent of the duty of a particular legislator in the world arena: does utility require the sovereign to maximise the interests of his own people or should his duty extend to all humankind?[3] Bentham did not come up with clear answers, but he did pose some questions which lie right at the centre of contemporary international ethics.[4] On questions centring on the concept of 'rights' Bentham started a line of analysis that was later developed by Austin, Hohfeld, Hart and others. And, of course, his famous attacks on natural rights and other non-legal rights still pose a challenge to rights talk.[5]

Even the notion of law as command is not entirely dead. It is one of the ironies of intellectual history that Professor H L A Hart, who first made his reputation by destroying Austin's command theory, was later responsible for bringing Bentham's version of the theory to light; and in one of his last essays Hart even conceded that there is an important core of truth in Bentham's idea of law as command, as 'a content-independent peremptory reason for action'.[6]

This brings us back to Bentham's positivism. Whatever else one thinks of it, it is not apolitical or sterile or the basis for the idea that might is right or that law is simply a matter of brute fact or some of the other crude views that are sometimes attributed to legal positivism. Bentham's idea of law is that it is an instrument of power which ought to be, but often is not, exercised to maximise the happiness of the greatest number. The idea is still widely influential today and is, of course, perennially controversial. In my judgement, Bentham is here best treated as an important historical forerunner of modern positivism rather than as a good starting-point for considering contemporary issues. The debate has moved on.

1   These ideas are perceptively analysed in Oren Ben Dor, *Constitutional Limits and the Public Sphere: A Critical Study of Bentham's Legal and Constitutional Theory*, PhD thesis, (London, 1997) Chs 2 and 3.
2   Neil MacCormick, 'Beyond the Sovereign State', (1993) 56 MLR 1.
3   *Works*, II, 537, discussed *RB*, pp 133-138.
4   Above, Ch 3. 4.
5   The main text is *Anarchical Fallacies*, which has generated an extensive literature. See above, Ch 3.3.
6   Hart, op cit (1982), pp 20, 261.

(d)   Democratic Theory and Constitutional Law[7]

In his early writings Bentham was more concerned with how legislators should govern than with who should govern. He was prepared to deal with aristocrats, enlightened despots, and revolutionaries as well as with liberals and democrats in promoting his ideas for reform. His constitutional theory was only fully developed toward the end of his life. There has been much debate about the timing and the reasons for his 'conversion to democracy'.[8] He was sympathetic to democratic ideas during the French Revolution, but his interest in political reform was strongly reinforced after 1809 by the failure of the Panopticon scheme and general resistance and indifference to reform. Bentham firmly located sovereignty in the people, but he was not an instinctive democrat. He recognised the problem of the tyranny of the majority, but John Stuart Mill and other critics have argued that he never satisfactorily solved the problem of adequate securities against misrule by the majority, perhaps because of his virulent antipathy to talk of natural and other non-legal rights.

Bentham was like a fox in respect of administrative and logistical detail, but he was essentially a hedgehog in respect of constitutional design. That is, he had one big idea: that the interests of the rulers, however they are chosen, are in all respects potentially opposed to the interests of the governed. It is the function of constitutional arrangements to bring about an identity of interests so far as is feasible so that the greatest happiness of the greatest number will be maximised. The main solution is to give continuing and effective control over the exercise of power to the whole community, the people, and to provide a number of securities against misrule. By far the most important of these securities is publicity – a wide term which embraces such contemporary ideas as transparency, accountability, and freedom of information. The basic idea is embodied in three axioms:

1. 'The right and proper end of government in every political community is the greatest happiness of all the individuals of which it is composed.'[9]
2. 'The actual end of government is in every political community the greatest happiness of those, whether one or many, by whom the powers of government are exercised.'[10]

---

7   See generally, F Rosen, *Jeremy Bentham and Representative Democracy* (1983) and the recent volumes on political theory and the Constitutional Code in the *Collected Works*.
8   See John Dinwiddy, *Bentham* (1989).
9   *Constitutional Code Rationale* (ed P Schofield, 1989) at p 232.
10   Ibid.

3.   The junction-of-interests prescribing principle: 'The nature of the
     case admits but of one method, which is the destroying the influence
     and effect of whatever sinister interest the situation of the individual
     may expose him to the action of ...' – that is to divest rulers of
     virtually all sinister interest, so that the interest of the rulers is in
     accordance with the interests of the ruled.[11] This is mainly achieved
     by giving real and sustained power to the people to locate, to monitor,
     and to recall (or dislocate) and to punish almost anyone who is
     entrusted with political powers as their deputies.[12]

Practically everything in the thousands of pages of constitutional and
political writings stem back to this basic theme.[13] The main elements
were 'expense minimised, aptitude maximised', near universal manhood
suffrage, secret ballots, frequent elections, a unicameral legislature,
limited judicial power, strong accountability and transparency, and a
power of recall of office-holders, including the military, vested in the
sovereign people. He supported ideas backed by other radical reformers
of the time. He rejected a property qualification, but required a test of
ability to read. In principle he favoured votes for women, but he
considered it inexpedient to press for this in the climate of opinion of the
time. In other respects, the Blair Government's allegedly radical reforms
of the United Kingdom Constitution in the late 1990s look cautious and
piecemeal compared to Bentham's scheme.[14] The Constitutional Code
was designed specifically for nation states, but many of the basic ideas
about such matters as corruption, transparency, aptitude, and securities
against misrule are relevant to constitutional design at international,
regional and supra-national levels.

(e)   The Concept of a Universal Science of Legislation

Through the efforts of Hart and others several aspects of Bentham's
jurisprudence have been explored in detail, for example: his version of
legal positivism; a more flexible and subtle conception of sovereignty
than Austin's; his penetrating attack on natural rights; his progressive
ideas on punishment; and his theory of adjudication. These are all
important topics, but they represent only a relatively small part of the

---

11   Ibid at pp 235-236.
12   Bentham distinguished between appointment (location) and dismissal
     (dislocation) of administrators and judges: the electorate only directly chooses
     legislators, but it has powers to dismiss a wide range of officials, including judges
     (*Constitutional Code* I, Ch. V, Art 5, 31-32).
13   The most convenient summary in Bentham's own words is *Constitutional Code
     Rationale* (ed P Schofield, 1989).
14   See (1998) 51 CLP 1 at 22-32.

whole. What is missing, above all, is a rounded account of the most comprehensive and radical vision of law in Anglo-American intellectual history.

Bentham adopted the standpoint of 'a citizen of the world' which is more in tune with modern globalising tendencies than the perspectives of most of his successors. He propounded a universal science of legislation, which he worked out in great detail at a number of levels. Overall his grand vision included the five pillars mentioned above: a general theory of value, a theory of knowledge and of language, a theory about the nature of laws in general, a theory of institutional design, and towards the end of his life a theory of constitutional democracy. Subordinate to these were more or less developed sub-theories of codification, adjective law (evidence and procedure), rewards and punishments, indirect legislation and much else. No English-speaking jurist before or since has had such an ambitious intellectual agenda.

Philip Schofield has dealt in detail with the idea of a universal science of legislation.[15] Let me just add one footnote: One reason for the modern tendency to shy away from general jurisprudence is a greater sensitivity to differences of history, tradition, language, culture, and circumstance that make some of us chary of global generalisations, cultural universals, or universalisability, even if we hesitate on the path towards strong cultural or ethical relativism. But looking at law from a global perspective and constructing a general jurisprudence that looks at law in a global context involves no commitment to naive universalism: rather it puts issues about interdependence, cultural and ethical relativism, and multi-culturalism near the top of the agenda. Bentham was aware of issues of the influence of time and place on matters of legislation, but for my taste he underestimated the importance of history, language and other factors that go to make up the complex matters that we tend to talk of in terms of 'culture' and 'identity'. In this instance, some of his less known texts may make a good starting-point for thinking about a revived general jurisprudence, but too much has happened in the world and the realm of ideas for them to be more than that.

Much has happened since Bentham's time in respect of conditions, ideas and so on. The historical Bentham was a pioneer, the extent to which his ideas exerted a direct influence on subsequent events has been much debated, but there is a view that in so far as he was successful his ideas have been absorbed and developed by others and in so far as he was not influential, he is of no more than historical interest.[16] So the question

---

15 Philip Schofield, 'Bentham: Legislator for the World' (1998) 51 CLP Ch 4. See also J Bentham, *Legislator of the World* (ed P Schofield, 1998).
16 In 1876, Fitzjames Stephen wrote: 'During the last generation or more Bentham's influence has to some extent declined, partly because some of his books are like

arises, is Bentham still of continuing significance or is he best treated as an historical figure? One way of answering that question is to ask: is it possible for a jurist to be an unequivocal Benthamite as the Millennium approaches? I believe the answer is yes, but we must be careful not to look at late twentieth century issues through early nineteenth-century lenses. Benthamism, too, requires interpretation and imagination, because within certain parameters there are many possible Benthamites to be imagined: combine Benthamic ambiguity with room for interpretation of our post-modern condition and one has plenty of leeway for constructing different visions.

3   A JURIST AS CITIZEN OF THE WORLD: A MODERN BENTHAMITE

So let me construct one version of a possible Benthamite jurist at the end of this millennium, bearing in mind that this is my imagining and that I am not that committed disciple. The main outlines of the agenda and ideas of such a person fit the five pillars of Bentham's jurisprudence, as I have interpreted them. She is an unequivocal utilitarian, a liberal democrat, a legal positivist, a feminist, a humanitarian, possibly ambivalent about endangered species and endangered cultures; her epistemology treats knowledge and language as intimately related human constructs; and she aspires to recreate a general normative jurisprudence that is concerned principally with the design and implementation of legal institutions, codes, laws, practices and discourses. Knowledge, language and law should all be treated as tools created by humans for the maximisation of utility. As a democrat, she believes that sovereignty must lie with the people at all levels, not only as a last resort, but in terms of continuing accountability of and control over those to whom power is temporarily entrusted as a matter of practical necessity. Her standpoint, less equivocally than Bentham, is that of a citizen of the world: that is to say the extent of her concern in respect of every important calculation is the welfare of all humankind, including future generations, possibly extended to all sentient beings. For her, with increasing interdependence and possible outreaches into space, the only self-contained community is the world.

Such a global jurisprudence is both Utopian and intensely concerned with practicalities. It sets forth an aspirational ideal, but it focuses on the

exploded shells, buried under the ruins which they have made, and partly because, under the influence of some of the most distinguished of living authors, great attention has been directed to legal history and in particular the study of Roman Law.' *Digest of the Law of Evidence* (1879), Introduction.

details of the politics, the technology, and barriers to the attainment of the ideal.

While true to the Benthamite spirit, one can envisage some adjustments in the light of developments since 1832. To give just a few examples: First, in an inter-dependent world 'legislation' in Bentham's broad sense must concern itself not just with the municipal legal systems of sovereign states and the relations between them (old style international law), but also with global, transnational, regional, and various local and networked legal orders. This requires giving special attention to the concepts of sovereignty and of vertical hierarchical authority,[17] and to problems of sanctions and enforcement. It does not, however, necessarily point in the direction of a monistic conception of world governance.

Secondly, within the utilitarian positivist tradition due account can be taken of refinements of utilitarianism in the light of criticism and controversy over the past 150 years. Our modern Benthamite might follow J J C Smart or R M Hare at the level of philosophy and, even more important, Peter Singer in respect of applied ethics.[18] Similarly in jurisprudence, Herbert Hart's substitution of 'rule' for command, habit and a personalised sovereign can be accepted as a refinement within legal positivism, even though Hart himself was a modified, indeed ambivalent, utilitarian.[19]

Thirdly, our Benthamite jurist would fight for a revival of analytical jurisprudence as part of general jurisprudence, that is the elucidation, refinement and construction of key concepts. In recent years this has gone into decline. For her, Bentham's notion of a legislative dictionary was not a naive semantic obsession. Without concepts we cannot think. Rigorous rational thought involving a combination of a general vision and 'the method of detail', which was the basis of his whole enterprise. In other words, there is a need for a sophisticated conceptual apparatus which can form both a meta-language for talking about laws in general and a tool-box for expressing laws with precision.

Fourthly, our jurist can take into account other developments in ideas within her basic theoretical framework: for example, she can try to accommodate criticisms of naive conceptions of social engineering,[20]

17 On the diversity of meanings of 'subsidiarity' in discussions of European Law see Ian Ward, 'The Limits of Comparativism: Lessons from UK-EC Integration', (1995) 2 Maastricht Journal of European and Comparative Law 23.
18 J J C Smart and Bernard Williams, *Utilitarianism For and Against* (1983); R M Hare, *Freedom and Reason* (1963); Peter Singer, op cit (1975) and (1993) and *The Expanding Circle* (1981).
19 See generally, Neil MacCormick, *H L A Hart* (1981).
20 Roger Cotterrell, *The Sociology of Law* (2nd edn, 1992), Ch 2.

or of the significance of time, place and culture in legislation,[1] or developments in the social sciences, without abandoning the essentially rationalist, instrumentalist, and consequentialist vision of her subject.

She can find some support from contemporaries – for example, Peter Singer in applied ethics; David Held (although a Kantian) in respect of global democracy;[2] and, with some reservations, Harold Lasswell, Myres McDougal and Michael Reisman in respect of law.[3] However, such support is limited and fragmented. Nowhere will she find a conception and agenda for jurisprudence as comprehensive and ambitious as that envisaged by Bentham in his universal science of legislation and the pannomion. She might almost find illumination in the literature of economic analysis of law, but would cavil at the focus on common law doctrine within the confines of the nation-state and would consider subsuming all pleasures under 'wealth' to be an impoverishment. However, today many of the central tasks of a Benthamite jurisprudence remain only half-done or, as with the jurisprudence of the World Bank, seem half-baked, confused and used largely in support of minority interests.

In the present condition of humanity, some obvious items might be at the top of her Benthamite agenda. Perhaps the most important is democracy at the global, international, regional and transnational levels. If there is a democratic deficit at national level even in the most 'advanced' liberal democracies, how much greater is that deficit in respect of arrangements of governance and the control of power at supra-national levels.

I consider this to be both a grand and a challenging vision. However, I am not a committed Benthamite: I am not a utilitarian; I am only a weak positivist; and I would place more emphasis on history, tradition, intuition and local knowledge than most Benthamites would accept. There is more complexity and pluralism in 'the crooked timber of

1   See especially, Bentham's 'Essay on the Influence of Time and Place in Matters of Legislation', *Works*, I, p 169. Oren Ben Dor ((1997), op cit, Ch 6) advances an interpretation which gives a much greater place to time and place and culture in Bentham's constitutional thought: '… constitutional limits are conceived as a medium through which a community might evolve from being a community of law into what Bentham called a 'community of sympathy', the latter being based largely on self-government' (at p 1).

2   David Held, *Democracy and the Global Order* (1995).

3   Myres S McDougal and W Michael Reisman, *International Law Essays* (1981). In respect of perspective, intellectual ambition and general approach, Harold Lasswell and his associates in many respects came closest to being the twentieth century heirs of Bentham's jurisprudence. However, their espousal of a particular set of values, especially human dignity, which they associated with one version of 'the American Dream' and their emphasis on process represent significant departures. For a more recent development, see W Michael Reisman and Aaron M Schreiber, *Jurisprudence: Understanding and Shaping Law* (1987).

humanity'.[4] I suspect in some of these matters I am closer to Eckhoff than to Bentham.

4 ECKHOFF AND BENTHAM

If Torstein Eckhoff was with us, what would he make of this interpretation of Bentham's ideas? With some local guidance, let me offer some suggestions.[5] First, there is a clear affinity in their general approach to law and legal theory. Eckhoff was one of the first Scandinavian jurists to recognise Bentham's importance as a jurist and a precursor of analytic philosophy.[6] Like Bentham, Eckhoff was an analytic jurist with strong utilitarian and anti-metaphysical tendencies. He would probably have been in tune with Bentham's secularism and his later democratic theory. Secondly, both thinkers rejected a sharp distinction between theory and practice.[7] They shared a practical approach to technical questions, to reform, and to transparency, as is illustrated by their writings on the theory of evidence.[8] Thirdly, Eckhoff might have found the theory of fictions surprisingly close to key ideas in Scandinavian Realism, except that both thinkers treated analysis of concepts more constructively and pragmatically than was the case with the more negative proponents of the Scandinavian school. Fourthly, though each was located in a particular time and place, they shared a cosmopolitan outlook. I also suspect that Eckhoff would have been quite sympathetic to Bentham's idea of general jurisprudence as I interpret it.

On the other hand, Torstein Eckhoff was never an out-and-out utilitarian. He was more like Hart than Bentham in this respect.[9] Eckhoff

4   Isaiah Berlin, *The Crooked Timber of Humanity* (1990).
5   I am particularly grateful to Gert-Fredrik Malt for help with this section, but the responsibility for the interpretation is mine.
6   'In my view Bentham went deeper into these problems [concerning the analysis of fundamental legal conceptions] than anybody else among English and American legal authors in the 18th and 19th century have done'. T Eckhoff, *Rettsvesen og Rettsvitenskap i U S A* (1953) at pp 277-278.
7   Bentham, *The Book of Fallacies 2 Works* (Bowring ed) p 378, esp pp 457-462 (anti-Rational Fallacies).
8   Eckhoff's first book was on evidence: *Tvilsrisikoen* (1943). Bentham wrote more on evidence and procedure than on any other topic, see generally *TEBW*.
9   Hart was a 'modified utilitarian'. See especially, H L A Hart, *Punishment and Responsibility* (1968)), and *Essays on Bentham* (1982). Cf Eckhoff: 'However, I do not think that we should refuse to pay any regard to our sense of justice and fairness when evaluating the criminal law. Our conceptions of what is useful to society are often based on uncertain guesses: we are thus liable to make mistakes when we try to justify a certain use of punishment on utilitarian grounds. If we adhere to the principle that one should not inflict pain on other people without

was concerned with justice and legal and extra-legal limitations on utilitarian solutions. Like Bentham, he was critical of the metaphysical foundations of natural law and natural rights theories, but he would not have dismissed all talk of non-legal rights as 'nonsense upon stilts'. He was sympathetic to talk of 'rights', but this was not central to his concerns. Whether Eckhoff could have been counted as a 'weak' positivist is an open question, but he would have rejected Bentham's strong version as embodied in the command theory.[10] And he was more concerned with sociological perspectives and the 'realities' of the law in action than was Bentham. He would have placed more emphasis than Bentham on history, culture and social context.

Finally, Torstein Eckhoff was intensely concerned with contemporary problems that were unknown to Bentham. Eckhoff was greatly exercised by the cruelties of modern warfare, the risks of atomic disaster, ecology and environmental issues. He was intensely aware of the distortions and deceits of twentieth century democracy and mass communications and, while sharing Bentham's concern for transparency, he might have been less uncritical of publicity as the main security against misrule. Eckhoff was opposed to NATO, the European Union, and American dominance in world affairs[11] – and he would no doubt have been sceptical of the idea

---

having good reason to do so, we should play for safety by restricting the use of punishment to cases in which we find it both useful and just.' 'Justifications of punishment' (1983) at p 18.

10 In this context 'strong' positivism refers to an insistence on maintaining a sharp distinction between the is and the ought especially as a basis for what Hart called 'descriptive jurisprudence'. This is a position that is attributable to Bentham, Austin, Holmes and Hart – though not in all contexts. 'Weak' positivists (such as Neil MacCormick and myself) acknowledge the difficulties of maintaining the distinction in some contexts, and Eckhoff's ideas on legal reasoning have some affinity to MacCormick's; both would give some place to moral arguments within legal reasoning, though Eckhoff was probably more emphatic on this issue than MacCormick. See generally, Eckhoff's influential *Rettskildelaere* (3rd edn, 1993) and D N MacCormick, *Legal Reasoning and Legal Theory* (2nd edn, 1994). The term 'strong' positivism is sometimes used to refer to a belief that might is right, a view held by few jurists, and certainly by none of those mentioned in this note. See further Ch 5 below.

11 Gert-Fredrik Malt has kindly supplied the following note: 'His defence of objectors of conscience and his scepticism towards NATO and the American influence, may have arisen as a consequence of or in co-operation with his radical friends in the 1950s, in and around the independent newspaper "Orientering" (Information) and the Institutt for Samfunnsforskning ("The Independent Research Department of "Investigation of Society"), like Vilhelm Aubert, Arne Naess, and Johan Galtung. Some of his articles on the subject were published in newspapers in the early 1960s (eg "Atomic Weapons" in Aftenposten, Feb. 25th, 1060). An important article of this period was his criticism of a decision of the Supreme Court, touching on the rights of conscientious objectors to be treated as independent of the military service (in "Havnas-dommen – krittik og refleksjoner", 1962). This strand in his thought was continued all through his

of the jurist as 'legislator for the world'.[12] In short, each was a man of his time – one an optimistic child of the Enlightenment, the other a more cautious and sceptical witness of the complexities of the twentieth century. On this interpretation, Professor Gert-Fredrik Malt has suggested that Eckhoff could be represented as being, not so much a modern Benthamite, but rather as someone who provided some important twentieth century corrections and supplements to classical Benthamism.[13] I only wish that Torstein was here to debate some of these issues.

life; like his steady interests in alternative peace research; in dangers of political (and just formally "democratic", but often secret) supervision and control of opponents; and in the need to calm down the international conflicts involving risks of atomic warfare, like the conflicts with Russia. Some of his last important works were on this subject ...' Eckhoff was active in peace research for many years; he probably did not consider himself a 'pacifist', but he was decidedly anti-militarist (communication from Professor Nils Petter Gleditsch, November, 1998). Bentham and Eckhoff had shared concerns about war, but in significantly different contexts. On Bentham's position, Dr Stephen Conway has written: 'From the outset it must be stressed that he was not a "high" or "pure" pacifist. He disapproved of war, and sought its elimination, but he was not a non-resister.' 'Bentham on Peace and War' (1989) Utilitas 82. An in-depth comparison of their respective views in this area could be illuminating, and possibly surprising.
12 P Schofield, 'Jeremy Bentham: Legislator of the World' (1998) op cit.
13 G-F Malt, private communication to the author (October, 1998).

Chapter 5

Other people's power: the bad man and English positivism, 1897-1997*

I 'THE PATH OF THE LAW'

When we study Holmes, we are studying a mystery, a Delphic oracle, an ambiguous icon. We are studying him not solely as a historical phenomenon, or as an intriguing character, but also for illumination about current concerns. Dead jurists have their uses. They can be treated not only as straw persons or as perpetrators of interesting errors, but also as sources of ideas that have a potential significance that transcends the particular context in which they were introduced. If a text is worth studying, it is usually fruitful to subject it to charitable interpretation, even to try to make it the best it can be. Holmes's critics have not always observed this precept. The object of our study is understanding, in particular the use of a powerful idea to illuminate current concerns. The bad man is just such an idea.

'The Path of the Law' is still treated as one of the great legal classics.[1] Like *Hamlet*, it is the source of many epigrams and provocative phrases that are so well known that they have become clichés. 'Wash in cynical acid',[2] 'commit a contract',[3] and 'the fallacy of the logical form'[4] were absorbed into common law discourse, often without attribution.

* A shortened version of a paper delivered at Brooklyn Law School in 1997 on the occasion of the centenary of the publication of 'The Path of the Law' and published in (1997) 63 Brooklyn Law Review 189. It is reproduced here by kind permission of the Editors of the *Brooklyn Law Review*.
1 'The Path of the Law' (hereafter *Path*) was published in (1897) 10 Harvard Law Review 457. The references to the text used here are from O W Holmes, *Collected Legal Papers* (1920).
2 *Path*, op cit, p 174.
3 Ibid, p 175.
4 Ibid, p 180.

Examples of well-known quotations that originated in this short essay include the following:

'The law is the witness and external deposit of our moral life.'[5]

'The training of lawyers is in logic ... And the logical method and form flatter that longing for certainty and repose which is in every human mind. But certainty is generally an illusion, and repose is not the destiny of man.'[6]

'For the rational study of the law the black-letter man may be the man of the present, but the man of the future is the man of statistics and the master of economics.'[7]

'We must beware of the pitfall of antiquarianism, and must remember that for our purposes our only interest in the past is for the light it throws upon the present.'[8]

'We have too little theory in the law rather than too much.'[9]

These statements – and many more – give the flavour of the essay. They also suggest why it has been controversial. 'The Path of the Law' is the classic text of legal positivism, which also lives on as an object for some powerful lines of criticism. It is at once a talisman and a target within the positivist tradition. This is especially true of the bad man: he is sometimes treated as a symbol of a radically impoverished view of law.[10] I shall argue that he is more fruitfully interpreted today as one device for enlarging and enriching our vision of our subject in a broad geographical frame. The most-quoted passage of all in this much-quoted essay provides the basic text:

'Take the fundamental question, What constitutes the law? You will find some text writers telling you that it is something different from what is decided by the courts of Massachusetts or England, that it is a system of reason, that it is a deduction from principles of ethics or

5   Ibid, p 170.
6   Ibid, p 181.
7   Ibid, p 187.
8   Ibid, pp 194-195.
9   Ibid, p 198.
10 Yosal Rogat, 'The Judge as Spectator', (1964) 31 University of Chicago Law Review 213, at 225; cf Ronald Dworkin, *Law's Empire* (1986), p 14, calling 'external theories', which he associated with Holmes, 'perverse ... .impoverished and defective'.

admitted axioms or what not, which may or may not coincide with the decisions. But if we take the view of our friend the bad man we shall find that he does not care two straws for the axioms or deductions, but that he does want to know what the Massachusetts or English courts are likely to do in fact. The prophesies of what the courts will do in fact, and nothing more pretentious, are what I mean by the law.'[11]

Twenty-five years ago I wrote an essay entitled 'The Bad Man Revisited' which was later published in *The Cornell Law Review*.[12] My purpose was twofold: first, to explore the concept of standpoint as a tool of juristic analysis. For the bad man is a classic example of a significant switch of standpoint. Secondly, to rescue Holmes and the Realists, especially Llewellyn, from the charge of advancing a vulnerable general theory of law based on ideas of prediction or official behaviour or other 'brute facts'. British commentators, especially Hart, had had a field day in first setting up and then demolishing 'the prediction theory of law' and 'rule scepticism' as soft targets. I set out to show that neither Holmes's dictum nor Llewellyn's famous sentence in *the Bramble Bush* were intended as general definitions of law; rather they were advanced as deliberately provocative statements in specific educational contexts. The main points made by the critics were valid, but the interpretations of the two texts were caricatures.

I argued that the occasion, the broader context, and the actual wording all support the view that 'the Path of the Law' should be interpreted more as a contribution to legal education than to legal philosophy.[13] Holmes's purpose was to criticise several weaknesses in the approach to legal education that he felt had gained sway, especially at Harvard:[14] the fallacy of the logical form (anti-formalism);[15] the tendency of students to substitute their personal moral or other value predilections for rigorous legal analysis and thereby to confuse law and morality; and the distorted view of the reality of law which is promoted by viewing it from the

11 *Path*, pp 172-173.
12 'The Bad Man Revisited', (1973) 58 Cornell Law Review 275 (hereafter *BMR*).
13 In addition to the text itself, which is explicitly about the study of law, there is extrinsic evidence in support of this interpretation, for example, Holmes to Lady Castletown, 17 September 1896: 'I ought to get to work on a discourse on legal education'. However, he also refers to it as a general discourse on the law: ibid and letter to Lady Castletown, 11 January 1897. For further examples, see David Seipp, 'Holmes's Path' (1997) Boston University Law Review 515.
14 In 'The Path of the Law' Holmes scattered his shot quite widely; by no means all of the targets of his criticism were attributable to legal education at Harvard. See *BMR* at 277, n 6.
15 See above, p 109.

elevated standpoint of appellate judges.[16] These three lines of argument, which are analytically separable, might be labelled the anti-formalist, the positivist, and the realist argument. The bad man is not directly relevant to 'the fallacy of the logical form'. Holmes used the device to suggest that law students could be cured of the other two diseases by a simple switch of standpoint: substitute for the point of view of the appellate judge the lowly one of an ordinary citizen or his/her legal adviser (counsellor) and make that citizen amoral and one could see law from a perspective that is both hard-nosed and closer to the realities of everyday legal practice.

Here I shall gloss my original thesis by suggesting that the significance of the bad man goes beyond these specific concerns to provide an enduring symbol of a positivist view of law seen as other people's power. In the context of addressing American law students, who were assumed to be intending private practitioners,[17] it was natural and appropriate that Holmes should choose a notional participant as his symbolic character; but for the purposes of general jurisprudence it may also be appropriate to view the bad man as a relatively detached spectator or observer. As we shall see, this transition from actor to spectator is not unproblematic.

2   ENGLISH LEGAL POSITIVISM

It is commonplace that '*ius positum*' has been associated with a number of ideas that are not necessarily connected. Here I shall confine the term 'positivism' to the separability thesis – in Hart's words, 'the contention that there is no necessary connection between law and morals or law as it is and ought to be'.[18] Insistence on a sharp distinction between is and ought has characterised the English analytical tradition from Bentham, through Austin, Holland, Pollock, Buckland, Hart and Raz. The connecting thread has been 'clarity', but the predominating reasons behind this insistence have been quite varied. For example, Bentham distinguished the is and the ought for the sake of the ought – in order to criticise and construct (universal censorial jurisprudence); Austin (and Holland) distinguished the is and the ought for the sake of the is: as a foundation for an objective general science of positive law distinct from

---

16   Holmes only explicitly attacks two fallacies, but the realist argument is implicit in much of the essay. However, this aspect of his position was never fully developed, see below, p 121.

17   This is made clear in the opening words of the address.

18   H L A Hart, 'Positivism and the Separation of Law and Morals', (1959) reprinted in *Essays in Jurisprudence and Philosophy* (1983), Ch 2 at n 57 (hereafter Hart, *Essays*).

the science or art of legislation (general expository jurisprudence).[19] Pollock and Buckland were expositors who favoured particular analytical jurisprudence for pragmatic pedagogical reasons;[20] others, especially in the Nazi and Cold War periods, saw positivist legal science which emphasised objectivity and certainty as an essential part of the idea of the rule of law, conceived as a bulwark against tyranny and official administrative discretion.[1] Hart, following Austin, wished to revive a descriptive jurisprudence about laws and legal systems in general, not just English or Anglo-American or common law.[2] But, accommodating the 'hermeneutic turn', Hart recognised that external description of social institutions and practices had to take account of the 'internal point of view'.[3]

English positivists have shared with Holmes the idea that distinguishing the is and the ought promotes clarity of thought. In 'The Path of the Law', Holmes explicitly linked his distinction between law and morality to 'clearness of thought' for the purpose of learning and understanding law. However, most English analytical jurists including Bentham, Austin, Hart, and Raz, can be distinguished from Holmes in two key respects: first, most leading English positivists have been moralists. They were not moral sceptics or agnostics. Indeed, for most, their concern for clarity had a moral basis – for none more clearly so than Bentham.[4] Others were concerned with setting up an objective science of law as it is. Whether Holmes' concern for clarity had a moral basis is more debatable.[5]

19 Austin did not use the term 'analytical jurisprudence'. For rather obscure reasons in American usage the term has acquired connotations that have little to do with the ideas of Bentham or Austin. For a useful critique of American interpretations that conflate positivism, formalism, and analytical jurisprudence, see Anthony Sebok, 'Misunderstanding Positivism' (1995) 93 Michigan Law Review 2054.
20 On the history of the distinction between general and particular jurisprudence in the English tradition, see above, Ch 2.
1   On the complex historical roots of classical Continental 'Rule of Law' positivism, see Franz Wieacker, *A History of Private Law in Europe* (trs Tony Weir, 1995) especially Ch 23.
2   H L A Hart, *The Concept of Law* (Postscript) (1994); pp 239-241.
3   Ibid, pp 88-91.
4   Stephen Guest, in S Guest (ed) *Positivism Today* (1996) at pp 29-31; cf Neil MacCormick, *H L A Hart* (1981) at p 160. Attempts to establish the discipline of law as an autonomous science, exemplified by Austin and Holland, were not necessarily rooted in this kind of moral concern.
5   A good discussion is Stephen Diamond, 'Citizenship, Civilization, and Coercion: Justice Holmes on the Tax Power' in Robert Gordon (ed) *The Legacy of Oliver Wendell Holmes Jr* (1992), p 115. Some of the hostility directed at 'The Path of the Law' is probably attributable to negative interpretations of Holmes's moral views, which are notoriously problematic. See for example, Mark de Wolfe Howe, 'The Positivism of Mr Justice Holmes', (1951) 64 Harvard Law Review 529 at 544.

Holmes is also prototypically American in putting courts and adjudication at the centre of his jurisprudence. One reason why Americans often misread English positivism is that they interpret it as being, or as being centrally concerned with, a theory of common law adjudication. The focus on adjudication as central to legal theory seems to many outsiders to be peculiarly American, and not just because of the special position of courts in the American polity.[6] Such a concern belongs more to particular than to general jurisprudence, because litigation, judges, and courts are institutionalised in ways that tend to be historically contingent and culture-specific. Bentham and Hart, and to a lesser extent Austin, when doing general jurisprudence, marginalised and hardly developed theories of adjudication – in my view, rightly so.

It has been American commentators, for example, Fuller in 'The Case of the Speluncean Explorers'[7] Dworkin on Hart,[8] and Postema on Bentham,[9] who have tried to put adjudication at the centre of legal theory, sometimes in a quite ethnocentric fashion. A few particularistic English common lawyers, like Pollock and Goodhart (an adopted American), have followed suit, but most modern English jurists from Bentham through Hart, Raz and Finnis have been mainly concerned with general

6   Hart, *Essays* at p 123. Earlier English theorists of the common law, such as Blackstone and Coke, naturally emphasised adjudication, but they were doing particular jurisprudence before the rise of modern legislation. Bentham and Austin put legislation at the centre of their theories. The relative neglect of legislation by American academic lawyers and theorists cannot be explained solely or even mainly by the relative importance of courts in the United States. On issues surrounding the 'centrality' of adjudication see *RE*, pp 112-116; *TAR*, p 350.

7   L. Fuller, 'The Case of the Speluncean Explorers', (1949) 62 Harvard Law Review 616. Fuller's famous piece is an excellent introduction to some central issues in legal theory, but because it is centred on adjudication it hardly serves as a balanced overview of the whole field of legal theory. For example, one can reasonably ask students to write opinions for the case in the style of most American jurists, such as Holmes, Llewellyn, Posner, Dworkin, Kennedy, and Fuller himself. It works for utilitarians, such as Bentham, and for any jurist interested in reasoning about questions of law; but it just does not fit Maine or Hart or Weber or Raz or most feminist or Marxist or historical or sociological jurists, who generally have quite different agendas of issues. See further, *LIC*, pp 213-221. See now, James Allan, (ed), *The Speluncean Case* (1999), an anthology of fictional cases which are based on or extend Fuller's oiginal text.

8   Dworkin's first criticisms of Hart centred mainly, but not exclusively, on judicial discretion: 'Judicial Discretion' (1963) 60 Journal of Philosophy 624; cf *Taking Rights Seriously* (1967), Ch 2. Hart dealt with adjudication quite briefly in *The Concept of Law*. (pp 141-147). It is striking that a majority of references in the index to 'adjudication' and 'discretion of courts' relate to the Postscript.

9   G J Postema, *Bentham and the Common Law Tradition* (1986). Given Postema's focus on Bentham's attacks on common law ways of thought, the emphasis on judges is justified; but one wonders whether Bentham ever had quite as developed a theory of adjudication as Postema attributes to him.

jurisprudence. For that enterprise, questions about the structure and function of courts, styles of reasoning, the role of judges, the legitimacy of a given system, one's loyalty to it, even the concept of 'judge', and the relationship between different kinds of functionary tend to be more or less historically context-specific. They can best be dealt with in detail in relation to a particular system or culture in a given phase of its history. In this view, one of the main tasks of general analytical jurisprudence is to develop a meta-language that transcends particular legal systems. General descriptive analytical jurisprudence focuses on the form and structure of legal systems in general. It needs general concepts and patterns that transcend local differences in the content and institutionalisation of laws. How far one can generalise about the content and function of laws and legal institutions may be an empirical question, as Buckland suggested, requiring both detailed research and relatively sophisticated comparative interpretation.[10]

Herbert Hart's treatment of Holmes exhibits an illuminating ambivalence. It can be treated as fairly representative of English reactions. Shortly after Neil MacCormick's book on Hart had been published,[11] I travelled with Hart on a train from Oxford to London. I asked him what he thought of MacCormick's book. He replied that he liked it, but he considered himself to be a more died-in-the-wool positivist than MacCormick made him out to be. I took this to mean that Hart, like Holmes, wished to emphasise the is/ought distinction, not just for the sake of abstract clarity, but also in order to bring out the close connection between law and power. I believe that Hart felt strongly that one needs to cast a cold eye on how such power has been exercised in the name of law. Accordingly, it is a mistake to present law as an inherently attractive phenomenon. For Hart, as well as for Holmes, for the purpose of detached description, it is useful to conceive of law in terms of other people's power.[12]

In this respect, Hart was a positivist in the Holmesian mould; but he was also one Holmes' sharpest critics. His critique has four main themes.

First, in *The Concept of Law* Hart makes powerful criticisms of an alleged prediction theory as a general theory of law. The main criticisms

10 Above, Ch 2.3.
11 Neil MacCormick, op cit (1981), esp pp 158-162.
12 The terms 'weak' and 'strong' positivism have recently crept into juristic discourse, but they do not seem to be used consistently or precisely. The terms have been used in different contexts, and 'strength' sometimes seems to refer to tenacity, sometimes to degree of emphasis, and sometimes to the range of contexts in which the separability thesis is defended. Hart is surely both tenacious and emphatic in distinguishing the is and the ought for purposes of describing the form and structure of legal systems in general. He acknowledges being 'a weak positivist' in respect of the content of the rule of recognition (Hart, 1994, Postscript, pp 250-254). Holmes should have had no difficulty with that.

made by Hart and others were that (a) concepts such as 'court' and 'official' presuppose the existence of a legal system, so cannot be used to define law; (b) the prediction theory confuses prophesies (empirical) with rules (normative) and legal systems cannot be described solely in terms of brute fact; (c) the prediction theory is inadequate because it does not take account of or fit standpoints, such as that of judges, advocates, and legislators, for whom prediction is not the central concern. In my view, the criticisms of such a theory are valid, but Hart had to indulge in decontextualised readings of the flimsiest of texts – a few passages in 'The Path of the Law' and *The Bramble Bush* – in order to back the claim that anyone seriously advanced such a general theory.[13] More generally, I have argued, Hart's treatment of 'rule scepticism' in *The Concept of Law* is an example of an unwarranted misreading of the nature and concerns of legal realism generally and of American Realism in particular.[14]

Secondly, as part of particular (English, Anglo-American, perhaps common law) jurisprudence, Hart made cogent criticisms of Holmes' 'objective theory' of liability.[15]

Thirdly, and equally convincingly, Hart defended English analytical jurists from the charge that they subscribed to 'the fallacy of the logical form'.[16] He acknowledged that closed system reasoning is a chimera, but exempted the leading English positivists from the charge that they believed in it. Bentham and Austin were not 'formalists' in the Germanic sense that Holmes was attacking. To be fair to Holmes, he was probably not responsible for this attribution.

More generally, Hart praised Holmes for his specific insights as an historian and as a lawyer, but dismissed him as a poor philosopher. The aperçus and epigrams were diamonds, but they were held together by rather flimsy unphilosophical string.[17]

---

13   Hart, 1961, ch vii; *BMR*, pp 280-287. Hart later acknowledged that 'the Nightmare view of law' that he had criticised was often embodied 'in provocative slogans almost always meant to say something less extravagant than what the slogans seemed to say' (*Essays*, at p 128, specifically referring to the key passages by Holmes and Llewellyn). However, as so often happens in jurisprudence, this partial retraction is almost always ignored.
14   American Legal Realism refers to a specific historical movement; 'legal realism' refers to ideas that have a less local provenance and more general significance. Neither Realism nor realism is solely or mainly concerned with judicial decisions on questions of law. (*TAR*, at p 333 n 2, pp 359-371).
15   Hart, *Essays*, 1983, Ch 13.
16   Hart, *Essays*, 1983, Ch 12.
17   'The diamonds are the marvellous insights into the genius of the common law and the detailed explorations of its growth ... The string is the sometimes obscure and hasty argument, the contemptuous dismissal of rival views, and the exaggerations with which Holmes sought to build up the tendencies which he found actually at work in the history of the law into a tough, collective philosophy of society' (ibid at p 278).

Thus, if one accepts that 'The Path of the Law' did not launch a general theory or definition of law, Hart's arguments have little bearing on the main thesis of the address. On this interpretation, Hart's arguments are valid, but they do not damage the bad man. Hart exonerates English analytical jurisprudence from 'the fallacy of the logical form', ignores the realist argument, and endorses the positivist argument.

3   THE BAD MAN IN 1897

(a)   Uncharitable Readings

Hart may have misread Holmes, but at least he produced illuminating criticisms of the idea of law as prediction or as brute fact. Few other misreadings have been so fruitful. Indeterminate attribution, crude ism-atising, reading out of context, ignoring retractions and revisions, and both conflating and exaggerating difference and disagreement, are endemic bad practices in jurisprudence. 'The Path of the Law' has had more than its share of such unscholarly or uncharitable readings, most of which ignore the context of the relevant passages. One can clear away some unnecessary polemics by dealing peremptorily with four prime examples.

(i)   The bad man as the basis for a general prediction theory of law

There is little room for doubt that defining or conceptualising 'law' solely or mainly in terms of prediction is vulnerable to several strong lines of criticism, provided that the relevant passages are interpreted as launching a comprehensive general theory of law. Such an interpretation can only be sustained if one ignores the context, internal and extrinsic evidence of Holmes's intentions, and other more charitable interpretations. A better-grounded alternative interpretation is that Holmes intended to use a striking image to illustrate the point that prediction is a central concern of those subject to the law and their legal advisers. It is difficult to see how any careful reader can attribute to Holmes the view that legislators, judges or advocates are centrally concerned with prediction. A 'top-down' perspective, such as a prescriptive theory of legislation or adjudication, is no less vulnerable to charges of partiality and can no more claim to be a 'comprehensive' general theory of law than a 'bottom up' subject perspective. A more charitable reading of Holmes is that he was recommending to law students that one can get a more realistic, down-to-earth idea of ordinary private practice by adopting a bad man standpoint rather than some more lofty one.

(ii)   Holmes was urging students to adopt a cynical or immoral attitude to law and legal practice[18]

This uncharitable interpretation does violence to text and context. Holmes explicitly denied that he was speaking 'the language of cynicism'.[19] It is extremely unlikely that he intended to recommend that students should adopt such an attitude to law or its practice. It has been suggested that 'The Path of the Law' has a similar structure to Dante's *Divine Comedy*.[20] Holmes may have had a rather jaundiced view of legal practice, but it is hardly likely that he wished to equate entering private practice with a descent into Hell. It can readily be conceded that the bad man could be, and sometimes has been, used as a model for a private practitioner who views his or her role as furthering the client's goals without regard to morality or the public interest.[1] It is reasonable to criticize this view of a lawyer's role. A more charitable reading of Holmes is that the bad man perspective is a cognitive rather than an affective device, that is a way of looking at things rather than as a model for action.

(iii)   The emphasis on law as involving the power of the state is indicative of an attitude that venerates or glorifies power

It suggests that might is right or that brute power is the basis of political obligation. This is a standard caricature of 'positivism', exemplified by the notorious article 'Hobbes, Holmes, and Hitler'.[2] A more moderate version is the image of the state as 'the gunman writ large', which was so effectively criticised by Herbert Hart, though not in relation to Holmes.[3] A more charitable interpretation is that the bad man, far from venerating force, is confronted by institutions and laws that are threatening products of *other people's* power. These are as likely to be unattractive as attractive

---

18   Eg Henry Hart (1951) 64 Harvard Law Review at 932-934, see below n 1.
19   Quite apart from the context and Holmes' other writings this disclaimer is made explicitly in 'The Path of the Law' *before* he uses the phrase 'wash it with cynical acid' (*Path*, at p 170).
20   See the stimulating paper by Thomas C. Grey, 'Plotting the Path of the Law', (1997) 63 Brooklyn Law Review 19, 27.
1   On why it is inappropriate to treat the bad man as a role model, see below. Henry Hart is especially eloquent about the dangers of the bad man as a role model in respect of obedience, legal advice, judging, legislating, and scholarship: 'If we start with Holmes, where is the stopping place?', 'Holmes' Positivism: An Addendum' (1951) 64 Harvard Law Review 929 at 932-935.
2   Ben W Palmer, 'Hobbes, Holmes, and Hitler', (1943) 31 ABAJ 569. This was the culmination of a series of attacks, mainly from Catholics, in the 1940s. Cf Father John C Ford, 'The Fundamentals of Holmes' Juristic Philosophy' in *Phases of American Culture* (1942), p 51.
3   Hart, *The Concept of Law* (1961), Ch 2.

to him. Again, the linking of law to power is cognitive rather than affective.

(iv) The bad man is a role model for those subject to law in respect of obedience/political obligation

The bad man has been criticised as setting a bad example to ordinary citizens, taxpayers, civil servants, and the Chief Executive.[4] Again, one can concede that the bad man is not an admirable role model in respect of political obligation and civil disobedience. A positivist is not committed by the separability thesis to taking an amoral or immoral stance on obedience. Jeremy Bentham, Herbert Hart, Joseph Raz, and David Lyons are examples of positivists who treat political obligation as a normative question distinct from issues of the existence and validity of laws.[5] A standard positivist view is that there is no general moral obligation to obey or disobey the law just because it is law. From this perspective, one may have an obligation to obey some particular law or even a specific regime for many kinds of reason; conversely one may sometimes have an obligation to disobey the law. For positivists of this kind, questions about the nature of law and questions about political obligation are quite separate; the former are descriptive, the latter prescriptive.

In 'The Path of the Law' Holmes was not addressing directly the issue of political obligation. More important, there is a very good reason why the bad man cannot sensibly be treated as an example or role model for almost anyone: 'role model' is a normative concept, usually, but not invariably, involving a substantial ethical element.[6] The good professional, the upright or just judge, the lawyer-statesman, the enlightened law-maker are examples of personifications which combine

4   One example will suffice: 'The canons of ethics are not drawn for Holmes' bad man who wants to know just how many corners he can cut without running into trouble with the law. They are drawn rather for "the good man" or the ethical man as buoys to assist him in charting his professional conduct.' Irving Kaufman (1957) 70 Harvard Law Review 657 at 660 cited (*inter alios*) in *General Motors Corpn v City of New York* 501 F 2d 639 (1974) at 649.

5   Joseph Raz, *The Authority of Law* (1979), Ch 12, (arguing that there is no prima facie general obligation to obey the law, even in a good society whose legal system is just); Jeremy Bentham: 'Under a government of Laws, what is the motto of a good citizen? To obey punctually; to censure freely.' *A Fragment on Government*, Preface (J H Burns and H L A Hart eds, 1977) at p 399; David Lyons, 'Political Responsibility and Resistance to Government' (1995-96) Philosophic Exchange 5.

6   Some role models may exemplify qualities that do not involve an ethical element, for example, efficiency in a bureaucrat or skill in an athlete; but we generally expect our bureaucrats to have integrity and our athletes to be sporting. On moral constraints on partisanship within the adversary system see *LIC*, pp 322-325.

competence with ideals or standards that typically extend beyond what is formally required by disciplinary regulations or professional codes of ethics.[7] The bad man is by definition amoral, so it is very odd to interpret or use or criticise him as a role model.

(b)   A Charitable Interpretation

There is, of course, much scope for disagreement about what constitutes the best historical interpretation of a juristic text.[8] However, most would agree that attention needs to be paid to both text and context. The text and the context of 'The Path of the Law' both support the view that the bad man was introduced for quite limited purposes. In the text, the device had two manifest functions: (a) to dramatise a distinction between law and morals – the badness or amoral aspect; and (b) to focus attention on a more realistic standpoint for law students than that of appellate judges – the predictive aspect. One can clear away some unnecessary controversy by a brisk restatement of a moderate positivist interpretation.

In so far as the separability thesis is controversial, so is the bad man. However, I sympathise with the view, most recently expressed by several contributors to the volume on *The Autonomy of Law* , that much of the positivism versus anti-positivism debate is repetitious, trivial and almost entirely pointless.[9] Certainly, the debate tends to be trivialised if one discusses the so-called 'separability thesis' outside of particular contexts.

We can surely agree that there are some contexts in which distinctions between description and prescription, law and morals, is and ought (three different distinctions) can be both viable and useful.[10] For example, in discussing law reform in a particular system, or trying to give a relatively detached account of someone else's legal system, or assessing the human rights record of a foreign regime. For some purposes, a vocabulary is needed that aids description of existing situations in order to assess, criticise or recommend change. Such descriptions may not be entirely

---

7   *LIC*, Ch 16.
8   On interpretation and use of juristic texts, see *RB*, pp 104-128, (arguing for a pluralist approach). On historical reading my views are similar, but not identical, to those of Quentin Skinner.
9   Robert P George (ed), *The Autonomy of Law: Essays on Legal Positivism* (1996). Cf Klaus Fusser at p 120.
10   Few anti-positivists maintain that it is never possible and useful to distinguish 'is'-statements and 'ought'-statements. Ronald Dworkin claims that his best theory of law describes legal practice as well as prescribing best practice: 'Dworkin's idea of interpretation is not intended to dispense with these ideas of descriptivity and normativity. Rather, he wishes us to accept the idea that it is the nature of *some concepts* that they are not fully understood unless in an interpretive way.' Stephen Guest, *Ronald Dworkin* (1992), p 24 (italics added).

value-free or neutral, but we still need the distinction. It is not a concern of Amnesty International or Human Rights Watch to make a system the best it can be; even if they went out of their way to be charitable in interpreting 'the facts', they would need a language for giving an account of actual deviations from stated aspirations and international human rights norms. Proponents of the separability thesis maintain that rose-tinted spectacles filter out the seamy side of law and those elements that deserve criticism. What is done in the name of law can be pretty awful (or quite admirable). Furthermore, tools are needed for depicting both aspiration and reality – distinguishing what actually happens, from what is meant to happen. The bad man provides one such lens.

We can also agree that in some contexts the separability thesis is difficult to maintain: for example, an expositor advancing a theory of contract or responsibility in a particular legal system (as in Holmes's *The Common Law*) or a barrister advancing the best interpretation of a point of law on behalf of a client in court typically claims to be stating the law. The objective theory is advanced by Holmes as both descriptive and prescriptive; the theory goes far beyond the authoritative sources, but Holmes claims that this *is* the common law.[11] Hart criticises Holmes' theory because to impose liability on the basis of objective standards in criminal or civil matters is unfair or unjust. He also denies that it represents either English or American law. Hart interprets Holmes as trying to construct a theory based on first principles;[12] he points out that, while Holmes claimed that he was merely recording the law's use of 'objective standards', in fact 'he devotes much of this chapter to showing that the law here is reasonable and even admirable'.[13] Hart himself combines normative criticism of Holmes's theory with the claim that it has little support in American legal opinion. It seems that neither Holmes nor Hart strictly observes the is/ought distinction in this context. This is not surprising, because it is almost impossible to maintain the distinction when expounding the law. Even Kelsen recognised that, in stating or interpreting the substance of legal doctrine, ethical and other 'impurities' inevitably enter in.[14]

We can agree that reasonable persons can differ about the validity or utility of such distinctions in some contexts; including in respect of a

11 Holmes's 'objective theory' of liability has been generally discredited especially in relation to criminal law and contract: 'On Contract, Holmes is best remembered for his brilliant but generally rejected paradox that there is no duty to perform a contract, and for his bargain theory of consideration, which has left little mark on English law', Patrick Atiyah, 'The Legacy of Holmes Though English Eyes', in B Kaplan et al, *Holmes and the Common Law: A Century Later* (1981) at p 67.

12 *Essays* at p 279.

13 Ibid, 282.

14 R Tur and W Twining (eds), *Essays on Kelsen* (1986) at pp 26-33.

general theory of political obligation or about what constitutes a valid, cogent and appropriate argument on a question of law. There are some genuine, sometimes profound disagreements and some differences of concern underlying debates about positivism, but the range of disagreement is much narrower than decontextualised, repetitive discourse suggests.

The second function of the bad man is to focus attention on the standpoints of those subject to the law – including good citizens as well as bad men and the legal advisers of both – for whom predicting is often a central task or concern.[15] In the context of 'the Path of the Law' the device of the bad man can be interpreted as a means of urging intending private practitioners to adopt a *realistic* standpoint.

Surely we can agree with Holmes that: (i) there are some standpoints – both participant and observer – for which prediction is central or is one important aspect of a wider task;[16] (ii) that the standpoint of the office lawyer is at least as vocationally relevant for intending private practitioners as the standpoint of appellate judges; (iii) that the standpoint of those subject to the law is a significant and neglected one.

In respect of standard criticisms of Holmes we can agree about a number of points, independently of whether Holmes merited the criticism, including: (i) that there are many standpoints in which prediction is not central; (ii) that predicting is only one of the tasks of actual office lawyers; and (iii) that decisions of courts on points of law represent only one kind of a whole range of decisions and events that citizens, good or bad, and their legal advisers are concerned to predict.[17] To confine the bad man's concern to judicial decisions on questions of law is itself unrealistic – it smacks of 'court-itis' and leaves out important decisions and events that a rational actor within a legal system needs to consider.[18]

15 In practice, prediction is usually part of some broader operation such as drafting, or giving legal advice. Predicting is part of, but not central to, some standard judicial operations, for example anticipating the likely reaction of higher courts or judging the likelihood that a defendant may offend again.

16 *BMR*, pp 280-287.

17 In criminal cases, for example, the 'realistic' bad man contemplating a possibly unlawful act would be concerned with the likelihoods of observation, complaint, investigation, detection, decisions to prosecute, plea bargains and pleas, verdicts on questions of fact, procedural and jurisdictional issues, sanctions and so on. There have been other criticisms of the 'realism' of the bad man, [see below next note], for example: 'In ongoing relations, Holmes's "Bad Man" theory of law is quite removed from the realities of human conduct', Gidon Gottlieb, 'Relationism: Legal Theory for a Relational Society' (1983) 50 University of Chicago Law Review 567 at 602-603.

18 On one interpretation, Holmes focuses on interpretation and application of substantive law in particular cases and on sanctions and remedies, but not on pre-trial issues or fact-determination. He explicitly excluded 'the vaguer sanctions

4   THE BAD MAN IN 1997[19]

Since 1897 the bad man has to some extent become detached from the original text and has taken on a life of his own. We have seen that some decontextualised interpretations have treated him as a convenient target – what in England we would call an Aunt Sally. But what if we try to construct a more charitable interpretation, one which catches the positive part of his continuing appeal? I propose to argue that the bad man still has value both as an analytic device and as a metaphor, but within quite narrow parameters.

The bad man is a symbol, but what is the referent? And what is the context? In 1973 I wrote:

'Who is the Bad Man?
In the present context, the Bad Man is not a revolutionary nor even a reformer out to change "the system". The Bad Man's concern is to secure his personal objectives within the existing order as painlessly as possible; he is not so much alienated from the law as he is indifferent to all aspects that do not affect him personally. Unlike Sartre's Saint Genet, he is not one who has a problem of identity – who defines his being in terms of the system and who is driven to do acts *because* they are criminal or antisocial. Nor is he a subscriber to some perverse ethic which turns conventional morality upon its head. The Bad Man is amoral rather than immoral. He is, like Economic Man and Bentham's "civilized"

---

of conscience', and hence moral disapprobation, damage to continuing relationships, and other potential outcomes that would be the concern of prudent actors. This is because the focus is on understanding *law*. Fuller and others have made a different point: that in order to predict judicial decisions the bad man needs to take into account the motives and reasonings of 'good men'. (L Fuller, *The Law in Quest of Itself* (1940) pp 94-95.) This is no doubt true, but a comprehensive list of the factors that a prudent actor could usefully take into account as aids to prediction would be much longer and would vary according to context.

19 This section is similar in intent to that of William H Wilcox's interesting article, 'Taking a Good Look at the Bad Man's Point of View' (1981) 66 Cornell Law Review 1058. Wilcox states: '[M]y purpose is to develop the best theory possible in the spirit of Holmes' thought rather than to prove that Holmes' paper must be read in a particular manner' (p 1059). I agree with Wilcox that the most useful function of the bad man as an analytic device is to isolate prediction as a concern of all *prudent* actors, bad, amoral or good, and that prudence and prediction are central to understanding law. I also agree that the bad man is best interpreted as dramatising rather than providing a basis for the separation thesis. However, I argue that the bad man is also symbolic of some, but not all, subjects of the law whose viewpoints are essential for 'realistic' understandings of law, but are often neglected.

actors, a rational, calculating creature. In this and in other respects he does not necessarily reflect in a realistic manner the characteristics of actual deviants. Like Dahrendorf's *homo sociologicus*, "he can neither love nor hate, laugh nor cry. He remains a pale, incomplete, strange, artificial man".[20] Indeed, there appears to be no reason why the Bad Man should not be an artificial person, such as a corporation. In short he is a theoretical construct with as yet unexplored potential as a tool of analysis.'[1]

This passage bears repetition, but it needs further elaboration. First, in respect of context, it is important to distinguish between historical interpretation of the original text, and critical-constructive evaluation of the bad man today. As an historical interpretation this passage reads rather a lot into the original text, where, as we have seen, it served quite limited purposes. The passage is better read as addressing the continuing significance and utility of the bad man almost a century later.

Secondly, it is useful to distinguish between two main ways in which the bad man can be interpreted and used today. He can be treated either as a precise analytical tool or as a more diffuse metaphor for 'worms' eye views' or 'bottom up' perspectives. Let us call these the analytical and the symbolic uses.

For some purposes, it is useful to treat the bad man as an artificial construct analogous to *homo sociologicus* and economic man. On this interpretation the bad man is an analytical device that isolates the prudential concerns of those subject to the law. As Wilcox says: '[t]he prudent man's point of view is central to our understanding of law because everyone with an interest in law has at least a prudential reason for that interest'.[2] Predicting consequences is the core of prudence; detachment is a necessary, or at least an important, precondition for making good predictions. On this view, the bad man is amoral, rational and calculating. He is subject to the law, but he is different from *homo juridicus*. The latter is either just a legal person, whose existence according to one view is posited by law; or he is a personification of a purely legal perspective, ie depicting the lenses of the law from the point of view of legal science.[3] Both are creatures of law. The bad man, on the other hand, is conceived to exist independently of law; from his point of view the law is one of the facts of life that he has to cope with as an external force, to be avoided,

20 R Dahrendorf, 'Homo Sociologicus' in *Essays in the Theory of Society* (1968), p 76. This essay explores at length the relationship between constructs like *homo sociologicus* and actual people. See also H Lasswell and A Kaplan, *Power and Society* (1950), p 78.

1   *BMR*, pp 280-281.

2   Wilcox, op cit, p 1072.

3   Raz, op cit, Ch 7, pp 140-143.

evaded or perhaps used for his own purposes. *Homo juridicus* represents a top-down view of legal persons or purely legal perspectives;[4] the bad man represents a detached view by legal subjects. His main function is to isolate for purposes of analysis the concern for prediction of those confronted by law.

Because the bad man is neither created nor defined by law, it does not follow that the idea needs to be restricted to individual human beings. Indeed, the treatment of corporations in the quoted passage is too cautious. International drug cartels, multi-national corporations, businesses, whether incorporated or not, trade unions, political pressure groups, teenage gangs, and many other kinds of collective actors and agents may well fit the ideal type quite closely.[5] For instance, is not the perspective of a large bureaucratic corporation whose sole or primary aim is maximisation of profit very close to that of the bad man – amoral, rational, calculating, purposeful, pursuing its own agenda?[6] This may be especially significant for a realistic analysis of a given legal order in terms of distribution of power.

A less precise interpretation treats the bad man as a diffuse metaphor for 'bottom-up' perspectives and 'worms' eye views'. The analytical interpretation focuses on the practical concerns of prudent actors; the symbolic interpretation emphasises the position or vantage point of legal subjects, especially those subject to other people's power. The symbol is open to more than one interpretation. It could represent the viewpoint of all legal subjects, but insofar as it includes the main attributes of the analytic construct – rational, calculating, amoral – its scope is more restricted.[7] For example, a rational, calculating actor pursuing his own agenda is not an entirely appropriate symbol of the oppressed, the disempowered or the unempowered. In short there are many kinds of legal subjects, of which the bad man most appropriately represents only one species.

4   On the problematic aspects of the perspectives and role of 'legal scientists' see *BT* ch 6. The legal scientist as expositor is not a clear case of a top-down view: s/he is 'above' and 'outside' the law and is not in this sense a legal subject. How much power expositors or scientists actually exercise as participants within a particular system is a contingent matter, as Max Weber emphasised.

5   Cf Roger Cotterrell: 'the most important legal persons in capitalist enterprise in contemporary Western societies are *not* human individuals but *corporations*', *The Sociology of Law: An Introduction* (2nd edn, 1992), p 124.

6   Cf Lawrence E Mitchell, 'Co-operation and Constraint in the Modern Corporation: An Inquiry into the Causes of Corporate Immorality' (1995) 73 Texas Law Review 509 at 512 (arguing that certainty in respect of regulation of corporate governance encourages directors and managers to behave like a bad man in tailoring their behaviour to minimalist interpretations of fiduciary duties).

7   *BMR*, pp 288-289.

Let us illustrate this point in relation to two examples: gender and user perspectives on law.

(a)   Gender

Consider the bad man from a feminist perspective. What will result from a change of gender? Suppose a latter-day Holmes advised law students to look at law from the standpoint of a bad woman? Somehow the symbol loses its force. Why should this be? Several related reasons come immediately to mind: the stereotypical image of bad people is male: criminals, revolutionaries, naughty boys.[8] Even though we interpret 'bad' to mean amoral rather than wicked, the image is still more male than female. Becky Sharp is generally amoral as she manipulates her way through *Vanity Fair*, but it seems inappropriate to characterise her as a or the bad woman. If the gender is changed to meet feminist concerns it does not work. One reason for this might be that in so far as Holmes's bad man, like 'economic man', is a rational, calculating, bloodless creature he fits male rather than female stereotypes. Furthermore, the bad man does not seem to be a good symbol of subordination or victimisation. He does not share in and is detached from state power, but he is to some extent in control of his own destiny. In so far as feminist critiques of patriarchy focus on the subordination or victimisation or disempowerment or silencing of women, neither the bad man nor the bad woman seems to be appropriate as a symbol. The bad man may symbolize alienation, detachment or even of dislike of law; but is he an apt representative of all legal subjects – of victims, the oppressed, silenced voices, for example?[9] The same is true for other subjects whose concerns or interests relate to empowerment or fair treatment or other kinds of participation. The bad man better symbolises cool detachment and an amoral perspective rather than normative concerns about justice or oppression or power-sharing.

(b)   Users[10]

The bad man suggests an image of someone steering their own path through the legal jungle rather than seeing it as an aid or resource or

8   Eg Susan Estrich, 'Rape' (1986) 95 Yale Law Journal 1087 at 1091; Linda McClain, ' "Atomistic Man" Revisited: Liberalism, Connection, and Feminist Jurisprudence' (1992) 65 Southern California Law Review 1171, at 1228ff.

9   It is, of course, important to distinguish between victims *of* a legal system and victims *in* the legal system. For example, someone wrongly accused or wrongly convicted of rape or murder is a victim of the legal system; someone who has been raped may be both a victim in it and a victim of it. The bad man is not an appropriate starting-point for victimology.

10 On user perspectives see below, Ch 6.1 and 6.6.

habitat, to be used, manipulated or exploited for his own ends.[11] A user perspective can also be a form of worm's eye view, in the sense that the user does not necessarily have an authoritative say in the design, development or administration of the system. Thus, a user may also see law as a product of other people's power. Users may include complainants, plaintiffs, constructors of tax avoidance schemes, welfare recipients, debt collectors, health and safety inspectors, or successful disputants enforcing arbitration awards. Legal rules may be used to threaten, harass, or coerce, or for purposes different from those intended;[12] and, in so far as law is facilitative, entering a contract, making a will, or setting up a company is using the law. A user perspective is quite close to that of the bad man in that it can be rational, calculating, and detached. However, there are some significant differences between the two concepts: first, the user may be amoral or even immoral, but need not be so; secondly, the user in this sense is an active and willing participant; the bad man is not; and, thirdly, those in control of, or having significant influence on, the legal system may also be users, in which case the image of law as other people's power does not fit.[13] For these reasons the user is probably better treated as a close relative of the bad man, but separate from him.

Thus the bad man today still has value both as an analytical device, like economic man, that isolates the prudential concerns of those subject to the law and as a more diffuse symbol of bottom-up perspectives. As we have seen, differentiating the bad man from victims, the oppressed, women, and users signals some limitations of the metaphor. He represents only one 'bottom up' view among many. The next section illustrates how the bad man can be used to explore and question some currently fashionable ideas within legal theory.

11 On analogies between legal orders and jungles, see further below, Ch 6.6.
12 For example, large corporations using consumer courts as debt-collecting agencies.
13 This last point is important in respect of Laura Nader's sketch for 'A User Theory of Law', which emphasises the competition for power between different users: 'A user theory of law would embrace the view of law as being made and changed by the cumulative efforts of its users and would argue that law is being moved in a particular evolutionary direction by the dominant users. Such unconsciously generated cumulative movements may be considered as separate from yet equally important as any consciously created ones attributable to legal engineering.'Laura Nader, 'A User Theory of Law' (1984) 38 Southwestern Law Journal 951, at 52; cf Laura Nader (ed) *No Access to Law: Alternatives to the American Judicial System* (1980).

5   STANDPOINT: THREE DISTINCTIONS

The bad man usefully illustrates the elusiveness of three problematic, but useful, distinctions: general and particular jurisprudence; participants and observers; internal and external points of view. All three play a significant role in contemporary legal theory, but they have not been subject to much sustained critical analysis.

(a)   General and Particular Jurisprudence Again

Within the English analytical tradition a great deal of emphasis was placed on this distinction by Bentham, Austin, Holland and Buckland.[14] Later, Anglo-American Jurisprudence went through a strikingly particularist phase and the distinction was all but forgotten. In his early work Hart tended to be rather dismissive of the distinction,[15] although he can be credited with reviving general analytical jurisprudence. However, in his posthumous Postscript to *The Concept of Law*, Hart revived the distinction in order to try to narrow the range of disagreement between himself and Dworkin.[16] Another, more important reason for taking the idea of general jurisprudence seriously, is that some of the basic premises of particular jurisprudence, for example conceptions of municipal legal systems as discrete, self-contained orders, are under challenge in an increasingly interdependent world.

Particular jurisprudence deals with one legal system or culture. General jurisprudence deals with more than one legal system or culture. Generality and particularity are relative. General jurisprudence may claim to be universal (as with Bentham's universal censorial jurisprudence), it may address all developed or 'mature' legal systems (as with Austin's general expository jurisprudence), or it may deal with several legal systems or cultures. The geographical reach of much jurisprudential writing is strikingly indeterminate: is *Law's Empire* confined to American or Anglo-American law or does it apply to all common law systems or to the legal systems of liberal democracies or more generally?[17] The referent of such commonly used phrases as 'American jurisprudence' or 'Anglo-American jurisprudence' is not always clear. Sometimes such terms refer to provenance, sometimes to audience, sometimes to data and sources. More often than not they are indeterminate. This is especially true of 'common law' – do the phrases 'common law adjudication', 'common law reasoning', 'common lawyers',

14   Above, Ch 2.
15   Eg Hart, *Essays*, at p 88.
16   Postscript, pp 239-244, criticised Ch 2.4 above.
17   Above, Ch 3.4(a).

'the common law world' include Ireland and India and Sri Lanka and Mauritius? Similarly talk of 'legal culture' and 'legal families' is also vague: is there one American legal culture that encompasses California, and Boston, and Cripple Creek, Colorado? When is it meaningful to talk of 'Western legal culture' and what does it exclude? Jurisprudence may be the general part of law as a discipline, but how general is the reach of any particular text is often very vague.

In order to introduce more precision into talk about the geographical reach of a text or group of texts, it is useful to distinguish between provenance, audience, focus, sources, perspectives, and significance. It may also be illuminating to substitute for 'particular' such words as 'local' or 'parochial' which have somewhat different connotations.

The *provenance* of a text may refer to the nationality or locale of its author. For example, Holmes was an American jurist, Hart was an English positivist. It may also locate the origins of a school or movement: the Frankfurt School, the Chicago School of Law and Economics, American Legal Realism. More generally, it may associate a jurist or group with a nation or region – American or Icelandic or Scandinavian Jurisprudence. Such labels, though imprecise, may give an indication of the intellectual tradition or cultural context from which a jurist or a particular text or school or movement emerged.

The intended *audience* of a text may be local (as in a public lecture), specialised (as in a law review article which may have a modest circulation internationally), or it may be more general; the actual audience or readership may be wider or narrower than anticipated by the author. 'The Path of the Law' was seemingly addressed to Boston University law students; part of the sub-text may have been aimed at a professional audience – American practitioners and teachers of law. Holmes could hardly have anticipated that a century later it would continue to be frequently cited and occasionally read internationally in a variety of quite different contexts.

More important is *focus*: particular jurisprudence, in Austin's sense, refers to theorising about a single legal system: for example, English analytical jurisprudence is concerned with the basic concepts and principles of English Law. General jurisprudence, in Austin's usage, focuses on laws in general or at least in 'maturer systems'. A focus is strongly parochial if it is limited to local parish pump issues.

Juristic writing may be local or parochial in respect of *sources*. For example, much American writing cites only or mainly or almost exclusively American sources even when dealing with issues that are not merely local. Conversely, Pollock and Buckland were widely read in Roman and German literature, but explicitly argued that the focus of taught jurisprudence should be local or particular.[18]

18   Above, Ch 2.3.

Jurisprudence may be local or parochial in respect of *perspectives*. There are sometimes peculiarly English, or German, or French ways of looking at things. The pejorative term 'ethnocentric' is used when a writer allows the peculiar concepts, assumptions or 'blinders' of their own culture to cloud or distort their perception or interpretation of phenomena or ideas of another legal system or culture. This is quite commonly exemplified by foreign 'experts' who fly in to advise on legal development assuming that 'lawyers', 'courts', 'trials' or 'constitutions' have the same connotations and functions as in their own country.[19]

Finally, jurisprudence which is more or less local or particular in respect of provenance, audience, focus, sources, and perspectives may be of much more general or even universal *significance*. In jurisprudence, as elsewhere, one may see a world in a grain of sand.

Locating a juristic text is not an exact science. 'The Path of the Law' illustrates the limitations of such characterisations: one might say that it is American, even Bostonian, in respect of both provenance and audience. Its sources are mainly Anglo-American, but it is informed by a sprinkling of Roman and Continental European ideas. It is arguably mid-Atlantic in respect of style. Its focus ranges from the highly local to the universal. It is a classic of the common law and of jurisprudence generally, just because in important ways it transcends its peculiar roots in time and space to provide insights of general significance. The provenance of the bad man was Boston in 1897, but in 1997 he can sensibly be interpreted as a citizen of the world – for example, as a personification of positivism or realism or of some worms' eye views of law anywhere.

(b)   Participants, Observers, and Participant-observers

Law tends to be a participant-oriented discipline.[20] By this I mean that the culture of much legal scholarship, legal education and legal discourse generally is imbricated with practical insider attitudes. This is hardly surprising in what is for the most part an applied discipline closely associated with the world of affairs. What is surprising is how often one participant standpoint is equated with a whole view. The bad man and his critics illustrate the variety of participant standpoints in law: prediction fits bad men, good citizens, their advisers; decisions to prosecute; and some external observers (eg intelligence analysts), but not others. Prediction is not *central* to the role of legislators, judges, advocates, mediators, negotiators, but it plays a part in performing their tasks.[1] Holmes has been criticised for ignoring other standpoints;

19 On ethnocentrism and constitution-making, see *CCC*.
20 *BT*, pp 128-130; *LIC*, pp 126-128.
1   On prediction by lower court judges of potential decisions by higher courts see Richard Posner, *The Problems of Jurisprudence* (1990), pp 223-228.

accusations of confusing the part with some notional whole can at least as well be the basis for criticising theories of adjudication or legislation which claim to be comprehensive theories of law.[2]

It is a mistake to treat the distinctions between general and particular jurisprudence and between observers and participants as co-extensive. A stance of strong detachment fits the standpoints of some kinds of observers of other people's legal systems. However, one can observe a particular legal system, including one's own, and one can participate in foreign, regional, transnational and global operations. And general jurisprudence can be normative as well as interpretive or descriptive.

More important is the point that there are many kinds of observers, with different vantage-points, roles, resources, perspectives, and purposes.[3] Some people are observers by happenstance (a bystander, casual onlooker, or chance witness), but observing, describing, explaining and interpreting are *activities* undertaken for a variety of purposes from a variety of standpoints. Accordingly, some observers of legal systems are participants in some broader enterprise. For example, the CIA agent, the foreign correspondent, Amnesty International, the comparative lawyer, and 'the legal scientist' have different goals, roles, resources and situations. What lenses are appropriate depend on factors such as vantage point, purpose, and role.

Most such observers are not direct participants in the legal systems they are observing. There is, however, the social science concept of the participant-observer, who – leanly interpreted – participates in order to observe. The concept is notoriously fuzzy: in order to avoid the Hawthorne effect, the observer of a rain-making ceremony must be restrained about innovating or suggesting improvements in a subsequent de-briefing session.[4] The main point of participant-observation is to gain a better vantage-point and some first-hand experience of being part of the action. But a Moscow-watcher, whether journalist, diplomat, travel

2   On the alleged centrality of judges see above, pp 113-114.
3   The variety of types of observer and observing is illustrated by Rogat's splendid article. In discussing, mainly from a psychological perspective, the attitudes and postures of Holmes, Henry James and Henry Adams, Rogat uses *inter alios*: spectator (title *et passim*), Brahman, (p 230), observer (pp 230, 237, 239-240), outsider (pp 230, 243), onlooker (p 240), bystander (pp 241, 242), Olympian (p 245); audience (p 241); astronomer (p 243, Holmes Sr's image of his son); expatriate (p 243), disinterested technician (p 249). These nuanced characterisations are reflected in other nouns and adjectives: attachment, detachment, alienation, estrangement, withdrawal, indifference, disinterestedness, and fatalism. Rogat skilfully deploys these concepts, but he does not differentiate clearly enough between vantage point, role, perspective and purpose.
4   The Hawthorne effect refers to 'confounding influences on research outcomes caused by subjects reacting to being studied', Eric Lang *Encyclopaedia of Sociology* (1992) Vol 2, pp 733-734.

writer, or spy, usually needs to visit or live in Moscow, during which time, like the bad man, s/he too is subject to the Russian legal system and other local legal orderings.

The bad man illustrates the fluidity of such categories. Unlike the participant-observer, he does not participate in order to observe. But neither does he observe in order to participate; he is an actor rather than a participant, for participation in the legal system is only incidental to his purposes as actor.

Yosal Rogat, in his seminal article, 'The Judge as Spectator', pointed out a seeming paradox in 'The Path of the Law': Holmes advocates a standpoint of strong detachment for participants – not just for the bad man, but also for law students as intending practitioners, for citizens, and even for the judge.[5] However, the paradox is only apparent. The concerned insiders who are critics or reformers also need a language for describing existing institutions, rules, practices, and so on that they wish to evaluate, criticise, or change. In some contexts one describes in order to criticise. In many other participant roles, relative detachment is widely considered to be a desirable trait. Llewellyn's 'temporary divorce of the is and the ought for purposes of study'[6] and Holmes's 'dual lenses' seem sensible rather than paradoxical.[7] But Holmes, as a person, sometimes carried his detachment rather far.

Strong detachment does not fit so easily with the standpoints of most participants within their own legal system, such as legislators, judges, officials, advocates, good citizens, reformers, and expositors.[8] The image better fits one's academic colleague who throws away all administration circulars and directives without reading them; or the tax consultant who constructs wealth-maximising schemes for clients by calculating risks without too fine a regard for distinctions between evasion, avoidance and grey areas; or the ANC activist in the apartheid era who worked out when and how to use the South African legal system and when to operate outside the law in furthering the political goals of the movement.[9] Whether the image fits the standpoint of the bad man's legal adviser or a revolutionary or a spy or Saint Genet is debatable.[10]

The bad man is an actor: but he symbolises detachment from the system. He *disowns* it. For him there is no question of loyalty or fidelity or legitimacy or validity or correct interpretation or making it the best it can be. He is in the system, but not of it. It is a fact of life that has been

5   Rogat, op cit, at p 243.
6   Karl N Llewellyn, *Jurisprudence: Realism in Theory and Practice* (1962), pp 56-57.
7   On 'double vision' see Thomas Nagel's *The View from Nowhere* (1986) Ch 6.
8   On expositors as participants in their legal system see *BT*, pp 130-141.
9   See generally, Nelson Mandela, *Long Walk to Freedom* (1994).
10 *BMR*, pp 280, 288.

created, imposed, implemented (or not) by others – one can navigate or play the system or even benefit from it as one can a jungle or other external environment.

(c)   External and Internal Points of View

Much has been made of distinctions between 'internal' and 'external' points of view in modern jurisprudence. Hart made this a cornerstone of his hermeneutic interpretation of the concept of law. Dworkin claims for *Law's Empire* that 'This book takes up the *internal*, participants' point of view'.[11] Some sociologists of law, as different as Roger Cotterrell[12] and Donald Black,[13] claim that they are outside observers of legal systems. Even critical legal scholars frequently say that they are analysing law from the outside.[14]

It is a mistake to equate the distinction between observers and participants with the distinction between internal and external points of view. There are many types of observers and participants: some observe as part of participating; some participate in order to observe. The bad man is detached from the law and disowns it; but he is in the legal system as an actor, sometimes as a participant. At the very least, talk of 'internal' and 'external' needs to give a specific answer to such questions as: 'internal/external to what?'

Brian Tamanaha has convincingly shown that the internal/external distinction has arisen in a variety of contexts and 'remains obscure and largely unanalysed'.[15] I agree with most of his argument[16] and will not repeat it here. I would go further in differentiating vantage point, role, resources, purpose, and perspectives in relation to 'standpoint'. Suffice to say here that once again the bad man does not fit decontextualised distinctions between 'internal' and 'external' points of view and in the

---

11   Dworkin, *Law's Empire* at p 14.
12   Roger Cotterrell, 'The Sociological Concept of Law' (1983-4) 10 Journal of Law and Society 241, 242; cf Cotterrell, *The Politics of Jurisprudence* (1989).
13   Donald Black, *The Behavior of Law* (1976); *Sociological Justice* (1989), discussed by Cotterrell, *The Sociology of Law: An Introduction* (2nd edm, 1992), p 13.
14   For a perceptive critique of some examples see Tamanaha, op cit below at pp 188-191. It is natural for critical scholars to distance or dissociate themselves from authority, but a high proportion of critical literature is activist and hence participatory. For example, Ian Grigg-Spall and Paddy Ireland (eds) *The Critical Lawyers' Handbook* (1992); cf, from an earlier generation in the United States, K Boudin et al, *The Bust Book: What to Do Until the Lawyer Comes* (1970), discussed in relation to Holmes in *BMR*, pp 275-276, 299-303.
15   Brian Z Tamanaha, *Realistic Socio-Legal Theory: Pragmatism and a Social Theory of Law* (1997) 153-154.
16   Ibid at pp 153-195.

process illustrates why, in jurisprudence, it is essential to take clarification of standpoint seriously.[17]

Neither the distinction between general and particular jurisprudence nor distinctions between observer and participant standpoints or internal and external points of view can bear much weight. This does not mean that they are meaningless or useless. Holmes's bad man is local, participatory, and relatively detached. In 1896-97 he was introduced for quite narrow purposes. He has since become a symbol of wider significance. This standpoint usefully emphasises the power dimension of law. It fits quite comfortably with much of English legal culture. But, of course, the bad man represents only one juristic standpoint among many.

6 CONCLUSION

First, it is useful to distinguish between historical interpretations of Holmes's text and the potential uses of the bad man device today. An end to unscholarly interpretations of Holmes's text and uncharitable interpretations of the 'bad man' as a symbolic figure would be welcome. There never was a general prediction theory of law, except perhaps in the minds of some slapdash critics; the bad man was never intended to be nor should he be used or criticised as a role model; rather he represents one limited, but useful and neglected, perspective.

Secondly, Holmes's original intention was to use the bad man as a device to introduce a positivist and a realist perspective. It is a vivid way of illustrating the separability thesis, which was and to this day remains controversial. It was less successful as a realist move because real bad men, good citizens and their advisers are not solely concerned with prediction and they need to predict many kinds of decisions and events, not just judicial decisions on questions of law (and sanctions). Furthermore, real subjects of the law, whether good, bad, or amoral are not always rational, calculating or purposive. As an analytical construct, the bad man is no more realistic than 'economic' man. Rather, like *homo*

---

17 It is not a coincidence that Holmes was sensitive to the significance of standpoint. His friend Henry James was one of the first figures to develop self-consciously the idea of 'point of view' in fiction, see Percy Lubbock, *The Craft of Fiction* (1921, 1955 reprint): 'The whole intricate question of method, in the craft of fiction, I take to be governed by the question of point of view – the question of the relation in which the narrator stands to the story' (p 251). Earlier Lubbock states: 'Henry James was the first writer of fiction, I judge, to use all the possibilities of the method with the intention and thoroughness, and the full extent of the opportunity which is thus revealed is very great' (ibid p 172). A similar claim can be made for the significance of standpoint in legal theory.

economicus, it can be used as an analytic device for isolating the concerns of a prudent subject who is detached from both law and morality.

Thirdly, the bad man is a good example of the significance of switching standpoint. In particular, he reminds us of the significance of bottom-up perspectives. Even if broadly interpreted as a metaphor, he cannot be taken as fully representative of all legal subjects, such as victims, users, women, and the oppressed. But he does draw attention to the idea of law as other people's power and in the process to much that tends to be omitted from theories that are exclusively top-down. How law is perceived and used by subjects is as significant for the purpose of understanding as the motives, aims, and decisions of those who control a legal system. It also reminds us of the potential awfulness of much that is done in the name of law. Like *The Bonfire of the Vanities*,[18] the bad man draws attention to the seamy underside of law that is papered over or ignored by much legal scholarship.

Fourthly, distinctions between 'internal' and 'external' points of view, between participants and observers, between general and particular jurisprudence are recognised as important in contemporary legal theory. The bad man cuts across these distinctions: an outsider with an insider's vantage-point, an unwilling participant who is a relatively detached observer; a worm from Massachusetts who has become a citizen of the world. In transcending these dichotomies he shows up their fragility and their crudity. Here, legal theory needs a more nuanced vocabulary.

Finally, there are some genuine issues worth debating between positivism and its critics; but these tend to be obscured by unnecessary, often unscholarly, polemics. I personally believe that both positions are largely complementary and that jurisprudence is impoverished by obsessive preoccupation with the rather narrow range of issues that are the focus of such debates. For if the purpose of legal theory is understanding, how can anyone claim to have a balanced theory of law who only looks at one side of the admittedly rough distinctions between the local and the universal, between the law in books and the law in action, and between aspiration and reality? Any legal theory that focuses solely on aspiration or solely on the often brutal facts of the realities of

---

18   Tom Wolfe, *The Bonfire of the Vanities* (1987). While works of this genre may be poor sociology, as Judge Posner has suggested, they can vividly illuminate problems and practices that deserve serious attention. In *Overcoming Law* (1995) Posner partially retracted his original opinion ((1989) 98 Yale Law Journal 1653) that one learns almost nothing about law from Tom Wolfe's novel. However, he concludes that '*The Bonfire of the Vanities* is a fine novel with limited relevance to the deep issues of jurisprudence' (*Overcoming Law* 489). I respectfully disagree; like the bad man, it focuses on some neglected points of view, not least the experiences of people who become enmeshed in criminal process as suspects.

law is radically incomplete. Understanding law involves taking account of the 'realities' of those with power over it and those who are subject to it and many others besides. Understanding law requires multiple lenses. The bad man, constructively interpreted, still provides one useful set of lenses.

Chapter 6

Mapping law*

'*He is no true town planner, but at best a too simple engineer, who sees only the similarity of cities.*' *(Patrick Geddes)*

'*Only the name of the airport changes.*' *(Italo Calvino)*

I INTRODUCTION

This chapter is one of a series of explorations about the implications of globalisation for the discipline of law and for jurisprudence or legal theory as its general part. My project is to explore the idea of, and possible agendas for, a revived general jurisprudence in a world characterised by conflicting tendencies of globalisation and fragmentation; of homogenisation and of emphasis on cultural diversity; of bureaucratic rationalism, on the one hand, and post-modern indeterminacy and other kinds of pluralism on the other.

The central question that I shall address here is just one part of that agenda: what is involved in depicting law in the world as a whole, or single legal orders, or specific legal phenomena? This may be interpreted as one way of rephrasing the central question of traditional jurisprudence: what is law? I shall approach this from the perspective of a rooted

* This a revised version of the text of the MacDermott Lecture, delivered at the Queen's University, Belfast in June, 1998 and published in 50 NILQ 12 (1999). The text is reproduced here with the agreement of SLS Publications (Northern Ireland) Ltd.

cosmopolitan, using the idea of mapping as a theme. I shall speak first of geographical maps, and then figuratively of mental maps and of mapping as a metaphor for one way of depicting – that is interpreting, describing, evoking and explaining – a subject-matter of study. The central thread of my argument will be drawn from Italo Calvino's wonderful fable *Invisible Cities*.[1] This takes the form of an imaginary dialogue between the ageing Emperor Kublai Khan and his ambassador, the young Marco Polo. Kublai feels that he can only recover the ability to rule his empire if he can understand, and thus grasp, its underlying pattern; Marco Polo tries to assist by evoking cities he has visited. His accounts can be interpreted either as depictions of fifty-five different cities or fifty-five depictions of one city, Venice.[2] Here, I shall lean towards the second interpretation.

The flavour of the work and the possibility of suggestive analogies between depictions of cities and legal orders can be illustrated by Marco Polo's account of Esmeralda:

'In Esmeralda, city of water, a network of canals and a network of streets span and intersect each other. To go from one place to another you have always the choice between land and boat: and since the shortest distance between two points in Esmeralda is not a straight line but a zigzag that ramifies in tortuous optional routes, the ways that open to each passerby are never two, but many, and they increase further for those who alternate a stretch by boat with one on dry land.

And so Esmeralda's inhabitants are spared the boredom of following the same streets every day. And that is not all: the network of routes is not arranged on one level, but follows instead an up-and-down course of steps, landings, cambered bridges, hanging streets. Combining segments of the various routes, elevated or on ground level, each inhabitant can enjoy every day the pleasure of a new itinerary to reach the same places. The most fixed and calm lives in Esmeralda are spent without any repetition.

---

1   Italo Calvino, *Invisible Cities* (tr W Weaver, 1974) (hereafter *IC*). I am indebted to Michael Froomkin for suggesting that I use Calvino's book in this context.
2   There is a third, more plausible, possibility – that Marco Polo was using Venice as an implicit point of reference, almost as an ideal type, against which other cities are compared and contrasted: 'There is still one of which you never speak'. Marco Polo bowed his head. 'Venice,' the Khan said. Marco Polo smiled. 'What else do you believe I have been telling you about?' Later he adds: 'To distinguish other cities' qualities, I must speak of a first city that remains implicit. For me it is Venice' (*IC* 86).

Secret and adventurous lives, here as elsewhere, are subject to greater restrictions. Esmeralda's cats, thieves, illicit lovers move along higher, discontinuous ways, dropping from a rooftop to a balcony, following gutterings with acrobats' steps. Below, the rats run in the darkness of the sewers, one behind the other's tail, along with conspirators and smugglers: they peep out of manholes and drainpipes, they slip through double bottoms and ditches, from one hiding-place to another they drag crusts of cheese, contraband goods, kegs of gunpowder, crossing the city's compactness pierced by the spokes of underground passages.

A map of Esmeralda should include, marked in different coloured inks, all these routes, solid and liquid, evident and hidden. It is more difficult to fix on the map the routes of swallows, who cut the air over the roofs, dropping long invisible parabolas with their still wings, darting to gulp a mosquito, spiraling upward, grazing a pinnacle, dominating from every point of their airy paths all the points of the city.'[3]

Does not this look like an account of a users' perspective on a legal system?[4]

I have chosen today's topic for two particular reasons. The first is pure nostalgia. Thirty years ago, when I was at Queen's I toyed with the idea of mapping law in the world, but I was left quite dissatisfied with my efforts. So for me this is unfinished business. Second, it is often said that it is easier to see a legal order as a whole in a small jurisdiction than in a large one. Northern Ireland illustrates very clearly that this is a half-truth. The last thirty years have made all the complexities of human relations and local legal ordering more visible than in most places; this jurisdiction is also a clear example of legal pluralism. No legally interested person – whether law student, practitioner, law teacher, judge, law-maker, Vice-Chancellor, or citizen – can understand law in Northern Ireland by focusing only on Northern Ireland municipal law. Multiple legal orders are part of the local legal situation. Like it or not, United Kingdom law, the law of The Republic of Ireland, European Union Law, Public International Law, Human Rights Law, and developments in the common law world all bear directly on interpreting local legal issues. So too do different kinds of 'non-state law', a contested idea which is open to several different interpretations. One consequence of globalisation is a tendency to loosen the association of the ideas of law, state, and nation and so to make more salient the multiplicity of legal orderings.

---

3   *IC*, pp 88-89.
4   Above, Ch 5.5(b).

2   LEVELS OF LAW

For present purposes I shall assume rather than argue that law is concerned with relations between agents or persons (human, legal, unincorporated and otherwise) at a variety of levels, not just relations within a single nation state or society. One way of characterising such levels is essentially geographical:

- global (as with some environmental issues, a possible *ius humanitatis* – e.g. mineral rights on the moon – and, by extension, intergalactic or space law);
- international (in the classic sense of relations between sovereign states and more broadly relations governed, for example, by human rights or refugee law);
- regional (for example, the European Union, the European Convention on Human Rights, and the Organisation of African Unity);
- transnational (for example, Islamic, Hindu, Jewish law, Gypsy law, transnational arbitration, a putative *lex mercatoria*, Internet law, and, more controversially, the internal governance of multi-national corporations, the Catholic Church, or institutions of organised crime);
- inter-communal (as in relations between religious communities, or Christian Churches, or different ethnic groups);
- territorial state (including the legal systems of nation states, and sub-national jurisdictions, such as Florida, Greenland, Quebec, and Northern Ireland);
- sub-state (eg subordinate legislation, such as bye-laws of the Borough of Camden) or religious law officially recognised for limited purposes in a plural legal system; and
- non-state (including laws of subordinated peoples, such as native North Americans, or Maoris, or gypsies[5]) or illegal legal orders such as Santos's Pasagarda law, the Southern People's Liberation Army's legal regime in Southern Sudan,[6] and the 'common law movement' of militias in the United States).[7]

5   Recent studies of Gypsy law have been pioneered by Walter Weyrauch. See especially, Weyrauch and Bell, 'Autonomous Lawmaking: The Case of the Gypsies' (1993) 103 Yale Law Journal 323 and Symposium on Gypsy Law (Romaniya) (1997) 45 American Journal of Comparative Law 2.

6   The Southern Peoples' Liberation Army has operated a system of courts dealing with both civil and criminal cases in areas which they occupy in the civil war in the Southern Sudan. Monyluak Alor Kuol, *Administration of Justice in the (SPLA/ M) Liberated Areas: Court Cases in War-Torn Southern Sudan* (Oxford, Refugee Studies Programme, 1997).

7   Susan Koniak, 'When Law Risks Madness' (1996) 8 Cardozo Studies in Law and Literature 65; 'The Chosen People in our Wilderness' (1997) 95 Michigan Law Review 1761.

I shall not discuss in detail which regimes or orders or traditions one might include in a map of world law,[8] but I shall assume that any conception of law that is restricted to the municipal law of nation states and classical public international law is extremely narrow and probably misleading. In so far as the role of the institutionalised discipline of law is advancing and disseminating understanding of the phenomena of law, one needs a conception of these phenomena that is reasonably inclusive. This categorisation of levels into global, regional, international, transnational, municipal and local is admittedly crude, but it will serve for present purposes. These different levels of relations with which law has to deal are not neatly nested in a single vertical hierarchy. So even this simple categorisation hints at the complexities of mapping law.

3   MAPPING[9]

A standard geographer's definition of a 'map' is 'A representation, usually on a plane surface, of all or part of the earth or some other body showing a group of features in terms of their relative size or position'.[10] The idea of a map is also applied metaphorically to 'the mental conception of the arrangement of something'.[11] I shall be concerned here with both geographical and mental maps.

In considering physical maps one needs to bear in mind some elementary points: what constitutes a good map depends on its purposes, such as navigation or depicting spatial relations and distributions. Maps can serve ideological functions, as exemplified by Peters' Projection[12] or the exaggeration of the size of communist countries in some American maps during the Cold War period. Small scale maps depict vast areas using limited information highly selectively; large scale maps, such as local Ordnance Survey maps, contain more detailed information for smaller areas. Maps cannot be exact representations of reality. As Santos

8   On borderline candidates for the designation 'legal orders' see p 260 below.
9   On cartography in general I have found the following particularly helpful: J S Keates, *Understanding Maps* (2nd edn, 1996); Norman J W Thrower, *Maps and Civilization* (1996); and Peter Whitfield, *The Image of the World: 20 Centuries of World Maps* (1994). By far the best discussion of legal cartography is Santos's essay 'Law A Map of Misreading …' reprinted in Santos, op cit (1994), Ch 7, discussed below, pp 233-9.
10   Thrower op cit (1996) at p 254.
11   The OED (2nd edn, 1989) treats this as a 'nonce use', but the metaphor is almost a cliché in legal discourse.
12   In 1973 Arno Peters 'reinvented' a form of cylindrical projection to counterbalance Eurocentric projections of Third World countries. For a critique see Thrower at p 224.

puts it, they are 'organized misreadings of territories that create credible illusions of correspondence'.[13] This is illustrated by Borges' parable of the Emperor who futilely demanded an exact life-size map of his domains.[14] Similarly, Harry Beck's classic map of the London underground deliberately involved distortion to help users of the system, but was nonetheless both accurate and reliable for its purposes. Modern technology has greatly increased the sophistication and possibilities of cartography, witness for example animated weather maps on television. But maps also have distinct limitations: space is privileged over time; geographical maps are concerned more with physical than social or other kinds of relations; and there are other, often better means of pictorially presenting complex data. It is widely assumed that law is one of the subjects least amenable to pictorial representation, perhaps because it is concerned with largely invisible ideas and social relations. Algorithms, flow charts, logical trees, vidoes, Wigmore charts and other devices have found their way into law and legal education, but in a televisual and computer-driven era we can expect huge advances in the pictorial presentation of complex ideas and data. Edmond Tufte has already shown some of the tantalising possibilities in his books.[15]

It used to be assumed that 'Geography is about maps, but Biography is about chaps'.[16] This is an outdated image. Human geographers in particular tend to treat cartography as a rather primitive aspect of their discipline. In recent years, as Kim Economides has shown, their interests have converged with those of socio-legal scholars.[17] Here, I shall resist the temptation to chase such enticing hares as geojurisprudence or virtual reality constructions of law. Rather I want to explore some rather old-fashioned concerns about why even elementary mapping of law in the world is difficult. I shall concentrate mainly on the theoretical complexities that underlie constructing quite simple overviews of law in large geographical areas through either physical or mental maps.

13   Santos, p 458
14   Jorge Luis Borges, *Obras Completas* (1974).
15   E Tufte, *The Visual Display of Quantitative Information* (1983), *Envisioning Information* (1990), and *Visual Explanations* (1997).
16   Edmund Clerihew Bentley, *Biography for Beginners* (1905).
17   Kim Economides. 'Law and Geography: New Frontiers' in Philip Thomas (ed) *Legal Frontiers* (1996); cf Chand Wije, 'Applied Law and Applied Geography', (1990) 8 The Operational Geographer 27; Nicholas K Blomley and Gordon L Clark, 'Law, Theory and Geography' (1990) 11 Urban Geography 433, Nicholas Blomley, *Law, Space and the Geographies of Power* (1994); Paul Wiles, 'A Future Research Agenda for Analyzing Crime in Cities', (1997) 31 Comparative Law Review 23; Keith D Harries, *The Geography of Laws and Justice* (1978) and *Serious Violence: Patterns of Homicide and Assault in America* (1990).

4   GEOGRAPHICAL MAPS

(a)   Khartoum, 1958-61

In my first year of teaching, I was responsible for a course called 'Introduction to Law' in the University of Khartoum. Ignorant of earlier precedents, and inspired by Karl Llewellyn's precept 'see it whole', I decided to begin by setting the Sudan legal system in the context of a picture of law in the world.[18] Instinctively I chose a map as the means of depiction. I was quite conscious of history, but in this context space was privileged over time. I obtained a blank map of the whole world and used a palette of coloured chalks to characterise the legal systems of different countries. The map marked the borders of countries, that is nation-states and various forms of dependency. I do not recall the exact details, but I might have used blue chalk for the common law (deliberately avoiding imperial pink), brown for civilian or Romanist systems, red for Socialist countries, yellow for Islamic Law, and green for customary or traditional law. Countries with 'plural' or mixed national legal systems were clumsily depicted by stripes in different colours.

This first attempt, though consciously crude, helped to make some useful points. First, there were discernible patterns – some countries had relatively pure common law or civilian systems, some were mixed or plural, including countries in the Soviet bloc. Secondly, these patterns were intimately linked to colonisation and colonialism. Japan, Turkey and Ethiopia were held up as relatively exceptional instances of 'voluntary' receptions.[19] Thirdly, Sudan at the time was a clear example of a plural national legal system that conformed to British colonial patterns even though it had officially been a condominium until independence: imported or imposed 'common law' in the form of off-the-peg statutes and 'codes', English precedents, a handful of reported local cases, and a catch-all reception clause. Both Mohammedan Law and customary law were recognised in limited spheres subject to various provisos.[20] Fourthly,

18   On the use of 'total pictures' as one form of context see *TAR* at 372-378 (1985); *LIC* at pp 57, 298-299.

19   At the time I treated as exceptional Liberia, Siam and parts of the United States and I did not challenge the idea of a 'voluntary' reception. See, eg, Robert Kidder in Barbara Harrell-Bond and Sandra Burman (eds), *The Imposition of Law* (1979) Ch 6.

20   Civil Justice Ordinance, s 5:

'Where in any suit or other proceeding in a Civil Court any question arises regarding succession, inheritance, legacies, gifts, marriage, family relations or the constitution of wakfs, the rule of decision shall be:

a   any custom applicable to the parties concerned, which is not contrary to justice, equity and good conscience and has not been by this or any other

the map communicated some simple patterns and yet hinted at some puzzling complexities, such as the relationship between official state law and 'living law' in most of the country, especially in rural areas.[1]

At the time I felt that this map served my immediate purposes. It gave first year students some sense of a wider world and of Sudan's place within it. It set an agenda both for studying Sudanese law as a 'plural' system and for discussing issues about future 'legal development' in a newly independent country. I continued to use it during my three years in Khartoum, but I was vaguely puzzled and dissatisfied. My first ground for dissatisfaction was quite mundane: how could I improve the colour scheme so as to incorporate Public International Law, different constitutional patterns, and a more refined picture of legal pluralism? Such questions are not trivial, but they only scratched the surface.

In time I learned that many others had made similar attempts. For example, John Henry Wigmore had devised a neat solution to my problem about colours. By using a quite simple mixture of letters and numbers he was able both to depict mixed systems and to give an indication of the Age and Duration of legal systems.[2] But Wigmore's 'solution' compounded my doubts, for his presentation seemed naive and simplistic. Wigmore was a committed populariser and his three volume *Panorama of the World's Legal Systems*[3] and his *Kaleidoscope of Justice* were both overtly directed at general audiences.[4] These two works are fairly characteristic of Wigmore's strange mixture of the folksy and the methodical: on the one hand he had an insatiable curiosity and fascination with the variety of things; but Wigmore was known as 'the Colonel' and his simple military mind required that all phenomena, however complex, should be reduced to order and paraded in neat, simple patterns.[5] In *Invisible Cities* 'Kublai Kahn had noticed that Marco Polo's cities resembled one another, as if the passage from one to another

---

enactment altered or abolished and has not been declared void by a decision of a competent court;

b   the Mohammedan Law, in cases where the parties are Mohammedans, except in so far as that law has been modified as is above referred to.'

On the difficulties experienced by the courts in interpreting 'custom' during the condominium period, see C d'O Farran, *Matrimonial Laws of the Sudan* (1963), pp 88-91. A useful overview of the official legal system in the period is Zaki Mustafa 'Sudan' in Anthony Allott, *Judicial and Legal Systems of Africa* (1st edn, 1962; 2nd edn, 1970); cf Akolda Tier, 'The Legal System of the Sudan' in K Redden (ed) (1985) 6 *Modern Legal Systems Cyclopedia: Africa* Ch 12.

1   On the unrealities of teaching English Law in the Sudan, see *LIC*, Ch 2.

2   J H Wigmore, *A Panorama of the World's Legal Systems* (3 vols, 1928; 2nd edn, 1 vol, 1936).

3   Ibid.

4   J H Wigmore, *A Kaleidoscope of Justice* (1941).

5   *TEBW*, pp 110-111.

involved not a journey but a change of elements'.[6] Wigmore compared the legal cultures of the world to a kaleidoscope: 'When the Basic Pattern revolves, the Prisms Cause Variant Patterns in Different Communities; But the Latent Elements Remain the Same Throughout'. He illustrated this cryptic statement with an incomprehensible picture without any serious attempt at explanation.[7]

I was not alone in feeling uneasy about Wigmore's efforts. Indeed, he had been the butt of such mocking criticism by Plucknett and Goodhart in the *Harvard Law Review* and the *Yale Law Journal* that he had instructed his publishers, Little, Brown, not to submit any of his future publications for review in these journals.[8] In the eyes of some, armchair legal tourism in the style of *The National Geographic* was not academically respectable. This is just one example of a more general tendency to dismiss attempts to give a picture of law in the world as inevitably superficial.[9] My concern is to challenge this view.

A second puzzlement about my map was more theoretical: in a reception what is received and who were the main agents of reception? My first venture into print as an academic was an attempt to answer such questions. Drawing on Weber and Llewellyn, I concluded that rules are not the only, nor even the main, phenomena that are transplanted; that the reception of 'lawyers' law' and legal techniques is less problematic than matters that are closely related to local *mores* or political issues of the day; and that the main agents of reception of law as technology are the legal *honoratiores*, Weber's ironic term for the dominant legal élite.[10] This might be interpreted today as an early and moderate version of Alan Watson's famous transplants thesis.[11]

6   *IC*, p 43.
7   *Kaleidoscope*, Frontispiece. While Wigmore's *Kaleidoscope* and *Panorama* each contains some useful tid-bits of information and occasional insights, they are in many respects naive, prejudiced and inaccurate. They are probably best treated as curious period pieces.
8   Wigmore also had his defenders, including W Holdsworth and B A Wortley. For an account of the episode, see *TEBW* (1985) at pp 218-219, n 3.
9   It is no coincidence that Wigmore's chief critics were based in England, for the first half of the twentieth century was a period in which the intellectual climate was generally hostile to grand theory, historical jurisprudence was marginalised, and the first Professor of Comparative Law at Oxford, Harry Lawson, could say in his inaugural lecture: '... nowadays to be universal, is to be superficial'. (F H Lawson, 'The Field of Comparative Law' (1950) 61 Juridical Review 16). In the United Kingdom micro-comparative studies have almost invariably been preferred to the Grands Systèmes approach.
10   William Twining, 'Some Aspects of Reception' (1957) Sudan Law Journal and Rep 229.
11   Alan Watson, *Legal Transplants* (1974; 2nd edn, 1993). This thesis, that reception and imitation are the main influences in legal change, has occasioned a great deal of controversy; for a sympathetic appraisal, see William Ewald, 'The Logic of Legal Transplants: Comparative Jurisprudence Part II' (1995) 43 American

This may have been passable as a first effort, but it did not advance the topic very far either analytically or empirically. In retrospect, I think that I missed an opportunity. I might have developed the ideas much further if I had made issues raised by mapping and reception the focus of a research programme or as part of a final year course in Jurisprudence. The latter would almost certainly have provided a better basis for a theoretical understanding of law in the Sudan than rehearsing the ideas of a somewhat random selection of Western jurists. However, at this stage rather than pursue the matter further, I concentrated on the more 'practical' task of developing local law reporting and thereby missed out on a career in legal cartography.

(b)   Comparative Common Law: Belfast 1967-72

I was left vaguely puzzled by this youthful effort, but during the next five years my attention was directed elsewhere. However, shortly after I moved to Belfast in 1966, I revived the idea as part of our LLM course in Comparative Common Law. A number of factors stimulated this enterprise apart from my African background: first, teaching in Northern Ireland made one acutely conscious that we were continuously involved in making more or less explicit comparisons with England and Wales, the Republic of Ireland, and more broadly with American and Commonwealth sources and literature. This presented a challenge to Harold Gutteridge's dismissal of the idea of comparative common law.[12] I was also struck by stories about Montrose's introductory lectures in which he had tried to place law in the context of a map of all learning.[13] This typically bold vision had impressed many Queen's graduates, who reported that they had found it both memorable and way above their heads. Here was a recurrence of the mapping metaphor – another attempt to set a broad context at the start of one's legal education.

Thus stimulated, I devised a group exercise for the postgraduates taking the course on 'Comparative Common Law'. Recently I discovered the relevant handout among my papers. It is worth quoting from it at

Journal of Comparative Law 489; cf Gunther Teubner, 'Legal Irritants: Good Faith in British Law or How Unifying Law Ends Up in New Divergences' (1998) 61 MLR 11.

12 'No special form of technique seems to be called for if the comparison is, for instance, between Australian and Canadian law or between English law and the law of the United States.' Preface to *Comparative Law* (1946). Gutteridge also doubted the value of comparing legal systems at different stages of development. (justifying his focus on differences between civil and common law systems).

13 Some idea of his vision can be obtained from J L Montrose, *Precedent in English Law and Other Essays* (Hanbury ed, 1968) Ch 2 and Ch 7.

some length. Headed 'Taxonomy: "The Common Law World"', the opening paragraphs read as follows:

'Your course takes "Comparative common law" as its organising concept. Presumably "common law" in this context is contrasted with "civil law", "Hindu Law", "Islamic Law", "African customary law" and so on. Presumably "common law" is *not* contrasted with "equity" or with "statute law". To what extent can we give a precise meaning to "common law" in this usage? To what extent can we make universal generalisations about "the common law world"? or broad generalisations, admitting of a few exceptions? What jurisdictions comprise "the common law world"? Are there useful distinctions to make between "common law jurisdictions?" Are there distinctive features of some or all of the legal systems in "the common law world" which are not to be found outside it?

You are asked as a group to look into these and related questions. A possible, but not the only, way of approaching the subject would be to try to plan a map of "the common law world" within the general framework of a map of the world's legal systems. It is suggested that as a preliminary you need to give careful thought to such questions as: Is it possible to construct a working taxonomy of world legal systems? If so, how? If not, why not? Some of the factors that might be considered as possible bases for classification might be: historical factors (The British Empire? The Commonwealth? Voluntary importation of "common law", of "civil law"?) linguistic factors (does the common law operate anywhere in a language other than English?); values (does the common law have a necessary or regular association with certain ideals?); personnel (career judiciary? split profession? juries?); procedures (adversary v inquisitorial?); substantive doctrine (the doctrine of precedent? the trust concept? consideration in contracts?); methods... and so on. From detailed consideration of such factors (the above are only a sample) certain patterns may become apparent. Are these patterns sufficiently clear and sufficiently significant for it to be possible to construct a map, or a series of maps, based on a relatively precise taxonomy?'

In retrospect, this appears to me to be a rather demanding exercise in applied jurisprudence. Many of the questions are still worth asking. I have not kept the products of the group projects, but I do recall that discussions of these issues extended over several weeks and, at a general level, we did not get much further than some healthy, but essentially elementary, lessons of complexity: that a single 'scientific' classification of legal systems is impossible even if one has a clear purpose and specified units of comparison; that elucidation of concepts, such as 'legal system', 'legal tradition', 'common law', 'reception', and 'lawyers' law', is an essential precondition to mapping; and that generalisation is dangerous even within the common law 'family'. At least it legitimated the claim that 'comparative common law' deserves recognition as a viable form of comparative law, but I was still left with a nagging sense of dissatisfaction, which was not helped by the existing literature.

At Khartoum I had proceeded largely by instinct. For the Queen's seminar I was better prepared. There was a quite extensive literature on the spread of the common law, on receptions, on commonwealth and colonial law; and almost nothing on multi-lingual legal systems. There was some quite useful but uninspired writing about comparative law theory. The most immediately relevant literature concerned the 'legal families' debate in comparative law. Since the latter is the most obvious precedent it is worth commenting on it briefly.

The classification of legal systems or legal orders into 'families' has been one of the main concerns of macro comparative law exemplified by René David's *Grands Systèmes de Droit Contemporains*, Derrett's *An Introduction to Legal Systems*,[14] and Arminjon, Nolde and Wolff, *Traité de Droit Comparé*.[15] The debate has rumbled on for almost a century and continues today.[16] Perhaps the most sophisticated discussion is that of Zweigert and Kötz who frame the issues as follows:

'Can we divide the vast number of legal systems into just a few large groups (legal families)? How can we decide what these groups should be? And, supposing we know what the groups should be, how do we decide whether a particular legal system belongs to one group rather than another?'[17]

Comparative lawyers have struggled in vain to produce a neat taxonomy of 'legal families' in response to such questions.[18] Zweigert and Kötz

14 Op cit.
15 P Arminjon, B Nolde, and M Wolff, *Traité de Droit Comparé* (3 Vols, 1950-51).
16 A recent example is Ugo Mattei, 'Three Patterns of Law: Taxonomy and Change in the World's Legal Systems' (1997) 45 American Journal of Comparative Law 5. The debate about classification of legal systems has been taken more seriously in Continental Europe where the Grands Systèmes approach to Comparative Law has been quite influential especially in legal education. Most of the debate is rather tedious and repetitive: the main context is discussion of introductory courses on Comparative Law, and there seems to be a general consensus that legal systems are not susceptible to Linnean type scientific classification and any one of several possible schemes may be adequate for this modest purpose.
17 K Zweigert and H Kötz, *An Introduction to Comparative Law* (3rd edn, trs Tony Weir, 1997) 63-64.
18 Early attempts to classify by race or geography or solely by origin have generally been rejected by modern comparatists in favour of multiple criteria (eg Zweigert

having rejected attempts to use race or geographical location or relations of production or ideology as the main criterion, limited the idea to the predominant *styles of legal thought* of contemporary living legal systems. On this basis, they identify five factors as central to the style of a legal family:

'(1) its historical background and development, (2) its predominant and characteristic mode of thought in legal matters, (3) especially distinctive legal institutions, (4) the kinds of legal sources it acknowledges and the way it handles them, (5) its ideology.'[19]

Zweigert and Kötz, like other scholars, emphasise that there is no single right way of classifying systems. For the purpose of introducing 'the great legal systems of the world' their multiple criteria lead to a seven-fold classification: (1) Romanistic family; (2) Germanic family; (3) Nordic family (4) Common Law family, (5) Socialist family, (6) Far Eastern systems; (7) Islamic systems; and (8) Hindu law.

Given that they acknowledge some of the difficulties and that there are many hybrids (which include the People's Republic of China, Israel, South Africa, Louisiana, and Quebec), this classification probably serves their limited purpose as well as any other. But it is still deeply unsatisfying.[20] For if the enterprise of picturing law in the world is a necessary part of understanding law, it seems that something more intellectually ambitious is required.

---

and Kötz, op cit, Ch 5). Arminjon, Nolde and Wolff favoured 'substance', paying due regard to originality, derivation, and common elements. They produced a division into seven legal families, French, German, Scandinavian, Russian, Islamic, and Hindu. Eorsi constructed a Marxist classification in terms of relations of production, the major division being between socialist and capitalist, the latter being sub-divided into systems at different stages of evolution and different outcomes in the struggle between the bourgeoisie and the feudal class. G. Eorsi, *Comparative Civil (Private) Law* (1979) criticised by Kötz, RabelsZ 46 (1982); René David's revised classification was into late Romano-Germanic, common law, Socialist and 'other systems', which included Jewish, Hindu, Far Eastern and African; cf. the subtle analysis of differences between East and West German doctrine before the fall of the Berlin Wall, which doubts the explanatory value of differences between 'grand ideology'. Inga Markovits, 'Hedgehogs or Foxes?' (1986) 34 American Journal of Comparative Law 113. Other possible bases for classifying legal systems (but not traditions?) would include wealth (rich/poor countries), form of government (democratic/dictatorship/aristocratic etc), language (anglophone, francophone, other), religious/secular, or climatic.

19 At pp 69-75.
20 One obvious point is that the items on the list are not species of a single genus: (1)-(5) could refer to national state legal systems – so could (6), but that raises questions about the reason for choosing this as a category; however, there is no single state whose legal system is today based mainly on Hindu Law. Similarly, Islamic Law has a much wider ambit than the few Islamic states. During the

(c)   Boston 1996

Nearly thirty years later, at the start of a seminar on 'Globalization and Legal Theory', I set the students an exercise. I first asked the class to draw a map of the main legal orders in the world, next to draw an historical chart of the rise and fall of the main legal cultures in the world, and then to consider the relationship between the two. This was a modification of the Queen's exercise, but it was more explicitly linked to contemporary legal theory. At our second meeting the students asked for an extension. I granted this, subject to the proviso that their maps or pictures should include classical Roman Law and Islamic Law. At the next meeting, I granted a further extension, but added in the *lex mercatoria*, *ius humanitatis*, and Pasagarda Law – that is the legal order of illegal squatter settlements in Brazil as depicted by Santos. Each time they asked for an extension, I added further candidates for inclusion. After about six weeks they gave up and we discussed why the exercise was problematic.

Rather than reconstruct our discussions, let me state my own position on the reasons why earlier attempts have been flawed, my own as well as those of Wigmore and the Grands Systèmes comparatists.

(d)   Geographical Mapping: A Post-mortem

I have now reported a sense of dissatisfaction with several previous attempts to present an overview of law in the world through maps. What are the main sources of this dissatisfaction? Can anything constructive be rescued from such exercises? Or is legal cartography as an enterprise doomed to failure? Each of the examples considered involves illuminating errors.

To start with my first effort in Khartoum. Aside from my conscious puzzlements, at the time I did not question a number of assumptions that I would now reject. Three in particular are significant:

Cold War period it made sense to treat the Eastern bloc as a group, based on ideology and Soviet power, but mixed in with a strong civil law tradition. Since the collapse of the Soviet bloc the situation is more complex. 'Far Eastern systems' refers to a geographical grouping of states which seems rather diverse in respect of style. 'Common law' can refer to historical origin, or a legal culture (ideas and practices and possibly institutions), or tradition, or factors to do with colonialism on the one hand and the growth in importance of English as a world language on the other. Civil law, partly because of its perceived greater translatability, was received in a wider variety of historical situations. But there it is now widely acknowledged that in some respects there may be more important differences within 'the civil law family' than between that family and 'the common law'.

First, I just assumed that what was to be mapped was the national legal systems of 'countries' and that the starting-point for classification was national and state borders. My map included colonies, and subordinate jurisdictions, such as Canadian provinces, but did not provide for public international law or even for Islamic Law, except as a subordinate part of the law of secular states. It completely omitted candidates for the appellation 'legal orders' at the global, regional, transnational, communal and local or sub-state levels. Most legal maps that I have come across make the same dubious assumption.[1]

Secondly, I unconsciously privileged common law and civil law by depicting almost all national legal systems as belonging to one or other of these two 'parent families'. Indeed, I used this to emphasise the importance of colonialism in the spread of law. This same assumption still dominates the study of comparative law today. From an historical perspective the idea of 'parent' legal systems has some justification, even if it is patronising.[2] But the concept is past its sell-by date. For example, in 1998 who is the 'parent' in matters legal as between Scotland and England, or the United States and the United Kingdom? Or between the international community and nation states in respect of bills of rights? If Alan Watson is even half-right in suggesting that imitation is the main engine of legal change, the interaction between legal systems today can hardly be characterised as being like that between parent and child.[3]

Thirdly, in Khartoum I had glossed over the problem of taxonomy of legal systems. By the time I revived the idea in Belfast, I was familiar with debates among comparatists about legal families and they featured in our discussions about comparative common law. In raising questions about how far one can generalise across the common law world, we went beyond state legal systems to include the more elusive ideas of 'culture' and 'tradition' and we had a stab at exploring the relationship between law and language in multi-lingual societies – still a seriously neglected topic.[4] All of this was an advance, but the focus was still on state law; for example 'legal pluralism' was still conceived in the weak sense of pluralism within official legal systems rather than in the strong sense of

1   Santos, op cit, is a notable exception.
2   Another standard justification is one of economy. The argument goes that 'parent systems' can conveniently be treated as representative of their respective 'families'. However, this argument too is becoming increasingly questionable.
3   Above p 144.
4   In many countries only a minority of the population speak the official language(s) of their state legal system. This is a neglected issue which is quite different from the much more discussed topic of the comprehensibility of legal language to ordinary speakers of that language. On the politics of official languages, see David Crystal, *English as a Global Language* (1997) and references there. The most extended account of language policy in relation to law is L J Mark Cooray, *Changing the Language of the Law: The Sri Lanka Experience* (1985).

a multiplicity of overlapping orders co-existing within the same territorial or social space.[5]

We recognised that all the standard taxonomies, such as those of René David, or Arminjon, Nolde, and Wolff were unsatisfactory, but we did not get to the root of why this might be so.[6]

This account of some previous attempts to use geographical maps to depict legal phenomena suggests a number of lessons.

First, if one accepts that there are different levels of legal relations and legal ordering, the phenomena of law are probably too complex to be depicted on a single map or picture. At the very least one would need something more like an historical atlas, with a series of different kinds of maps and charts, using different projections, scales, time frames and classifying categories. Some maps could use countries or nation states as an important unit of analysis, some would be better to ignore national boundaries. In *Invisible Cities*, Kublai Khan in his search for order and patterns, has an atlas that depicts continents, sea routes, and particular cities that Marco Polo has visited or heard described. It also reveals possible cities that do not yet have a form or name.[7] 'In the last pages of the atlas there is an outpouring of networks without beginning or end, cities in the shape of Los Angeles, in the shape of Kyoto-Osaka, without shape.'[8]

A second lesson of my tour has been that geographical maps are just one means of depicting mainly spatial relations. They have their uses. Indeed, a reasonably sophisticated historical atlas of law in the world could be quite illuminating. I know of serious scholars who have contemplated such a project. But maps mainly depict physical relations and distribution and, as such, they have a restricted application to legal phenomena.

After nearly a century of unsatisfactory debates, it is natural to ask: are all attempts at a systematic classification of legal systems or legal families doomed to fail? If so, does it matter?

The 'Grands Systèmes' approach of macro-comparison has sometimes been dismissed as superficial or unscholarly or of little or no utility.[9] Such criticism may be valid when applied to poorly executed examples or to very general treatments that never get down to concrete details.

---

5   Above, Ch 3.5.
6   For an attempted diagnosis, see below, Ch 7.3.
7   *IC*, pp 137-139.
8   *IC*, p 139. It has been pointed out that Kublai Khan's atlas does not produce a single overall order: 'There is no global map, only a sheaf of insets of hypothetical cities in an atlas whose order is either unknown or fanciful', Albert H. Carter III, *Italo Calvino: Metamorphoses of Fantasy* (1987), pp 120-121.
9   Eg Watson, *Transplants*, Ch 1; cf Basil Markesenis, *Foreign Law and Comparative Methodology* (1997) Ch1.

However, there are good reasons for taking the enterprise of mapping the phenomena of law in the world quite seriously.

First, setting the local in the context of the global serves the values of any form of contextual study. For example, my attempt to get Sudanese students to see their national legal system as part of a broader world picture had a worthy aim, even if the execution was faulty. Secondly, micro-comparison presupposes macro-comparison; they are complementary rather than alternatives. Thirdly, if one task of jurisprudence is to construct a coherent 'total picture' of law; one job for general jurisprudence should be to construct such a picture for legal phenomena in the world as a whole. This is not just an exercise in abstract theorising. A skewed vision of law can have all sorts of practical implications – witness, for example, the incredibly delayed response of our systems of legal education and training to human rights law and membership of the European Community; the confusion created by ad hoc responses to quite predictable aspects of the internationalisation of legal practice; and the naivety of some attempts at harmonisation of laws.

The debate about 'families' and mapping world law has taken place largely within comparative law with almost no help from legal theory. Yet the problems of mapping law are essentially jurisprudential. The difficulties that face anyone trying to construct a map of law in the world are familiar problems of legal theory. The key point is is that geographical maps presuppose mental maps. That is to say they are means of presenting and ordering pre-existing concepts and data. The main weakness of my own early attempts and those of Wigmore and others, is that they were jurisprudentially naive. The problems underlying the 'legal families' debate are almost entirely conceptual; the debate brings out the point that there are questions and doubts about purposes, levels, units of comparison, differentiae, and over-generalisation that need to be addressed before one can produce a satisfactory overview of law in the world.[10] This seems to me to be a neglected job of analytical jurisprudence. So we need to proceed from geographical to mental mapping.

5   MENTAL MAPPING

The metaphorical use of 'map' as 'a mental conception of the arrangement of something' is quite common in legal theory. For example,

10 For a fuller discussion, see below, Ch 7.3.

Leibniz talked of a *theatrum legale mundi*;[11] Blackstone[12] and Austin[13] used mapping as a metaphor for providing general overviews of English law. More recently post-modernists, such as Santos and Goodrich, have used the metaphor in more complex ways. Perhaps the most important example is Santos's well-known essay 'Law a Map of Misreading'[14] in which laws themselves are presented as maps that both distort and construct social relations. Mainstream theories of law, such as those of Kelsen, Hart, Llewellyn or even Dworkin, can be interpreted as attempts to construct one kind of mental map of state legal systems.

In Chapter 3 I began to explore how far mainstream theories that have focused on municipal legal systems and that treat societies as enclosed units can be adapted to apply to other levels of legal ordering and deal with the complexities of the phenomena of legal pluralism. There is much more to be said about legal theory as mental mapping, but here I shall confine myself to some less obvious examples: global statistics; the increasingly fashionable use of rankings at global, national and other levels; and some different ways of profiling a legal system or order. What these have in common is that they are all examples of mental maps.

(a)   Global Statistics

Almanacs, encyclopaedias, and world surveys are a long-established phenomenon. The first edition of the *Encyclopaedia Britannica* was

11 Leibniz, *Nova methodus discendae docendaeque jurisprudentiae* (1667); *Theatrum legale* (1675); Patrick Riley, *Leibniz' Universal Jurisprudence: Justice as the Charity of the Wise* (1996).

12 W Blackstone, *Commentaries on the Law of England* (1st edn, 1765) I.1.35. Blackstone's concern was to present English law, especially the common law, in a systematic or scientific fashion by identifying the basic principles that gave it coherence. The most germane passage is worth quoting: '[The academical expounder] should consider his course as a general map of the law, marking out the shape of the country, its connections and boundaries, its greater divisions and principal cities: it is not his business to describe minutely the subordinate limits, or to fix the longitude and latitude of every inconsiderable hamlet.'

13 J Austin, 'The Uses of the Study of Jurisprudence' in The *Province of Jurisprudence Determined Etc* (Hart ed, 1954) 379. Austin began his lecture series with this lecture, but it was not published until 1863. Interestingly, like Blackstone, Austin used this not in relation to general jurisprudence, but rather to the need of the student for a map of English law, in order to have an overview of basic concepts and principles as a system or organic whole.

14 'Law: A Map of Misreading. Toward a Post-modern Conception of Law' (1987)14 Journal of Law and Society 279, now incorporated in *Toward a New Common Sense*, op cit, discussed below, pp 233-39.

published in 1768-71.[15] In the last twenty years there has been a striking increase in the production of data, mainly but not entirely statistical, presented in standardised forms that provide, or purport to provide, a basis for world-wide comparison. Tabulated information is widely used in fields such as population, economics, health, and education. Well-respected examples include the *Britannica Yearbook*, *The World in Figures* (published by the Economist) and reports by United Nations agencies, the World Bank and IMF. Some of the best-known are very general, but there are, of course, many more specialised publications dealing in greater detail with narrower areas.[16]

Someone might ask: what has this to do with law? A survey of this general literature brings out a number of related points: first, these kinds of data are almost totally absent from the literature of mainstream comparative law;[17] conversely, law is strikingly absent as a significant category from most of the general statistical literature. With one major exception, crime statistics, law as such is hardly treated as a significant category. To take a fairly representative example: *The Britannica Yearbook* uses over 20 categories for organising its presentation of global data, including agriculture and population, language, religion, employment and labour, manufacturing industries, communications, trade, housing and construction, household budgets, health services, and education. The only explicit mention of a legal category is crime, which is one of

15 *Whittaker's Almanac* dates from the late 1860s; the 1997 edition is the 129th annual volume; the *World Almanac and Book of Facts* (formerly *World*) can be traced back to 1860.

16 The trend is towards not only greater sophistication and standardisation, but also an increase in the range of producers. While the great majority of such data is based on official statistics, with their own particular criteria for selection and biases, governments do not have a monopoly on the production of global data. Non-governmental organisations, corporations and commercial publishers have contributed to the trend. With the communications revolution the range of producers is proliferating, exemplified by the range of conventionally published reference works now on the market, especially in the United States. Some of these are addressed to the general public, others are aimed at quite specific commercial, educational, and professional audiences. One of the main publishers in this area, Facts on File, explicitly targets secondary schools and public libraries. The variety of such works is illustrated by their titles. Atlases include The *Macmillan World Reference Atlas* (1994), *The State of the World Atlas* (1995) and a great variety of specialised atlases. There are a few legal atlases, for example, *The Legal Atlas of the United States* (1996); Galgano (ed) *Atlante di diritto comparato* (1992) – I am grateful to Giovanni Sartor for this reference. See *The World Map Directory: A Practical Guide to US and International Maps* (1992-93).

17 CLLT. Two exceptions are the intelligent use of statistics by Basil Markesenis, *Foreign Law and Comparative Methodology* (1997) Ch 20 (on 'litigation mania') and Inga Markovits in her studies of East and West Germany before the transition, eg 'Hedgehogs or Foxes?' (1986) 34 American Journal of Comparative Law 113.

three sub-categories of social protection and defence services along with welfare and security forces. It takes up less than 2% of the volume for 1997.[18] There are international statistics for crimes, police and prisons and a few more items can be extracted from tables of 'social indicators' and the like.[19]

It might be objected that law is a cultural phenomenon of a kind which is less prone to statistical analysis than areas such as economics, health and education. Indeed cultural and legal relativists, including some leading members of the new generation of comparative lawyers, who wish to emphasise *différance*, may argue that most legal statistical data is likely to be unhelpful, misleading or just meaningless.[20] They can point, with some justification, to the unhappy history of attempts to subject legal institutions and processes to allegedly 'scientific' quantitative analysis, from the Johns Hopkins Institute in the 1920s through to the abortive Stanford Studies in Law and Development of the 1970s that tried to produce Legal and Social Indicators for Comparative Study in Latin America and in Mediterranean Europe.[1] I shall not enter

18 Other examples include *The Sourcebook of Global Statistics* (1998) which draws on over 200 sources, only about 1%-2% of which are explicitly legal, mainly in respect of crime.
19 It might be objected that this downplaying of law is mainly a matter of taxonomy; a great deal of data can be extracted from these sources about legal activities, institutions, processes and personnel. After all, since law is a generally pervasive feature of most aspects of social life many statistics about accidents, divorce, employment, housing, homelessness, immigration, the police and so on are more or less directly 'legally relevant'. However, even international crime statistics appear to be less developed than most of these other fields and fundamental questions about the comparability of legal phenomena across nations and cultures need to be addressed.
20 Cf L Zedner, 'In pursuit of the vernacular: comparing law and order discourse in Britain and Germany' (1995) 4 Social and Legal Studies 517; Cf Pierre Legrand's scepticism about the use of economic analysis as a basis for comparative law on the grounds that it excludes or underplays the importance of history and culture, review of Ugo Mattei, *Comparative Law and Economics* (1997) in [1997] CLJ 638; Richard Hyland, 'Comparative Law' in Dennis Patterson (ed.) *A Companion to Legal Philosophy and Legal Theory* (1996), Ch 11.
1   On the generally sad story of such studies in the United States see J H Schlegel, *American Legal Realism and Empirical Social Science* (1995). A rather striking example in comparative law is J H Merryman, D Clark, and L Friedman, *Law and Social Change in Mediterranean Europe and Latin America: A Handbook of Legal and Social Indicators for Comparative Study* (1979). This was an attempt by distinguished legal scholars at Stanford to break away from the unempirical approaches that had characterised 'Law and Development' studies by providing 'quantitative descriptions of legal systems'. Collections of statistical tables, devoid of any context or commentary and without discussion of issues of comparability and concepts, proved to be singularly unilluminating. Merryman has acknowledged that the project 'was a failure in a number of ways' and attributes this in part to trying to get too much data and to refusal of funding for the next

here into the debate in comparative law between universalists and
difference theorists, that is to say those who emphasise the unique aspects
of each legal system and culture.[2] Questions of cultural relativism of law
are central to contemporary jurisprudence.[3] So too are questions about
the extent to which legal institutions and practices are susceptible to
economic or other kinds of quantitative analysis.

Such questions need to be addressed as preliminaries to the
compilation of meaningful global statistics about law. However, these
kinds of data are in fact already becoming increasingly important in
policy formation and other decision-making at local, regional,
international, transnational and global levels. Comparators and standards
for assessing the health of aspects of legal systems exist and are being
used either explicitly or implicitly for all sorts of purposes. A few well-
established standards or comparators do exist in law but they tend to be
fragmented: for example, Amnesty International, the International
Committee on Human Rights and numerous other bodies assess the
human rights record of different nation states and regimes by reference
to general human rights norms.[4] The World Bank, the IMF, and donor
states and agencies subject potential recipients to notional standards
implied by the phrase 'democracy, good governance and human rights'.
'Democratic audit' is becoming a fashionable phrase.[5] Recently,
Transparency International has developed a quite sophisticated
methodology for analysing the extent of corruption in a given country
and for constructing 'national integrity systems'.[6] At a national level,
courts and legal services are becoming increasingly subject to

---

phase of the project. Pierre Legrand, 'John Henry Merryman and Comparative
Legal Studies: A Dialogue' (1999) American Journal of Comparative Law 3 at
25-26. [Merryman has promised an article on the project, ibid.] In 1999 a
follow-up conference was convened at Stanford to consider and to update the
project. See also, Heinz Schaffer and Attila Racz (eds) *Quantitative Analysis of
Law: A Comparative Empirical Study* (1990). This Budapest-based project involves
a quantitative comparative analysis of 'sources of law in Eastern and Western
Europe', mainly in relation to 'normative acts' of different kinds.

2   Richard Hyland, op cit.
3   LIC, Ch 8; Richard A Wilson (ed) *Human Rights, Culture and Context* (1997).
4   For example, Amnesty International, Annual Reports; Freedom House, *Freedom
in the World: The Annual Survey of Political Rights and Civil Liberties* (1978-); US
Department of State, *Country Reports on Human Rights Practices* (annual) regularly
reviewed by Lawyers Committee for Human Rights in *Critique* (1978-); Charles
Humana, *World Human Rights Guide* (3rd edn, 1992). For general discussions of
this literature see J C McCrudden and G Chambers, *Individual Rights and the
Law in Britain* (1994), Ch 16; Youcef Bouandel, *Human Rights and Comparative
Politics* (1997); Francesca Klug, Keir Starmer and Stuart Weir, *Three Pillars of
Liberty* (1996).
5   Eg F Klug, K Starmer, and S Weir (1996), op cit, D Beetham, *Auditing Democracy
in Britain* (Democratic Audit Paper No 1, 1993).
6   Jeremy Pope, *The TI Source Book* (Berlin 1996), TI annual reports.

bureaucratic evaluation.[7] Educational institutions, including law schools, are also becoming aware of the uses and misuses to which performance indicators and other external criteria of evaluation can be put – on which more later. Some agencies have formulated performance indicators for different sectors of a legal system, not all of which are published.[8] Some of the formulated standards are explicitly qualitative; some are based on carefully constructed statistics; some are artificially or dubiously quantified.[9] Other standards for evaluation are left implicit, which may be even more dangerous. Like it or not, most public institutions are now part of a performance culture. We have to live with such evaluations, whether explicit or implicit. We need to assess their uses, limitations and dangers and to examine critically their intellectual foundations. So far as law is concerned, the underlying jurisprudential assumptions need careful scrutiny.

(b) Rankings

A relatively new phenomenon, rankings, has grown up on the back of the increasing standardisation of statistical data. A familiar example is educational 'league tables', such as the notorious *US News and World Report* rankings of graduate (mainly professional) schools,[10] the Norrington Table in Oxford and the more recent, and only slightly less controversial, London *Times Good University Guide*.[11]

Educational rankings are only one small part of the rapidly expanding rankings game. The American passion for statistics linked to the relative easiness of standardising data relating to the 50 states makes the United States the clear leader in the field. For example, the *Gale State Rankings*

---

7   Probably the most developed in respect of courts is the US National Center for State Courts, eg *Trial Court Performance Standards* (1990); cf publications of the New South Wales Bureau of Crime, Statistics and Research. In England there has been significant recent work in respect of franchising legal aid, eg Richard Moorehead, Avrom Sherr, and Alan Paterson, 'Judging on results? Outcome measures: quality, strategy and the search for objectivity' (1994) 1 International Journal of the Legal Profession 191.

8   A general example is Roberto Mosse and Leigh Ellen Sontheimer, *Performance Monitoring Indicators Handbook* (World Bank Technical Paper No 334, 1996).

9   Cf David Braybrooke's 'Scale of Scientificity': *Philosophy of Social Science* (1987), pp 43-46.

10 The *US News and Report* 1998 *Annual Guide* covered Business, Law, Medicine, Health, Education, Engineering and Public Affairs (2 March, 1998). This is, of course, only one salient example from a very extensive and controversial literature.

11 John O'Leary (ed), *The Times Good University Guide* (1998) is subtitled *For Students Entering University in 1999*.

Reporter for 1994 features over 300 tables comparing the 50 states, with no less than 5,200 specific sets of rankings.

Under American leadership the rankings game has spread to largely popular attempts to produce global rankings – with titles like *The New Book of World Rankings* or *World Facts and Figures*.[12] At present the lack of availability and standardisation of statistics make such tabulations much cruder and less detailed than those confined to the United States, but no doubt that will change over time.

Global legal rankings do exist in a number of fields. There have been a few published league tables in respect of human rights, corruption, and various kinds of democratic audit – for example, those produced by Charles Humana and Freedom House on national human rights performance,[13] Transparency International's Corruption Perception Index,[14] and various organisations' reports on crime trends.[15]

One is tempted to dismiss such rankings as ridiculous and not worth the attention of serious academics. That was my first reaction. But I have changed my mind for three reasons: first, even the cruder ones are not entirely meaningless; second, rankings are becoming increasingly

12 Examples include *The New Book of World Rankings* by George Thomas Kurian, (now in its third edition, (1991)) and Victor Showers, *World Facts and Figures* (3rd edn, 1989); cf IBRD, *The Development Data Book: a guide to social and economic statistics* (1995) and UNESCO *Statistical Digests* (annual). An example of compiling international rank orders for scholarly purposes is W Muller (op. cit., 1998) who states: 'One of the three principal purposes for which this compendium has been prepared is the analysis of *international rank orders*. International rank orders are the result of *differences* with regard to national participation in *highly valued scarce goods* such as military strength, national wealth, or human capital. This means that *international rank orders* are much more than theoretical constructions. They constitute *social stratifications* of national societies which are relevant for these societies in terms of their collective fears and aspirations. This stratified nature of the world system has led us to focus the contents of the compendium on research questions of the following kind:
    -    What is the shape of the stratification pyramid of a given rank order?
    -    Which are the nations belonging to a given stratum of the international system?
    -    Are certain strata or groups of nations more mobile than others and what are the reasons for this mobility?' (ibid 15. Italics in the original).
    Note that the basic unit of comparison is assumed to be the nation-state.
13 Op cit, p 156. Amnesty International and the US Department of State provide some contextual information and avoid some of the cruder pitfalls by not producing 'league tables'; but they nevertheless use implicit comparators with all the problems of comparability and potential bias that these entail.
14 Op cit, p 156.
15 Eg United Nations, *Trends in Crime and Criminal Justice 1970-85, in the Context of Socio-Economic Change* (1992); *Crime Trends and Criminal Justice Operations at the Regional and International Levels* (1993).

influential in many types of practical decision-making; and third, they are often used or misused for purposes quite other than those for which they were intended.

The first point can be illustrated by an example that is at first sight quite absurd. I recently came across an American book entitled *Where We Stand*, the sub-title of which is *Can America Make it in the Global Race for Wealth, Health and Happiness?*[16] The opening words of this bizarre publication are: 'America is as competitive as a Chevrolet'. It produces a series of league tables centred around seven themes: Who is the wealthiest? Who is the smartest, healthiest, busiest, freest? Who are the best lovers? Who has the best home? The bottom line, a combination of all factors into a single index, concludes that the United States is only the sixteenth 'most habitable' country and that 'THE WINNER IS JAPAN'.[17]

At first sight this looks like no more than a piece of enjoyable nonsense. The style is breezy, iconoclastic and tongue in cheek. The book seems to be designed to shock American readers out of a sense of complacency about their society by banging them over the head with figures about gun ownership, murder, oil spills, clean air, teachers' salaries, and over one hundred other matters. Interestingly, and perhaps worryingly, it is actually quite informative: the sources are generally the best available, the rankings are fairly plausible, and some of the findings are quite surprising. The final composite index is blatantly subjective in its weightings of different variables, but at least readers are given the opportunity to give their own weightings to different factors.

Where We Stand is not nearly as silly as it looks. Read with the more sophisticated American books of rankings it suggests what might be achieved if a greater amount of reliable international data were available in relatively standardised form, as has already happened in some fields. With the rapid increase of international and global standardisation we are not far off reaching such a situation.

So let us look briefly at one law-related example. Transparency International (TI) is a non-profit non-governmental organisation established in 1993. Its mission is to combat corruption world-wide.[18] TI publishes an annual Corruption Perception Index, based on the

---

16 Michael Wolff, *Where We Stand: Can America Make it in the Global Race for Wealth, Health and Happiness?* (1992).

17 Ibid.

18 Its purpose is 'To curb corruption by mobilising a global coalition to promote and strengthen international and national integrity systems'; Transparency International, (TI) Mission statement 1997. 'Corruption' is broadly defined as 'the misuse of public power for private profit', Jeremy Pope, *The TI Source Book* (1997), Ch 1.

perceptions of multi-national firms and institutions.[19] Although this is only a small part of TI's many activities, it is by far the best known, largely through highly condensed reports in newspapers and other media.[20] On closer examination one finds that TI is a small, but highly professional organisation that concentrates largely on specific issues in particular countries. It uses sophisticated and seemingly effective techniques for analysing a local situation,[1] devising tailor-made strategies for reducing corruption, and mobilising practical support for the effort. The simplistic composite league tables, as reported in the press, mask the professionalism of the organisation.[2] The TI indexes have provoked protests and have had some unintended political consequences. Although vulnerable to many of the standard objections to league tables, these eye-catching publicity devices seem to have served several useful functions in generating public awareness about corruption issues, in raising the profile of the organisation, and in putting pressure, both directly and indirectly, on governments, organisations, and individuals in countries that have fared badly in the ratings. They have also had a number of unintended consequences, such as being used in election campaigns. Publicity, as Jeremy Bentham repeatedly proclaimed, is the most potent tool for controlling the abuse of power. League tables are crude, but they can also be effective attention-getting tools for publicity and shame.[3]

The question arises: would it be possible to produce a theoretically sound source book of global legal statistics or a book of rankings of the health of national legal systems of the world that could be of real value? A short answer is that there is a mass of data already available, but they

19 The methodology is discussed at length in *The TI Source Book*, Ch 6, which emphasises that this is an index of perceptions based on a poll of polls. The popularity of the index has surprised those responsible who are investigating ways of refining it.

20 In 1996 Nigeria came first (out of 54 countries) on the index as the country perceived to be the most corrupt, and New Zealand came bottom of the league at 54th. Britain, at 43rd, was rated as being thought to be less corrupt than the United States, Austria, and Germany, but fared worse than Ireland, Austria and the Netherlands. It may come as no surprise that Nigeria or Pakistan or Venezuela fared worse than New Zealand and the Scandinavian countries, but it is difficult to take seriously the idea that within Scandinavia Denmark, Sweden, Finland and Norway can be precisely ranked.

1   Part A of *The TI Source Book* outlines a general analytical framework, which draws heavily on a wide range of sources and, as far as I can tell, is the most sophisticated attempt to establish a method for analysing and constructing a 'national integrity system'.

2   Eg The Wall Street Journal Europe Fri-Sat 3-4, Jan 1997 (one of the most substantial press reports).

3   See Philip Schofield, 'Jeremy Bentham on Political Corruption' 49 *Current Legal Problems* Part 2, 395 (M. Freeman ed, 1996).

are patchy and scattered and most are not standardised. Even international criminal statistics are far less sophisticated than in other cognate fields. There are some areas, for example judicial statistics, delay, legal services, levels of compensation for personal injuries, lawyers' earnings, most of which raise difficult questions of comparability. But before contemplating such a possibility one would need to address some fundamental theoretical questions, such as: What might be acceptable indicators of the health of a legal system analogous to social or economic indicators? To what extent is it possible to standardise such comparators in a meaningful way? What might be the uses, abuses, limitations and dangers of such indicators? These seem to be significant theoretical questions that need to be addressed by legal theorists and comparative lawyers. It is beyond the scope of this essay to address such questions in detail, but it is worth pausing to consider briefly one familiar example which may serve as a cautionary tale.

(c) The Law Schools Rankings Controversy

To illustrate the methodological problems let us look at a familiar, reasonably developed and highly controversial area: national law school rankings in the United States.

The first *US News* rankings of law schools were published in 1987, but the present series started in 1990. There is a longer history of educational rankings, but what is relatively new is the phenomenon of national journals publishing rankings that claim to be methodologically sound. A prolonged, often heated controversy, has been stimulated by these league tables in many disciplines.

Among the many objections to the *US News and Report* law school league tables, five are particularly significant in the present context.[4]
(i)   More emphasis is given to simple data that are easily quantified and standardised – such as Law School Admission Test (LSAT) scores – rather than to more complex or qualitative measures. Hard variables

4   From the extensive literature I have learned most from an unpublished paper by Richard Lempert and a series of short articles in the *National Law Journal*, 1997-98, and various contributions on the Internet, mainly discussing the relative merits of the *US News* and Leiter methods of ranking. On the latter see Brian Leiter, *The Legal Gourmet Report, 1997-8, Ranking of Law School by Educational Quality* on the website of the University of Texas Law School and *Press Release* by Leiter on New Educational Quality Ranking of US Law Schools for 1998-99 (bleiter@mail.law.utexas.edu); see also Leiter, 'Why US News Makes State Law Schools Angry' (1997) 19 National Law Journal, March 24 A24; David E. Rovella id v. 19 n. 40 June 2 A1 col 3. A useful survey of five leading sets of US law school rankings is found in ABAJ, March 1998, at 50. See generally David S Webster, *Academic Quality Rankings of American Colleges and Universities* (1986).

tend to push out soft variables.[5] A striking example of an omission is that *US News* does not include quality of teaching as an indicator.

(ii)   The choice of indicators and the weighting given to each is arbitrary, so that composite scores are at least biased,[6] at worst meaningless or positively misleading.

(iii) Detailed league rankings involve false precision: to say that Harvard, Stanford, Yale and Chicago are near the top of the Premier League is not news; to say that Yale or Stanford is better than or 'beats' Harvard is newsworthy but almost meaningless. Unfortunately it is just these close calls that may be the most important. For example, in the United Kingdom, a potential applicant might be unduly influenced by meaningless small gradations in choosing between the three leading London law schools or between say Sheffield, Warwick and Leicester, three quite different institutions ranked 8th, 9th and 10th by *The Times* in 1998.[7]

(iv)   The tables are full of insidious hidden assumptions: for example, that all law schools have identical missions and functions;[8] that full-time first degree students are the only significant beneficiaries of legal education; that the quality of entrants and their immediate employability is more important than the quality of their educational experience or the 'value added' factor, or longer-term benefits, or research record.

(v)   Perhaps the most important point is the danger that league tables prepared for one purpose are used or misused for other quite different purposes. *US News* justifies its rankings – as does the *Times Good University Guide* – on the ground that they are meeting a genuine

5   The most influential variable is LSAT scores; opinions of peers and of the legal profession are given a place, but weigh less heavily. The biggest single difference between *US News* and Leiter's rankings is that the latter gives greater weight to assessment of the quality of the faculty and of teaching.

6   *US News* is said to be biased in favour of small, private schools and those oriented to success in bar examinations., see Leiter, op cit, n 4.

7   Times *Good University Guide* (1998) at 42. In the same table Queen's is sandwiched between the Law Departments at SOAS and East Anglia – an even more motley trio.

8   Professor Martin Harris, Chairman of the Committee of Vice-Chancellors and Principals commented as follows: 'Naturally these students demand more information about the range of universities in this country and what they can offer. The *Times Good University Guide* goes some way towards meeting this demand. But vice-chancellors believe that single "super" league tables, attempting to cram all universities into one mould, cannot do justice to the needs of such a wide variety of students, and to what we can justifiably boast is one of the world's most diverse higher education providers' (*The Times*, 11 May 1998). On the plurality and multi-functionalism of law schools, see *BT*, op cit, Ch. 3 and 'Thinking About Law Schools: Rutland Reviewed', (1998) 25 Journal of Law and Society 1.

need in providing a guide to potential applicants in making important choices.[9] But the American league tables are said to have a disproportionate influence on alumni, university administrators, employers, fund-raisers, donors, and even faculty. Rankings can affect policies on such matters as admissions, library, curriculum, preparation for bar examinations, and activities that do not count for the purpose of ranking, such as postgraduate work, continuing legal education, or contributions to the local community.[10]

US News, it is said, conscientiously tries to listen to criticism and improve its methodology. But it is caught in two dilemmas: as its methodology changes, the validity of comparisons over time is undermined; and, more important, US News is a business and its rankings issue is one of its best-sellers. There is an apparently insatiable demand for simplistic, composite rankings that are the modern substitute for the mixed metaphor.[11] The weakest aspect, the composite table, is the most popular.

There is a need to explore further possible analogies between law school rankings and other legal rankings such as those produced by Freedom House [12] and Transparency International.[13] The debate on law school rankings deserves attention because of its detail and relative sophistication. Here, I shall confine myself to two points:

First, the phenomenon is not entirely unhealthy. The febrile US News debate has at least stimulated systematic collection and construction of data, sophisticated discussion of methodology, and alternative schemes for evaluating and comparing US law schools. While crude league tables have sometimes distorted policy, they have also provoked critical reappraisal of some institutional arrangements that to an outsider seem to be locked into rigid and often self-stultifying sets of practices and

9   Clearly applicants need guidance and rounded works like the *Times Good University Guide* are helpful, if imperfect. In a recent *Times* survey only 11% of sixth formers in 1998 gave league tables as their main source of advice in choosing a university (*Times*, 12 May, 1998). In practice, probably few applicants would rely on only one source.

10 *The National Law Journal* (May 11, 1998) reported that during the academic year 1997-98 no less than seven law school deans had been squeezed out of office and it has been suggested that a major factor was *US News* ratings. To an outsider one of the puzzles is why such a simplistic measure should have so much influence upon informed insiders.

11 League tables invite sporting metaphors. Criticism of the Research Assessment Exercises in the United Kingdom is sometimes expressed in terms that suggest that the goal posts keep moving, the system of scoring is kept secret from the players, and the prizes and penalties are determined after the event. In so far as law schools have different missions, functions, situations etc, ranking them in a single league is more akin to popularity contests in which footballers, cricketers, swimmers, politicians, and pop stars compete for 'personality of the year'.

12 Op cit.

13 Op cit.

assumptions.[14] They have increased self-criticism and public accountability, but at a price.[15] Similarly, a reflective approach to evaluating the health of national legal systems, other legal orders or parts thereof may be stimulated by even the cruder efforts at producing national rankings. What is involved in seriously evaluating a legal system or order, a national criminal justice system, or any particular legal institution is a neglected job of jurisprudence.

The second point is more worrying. The rankings phenomenon tends to make explicit, often in simplistic and sensational form, what has been going on implicitly in arcane ways that may be equally crude. In a recent review of secondary and tertiary literature about comparative law, I concluded that one of the most striking omissions is that there has been hardly any discussion of comparators, that is standards or measures for comparison.[16] On one standard model of 'comparing' – that is analysing similarities and differences between comparable phenomena – analysis requires both clear conceptions of comparability and standards or indices for comparison. Such indices may in first instance be descriptive, such as a tape measure or weighing scale or an index for measuring mortality rates; they may be explicitly evaluative, such as a marking system, or performance indicators, or international human rights norms; more often than not they are a combination of the two or implicitly evaluative, such as indexes of infant mortality or GNP. We use comparators not only to compare two or more objects, but also to describe individual phenomena. When one describes a city or a legal system in terms of its salient features one is more or less explicitly comparing it to some general norm or standard or ideal type. Any description involves selection and comparators are the main, but not the only, criteria for selection.[17]

One reason why I have dwelt on the phenomenon of rankings is that they dramatise the use and difficulties associated with comparators – in law as elsewhere. The controversy about American law school rankings raises fundamental questions about the comparability of law schools as institutions, their nature and functions, and what are possible criteria for the evaluation and comparison of the health of such institutions, if indeed they all belong to a single genus. Similar problems arise about the description, comparison, and evaluation of legal systems or indeed of

---

14 W Twining, 'Rethinking Law Schools', (1996) 21 Law and Social Inquiry 1007.
15 However, league tables confirm part of the orthodoxy, for example that only those reading for first degrees in law count as 'law students'. American law schools have long had to take internal and external evaluation seriously, but the main standards set by the ABA have been criticised as being cosy and self-serving. On the history of ABA accreditation, see Robert Stevens, *Law School* (1983).
16 CLLT.
17 Cf Charles Taylor, 'Comparison, History, Truth' in *Philosophical Arguments* (1995).

any legal phenomena. Legal institutions and practices are increasingly subject to the kinds of analysis and evaluation associated with management consultants – what may be called 'bureaucratic rationalism'.[18] Like it or not, they are increasingly important and the methodological problems and the underlying assumptions need to be examined critically. Within the discipline of law these problems are primarily jurisprudential because they raise issues about abstract concepts and general assumptions and presuppositions.

I have suggested that geographical maps involve selection from pre-existing data that themselves presuppose conceptual schemes and taxonomies. In this context such maps are little more than one technique for visual presentation of, typically simple, data.[19] Statistical tables are similarly just one kind of mental or metaphorical map, which have similar presuppositions. Rankings are just one, usually crude, form of pseudo-statistical mapping that help to dramatise some of the underlying theoretical problems. Statistical tables and ranking involve comparison; but comparison in turn assumes description or at least giving an account of salient characteristics or differentiae. Questions about comparing and evaluating legal orders and other phenomena presuppose answers to questions about what is involved in giving an account of one such system or phenomenon.

(d)   Profiling Legal Orders

So let us move from ranking and comparison to profiling. My argument suggests that even a description of a single system or other phenomenon typically involves the use of comparators that may be explicit or implicit. So, what is involved in depicting (i.e. interpreting, describing and explaining) a single legal system or order? It is to such questions that a substantial part of our vast heritage of jurisprudential writing is ostensibly addressed. Most of our mainstream jurists – Kelsen, Hart, Llewellyn, and Dworkin, for example – purport to give accounts of the nature of law and legal systems.

So is not my question the central question addressed by general theories of law? Up to a point the answer is 'Yes'. I have from time to time in teaching jurisprudence set an exercise in which a motley team of jurists are planning an expedition to Xanadu – a mythical country, more like that of Coleridge or Calvino than the real place – in order to construct

18 W Twining, 'Bureaucratic Rationalism and *The Quiet (R)evolution*' (1996) 7 Legal Education Review 291.

19 On modern methods of increasing data density in presentation of information, including on maps, see Tufte (1983), (1990) (1997), op cit.

an account of its legal system for a new Encyclopaedia of Comparative Law. They are behind a veil of ignorance about Xanadu and they are discussing how they should go about their task. The exercise usually leads to the conclusion that each jurist would ask somewhat different questions, and that for the most part they would complement rather than conflict with each other. In short, they would bring different conceptual schemes to bear. Hart, Kelsen and Fuller might on investigation differ as to whether Xanadu has a legal system at all;[20] or, if it satisfies each's criteria for the existence of a legal system, they might give different accounts of its salient features. A disciple of Hart and Kelsen might describe, with slight variations, the basic form and structure and criteria of validity of a system of rules or norms. A Fullerite might assess how far the norms satisfy his principles for the internal morality of law.[1] A Dworkinian would try to divine the fundamental principles of political morality – the ideology in a non-pejorative sense – that give the legal order coherence or integrity. She might also provide an account of the local modes of reasoning in adjudication (and interpretation generally).[2] A follower of Karl Llewellyn would try to find out empirically how the law-jobs were in fact done through asking about actual disputes and how they were in fact handled;[3] if there were judges, the Llewellynite would ask questions about their styles of justification – perhaps coming up with not very different answers from Dworkin.

Each of these general theories might provide a basis (or at least a starting-point) for giving a particular account of the legal order in question. In our discussions, we usually conclude that far from providing rival or radically different interpretations, a richer account of legal

20 In teaching, these exercises raise familiar questions about the definition or, better, the boundaries of the concept of law. In this context I have generally not had great difficulty in persuading a class that for the purposes of the enterprise of understanding law there will always be some borderline cases, but that if one wishes to understand law in Brazil one is going to miss a great deal if one omits or overlooks the institutionalised orders of the squatter settlements which affect the property and other day to day relations of many thousands of people. In 1970 'Pasagarda', one of the squatter settlements outside Rio de Janiero, had an estimated population of 50,000 (Santos, 1995, p 158). A jurisprudential basis for this view can be found in the ideas of Llewellyn and Honore. Eg 'The first question in descriptive legal theory is then not "What is a rule?" but "What is a group?" A Honoré, *Making Law Bind* (1987), p 33.

1   L Fuller, *The Morality of Law* (1964), Ch 2.

2   I have suggested elsewhere that Dworkin's 'theory of adjudication' is better characterised as a theory of interpretation, because it can apply to non-judicial interpreters and potentially might be applied to legal orders without courts, and the legal traditions such as Islam (above, 64). For an extension to the European Union, see J. Bengoetxea, *The legal reasoning of the European Court of Justice: Towards a European Jurisprudence* (1993).

3   K Llewellyn and E Adamson Hoebel, *The Cheyenne Way* (1941).

ordering in Xanadu might emerge through subjecting it to such multiple perspectives. We also sometimes come to other, less banal, conclusions. First, on their own, these general theories are too abstract to give much guidance on the handling of detail. Kelsen and Hart would end up with rather thin descriptions of form and structure. Llewellyn would point to thicker and more realistic accounts, but his law-jobs theory and his extended case-method are suggestive ideas that need to be refined and fleshed out to provide an adequate methodology.[4] How far Ronald Dworkin's theory of law is applicable to different kinds of legal orders and cultures is still largely unexplored.[5]

This exercise also brings out the point that most standard accounts of actual legal systems do not draw explicitly on our stock of legal theories. Rather such accounts tend to be conventional and pragmatic, based on generally unarticulated and not very coherent or precise assumptions about law students' or foreigners' needs at the start of their studies. For example, standard introductory accounts of 'The English Legal System' rarely articulate their basic assumptions or any criteria of selection; they do not talk of basic norms or rules of recognition or interpretive concepts or 'law-jobs', nor do they pause to clarify what is meant by a legal system, an institution, a process, a dispute, a court, or a profession.[6] Writers of such works do not draw much more directly on legal theory than writers of guide books refer to the literature of urban sociology. Similarly the *International Encyclopaedia of Comparative Law* (and similar less scholarly works) has a standard format which is based more on common sense and the conventions of comparatists than on explicit theory.[7] In short, there appears to be only a tenuous connection between our stock of general theories and standard accounts of actual legal systems.[8]

4   A L Epstein (ed), *The Craft of Social Anthropology* (1967); cf JJM.
5   *LIC*, Ch 8.
6   Even a more theoretically informed text, such as Fiona Cownie and Anthony Bradney's *English Legal System in Context* (1996), which explicitly espouses legal pluralism, makes so many concessions to traditional syllabuses, especially in respect of providing basic (ie orthodox) information, that its coherence and originality seem to me to be artificially restricted; cf Julian Webb, (1998) 32 The Law Teacher 344.
7   One attempt at theorisation is the Introduction by René David in Vol II of the *International Encylopedia*: *The Legal Systems of the World: Their Comparison and Unification* which is mainly concerned with problems of internal division and classification of legal doctrine.
8   Moreover, such accounts make very little use of either maps or available statistical data. For example, *The Legal Atlas of United States Law* (1996) contains substantially different information from standard descriptions. Compare for example two very different attempts to introduce their own legal systems to foreigners: E Allan Farnsworth, *An Introduction to the Legal System of the United States* (1963) and E Blankenburg and F Bruinsma, *Dutch Legal Culture* (2nd edn, 1994). Only exceptionally are statistics used in a systematic way as part of a profile of a

A quite different perspective on the institutions of a municipal legal system is to be found in the context of foreign aid. Development agencies, foreign donors, and institutions such as the World Bank often employ techniques of institutional analysis that are much more systematic than those used in accounts of legal systems by academic lawyers. Some of the basic ideas of institutional appraisal appear to be inspired by management consultancy perspectives, with a strong tendency to bureaucratic rationality. In my experience they tend in practice to be stronger on prescription than diagnosis, but they do sometimes pose illuminating questions about goals, structures, 'stakeholders and beneficiaries', outcomes, performance indicators and costs. There is much that could be said about what might be termed 'the Jurisprudence of the World Bank'. In the present context, the relevant point is that such perspectives and methodologies when applied to legal institutions contrast quite sharply with orthodox academic accounts of 'legal systems'. There are, of course, many other perspectives – human rights 'auditing', economic, anthropological, linguistic, historical, evocative, for example – that can be employed in depicting a legal system or order.

6   CITIES AND LEGAL ORDERS

Detailed analysis of particular examples must await another occasion. Instead, I shall conclude by suggesting that depicting a legal system or order is closely analogous to depicting a city. If one is about to visit Venice or Oxford or Hong Kong for the first time and wants to do some reading in advance, there are many different kinds of literature to choose from. One might start with a map of the country and of the city. One might move on to a tourist guide – Rough for the economically disadvantaged; Blue for culture vultures or gastronomes. For setting a tone, one might turn to evocative works that report personal impressions – by a Jan Morris or a Bill Bryson – or some more orthodox travel writer. Depending on one's purposes or interests one might proceed to histories, or novels, or specialist works on politics or economics or transport or architecture or folklore or drains or even law.

I suggested earlier that Calvino's *Invisible Cities* could be interpreted as 55 accounts of Venice; it would not be difficult for an avid reader to

---

national legal system. A partial exception is Michael Zander, *Cases and Materials on the English Legal System* (8th edn, 1999) which makes quite extensive use of statistical data. Combine these sources and one will have quite different, mainly complementary, accounts.

find more than 55 different treatments of Venice or Oxford or Belfast.[9] Some of the accounts might be thicker and overlap more than Calvino's spare evocations; but the outcome would be similar – a complex, multi-layered cumulation of accounts, built up from multiple perspectives. This is the opposite of reductionism.

Cities attract metaphors. Calvino uses labyrinths, mazes, chessboards, bridges, canals as symbols of aspects of invisible cities. A legal order, like a city, is typically a human construct, but not the work of a single mind;[10] rather it reflects the beliefs, decisions and practices of generations of its inhabitants. Both are complexes of muddle and order.[11]

There are some suggestive parallels between debates and divisions within urban sociology and within the discipline of law.[12]

(i)   For example, a central theme of talk about cities is that they are all similar and yet all unique. Sir Patrick Geddes wrote:

'Though the woof of each city's life be unique, and this may be increasingly with each throw of the shuttle, the main warp of life is broadly similar from city to city.'[13]

One could substitute legal order for city without changing the rest of the wording.

(ii)   Classical writers have been criticised for presenting top-down perspectives and for neglecting the points of view of the inhabitants and users.[14]

9   This is a very modest assessment. According to Peter Ackroyd there have been more than 25,000 printed works on London's history (Book review, London Times 13 August 1998, at p 35).

10   Contrast the insistence of the arch-planner, Jeremy Bentham that 'each code should be drafted by a single individual' so that it would systematically conform to the principle of utility and responsibility for it should be clearly located, on which see Philip Schofield, 'Jeremy Bentham: Legislator of the World' (1998) 51 Current Legal Problems 115. Bentham did, of course, allow for participation in discussing drafts.

11   As Weis puts it: 'Calvino regards the city as a "complex symbol" which allows him to express "the tension between geometric rationality and the entanglements of human lives" (Six Memos, p 71). In fact, in order to understand fully his interest in cities and their evolution and decline, one must see them as a representative symbol of human behavior. Going back to the beginning of civilization, since their designs and disposition are never arbitrary, cities reflect the doctrine and practices of the society which creates and maintains them.' Beno Weis, Understanding Italo Calvino (1993), pp 156-157.

12   Describing cities is a good metaphor for mental topography. We are comparing the problems of depicting cities and legal orders, not the objects of depiction. Calvino reminds us that a city is not its description; the idea of a city is abstract and a map of a city is at a higher level of abstraction. Albert H Carter, op cit (1987), pp 120-121.

13   Patrick Geddes, Cities in Evolution (rev edn, 1969); cf the quotations by Geddes and Calvino at the start of this essay.

14   Above, Ch 5.

(iii) There is much debate about whether cities are 'systems'; so too with law: Brian Simpson has memorably characterised the common law as more a muddle than a system.[15]

(iv) Urban literature is characterised by deep ambivalences, with strong strains of extreme pro- and anti-urban views; leading theorists, such as George Simmel take centrist and ambivalent positions. There is also pervasive ambivalence about the costs and benefits of a well-ordered and efficient urban system.[16] Similarly, in law the natural law tradition and its successors idealise our subject and present aspirational perspectives, some theorists emphasise the benefits of efficiency and order, whereas Marxists, realists and others point to the repressive, problematic, or seamy side of actual legal orders.

(v) Many of the unique or distinctive characteristics of a city or a legal order can only be explained in terms of its particular history.[17]

There is another suggestive analogy between cities and legal orders. Urban sociology is replete with different images of 'the city'. For example, Peter Langer identifies four recurrent images of the city as 'organized diversity.': Bazaar, Jungle, Organism, and Machine.[18] The first two are associated with bottom-up perspectives; the others seem to be more top-down. 'The city as bazaar imagines the city as a place of astonishing richness of activity and diversity unparalleled in nonurban areas.' This place offers opportunity, choice, and liberation.[19] The jungle is densely packed, intertwining and threatening. The city as organism, normally a favourable functionalist image, conceives of the city as a body of diverse organs generally co-operating together without any central direction. The image of city as machine represents social engineering, typically controlled by a small group which runs it largely in the interests of one section of the population.

Images of law as an organic growth, not just the product of a single mind, or as the product of social engineering (typically presented as benevolent), are familiar within jurisprudence. A legal order seen as an essentially hostile environment is typified by Holmes' Bad Man, who – to mix metaphors – has to learn to be street-wise to survive in the legal

---

15 Brian Simpson in Simpson (ed) *Oxford Essays in Jurisprudence*, 2nd series, (1973); cf Charles Sampford, *The Disorder of Law* (1989).

16 Andrew Lees, *Cities Perceived* (1985).

17 H Molotch 'The City as Growth Machine', (1976) 82 Am Jo Sociology 309.

18 Peter Langer, 'Sociology Four Images of Organized Diversity' in Lloyd Rodwin and Robert M Hollister (eds) *Cities of the Mind* (1984), Ch 6. I have discussed all four images elsewhere, especially 'The Great Juristic Bazaar' (1978) 14 JSPTL (NS) 185; Holmes' Bad Man and the legal jungle, Ch 5.3(b); functionalist and technological views of law in JJM.

19 Langer, op cit, pp 101-105.

jungle. The image of a legal order as a bazaar is less explicitly developed in Jurisprudence, but fits quite closely with free-market ideology. The legal order provides a stable environment which, through largely invisible mechanisms, enables individuals to choose freely from life's goods and facilitates the pursuit of different individual life-plans or more limited objectives with settled expectations.[20]

Each of these images is primarily associated with a particular kind of standpoint, the bazaar with merchants and consumers, the machine with planners and engineers, the organism with traditionalists and functionalists, and the jungle with the more or less powerful, the hunter and the hunted. However, such associations are neither necessary nor exclusive. Real jungles, for example, can be viewed from the standpoints of ecologists, foresters, developers, entrepreneurs, hunters and zoologists, among others. Similarly, machines can be seen from the point of view of designer, boss, machine worker, accident victim and so on. Langer's four images point to different ways of conceiving of a city or a legal order; each image can be looked at from multiple standpoints.[1] The bazaar and the jungle suggest diversity; the organism and the machine suggest reductionist tendencies at work.

It might be objected that cities are physical phenomena, but legal orders have no physical existence. This is only partly so. On the one hand it is trite that to depict a city it is not enough to describe its physical characteristics. One needs to be take account of its history, traditions, myths, customs, dramas, festivals, power relations, ideologies, languages, conflicts, 'spirit' and, above all, people. Conversely, legal orders do have physical embodiments in documents, dress, more or less photogenic activities and events, and even geography and architecture.[2] Accounts of

---

20 On modern invisible means of social control, using Disney World and shopping centres as examples, see Clifford D Shearing and Philip C Stenning, 'From the Panopticon to Disney World: The Development of Discipline', in A N Doob and E L Greenspan (eds), *Perspectives in Criminal Law* (Aurora, Ont, 1984). I am grateful to Jonathan Simon for this reference.

1   Langer suggests that the relative salience of any imagery is dependent on its ability to provide guidance in two different directions. The first is a theoretical insight into issues of *social process* as well as insight into social structure. Second, the imagery is helpful to the extent that it has problem-solving relevance' (at p 114). Langer's four images – each of which suggests an underlying order – are by no means the only ones to be found in urban sociology. Legal theory, more prosaic and generally dominated by top-down, statist perspectives may have had a rather less rich heritage of metaphors, but one can add trite examples like 'a seamless web' and 'the King's True Body', and many others scattered in the literature.

2   A striking modern example of the use of symbolism in legal architecture is Israel's Supreme Court Building, see Yosef Sharon, *The Supreme Court Building, Jerusalem* (trs A Mahler, 1993).

both legal orders and cities have to be expressed in terms of ideas, ideologies, stories, history, mores, people and so on.[3]

Calvino's book depicts invisible cities. Legal orders, too, are largely invisible, that is only a few aspects are susceptible to geographic mapping, pictures or videos – or even to statistical analysis. Law is not particularly photogenic, although watching trials on television reminds one that the common law is more telegenic than the civil law. Legal orders are made up of complexes of social relations, ideas, ideologies, norms, concepts, institutions, people, techniques and traditions. Calvino's concern is 'to portray the diversity and at the same time universality of human experience'.[4] He captures brilliantly what is involved in describing and understanding a city – the elusive mixture of patterns, complexity, and arbitrariness, and the capacity and the limitations of the human mind to grasp these realities.[5] Kublai Kahn's dialogue with Marco Polo revolves around how and whether the diverse cities of his empire can be mentally reduced to order. The great Khan hopes to master the invisible order by learning the rules as if they are like chess. His is a reductionist temperament.[6] Marco Polo emphasises hidden complexities, exceptions, contradictions, the elusiveness of hidden orders. He accepts that there are patterns, but they are too complex to capture from a single perspective. He even acknowledges that a basic design exists, but it is too elusive to be understood through the logic of a game, even one as complex as chess. Rather, the order that structures human attributes and relationships ought to be compared to the logic and structure of dreams:

'With cities it is as with dreams: everything imaginable can be dreamed, but even the most unexpected dream is a rebus that conceals a desire, or its reverse a fear. Cities, like dreams, are made of desires and fears, even if the thread of their logic is secret, their rules are absurd, their perspectives deceitful, and everything conceals something else.'[7]

3   Cf Llewellyn, who suggests that the institution of law plays between six poles – Might, Right, Skills, Rules, Results, and Law's People (*My Philosophy of Law*, 1941) at p 197.
4   Sara M Adler, *Calvino: The Writer as Fablemaker* (1979) at p 49.
5   Albert H Carter (op cit, 1987), pp 123-124.
6   Kublai Khan, the pessimist, sees his chessboard as a reduction to nothingness; Marco Polo, by contrast, treats each square as a starting-point for seeing a multiplicity of things in a little piece of smooth and empty wood, for example: 'Your chessboard, sire, is inlaid with two woods: ebony and maple. The square on which your enlightened gaze is fixed was cut from the ring of a trunk that grew in a year of drought: you see how its fibres are arranged? Here a barely hinted knot can be made out: a bud tried to burgeon on a premature spring day, but the night's frost forced it to desist' *IC*, pp 130-131.
7   *IC*, p 44.

A similar tension between geometric rationality and the messy complexities of human relations runs through our discourses about law. In jurisprudence we have our Kublai Khans and our Marco Polos. Like Calvino, I side with Marco Polo. Calvino is sometimes identified as a 'post-modernist'. If that label implies disregard for facts, or extreme subjectivity or indeterminacy in interpretation, or that all patterns are merely constructed by the reader, I think that this is a mis-reading. Calvino while emphasising complexity, paradox, the elusiveness of reality, agrees that there is a 'hidden "filigree of design" upon which all human experience is built'.[8] The idea of a city is a good metaphor for mental topography in general and for law in particular. Like Calvino, we need many mental maps of our invisible cities.[9]

8   Adler (1979), pp 51-52; *IC*, pp 5-6, 43-44.
9   'The Great Khan owns an atlas whose drawings depict the terrestrial globe all at once and continent by continent, the borders of the most distant realms, the ships' routes, the coastlines, the maps of the most illustrious metropolises and of the most opulent ports. He leafs through the maps before Marco Polo's eyes to put his knowledge to the test' (p 136). After Polo has given accounts of cities he has seen, cities he knows by hearsay, and possible cities that he does not know whether they exist or where they are, the Great Khan says: 'I think that you recognize cities better on the atlas than when you visit them in person'. And Polo answers: 'Traveling, you realize that differences are lost: each city takes to resembling all cities, places exchange their form, order, distances, a shapeless dust cloud invades the continents. Your atlas preserves the differences intact: that assortment of qualities which are like the letters of a name' (p 137). Cf Richard Hyland on 'difference theorists' in comparative law in Dennis Patterson, op cit (1996), Ch 11.

Chapter 7

Globalisation and comparative law*

I MR PALOMAR

Italo Calvino's Mr Palomar is a nervous man who lives in a frenzied and congested world.[1] In order to escape the general neurasthenia he seeks 'the key to mastering the world's complexity by reducing it to its simplest mechanism'.[2] On the beach he tries to see and fix in his mind one individual wave as a limited and precise object. The task eludes him again and again. Eventually he loses patience and gives up, as 'tense and nervous as when he came, and even more unsure about everything'.[3]

Mr Palomar wants to eliminate every single weed from his lawn.[4] To work out a method he shifts his focus from the lawn as a whole to a single

---

*   This is a shortened version of a paper published in 6 Maastricht Jo. of European and Comparative Law 217 (1999). The relevant parts are reproduced here by kind permission of the publishers.
1   Italo Calvino, *Mr Palomar* (1983, trs William Weaver, 1985), 1.1.1, 'Mr Palomar on the Beach: Reading a Wave'.
2   Ibid, p 6.
3   Ibid, p 8. Mr Palomar is an intellectually honest reductionist. In Calvino's *Invisible Cities* (trs W Weaver, 1974) the central contrast is between Kublai Khan, who is a reductionist, and his young Ambassador Marco Polo, who sees even a single object, such as a chessboard, as opening up a universe of possibilities. See above, Ch 6.
4   'Mr Palomar in the garden: The infinite lawn', Calvino, op cit, pp 29-33. As with *Invisible Cities*, the text of *Mr Palomar* is highly schematic, involving different combinations of three kinds of experience and enquiry (1) description of natural objects; (2) stories containing elements that are anthropological or cultural, 'and the experience involves, besides visual data, also language, meaning, symbols'; (3) meditation about 'the cosmos, time, infinity, the relationship between the self and the world, the dimensions of the mind' (p 126). 'On the Beach' involves mainly (1), the difficulties of describing one wave; 'The Infinite Lawn' involves all three, combining description, narrative and interpretation.

section one metre square and tries to count 'how many blades of grass there are, what species, how thick, how distributed'.[5] He tries to arrive at a statistical knowledge of the lawn as a whole. But counting the blades of grass is futile, the lawn has no precise boundaries – indeed it is infinite – and he is again defeated. He tries to apply to the universe everything he has thought about the lawn. 'The universe perhaps finite but countless, unstable within its borders, which discloses other universes within itself. The universe, collection of celestial bodies, nebulas, fine dust, force fields, intersections of fields, collections of collections ...'[6]

As a jurist, I often feel like Mr Palomar. One's efforts to master even a single legal phenomenon – to obtain a comprehensive understanding of it – seem futile. Even a single rule or concept can be as elusive as a wave or a tuft of grass. Yet, in an era of globalisation, we are under increasing pressure to focus on the whole universe of legal phenomena.

My thesis is simple. In an increasingly interdependent world nearly all legal studies are inevitably more or less cosmopolitan. For cosmopolitan legal studies there is a need both for a revival of general jurisprudence and a rethinking of comparative law from a global perspective. The project is simple: its achievement may be as elusive as describing a wave or mastering a piece of lawn en route to understanding the universe.

The essay is organised as follows. After summarising my standpoint, I report on my impressions as a non-specialist of some of the secondary literature about comparative law and how macro- and micro-comparative legal studies appear from the point of view of an outsider adopting a global perspective. Finally, I outline one possible agenda for rethinking comparative law in a global context and put forward some general conclusions. The presentation may seem rather staccato, for this paper synthesises several themes that have been developed at greater length elsewhere.[7] The conclusion is a programme for future work calculated to daunt many Mr Palomars.

My standpoint is that of an English legal theorist concerned about the health of the institutionalised discipline of law in the common law world, in Europe and beyond. A legal theorist is a hired subversive and a professional dilettante. During the past two years or so, I have trespassed into the field of institutionalised comparative law, especially writings in English by reflective practitioners about the objectives, nature and scope of their enterprise. On this occasion I want to report on some of my impressions as a non-expert about the strange world of comparatists: I

---

5   Calvino, op cit, p 31.
6   Ibid, p 33.
7   See Chs 1-6 above and 'Comparative Law and Legal Theory: The Country and Western Tradition' (forthcoming) (hereafter CLLT).

say non-expert, because on this foray into the literature of what many consider an esoteric subject, I have realised that I have been involved in comparative work all of my professional life: I was taught by Barry Nicholas, Harry Lawson, Max Rheinstein and Karl Llewellyn, (who was perhaps an honorary comparatist); I knew Fritz Kessler, Wolfgang Friedmann, Otto Kahn-Freund, Rudolf Schlesinger and Ulrich Drobnig; I have studied and taught in several countries, and I have enjoyed many of the privileges of the modern jet-setting jurist. Yet I do not consider myself to be a comparatist and members of that guild can point out that I do not have the credentials to be one. This raises the question whether within academic law one can sustain a distinction between being a comparatist and a cosmopolitan?

2   COMPARATIVE LAW: AN OUTSIDER'S VIEW[8]

In earlier papers I have reported on my impressions of comparative law as an institutionalised sub-discipline and how it has been conceptualised by some of its leading practitioners. My project was to examine how leading comparatists have envisioned their enterprise – its history, scope, objectives, methods, problems and so on. In order to make the project manageable, I concentrated on a limited range of texts in the English language: (a) standard general and introductory works; (b) inaugural and valedictory lectures and general statements about their subject by pioneers and 'reflective practitioners' in the enterprise and by its recent internal critics; and (c) a selection of examples of 'best practice' over the past 50 years.[9] This then is no more than a report of first impressions by an outsider with a distinct Anglo-Saxon bias. As we shall see, my main impression is that best practice in the field has outstripped its theory, but that there is a need for a quite radical rethink in changed circumstances.

My first impressions of the secondary literature about comparative law can be summarised in four broad propositions or hypotheses: first, the secondary literature exhibits the symptoms of a young, marginal discipline straining to establish its credentials in terms of intellectual respectability, practical utility, and 'relevance'. Secondly, in the past 20 years comparative law has in practice diversified to cover many fields of law beyond the traditional focus on private law, especially obligations;

8   For a more detailed discussion, see CLLT.
9   For a more detailed bibliography see CLLT. In addition to standard students' works and classics of comparative law, I have canvassed secondary writings by, among others, Ancel, Bell, David, Drobnig, Gutteridge, Hall, Hamson, Hyland, Kahn-Freund, Kötz, Lawson, Markesenis, Mattei, McDougal, Merryman, Rheinstein, Schlesinger, Watson, Zweigert and recent critics.

but theorising about the subject has not kept pace with these developments. Thirdly, micro-comparative studies have dominated institutionalised comparative law, especially in the Anglo-American tradition. And, fourthly, in modern times comparative law and legal theory have drifted apart: few modern canonical jurists have paid much sustained attention to comparative law and its theoretical problems; conversely, few mainstream comparatists have made much use of contemporary jurisprudence. For example, the dominant tradition from Rabel, through Kahn Freund and Kessler to Zweigert and Kötz and Markesenis[10] appears to espouse a rather simple form of functionalism that has echoes of the 1920s and 1930s.[11] One major exception is that some internal critics complain that comparative law is 'atheoretical'. They bring to bear more recent theoretical perspectives, post-modernism in the case of Legrand[12] and neo-Kantianism in the case of Ewald.[13]

These sweeping generalisations are just first impressions. In so far as they are broadly true, this is a matter for regret. Comparative studies should be central to a cosmopolitan discipline at the end of the twentieth century; building an accurate and coherent picture of law in the world is a central task of general jurisprudence; comparison and generalisation in law are fraught with theoretical difficulties and, in turn, legal theory needs to draw on the insights provided by detailed comparative work. In short, comparative law and legal theory need each other.

Comparative legal studies have a long and complex history. But modern comparative law did not become institutionalised or attain critical mass until after World War II in the common law world, somewhat earlier in Continental Europe. Standard secondary writings about comparative law distinguish between two main approaches: macro-comparative studies exemplified by the Grands Systèmes approach of René David and others, and micro-comparative studies, which are usually depicted as approximating to an ideal type that I have mischievously

---

10 See especially, K Zweigert and H Kötz, *Introduction to Comparative Law* (3rd edn, trs Tony Weir, 2 vols, 1997/1998) and Basil Markesenis, *Foreign Law and Comparative Methodology: A Subject and a Thesis* (1997).

11 See, eg Richard Hyland, 'Comparative Law', in Dennis Patterson (ed) *A Companion to Philosophy of Law and Legal Theory* (1996); Jonathan Hill, 'Comparative Law, Law Reform and Legal Theory' (1989) 9 OJLS 101. This theme is touched on in CLLT, but I propose to explore it in more detail in a future paper.

12 Eg Pierre Legrand, 'Comparative Legal Studies and Commitment to Theory' (1995) 58 MLR 262; Pierre Legrand, 'European Legal Systems are Not Converging', (1996) 45 ICLQ 52; 'How to Compare Now' (1996) 16 *Legal Studies* 232.

13 William Ewald, 'What Was it Like to Try a Rat?' (1995) 143 University of Pennsylvania Law Review 1889.

called 'the Country and Western Tradition'.[14] I shall consider each in turn.

3   MACRO-COMPARISON: THE GRANDS SYSTÈMES DEBATE

A distinction is sometimes drawn within comparative law between the study of 'legal families' and the detailed comparison of particular aspects of legal doctrine.[15] This reflects the distinction between macro- and micro-comparative studies. These are sometimes treated as two distinct enterprises,[16] but any serious comparatist knows that there are many inter-related levels of comparison and that most work has to proceed on a number of levels that cannot be kept artificially separate.[17] However, it is useful to distinguish between the two types, because in practice they often have quite different objectives and are presented to different audiences.

The study of 'legal families' is sometimes equated to 'The Grands Systèmes approach'. This seems to have developed in two main contexts: introductory courses designed to give law students an overview (or map) of law in the world and the *International Encyclopaedia of Comparative Law*. In both enterprises René David and Konrad Zweigert played leading roles. Anglo-American commentators have generally been dismissive of the tradition: the more outspoken ones, such as Alan Watson, have criticised it as too broad and superficial to deserve the name of scholarship.[18] The majority have voted with their feet by concentrating on micro-comparative work.

I believe that such dismissiveness is mistaken. There are indeed examples of muddled taxonomies or very general treatments that deserve such strictures. However, there are good reasons for taking seriously the enterprise of constructing total pictures or maps of law in the world. It is admirable to give beginning law students a broad overview of their field,

---

14   CLLT.
15   Pierre Legrand, (1995) at p 263. This was a critical review of Peter de Cruz, *A Modern Approach to Comparative Law* (1993), which was later revised and published as *Comparative Law in a Changing World* (1995).
16   The two approaches are sometimes combined in leading introductory students' works, such as those by Zweigert and Kötz, and Schlesinger. Indeed, as de Cruz remarks: 'The writer cannot really imagine that any teacher of comparative law in any institution, apart from perhaps one teaching it as a part of a global study subject in school, would leave the matter to rest after the introduction to the legal systems has been completed' (7).
17   Eg Zweigert and Kötz, op cit, p 5.
18   A Watson, *Legal Transplants* (1974) Ch 1. There have been common lawyers who have been more enthusiastic, including J H Wigmore, B Wortley, and J D M Derrett.

not least because it can help them to set more particular studies in a broad geographical and historical context. It can also provide them with an initial framework for organising their understandings of law.

An elementary overview need not be intellectually ambitious or even particularly rigorous, but laying a sound theoretical foundation for the study of law needs to aim higher. If the main objective of the discipline of law is to advance knowledge and understanding of its subject-matter, then surely one aspect of this must be the aspiration to build up an accurate and sophisticated total picture (or series of pictures) of law-in-the-world. Such an enterprise is often talked about in terms of mapping. Maps presuppose usable concepts and reliable data. My own view is that what is involved in mapping law for intellectually ambitious purposes raises some important and potentially interesting theoretical questions. In this enterprise general jurisprudence needs to provide the conceptual framework and comparative law to produce reliable and comparable data.

The Grands Systèmes tradition has generally not managed to achieve this. One reason is that it has become entangled in a protracted and unsatisfying debate about how to classify the main legal systems (or orders) of the world.[19] This debate is theoretically flawed. Here let me confine myself to one example. Within the Grands Systèmes debate about taxonomy, the scheme advanced by Zweigert and Kötz, is widely considered to be the most satisfactory, or rather the least unsatisfactory. Even the usually critical Santos acknowledges this and adopts it for his own purposes.[20] Zweigert and Kötz, having rejected attempts to use race or geographical location or relations of production or ideology as the main criterion, limited the idea to the predominant *styles of legal thought* of contemporary living legal systems. They identify five factors as central to the style of a legal family:

'(1) its historical background and development, (2) its predominant and characteristic mode of thought in legal matters, (3) especially distinctive legal institutions, (4) the kinds of legal sources it acknowledges and the way it handles them, (5) its ideology.'[1]

19 It is significant that the main protagonists in the debate are from Continental Europe. This may be due to the mundane reason that providing beginning law students with an overview of law in the world requires some sort of taxonomy, however rough, or it may be due to a more profound urge to establish the scientific 'autonomy' of fields of study, what Günther Frankenburg has called 'Continental "cartographic practice"' (1998) 18 *Legal Studies* 177.
20 Santos, at pp 273-274.
1   At pp 69-75.

On the basis of these criteria Zweigert and Kötz classify 'legal systems' into eight groups or families: Romanistic family, Germanic family, Nordic family, Common law family, socialist family, Far Eastern systems, Islamic systems and Hindu law.[2]

One does not need to be a logician to recognise that this is a strange categorisation. For one thing it looks like a list by Borges[3] – more of a muddle than a systematic taxonomy. Zweigert and Kötz's scheme is widely considered to be the least unsatisfactory. All the standard taxonomies, such as those of René David, or Arminjon, Nolde, and Wolff are at least as vulnerable to criticism.[4] What is wrong with them? A satisfactory taxonomy needs to have a clearly defined purpose or purposes; clear units of comparison; precise and definite differentiae; and, ideally, non-overlapping species that exhaust their genus.[5] Within the legal families debate these conditions are generally not satisfied.

First, *purpose*. The most common use has been to introduce law in general or a particular legal system to beginning law students or as an elementary introduction to comparative law or to a non-specialist readership. Such *introductory mapping* can serve a very useful function in providing a general context for particular studies. For such modest purposes a relatively crude overview is probably adequate; it can take many forms, and the relative merits of different taxonomies hardly deserve serious theoretical attention.

However, for the purposes of developing a modern general jurisprudence the approach to constructing total pictures of law in the world needs to be more systematic and rigorous. The more intellectually ambitious enterprises of a Leibniz or Blackstone or Austin are designed to provide a conceptual basis for systematic enquiry.[6] Such *foundational mapping* is a more serious matter: for example, Duncan Kennedy in his critique of the structure of Blackstone's *Commentaries* argues that what purports to be a systematic presentation of an internally coherent system is really a justificatory apologia that masks the inherent contradictions of the common law.[7] The general part of Austin's ideas, especially his

---

2   K Zweigert and H Kötz (1998) vol 1 at pp 69-75. By 'institutions' in this context the authors mean doctrinal constructs such as contract, trusts and restitution, rather than social and political institutions such as courts, the police and legislatures.

3   Eg Jorge Luis Borges, *Other Inquisitions* (trs Ruth L Simms, 1952), discussing the analytical language of John Wilkins. Cf M Foucault, *The Order of Things*.

4   See above, Ch 6.4(b), n 37.

5   Max Black, *Critical Thinking* (2nd edn, 1952). However, Black observes of the last requirement that 'in practice this ideal is seldom attained', at p 224.

6   Above, p 153.

7   Duncan Kennedy, 'The Structure of Blackstone's Commentaries' (1979) 28 Buffalo Law Review 205.

agenda for jurisprudence and his command theory of law, have attracted the most criticism. His defenders may argue that these can be interpreted as little more than general prolegomena to the detailed analyses which represent his most worthwhile contribution. My own view is that some such prolegomena are not best treated as mere prefatory grace notes. In legal theory, as in political and social theory, elucidation of abstract concepts is a critically important task. It is particularly difficult to identify or construct concepts that transcend different cultures and, for this reason, the decline of general analytical jurisprudence – at least in the English-speaking world – is a matter for regret.

Secondly, *levels of comparison*. If one's list of candidates for mapping includes various kinds of non-state law as well as national and sub-national state systems, then it is difficult if not impossible to find a single basis for classifying them: Scots law, common law, New York law, Islamic law, Pasagarda law, and European Union Law are not species of a single genus. Many of the candidates for inclusion in a reasonably comprehensive map of world law do not respect national boundaries: Islamic law, *lex mercatoria*, canon law, or Roman law for example; other candidates, such as European Union Law and Public International Law transcend state boundaries but are intimately related to sovereign states; some, such as Mississippi law or Dinka or Maori law, are confined within national boundaries.[8] To depict legal orders dealing with global, international, transnational, regional, and local relations, as well as national, requires some differentiation of levels of classification. Each level will require its own differentiae. Most standard taxonomies are confined to one or two levels, usually municipal and religious law.[9]

Thirdly, even assuming that the focus is on state law, it is unclear whether the *units of comparison*, what is being compared, is systems, orders, cultures or traditions. Sometimes these are run together so that the classification does not consist of species of a single genus. In other words it is by no means clear what legal families are families of.[10] Most comparatists either explicitly or implicitly treat 'legal systems' as the unit of comparison.[11] However, the term is used ambiguously: German

---

8   See above, p 139.
9   But see, for example, R Dehousse, 'Comparing National and EU Law: The Problem of Level of Analysis', (1994) 42 American Journal of Comparative Law 761; a more sceptical view is being developed by Ian Ward, eg, 'The Limits of Comparativism: Lessons from UK-EC Integration' (1995) 2 Maastricht Journal of European and Comparative Law 23.
10 See, for example, Pierre Legrand, 'Comparative Legal Studies and Commitment to Theory' (1995) 58 MLR 262 at p 267.
11 Eg Ake Mälmstrom, 'The System of Legal Systems' (1969) 13 Scandinavian Studies in Law 129; Arminjon et al, op cit; David, op cit; Zweigert and Kötz, op cit, Ch 5; de Cruz, op cit, entitles his Chapter 2 'The Classification of Legal Systems into Families'.

law, Islamic law and African law are 'legal systems' in quite different senses. If 'legal system' is used in a precise sense, for example the state legal systems of all members of the United Nations or, more broadly, those legal orders that satisfy some recognisable juristic criteria for the existence of a legal system, such as those of Hart or Kelsen, then it is not possible to accommodate some of the standard candidates such as Islamic, Hindu, or African law. If one substitutes 'tradition' or 'culture', the terms are so vague as to raise serious doubts of their being used for any precise or useful system of classification.[12]

As we have seen, Zweigert and Kötz identify eight groups of legal families: Romanistic, Germanic, Nordic, Common Law, Socialist, Far Eastern Systems, Islamic Systems, and Hindu Law. Some schemes include African Law and Chinese Law. Whilst some of these categories could be interpreted as families of municipal or state legal systems, this is not the case with Islamic, Hindu or African law. Hindu law can be interpreted as a system of concepts and principles, but not as a state legal system anywhere. While there are a few officially Islamic states, Islamic Law is surely not confined to them. One can view Islamic law from a variety of perspectives: for example, as a system of norms, or as a body of ideas, or as a culture involving practices and interpretive styles as well as ideas, or as a tradition which involves change or development over time in respect of all of these – even in a system decreed by God. If one looks at Islamic law in Saudi Arabia or Sudan or Malaysia or England, in order to understand it one will need to consider local history, institutions, personnel, and practices as well as norms and concepts and culture.

Similar considerations apply to other bodies of religious law, such as Jewish or Buddhist law, or stateless cultures or traditions such as 'Gypsy Law'. The term 'African Law' was originally coined to refer to traditional or customary law of African peoples; it is hardly ever used to refer to the national legal systems of modern sovereign states in Africa.[13] Socialist law or socialist legal systems was always an uneasy category. Socialist legal systems were those state systems that were strongly influenced by a particular ideology at a particular period in their history – here the contrast should be with other ideologies such as a social democratic, liberal, or religious systems; and surely ideologies are directly relevant to all styles of legal thought.

Fourthly, part of the legal families debate has centred on the *differentiae* of classification. There are almost as many ways of classifying legal systems or orders as there are for cities and countries. Race,

---

12 See the discussions in David Nelken (ed) *Comparing Legal Cultures* (1997) esp Chs 1-4.
13 While there is a body of legal theory providing criteria for identifying the legal systems of sovereign states or parts therof, the same is not true for the vaguer 'legal traditions' and 'legal cultures'.

language, stage of economic development, ideology, historical origin, substantive concepts and 'institutions', and even climate are among the factors that have been suggested.[14] The more sophisticated attempts at constructing a taxonomy of legal families have insisted on multiple criteria of classification – for example, Zweigert and Kötz, in respect of styles.

While the emphasis on history and factors in addition to substantive doctrine is welcome there is a danger of reductionism in this approach. For example, the idea that there is a single characteristic or predominant[15] mode of thought in the English legal profession assumes that the profession is monolithic and that all that English lawyers think about is questions of law.[16]

It might be argued that the idea of styles of thought applies both to ways of thinking in both families of state legal systems and at least some kinds of non-state law, such as Islamic, Jewish and Gypsy law. There is some truth in this, but the idea of dominant 'styles of thought' needs to be approached with as much caution as reductionist phrases such as 'the legal mind' and 'thinking like a lawyer'. It has often been pointed out that many legal professions are highly stratified; that in so far as lawyers think, they do not only or mainly think about questions of law; and that within any given legal system or culture or tradition what constitute valid, cogent and appropriate ways of reasoning and interpretation about questions of law are regularly contested.[17] It is a plausible hypothesis that patterns of disagreement about legal reasoning and interpretation are repeated, with local variations, across cultures – for example, differences between purposive and literal interpretation, 'grand style' and 'formal style' reasoning, substantive and authority reasons, and more nuanced contrasts are debated in both common law and civilian legal philosophy. As important is the point that a problem that is treated as a question of law in one context may be treated as involving questions of fact or disposition by lawyers from a different tradition.[18] Generalisations about predominating or characteristic 'styles of thought' need to be treated with caution.

14 de Cruz, p 34; Zweigert and Kötz, pp 63-69. One could turn to classifications used in other disciplines, such as economics, politics, and geography.
15 de Cruz talks of the 'predominance principle' in relation to styles or mentalities, op cit, at pp 33-34.
16 On reductionism in respect of 'the lawyer', 'the legal mind', 'legal method', and 'skills' in the United States see *LIC*, Chs 16 and 17.
17 See *LIC*, Chs 16 and 17, especially pp 331-337, 348-350.
18 See the vivid account of differences of approach to international commercial arbitration by French professors, English barristers and Wall Street lawyers (all sub-groups within their own legal professions) in Yves Dezalay and Bryant Garth, *Dealing in Virtue: International Commercial Arbitration and the Construction of a Transnational Legal Order* (1996).

I have chosen the scheme of Zweigert and Kötz because I admire their book and think that their scheme is the least unsatisfactory. They are aware of the difficulties and struggle with them, but within a framework that really does not differentiate adequately between different levels of legal ordering. The difficulties are many. Some are conceptual, but more relate to the sheer complexity of the phenomena in question.

There are good reasons for taking seriously the enterprise of constructing total pictures or maps of law in the world. Setting the local in the context of the global serves the values of any form of contextual study – for example, maintaining a sense of scale and proportion; avoiding the dangers of parochialism; establishing the relationship of the subject of study to others. Furthermore, micro-comparison presupposes macro-comparison; they are complementary rather than alternatives. Even the most narrow formalist wishes to see a particular rule as part of a legal system or order; setting whole legal systems in a broader world picture is taking the process one stage further. One task for general jurisprudence is to construct such a picture for legal phenomena in the world as a whole. That is part of the synthesising function. This raises on a broader canvas some familiar, central problems of legal theory: what is the subject of our study? On what basis does one decide to draw a line between 'legal' and 'non-legal' phenomena? How can legal phenomena be classified? and so on. Most of the rather unsatisfactory debates about classifying 'legal families' have taken place very largely in the context of elementary introductions to courses on comparative law. Yet the problems of mapping law are essentially jurisprudential and their significance extends far beyond this limited context. It is a central part of understanding law from a global perspective.

4   MICRO-COMPARISON: THE COUNTRY AND WESTERN TRADITION

Let us now turn to micro-comparative studies. One of the attractions of focusing on smaller units is that they may seem to be more manageable. That is what Mr Palomar thought.

In taking stock of modern comparative law scholarship it is important to distinguish between the vast heritage of particular studies of foreign and comparative law that have been published since World War II and the way the field has been conceptualised in general terms by its more influential figures. The former is rich and very diverse; the latter is remarkably monolithic. It is my contention that the praxis of comparative law is much richer and more diverse than the predominant theory allows.

From the accounts of leading comparatists, especially in the formative period after World War II, we can construct an ideal type of the conception of mainstream 'Comparative Law' with the following characteristics:

(i)   The primary subject-matter is the positive laws and 'official' legal systems of nation states (*municipal legal systems*).

(ii)   It focuses almost exclusively on *Western capitalist societies* in Europe and the United States, with little or no detailed consideration of 'the East' (former and surviving socialist countries, including China), the 'South' (poorer countries) and richer countries of the Pacific Basin (Japan, Asian tigers).[19]

(iii) It is concerned mainly with the similarities and differences between *common law and civil law*, as exemplified by 'parent' traditions or systems, notably France and Germany for civil law, England and the United States for common law.

(iv)   It focuses almost entirely on *legal doctrine*.

(v)   It focuses in practice largely on *private law*, especially the law of obligations, which is often treated as representing 'the core' of a legal system or tradition.[20]

(vi)   The concern is with *description, analysis and explanation* rather than evaluation and prescription, except that one of the main uses of 'legislative comparative law' is typically claimed to be the lessons to be learned from foreign solutions to 'shared problems'– a claim that is theoretically problematic.[1]

This set of propositions is not a 'paradigm', nor is it intended as a caricature of actual practice.[2] Rather it is an ideal type to which most explicit *secondary accounts* of the nature and scope of comparative law and many implicit assumptions in the discourse approximate more or less closely. Here I shall assert rather than argue that this is a fair approximation to a recognisable set of ideas that have influenced the development of Western comparative law since World War II. In so far as this is correct, it is relevant to make a number of points in relation to it.

First, between about 1945 and 1980 this set of assumptions was very influential in respect of the conceptualisation of the sub-discipline and

19   A major exception was Soviet or Socialist law, which was treated as belonging to 'Comparative Law' in a way in which African, Indian, Islamic and Hindu law were not. J Barton, JL Gibbs and JH Merryman *Law in Radically Different Cultures* (1983) is an important attempt to break away from the Western model.

20   Again it worth emphasising that this is a model of the conceptualisation of 'comparative law', not of its praxis. Comparative constitutional, procedural, penal, labour law have developed rapidly in recent years.

1   On the relativity of problems, see *HTDTWR*, Ch 2.

2   Compare the ideal type of 'the Rationalist Tradition of Evidence Scholarship' *RE*, Ch 2. The models are similar in that they are rational reconstructions of widely held assumptions underlying secondary writings in two legal sub-disciplines. On the differences, see CLLT.

its institutionalisation in journals, textbooks, courses, projects, and above all ways of thought. It is still influential today. Just to take two examples. Most historical surveys of the field, including that of the admirable Zweigert and Kötz, do not include Western scholars of the stature of Derrett (Hindu Law), Schacht and Anderson (Islamic Law) and Allott, Schiller, and Read (African Law), even when they deal with these fields as part of macro-comparative law. Hardly any non-Western scholars feature in these histories. Perhaps even more remarkable is the fact that internal critics of the tradition, such as Ewald, Legrand, Markesenis and – perhaps less clearly – Alan Watson by and large do not challenge the main assumptions. Ewald, for example, in his fascinating philosophical critique of the tradition ('What was it like to try a rat?')[3] assumes throughout that comparative law is concerned with analysis of the doctrine (especially private law)[4] of 'parent' common law and civil law systems.[5]

Thus in so far as it has been influential, the model has served to exclude from the *concept* of 'comparative law' vast tracts of work, including the specialised study by Western scholars of non-Western law, studies of foreign law that were not explicitly comparative (on which more later), and cross-jurisdictional studies within the common law world – what may be termed comparative common law.[6] There is a long tradition of comparative studies within the civil law tradition. Since most legal scholars in the United States study a mythical subject called 'American law', dismissal of 'comparative common law' as methodologically uninteresting excludes most American legal scholarship, including that with an explicit comparative element. Since mainstream comparative lawyers and American legal scholars often exhibit a sophisticated awareness of the pitfalls and difficulties of comparative work, it is regrettable that there has not been a more sustained dialogue at the level of theory about such issues.

This narrow, often exclusive, concept of comparative law did not prevent more varied scholarly work from being undertaken; in recent years comparative legal studies have diversified in many directions – look, for example at the contents of the leading journals– but its conceptualisation may have marginalised some areas of work and held back theoretical development.

The Country and Western model is restricted in respect of each of its elements: municipal law, of Western nation states, with doctrine,

3   William Ewald, op cit (1995).
4   Ewald does consider the bearing of public law on the BGB, but in respect of focus does not really break out of the private law framework.
5   Apart from its colonial associations, the term is outdated: as between England and the United States, Scotland, New Zealand and Hong Kong who is 'parent'?
6   See above, Ch 6.4(b).

especially private law, and contrasts between so-called 'parent' civil and common law systems as the central focus. Each of these elements can be challenged as narrow. In some contexts such narrowing had pragmatic justifications: manageability, relevance to other subjects in the curriculum, academic respectability, and sharpness of focus. The comparative study of the French, German, and English law of obligations, for example, has attained a very high degree of sophistication and specificity. But the price has been a heavy one. Apart from the exclusions already mentioned, the label 'comparative law' has been appropriated by practitioners and critics of one particular tradition in ways that artificially isolate it from very similar work, especially in respect of shared problems of methodology. The result is that much of the secondary literature about comparative law as a field is narrowly focused, overlooks some examples of best practice, and underestimates the richness, diversity and unevenness of transnational and cosmopolitan legal studies. It neither draws on nor illuminates these neglected areas.

Comparatists sometimes insist on a quite sharp distinction between foreign and comparative law. This distinction is not sustainable for several reasons. Comparison covers a variety of activities and foreignness is a relative matter. At a theoretical level nearly all description involves comparison, which can be more or less implicit or explicit.[7] We make loose comparisons in everyday life, explicitly or implicitly, using analogies, models, metaphors, ideal types and a variety of other devices. So do comparatists. It is quite easy to show that explicit 'comparison' only exceptionally involves a precise analysis of the similarities and differences between comparable objects (molecular comparison). Some of the best work by comparatists includes examples of:

- parallel studies (eg the Bielefeld Kreis studies of precedent and interpretation of statutes);[8]
- explaining one's own system to others, such as Llewellyn's *Praejudizienrecht und Rechtsprechung in Amerika*;[9]
- looking at one's own system through foreign eyes – holding up a mirror to ourselves as in Montesquieu's *Lettres Persannes* or Lawson's *The Rational Strength of English Law*;[10]

---

7   Charles Taylor, 'Comparison, History, Truth', in *Philosophical Arguments*, (1995) at p 147.
8   Neil MacCormick and Robert Summers (eds), *Interpreting Statutes: A Comparative Study* (1991); *Interpreting Precedents: A Comparative Study* (1997). On the comparative element see below, p 191 n 2.
9   Materials linked to lectures in Leipzig (1933). The text (but not the cases) was translated into English as *The Case Law System in America* (ed Paul Gewirtz, trs M Ansaldi, 1989).
10 F H Lawson, *The Rational Strength of English Law* (1951).

- looking at a foreign system through the lenses of one's own culture; as in Lawson's *A Common Lawyer Looks at the Civil Law*;[11]
- applying foreign theories or ideas to one's own system as in Crombag, Van Koppen and Wagenaar's application of Anglo-American theories of evidence to Dutch criminal justice in *Dubieuze Zaken*, that was redacted into English as *Anchored Narratives*;[12]
- There are also admired works of Higher Legal Journalism, such as Sybille Bedford's narrative evocations in *The Faces of Justice* and Inga Markovits' marvellous East-West German diary.[13]

Comparatists tend to shy away from sustained molecular comparison. I think that this is for good reasons: on the one hand, they are aware of the many pitfalls and difficulties in dealing with complex and dynamic subject-matters; on the other hand, they have a wider range of tools than the mere cataloguing of similarities and differences. And as for foreign, whose law was 'foreign' to a Max Rheinstein or Otto Kahn Freund or Friedrich Kessler or Wolfgang Friedmann?

The Country and Western model is now out-of-date, but it has not been replaced by any coherent theory or theories. This is not to suggest that one should replace one reductionist theory by another, but rather that central issues relating to scope, method, comparability, explicit and implicit comparison, and the relationship to other enquiries need to be addressed.

This critique of the Country and Western model should not be taken as an all-out attack. Indeed, I think that it is a heritage to be valued and built on. First, there were good reasons for narrowing the focus, especially at the pioneering stage. This pragmatically motivated ideal type usefully guided development of a fragile new subject in a potentially hostile environment at a particular stage of its development. In England the pioneers such as Gutteridge, Lawson and Hamson had to emphasise the relevance, the respectability and the practical value of their field as part of their struggle for acceptance in the academy. Basil Markesenis, building on them, plays on similar themes in arguing for a more central place for comparative law in our legal culture.[14] Secondly, as I have already noted, there were benefits as well as costs, not least in the quality of some of the work done within the Country and Western framework.

---

11   F H Lawson, *A Common Lawyer Looks at the Civil Law* (1963, 1977).
12   Hans Crombag, Peter Van Koppen, and Willem Wagenaar, *Dubieuze Zaken* (1992), *Anchored Narratives* (1993).
13   Mirjan Damaska paid homage to Sybille Bedford in the title of his masterpiece, *Faces of Justice and State Authority* (1986), itself a rare legal work which uses ideal types as a tool of sustained comparative analysis. Cf Inga Markovits, *Imperfect Justice: An East-West German Diary* (1995). Sybille Bedford was a journalist and novelist; Inga Markovits is an outstanding comparative lawyer.
14   Markesenis (1997).

We should not just dismiss this part of our heritage. In my view work done within the Country and Western Tradition stands to comparative law as classical music stands to music: it is the best we have.

However, the model no longer fits what is being done in the name of comparative law, let alone work that has been excluded from the label. The Country and Western model has four main weaknesses: it is narrowly conceived; it has been artificially isolated from cognate fields; it is out of date; and it is under-theorised. What is lacking is a coherent view of the enterprise and above all sustained discussion of shared issues of comparability, method, levels, objectives and so on across a broader range of enquiries. One result of this is that those who do comparative work – that is most of us[15] – do not get sufficient help and guidance from theory by way of synthesis, conceptual clarification, middle order theorising, critical evaluation of assumptions and presuppositions. In short the jobs of jurisprudence are not being adequately performed for comparative or cosmopolitan legal studies. So the time is ripe for some quite radical rethinking.

5   RETHINKING COMPARATIVE LAW: A THEORETICAL AGENDA

I have suggested that one of the implications of globalisation for our discipline is that it requires a revival of general jurisprudence and a rethinking of comparative law from a global perspective as key elements in cosmopolitan legal studies. Rethinking comparative law will involve all of the main tasks of legal theory including synthesis, construction and elucidation of concepts, critical development of general normative principles, developing middle order theories, both empirical and normative, and working theories providing guidance to various kinds of participants, including comparatists, intellectual history, and the critical examination of assumptions and presuppositions underlying legal

15   Again, it is important to distinguish between provenance, audiences, focus, sources and significance. For example in the next 20 years one might hypothesise that: (a) most legal scholars will be rooted in one primary legal tradition and academic culture (provenance); (b) the processes of globalisation, such as the development of systems of communication, will tend to broaden and diversify potential *audiences*, but many consumers of legal scholarship will remain predominantly local; (c) while the *focus* of legal studies will rapidly extend to other levels than that of municipal law, a high proportion of legal studies will continue to be microscopic and local; and (d) few legal scholars will be able to be strongly parochial in respect of primary and secondary *sources* and hence of ideas; and (e) there will be increased transnational networking among scholars, but how that will play out in terms of significance of locally focused works is unpredictable. On the distinctions between provenance, audiences, focus, and sources see above at pp 128-129.

discourse.[16] This is a daunting programme that is beyond the capacity of a single Mr Palomar.

Even outlining such a programme is a large undertaking, which must be left to another occasion. But it may be appropriate to end by suggesting a few examples of the kind of tasks that I think are involved.

One goal should be to build up a total picture of law-in-the-world as the subject-matter of our discipline. This is the synthesising or mapping function of legal theory. But maps presuppose concepts and reliable, systematic data. So these tasks are to some extent anterior to developing such an overview.

Construction and elucidation of concepts has been the traditional concern of analytical jurisprudence. Bentham's list of terms which he saw it to be the task of universal jurisprudence to expound was quite short: '... obligation, right, power, possession, title, exemption, immunity, franchise, privilege, nullity, validity and the like'.[17] Austin's list of 'the principles, notions and distinctions which are the subject of General Jurisprudence' was only a little longer.[18] Their successors did not extend the list much further. English analytical jurists largely confined themselves to concepts involved in or presupposed by exposition of legal rules that is 'law talk' rather than 'talk about law'.[19] A broader conception of the discipline would have extended to analysis of concepts such as group, dispute, institution, process, function, decision, regulation, efficiency and effectiveness. Some of these are shared with and have been developed in neighbouring disciplines, but analytical jurisprudence also needs to extend its focus to key concepts in specialised sub-disciplines concerned with law, including constitutional theory, law and economics, legal sociology, and socio-legal studies.[20]

The brevity of the lists of the nineteenth-century analytical jurists exhibits some sensitivity to the difficulty of constructing a terminology that crosses cultures. As jurisprudence became more particular this problem became less of an issue. Some of the classics of modern analytical jurisprudence, such as Hart and Honoré's *Causation in the Law*, are understandably quite particular. Of course, questions of the translatability of legal concepts have long exercised the minds of comparatists and so there is a vast heritage of sophisticated analysis to

16 On the functions of legal theory within the discipline of law, see above, Ch 1.3.
17 *A Fragment on Government* (eds J H Burns and H L A Hart, 1977) at p 6; cf *Works*, iii p 217 (Bowring edition). He makes clear that this list is illustrative. See above, Ch 2.1.
18 J Austin, 'The Uses of the Study of Jurisprudence', (1863, ed Hart, 1954) at 367-369. See above Ch 2.2(b).
19 *LIC*, p 223.
20 *LIC*, pp 168-169.

draw on. However, most of this has taken place in the context of micro-comparative studies of only a few, usually two, Western legal systems. To date there has not been a sustained debate, comparable to the 'emics'/'etics' debate in anthropology,[1] about the difficulties, or even the possibility, of constructing a more general and broader meta-language for law. However, such a debate would not be starting from scratch.[2]

At a particular level there is room for a great deal of work on the transferability of particular concepts across different cultures. The harmonisation of global statistics about law requires reasonably transferable concepts. I find it intriguing, for example, that 'legal person' travels better than 'lawyer'; 'prison' is more transferable than 'court' or 'judge' or 'trial'; and that Transparency International claims to have developed a workable definition of 'corruption', a concept that one might expect to be culturally sensitive.[3]

Another task for analytical jurisprudence is to help to analyse critically the basic terminology of comparative studies. A common complaint is that comparatists claim that 'comparative law is a method, not a subject', but they do not tell us what the method is.[4] That may not be totally fair criticism, but as an outsider I have been struck by the relative lack of concern for the conceptual issues that bear directly on the methodology of comparison. For example, what is 'comparison' and how does it relate to description, abstraction, classification, induction, and generalisation?[5] What are the conditions of 'comparability'? Can a clear distinction be maintained between explicit and implicit comparison? Or between 'molecular' and 'holistic' comparison? Can 'parallel studies', 'seeing ourselves as others see us', or 'a common lawyer looks at the civil law', or

1 The terms are taken from linguistics, reflecting the distinction between phonemics (study of basics units of a given language) and phonetics (the general study of speech sounds). See above, p 43n.
2 There are some suggestive examples in the attempt of the Bielefeld Kreis to construct a meta-language for comparing precedent and interpretation of statutes in several Western societies, see especially MacCormick and Summers (1991, 1997) above, p 187n. Interestingly, Summers is quite sanguine about the possibilities in this context, but in an earlier work Atiyah and Summers concluded that even such basic concepts such as 'a rule' and 'legal validity' (surely strong candidates for inclusion in a meta-language for general jurisprudence) mean significantly different things in English and American legal cultures (1987) at p 420, cf pp 264-266.
3 Corruption is broadly defined as 'the misuse of public power for private profit.' Jeremy Pope, *The TI Sourcebook* (1997) Ch 1. See further Transparency International, *Annual Reports*. See above, Ch 6.5(b).
4 Watson (1974), pp 1-2.
5 See S M Mellone, *Elements of Modern Logic* (2nd edn, 1970) discussing J S Mill, Logic, *A System of Logic*, 2 vols, (1st edn, 1843).

explaining one's own legal system to a foreign audience, count as clear examples of 'comparison'?[6]

In my excursions into the literature, one point that has struck me quite forcibly is the absence of the idea of 'comparators' – that is standards, measures or indicators that provide a basis of comparison.[7] This seems particularly surprising because, in an era of increasing bureaucratisation, some standards have become extraordinarily influential. Comparators may be empirical, such as measures of weight or time or length; they may be explicitly normative, eg international human rights norms or they may be a mixture of the two, such as infant mortality rates. Standards may be applied to individual examples, or as a basis for comparing two or more phenomena, or in the process of compiling 'league tables'.[8] They may be explicit, as with the human rights industry,[9] or they may be arcane or largely implicit, as seems to be the case with many of the measures and indicators used by the World Bank and other Western agencies in determining whether a country is living up to the ideals of 'good governance, human rights and democracy'. Similar considerations apply to the growing movement for 'democratic audit'[10] and 'corruption'.[11] I find it quite remarkable that these phenomena are not generally perceived to fall under the rubric of comparative law; I find it disturbing that these alleged universal or general standards are not often subjected to sustained critical analysis.

There are many other topics deserving attention, such as the need for a more comprehensive intellectual history[12] or issues relating to

6   See above, pp 187-188.
7   There has been some discussion by comparatists of the idea of a 'tertium comparationis', eg R Sacco, 'Legal Formants II' 39 American Journal of Comparative Law 343 (1991). This debate deals with only one aspect of what is covered by the concept of 'comparators' as used in the text. I am grateful to John Bell for drawing my attention to the debate.
8   See further above, Ch 6.5.
9   Apart from governmental publications, there is an increasing number of private assessments of human rights performance, for example, Freedom House, *Freedom in the World: The Annual Survey of Political Rights and Civil Liberties* (1978- , 1996-7); Lawyers' Committee for Human Rights, *Critique*: Review of US Department of State's Country Reports on Human Rights Practices for 1995 (Annual, 1978 , 1996); Charles Humana, *World Human Rights Guide* (1983, 1986, 3rd edn, 1992).
10 See, for example, F Klug, K Starmer and S Weir, *Three Pillars of Liberty* (1996); D Beetham, *Auditing Democracy in Britain* (Charter 88 Trust, 1993).
11 See Transparency International, above Ch 6.5.
12 A historical account of the different histories of Western studies of foreign and comparative law in the twentieth century, including Roman law scholarship, studies of non-Western traditions and systems, law and development work, legal anthropology, and reports by foreign 'experts' could be of immense value in providing a solid basis for considering methodological issues involved in cross-cultural and comparative legal studies. I would personally favour a Collingwoodian

methodology, such as problems of cross-level comparison,[13] what basic guidance in the form of working theories that might be given to legal scholars and students about the pitfalls of handling foreign material, or to those involved in transnational law-making and unification. The disdain for concern with methodology expressed by Zweigert and Kötz in successive editions of their *An Introduction to Comparative Law*[14] may have had some justification in an introductory work in an earlier period, but hardly fits today's needs. If comparative law is to become the linchpin of the development of an intellectually ambitious and disciplined approach to cosmopolitan legal studies, we need to take theoretical problems of comparison more seriously.

---

approach that looked at the problems from the point of view of the authors and their primary audiences (see 'R G Collingwood's Autobiography: One Reader's Response' (1998) 25. *Journal of Law and Society* 603).

13 See Renaud Dehousse, op cit (1994), which could be usefully extended to comparison across other levels; cf Ian Ward, op cit (1995). The literature on problems of cross-level comparison is more developed in other social sciences, especially international relations, anthropology and sociology.

14 Repeated in the latest (1998) edition at p 33.

Chapter 8

Globalisation, post-modernism, and pluralism: Santos, Haack, and Calvino*

'*The symbolic cartography of law reinforces [my] conception of legal plurality – not the legal pluralism of traditional legal anthropology, in which the different legal orders are conceived as separate entities coexisting in the same political space, but rather, the conception of different legal spaces superimposed, interpenetrated, and mixed in our minds, as much as in our actions, either on occasions of qualitative leaps or sweeping crises in our life trajectories, or in the dull routine of eventless everyday life. We live in a time of porous legality or of legal porosity, multiple networks of legal orders forcing us to constant transitions and trespassings. Our legal life is constituted by the intersection of different legal orders, that is, by interlegality. Interlegality is the phenomenological counterpart of legal pluralism, and a key concept in a postmodern conception of law.*' (Santos)

'*The crucial question of how to reconstruct in postmodern architecture, the connections between the social and the legal finds a highly vague answer: interpenetrating, intertwined, superposed mutually constitutive, dialectical … We are left with ambiguity and confusion. After all this is the very charm of postmodernism.*' (Gunther Teubner)

'*Only in Marco Polo's accounts was Kublai Khan able to discern, through walls and towers destined to crumble, the tracery of a pattern so subtle it could escape the termites' gnawing.*' (Italo Calvino)

*   This essay is published here for the first time. Thanks are due to Terry Anderson, Christopher McCrudden and participants in seminars in Berkeley, London, Miami, and Warwick for comments on early drafts of the essay or particular sections, and especially to Susan Haack for patiently explaining her ideas and for saving me from error and imprecision, though not always from heresy.

1 INTRODUCTION

'Post-modernism', 'post-Marxism', 'post-structuralism' – such terms are boasts claiming superiority over the past. They imply: 'We know better now'. 'Globalisation' also suggests something grandiose. Post-modernism and globalisation are both in fashion. Combine the two and one has a dangerous liaison. But beneath these conceits may be some more modest truths that are worth rescuing.

In 'Globalisation and Legal Theory' I have attempted a preliminary exploration of how far the ideas of some mainstream Anglo-American jurists might be responsive to the challenges of globalisation and the need for a new general jurisprudence. The argument was essentially conservative in that it suggested that there is much in our heritage of canonical texts that is worth preserving and using in this changing situation.

This essay steps outside the canon to consider a rather different work, *Toward a New Common Sense* by Boaventura de Sousa Santos. This is perhaps the first major book to address directly central issues relating to globalisation and legal theory from a post-modern perspective. My essay has three main objectives: first, to try to make Santos's difficult, but important, work more accessible to non-specialist readers; secondly, to explore some ideas loosely associated with 'post-modernism' by considering Santos and Calvino in relation to one of the most trenchant critics of such ideas, Susan Haack;[1] and, thirdly, to clarify my own position in relation to some of Santos's main themes. This essay, then, is a 'conversational' reading of a work that I have found stimulating and irritating in almost equal measure.[2] I side with Haack in rejecting several of the more extravagant philosophical claims made by post-modernists, while being broadly in sympathy with some of their central concerns and ideas at less abstract levels. I shall argue that this does not quite amount to accepting Santos's conclusions while rejecting his premises, but there is a puzzle that needs teasing out.

'Post-modernism' is a notoriously vague label. Haack deliberately avoids using the term in her *Manifesto of a Passionate Moderate*. Calvino refused to be so categorised.[3] Santos, while acknowledging the ambiguity

---

1   The main works considered in this essay are Boaventura de Sousa Santos, *Toward a New Common Sense: Law, Science and Politics in Paradigmatic Transition* (1995) (hereafter *TNC*); Italo Calvino, *Invisible Cities* (tr W Weaver, 1974, hereafter *IC*) and *Mr Palomar* (tr W Weaver, 1985, hereafter *MP*); and Susan Haack, *Manifesto of a Passionate Moderate* (1998)(hereafter *Manifesto*).

2   On the distinction between historical and conversational reading see *RB*.

3   Calvino hated to be pigeon-holed, but some of his work, especially *Invisible Cities*, has several characteristics associated with post-modern style. It is playful, ironic, multi-layered, subversive of boundaries, and may even fit Santos's idea of the baroque.

of the term,[4] explicitly advances a 'post-modern theory of law.'[5] I shall treat Santos's ideas, as expounded in *Towards a New Commonsense*, as fairly representative of a congeries of ideas and attitudes now fashionable in academic law. I shall suggest that Santos combines two tendencies in post-modernism that need to be differentiated. First, *imaginative post-modernism* which emphasises the elusiveness of reality, the fallibility of what passes for established knowledge, the importance of attending to multiple perspectives and points of view, a resistance to closure, and a playful style that treats metaphor and imagination as necessary to understanding complex phenomena. Within certain limits, I find these tendencies both congenial and intellectually acceptable. However, these tendencies often spill over into *irrationalist post-modernism*, which seems to involve commitment to strong versions of cultural relativism, epistemological scepticism, anti-rationalism, and irrealism.[6] I say 'seems', because much of this kind of writing, illustrated by Santos's first two chapters, is characterised by a lack of clarity, so that one cannot tell whether what is being said is just meaningless or involves commitment to strong versions of scepticism or is an exaggerated way of expressing sensible ideas that can be articulated more clearly and simply.

In the next section I shall suggest that Santos combines both tendencies, that Italo Calvino can be interpreted as exemplifying imaginative post-modernism without being committed to anti-rationalist positions, and that Susan Haack convincingly steers a path between the two by robust debunking of the anti-rationalist version while allowing space for other strands, with some of which I am probably more in sympathy than she is.

In section 4 I shall suggest that Santos's views on many issues concerning globalisation and legal theory are quite close to mine, especially in emphasising the complexity, fluidity and elusiveness of legal phenomena, but that these views owe nothing to irrationalist post-modernism. Thus this essay can be read as an attempt to reconcile my rejection of some aspects of post-modernist metaphysics and epistemology with finding much affinity with Calvino's playful, sometimes melancholy, complexities and Santos's global perspective on law.

---

4   Eg at 1x-x.
5   Eg at p 473.
6   Haack links 'irrealism' with Nelson Goodman (*Manifesto*, Ch 9). In legal contexts the term is used with a conspicuous lack of clarity, see eg Kenneth Graham Jr's '"Irrealist Theory of Evidence" in '"There'll Always be an England": The Instrumental Ideology of Evidence', (1987) 85 Michigan Law Review 1204 (a satirical critique of my model of the Rationalist Tradition of Evidence Scholarship in *TEBW*).

2.   TOWARD A NEW COMMON SENSE

(a)   Standpoints and Concerns: Santos and Twining

Although our views converge on a number of specific issues in legal theory, Santos and I have different starting-points and concerns. The main difference is that my standpoint is that of an English jurist concerned with the health of the discipline of law; Santos is concerned with the development of law itself, as well as its study. We are writing within very different time-frames: my interest is in the future development of the study of law in the medium-term – say the next 10 to 20 years. Santos deals with the long-term future of law itself. The closing words of the book are: 'The patience of Utopia is infinite'.[7]

At the time he wrote the book, Santos was Professor of Sociology at the University of Coimbra in Portugal and a regular visitor at the University of Wisconsin Law School. He studied law first at Coimbra, then in Germany, and in the late 1960s at Yale Law School. In chapter 3 he gives an engaging autobiographical account of an intellectual odyssey that took him through legal dogmatics and criminology to law and development, to field work in the squatter settlements in Brazil, eventually developing a position of a post-Marxist, post-modern, sociologist of law and social theorist.[8] Substantial parts of the book had been published before and, although they have been extensively revised, the work moves among a variety of levels and has a feeling of fragmentation that makes it difficult to read. Unity is imposed on the contents in the first and last parts by an intellectually ambitious and abstract statement of a general social theory. The result is rather like a gigantic sandwich containing a variety of succulent ingredients held together by a less appealing outer casing. I usually advise my students to begin with the filling and only to chew through the outer casing later, if they feel so inclined.

Santos's standpoint is that of a sociologist and social theorist advancing a thesis about the breakdown of modernity and the emergence of a new 'paradigm'. '[I]t is the purpose of the book as a whole to identify some of the constitutive elements of a postmodern understanding of law.'[9]

The aims of Part II are stated more concretely:

---

7   At p 519.
8   An earlier version of Santos's memoir was published in Robin Luckham (ed), *Law and Social Enquiry* (1981). This is a collection of research autobiographies and case studies. It sets Santos's intellectual development in the broader historical context of early efforts to do empirical fieldwork in the sociology and anthropology of law.
9   At p 5.

'My purpose is to show (a) that the legal field in contemporary societies and in the world system as a whole is a far more complex and richer landscape than has been assumed by liberal political theory; (b) that such a field is a constellation of different legalities (and illegalities) operating in local, national and transnational time-spaces; (c) and finally that, thus conceived, law has both a regulatory or even repressive potential and an emancipatory potential, the latter being much greater than the model of normal change has ever postulated; the way law's potential evolves, whether towards regulation or emancipation, has nothing to do with the autonomy or self-reflexiveness of law, but rather with the political mobilization of competing forces.'[10]

Santos advances his explicitly political thesis from the vantage point of a sociologist of law who has read widely in several other disciplines, especially political economy, legal anthropology, and international relations. He also enters boldly, perhaps rashly, into debates in the physical sciences, but pays rather little attention to micro-economics,[11] socio-legal studies and mainstream legal theory, which he tends to lump together under the tendentious label of 'liberal legalism'.

My standpoint is that of a mainstream English jurist interested in the implications of globalisation for legal theory and the discipline of law. Since I am writing from within the tradition of modernity, and in a more modest time-frame, I shall unabashedly adopt what Santos calls a 'subparadigmatic perspective'.[12] Santos's work is politically committed; the sociological analyses in Part II claim to adopt the perspective 'of the oppressed social classes and groups';[13] the overall objective is to proclaim and to advance a utopian dream. Set beside this my own standpoint may seem mundane, cautious and rather apolitical.[14] We have different

10 At p 111. I have strong reservations about the philosophical underpinnings (see below), but generally agree with the more concrete formulations in (a) and (b); and I am sympathetic to, but not fully persuaded by (c).

11 Santos also tends to gloss over sceptical views about globalisation, such as those of Paul Hirst and Grahame Thompson, *Globalization in Question* (1996).

12 Eg pp 121-122. On the misuse of the Kuhnian idea of 'paradigm shifts' see below, p 200.

13 xi.

14 Santos and I both have commitments to certain values, but we are involved in enterprises of different kinds. On my general position see *LIC* at pp 23-25. I agree with Santos that there is an intimate connection between law and power and so the study of law is 'political' in a broad sense. As a scholar my commitment is to a set of values embodied in Peirce's notion of 'the scientific attitude', that is open-minded pursuit of knowledge and understanding and a belief that truth and reason are important. I have considerable reservations about talk of capitalist or sexist or racist science, unless this means that actual enquiries have sometimes been used to bolster such ideological commitments – which is, of course, a denial of the scientific attitude.

projects. Our standpoints, concerns, time-frames, and objectives clearly differ.[15] The meeting-point is looking at law from a global perspective.

(b) The Plot of Santos's Book

Toward a New Common Sense is divided into four parts. Part I, headed 'Towards a Paradigmatic Transition in Science and Law', is an ambitious exercise in social theory. Part II consists of a series of sociological studies or forays that range from the very local to the global. This includes accounts of his fieldwork in Brazil and the fragment of autobiography already alluded to, interleaved in playful mode in his report on Pasagarda law. Part III uses the metaphor of mapping to present in more detail his theoretical reconstruction of the many landscapes of law within modernity and beyond. This part includes his best-known essay 'Law: A Map of Misreading', which will be discussed below. Part IV returns to the visionary level to give an abstract and openly Utopian account of 'the main parameters of the emancipatory struggles in the paradigmatic transition'.[16]

It is worth emphasising that by no means all of the text is lumbered with sociological abstractions and jargon. The book, especially Parts II and III, is much more readable than this brief summary suggests.

In the following sections I shall first set out why I do not accept Santos's version of postmodernism at the level of philosophy. I shall then explore more positively our respective, and largely convergent, views on globalisation, legal pluralism, mapping, and an alternative agenda for general jurisprudence, suggesting that mine is more modest and more cautious, but is not necessarily incompatible with some aspects of Santos's bolder vision.

---

15 This does not mean that I necessarily *disagree* with Santos's diagnosis of modernity or his vision of the future. Much of his analysis seems to me to be at least plausible, if rather abstract and often unclear. On some aspects I am agnostic. For example, I simply do not know whether we are coming to the end of the age of capitalism or of an era of modernity, or whether there is about to be a genuine revolution in law and legal theory.

16 At p xii. Throughout the book Santos uses the word 'emancipatory' without precisely specifying emancipation from what. The main thrust throughout seems to be 'the emancipatory struggles of oppressed social groups ... from a societal paradigm, based on an unequal and unfair capitalist world system ...' (p 477).

3   TWO STRANDS IN POST-MODERNISM

(a)   Santos and Haack

'Post-modernism' is a term that originated in art, literature and architecture to designate a reaction against 'modernism'. Over time it has spread to most enclaves of intellectual culture, including law. 'Modernism' (or modernity) is a vague term and the reactions against modernism have been varied. In Jurisprudence, the term 'post-modernism', like 'positivism' and 'realism', is both vague and ambiguous. It has also been stretched and extended to cover almost any novel, or not-so-novel, idea. This leads to a tendency to bring together some incongruous bedfellows. It is sometimes claimed that we are all post-modernists now. If that means that all jurists participate in contemporary intellectual trends, that may be largely true, but is trivial. If it means that we are suckers for fashion, I hope that it is untrue.

Santos claims to be a post-modernist, but understandably distances himself from some of the ideas loosely associated with the term.[17] He explains his version largely in negative terms as representing a break from 'the socio-cultural paradigm of modernity'.[18] He gives a coherent, if rather abstract, account of 'modernity', and so defines in general terms what is being reacted against. Since his vision purports to be emancipatory, revolutionary, and utopian, the alternative is less specific. If, as I do, one deplores the current tendency to categorise almost any novel idea as a 'paradigm shift', one approaches his thesis with caution.[19]

For Santos 'modernity' is the label for the dominant mode of Western thought which began to emerge in the sixteenth century, received its greatest boost with the French Revolution and the Enlightenment, and remained dominant in the West until the middle to late twentieth century. Modernity preceded the rise of capitalism, but became closely associated with it. Modernity 'will disappear before capitalism ceases to be dominant'.[20] Santos claims that the main ideas associated with modernity

17   Eg he argues that 'the grain of truth' in post-modernity lies in the fact that in a period 'of paradigmatic transition' the new paradigm can only be defined inadequately *TNC* at p 1.
18   At p 1.
19   My personal ambivalence towards post-modernism is in part attributable to the fact that I assimilated some of the ideas associated with it from R G Collingwood over forty years ago in versions that now seem either more moderate or as cranky as those that are currently touted as 'novel' (see (1998) 25 Journal Law and Society 603). As I do not accept a reductionist concept of 'modernity', there seems to be no coherent 'ism' in the negative or reactive, let alone the positive, aspects.
20   Ibid.

are epistemological. They are rich, complex and internally 'contradictory':

'It is based on two pillars, the pillar of regulation and the pillar of emancipation, each of them constituted of three principles or logics. The pillar of regulation is constituted by the state, formulated most prominently by Hobbes, the principle of the market, developed by Locke and Adam Smith in particular, and the principle of the community, which presides over Rousseau's social and political theory. The principle of the state consists of the vertical political obligation between citizens and the state. The principle of the market consists in the horizontal self-interested or antagonistic obligation among market partners. The principle of the community consists in the horizontal solidary, political obligation among community members and associations. The pillar of emancipation is constituted by three logics of rationality as identified by Weber: aesthetic-expressive-rationality of the arts and literature, the cognitive-instrumental rationality of science and technology, the moral-practical rationality of ethics and the rule of law.'[1]

According to Santos, the rise of capitalism led to emphasis on instrumental-technical regulation in furthering an ideal of a social order based on science at the expense of the other two forms of rationality. In jurisprudence modernity is associated with legal positivism, liberal legalism, and the equation of legal science with legal dogmatics.[2] Under this paradigm law has had an important, but secondary place, as the main instrument of technocratic management of society. All of this looks like a nutshell of a vaguely familiar post-Marxist interpretation of the 'paradigm of liberal legal ideology'.

Santos's central argument is that modernity is in crisis. It has exhausted its potential and is in process of being replaced by a post-modern paradigm which could be built on the emancipatory possibilities of traditions and cultures that have been marginalised by the conjunction of modernity and capitalism. In Santos's view we now are in a position to diagnose this crisis in modernity in some detail. However, it is less easy to be precise about the likely characteristics of the new paradigm, since we are in a time of 'paradigmatic transition'. Santos's projection of the future is a remarkably optimistic and Utopian vision of the potential for a more democratic, just and communitarian world based on a *paradigm of prudent knowledge for a decent life*' or 'a re-enchanted common sense'.[3]

1   At p 2.
2   At p 39 and Ch 2 *passim*.
3   Preface, p ix.

'Common sense' here refers to the forms of knowledge that individuals and communities create and use to give meaning to their practices. Santos emphasises that 'common sense' is not monolithic; under capitalism different 'common senses' have dominated in at least six different contexts or loci: the household, the workplace, the marketplace, the community, the citizenplace (nation state), and the world. Refreshingly, he distances himself here from the tendency to set common sense and science in opposition to each other. This accords with the view of 'general experience' (a society's 'stock of knowledge' or stock of beliefs) which has been developed within evidence theory as providing warrants for inferences in argumentation about questions of fact. The standard concept of 'general experience' includes generalisations accepted by the scientific community, 'horse sense' based on experience, more speculative beliefs, proverbs, stereotypes and myths.[4] Santos's categorisation could usefully be applied in this more specialised context.

Santos interprets the 'crisis of modernity' largely in terms of epistemology. For him, the crisis is most clearly seen in modern science. He draws on contemporary debates in some natural sciences and mathematics which suggest that traditional claims to authority and knowledge are as sharply contested as they are in the arts and social sciences. Einstein, Heisenberg, Gödel and others, as well as developments in fields such as astrophysics, micro-physics, neuro-science and socio-biology, are invoked to illustrate the challenges to modernity to be found within the natural sciences. Few lawyers, myself included, can judge how far this is an accurate or balanced interpretation of such developments. If this suggests that sustained challenges to institutionalised claims to the authority of science based on well-warranted results are new, this seems rather dubious. It is part of the enterprise of science that its authoritative claims should be always susceptible to challenge. If this involves a denial of cumulation of knowledge or, dare one say it, progress in science, one has one's doubts.[5] One is also left wondering whether this display of erudition is really necessary as a prologue to a post-modern theory of law. It locates Santos's vision in a broad intellectual context, but for a legal audience it may set up some unnecessary barriers.

Far from seeing this crisis in modernity as a quagmire, Santos presents an apocalyptic, eloquent, unspecific, and romantic vision of the possible

---

4   See William Twining, 'Civilians Don't Try', (1997) 5 Cardozo Journal of International and Comparative Law 69 and 'Generalizations and Narrative in Argumentation about Questions of Fact', (1999) 40 Southern Texas Law Review 101.

5   On progress in science, see *Manifesto*, Ch 5, especially pp 99-100 (steering a middle course between the excessive optimism of the Old Deferentialists and the excessive pessimism of the New Cynicism).

realisation of an emancipatory communitarian legal and political order. Santos imagines his utopia not in terms of a programme, but rather through three linked metaphors: the Frontier, the Baroque and the South.[6] Each represents a form of 'subjectivity' that has been repressed or, at least marginalised, by modernity. The frontier mentality is fluid, open to strangers, new ideas and the reinvention of tradition, mixing heritages and inventions, weak on hierarchy, and disdainful of boundaries. The baroque represents the aesthetic, playful, ironic, irreverent, given to rhetorical exaggeration that 'resides in disproportion, laughter, and subversion'.[7] The South, less clearly articulated, represents the rise of an emancipatory consciousness of the oppressed, exemplified by Gandhi, but not specified in advance as to the form it will take. Santos urges his audience to recognise the South, go South, and learn from the South.[8] Santos's utopia involves a conjunction of the three metaphors, so that none is privileged.

Some readers may dismiss this part of *Toward a New Common Sense* as incomprehensible. I personally find the metaphors intriguing, but frustratingly vague. As one commentator put it, Santos's 'evocation of the baroque is, well, a bit baroque'.[9] Others have pointed out that each of these metaphors, especially that of the South, is open to quite negative interpretations.[10] I read these chapters (and Santos's subsequent address) with enjoyment and scepticism in equal measure.

Santos's account of the crisis of modernity is a highly compressed piece of potted history. Such sweeping generalisations about broad intellectual trends are difficult to assess. They are so abstract and so hedged around with qualifiers that they are not specific enough to criticise. Like generalised accounts of schools or movements in legal or political thought, they may seem broadly true, yet misleading in their

6   Santos subsequently developed the metaphors in an address to the Law and Society Association in Toronto in 1995. This, together with six comments, is published in a symposium in (1995) 29 Law and Society Review 569ff. As I understand it, Santos's three metaphors are his way of articulating his vision of utopia: 'By utopia I mean the exploration by imagination of new modes of human possibility and styles of will, and the confrontation by imagination of the necessity of whatever exists – just because it exists – on behalf of something radically better that is worth fighting for, and to which humanity is fully entitled' (*TNC* at p 479).

7   At p 503.

8   Ibid at p 580. Here Santos follows Chomsky, but gives more emphasis to 'learning from the South'. However, in this context he only discusses Gandhi, and that quite briefly, and does not take the opportunity to suggest what 'unheard voices' among 'southern' jurists merit more attention.

9   Ie, per Webster's Dictionary: 'extravagant or farfetched arguments in scholastic syllogisms ... odd, bizarre, grotesque, exaggerated, and overdecorated', Rosemary Coombe (1995), Symposium, op cit, 599, at 603.

10 Eg Coombe, op cit, J. Brigham, p 589.

simplicity. However, in the second chapter Santos commits himself to some specific ideas that have been fashionable in post-modern writings, but which I believe can be shown to be bad philosophy.

Rather than go into great detail about the philosophical underpinnings of a book that I think is of real value at a different level, I shall briefly contrast Santos's main philosophical claims with Susan Haack's *Manifesto of a Passionate Moderate*.[11] This is a formidable philosopher's debunking of 'recent fads, fashions, and false dichotomies',[12] and of anti-scientific exaggerations and irrationalist tendencies in the current intellectual climate. Her position seems to me to dispose of the core ideas of anti-rationalist post-modernism, while leaving space for what I find attractive in imaginative post-modernism.

Haack depicts herself as an 'old-fashioned prig', 'an old feminist', and, engagingly, as 'the still small voice that whispers "bosh"'. An admirer of Charles Sanders Peirce, she is mainly concerned with philosophy. She distances herself from some of the standard targets of post-modernism, such as 'foundationalism',[13] metaphysical realism (that there is one true description of the real world, which consists of a fixed totality of mind-independent objects),[14] and what she calls the 'Old Deferentialism', or 'scientism', that is the belief that there 'must be a uniquely rational method of inquiry exclusive to the sciences'.[15]

Haack draws a clear distinction between metaphysics and epistemology.[16] Her *Evidence and Inquiry* is a work of epistemology.[17] In *Manifesto of a Passionate Moderate* she further adopts a metaphysical

11   Ibid.
12   The false dichotomies are revealing: '*either* scientistic philosophy *or* philosophy as "just a kind of writing"; *either* metaphor as an abuse of language *or* metaphor as ubiquitous and philosophy, even the sciences, as genres of literature; *either* the Old Deferentialism, *or* the New Cynicism; *either* scientific knowledge as a mere social construction *or* a denial of the internal organization and external context of scientific work; *either* the scholastic rigidities of analytic epistemology *or* wild and woolly "feminist epistemology"; *either* preferential hiring of women, etc. *or* the Old Boy network; and so forth and so on' (at p 5).
13   On the ambiguity of 'foundationalism' see below, p 206 n 4.
14   At p 153.
15   At p 3.
16   'Epistemology' refers to theories of knowledge: evidence, the justification of beliefs, more or less warranted claims, procedures and methods of enquiry, and foundationalist versus coherentist theories of justification belong here. 'Metaphysics' refers to theories of reality, truth, the problem of universals, realism versus anti-realisms etc. 'Innocent realism' is a theory within metaphysics. Haack's *Evidence and Inquiry* (1993) is a work of epistemology, as is her 'foundherentism' which convincingly, in my view, steers a path between foundationalist and coherentist theories of justification (*not* of truth). Questions about what is true, and how we know what truth is, belong to metaphysics. Questions about what we know and justifications for belief belong to epistemology. *Manifesto* includes arguments that belong to both domains. Post-

position that she labels 'innocent realism'.[18] Since this articulates simply and much better than I can a more plausible metaphysics than one finds in fashionable post-modernism or its standard targets, it is worth restating it briefly:[19]

1. There is one real world.
2. This world is largely independent of us.
3. Whether a synthetic description is true or false depends on what it says and how the world is.[20]
4. There are many true descriptions of the world; such descriptions can be combined into a single conjunctive description; but incompatible descriptions cannot be jointly true.[1]
5. Innocent realism can accommodate three concerns of Hilary Putnam's thesis of 'conceptual relativity': viz that vocabularies may vary and may change; that no one vocabulary is privileged; and that perception involves conceptualisation and interpretation.[2]

---

modernists seem to tend to run epistemology and metaphysics together, almost invariably committing 'the passes for fallacy', (ie the argument that because what 'passes for' truth is often no such thing, therefore there is no objective truth. See further below, p 217 n 8). Haack attacks Richard Rorty and Stephen Stich for proclaiming the end of epistemology and dismissing the idea of objective truth as meaningless. Santos distinguishes epistemology and ontology at the start of the book (*TNC*, p 7), but seemingly conflates metaphysics and epistemology for the rest of the first two chapters, claiming to focus almost entirely on a new epistemology. It is not clear to me whether he clearly is guilty of 'the passes for fallacy'. I am grateful to Susan Haack for help with this note, but I am responsible for the formulation. Of course, our views may not be identical on all of the issues referred to here, but any significant differences (some not yet resolved) are not germane to this essay.

17 Op cit.
18 Haack's realism is 'innocent' because it is simple, commonsensical and unspecific. It was meant to convey 'not unnecessarily complex and loaded with strange metaphysical commitments, but not naive, either' (communication to the author). The lack of specificity is deliberate, leaving space for a variety of ideas and positions. Haack suggests that amplification of the caveat that the world is *largely* independent of us would involve 'some loss of innocence' (p 158). This seems a neat way of postponing some of the central questions of interpretive sociology which has to concern itself with internal points of view (see below, pp 216-217).
19 This restatement is based on *Manifesto*, especially Ch 9. Haack's views are further developed in 'Realisms and their Rivals: Recovering our Innocence' (unpublished paper, adapted from 'Realism' in *Handbook of Epistemology* (eds I Niiniluoto et al, forthcoming, Dordrecht, 2000).
20 Haack's starting-point, like that of Peirce, is that a description is true if 'something is So ... whether you or I, or anybody, thinks it is true or not'. (C S Peirce, *Collected Papers* 2.135. 1902), cited in *Manifesto* at p 22.
1 At p 157.
2 Haack at pp 153-156, discussing Hilary Putnam, *Renewing Philosophy* (1992). Haack reports that Putnam subsequently revised his position.

6.   That some statements are meaningful, but their truth-value is unknowable, and are epistemically idle if they are unknowable in principle.[3]

Haack's *Manifesto* is an eloquent defence and celebration of the values of reason, truth and the scientific attitude – especially open-mindedness, honesty, and 'the Will to Learn'. In *Evidence and Inquiry* Haack elaborates at much greater length a middle position between foundationalism and coherentism that she mischievously labels 'foundherentism' – in the process acknowledging that the supporters and critics of both positions make important points that need to be accommodated in a coherent epistemology.[4]

Haack's targets include feminist epistemology, deep philosophical forms of cultural relativism, and the excesses of some versions of the sociology of knowledge. She is especially harsh about those post-modernists, such as Richard Rorty, who claim to be 'pragmatists'. In an imaginary dialogue between Peirce and Rorty, she wittily shows Rorty's views on pragmatism to be almost the opposite of Peirce's.[5] While acknowledging that science is in an important sense a social enterprise,[6] she dismisses some of the claims made in the name of the social construction of knowledge:

'It is false that social values are inseparable from scientific inquiry; false that the purpose of science is the achievement of social goals; false that knowledge is nothing but the product of negotiation among members of the scientific community; false that knowledge, facts, reality are nothing more than social constructions; false that science should be more democratic; false that the physical sciences are subordinate to the social sciences.'[7]

In chapter 2, Santos makes a number of assertions that appear to be very close to Haack's targets. For example:

---

3   Ibid at p 164. At the level of philosophy, I am here prepared to follow Haack and Peirce, and hence to reject strong forms of epistemological scepticism, cultural relativism, and coherence theories of truth.

4   'Foundationalism' is another ambiguous '-ism'. Haack distinguishes three meanings, two of which she argues against, one of which she defends; *Evidence and Inquiry* (1993) Ch 9.

5   Ch 2 '"We Pragmatists": Peirce and Rorty in conversation.'

6   At p 3. Cf Ch 6, 'Science as Social? – Yes and No'.

7   At p 104. Cf 3. Haack also deplores the conflation of science, philosophy and literature, all of which she views as distinct enterprises with different primary objectives (Ch 3). Philosophy and science are both forms of *enquiry*; literature is not.

1. 'All Nature is Culture'.[8]
2. '... modern science, besides being modern, is also Western, capitalist, and sexist'.[9]
3. 'There are as many natures as there are cultures. This being the case, all natural-scientific knowledge is social-scientific'.[10]
4. 'The creation of knowledge in the emergent paradigm claims to be close to literary or artistic creation'.[11]
5. 'As the catalyst of the blending together of natural and social science, the neohumanities help us to look for global categories of intelligibility, warm concepts, capable of melting the frontiers from which modern science has divided and enclosed reality'.[12]
6. 'For postmodern emancipatory knowledge, truth is rhetorical, a mythic moment of rest in a continuous and endless argumentative struggle among different discourses of truth; it is the ever provisional result of a negotiation of meaning within a given relevant audience, which in the modern era has consisted of the scientific community, or rather, of a plurality of scientific communities'.[13]
7. 'Modern science built itself against common sense, which it deemed superficial, illusory and false'.[14]

8   Santos, p 30. On the ambiguity of 'culture' see Haack, Ch 8. Santos's claim is obscure, but Haack would probably reject all of the interpretations that can be most plausibly given to it.
9   At p 30, expanded at pp 30-32; contrast Haack, Ch 6.
10 Ibid, p 33. See Haack, Ch 9, especially p 156ff; cf ibid, Ch 6.
11 Ibid p 35, Haack explicitly distinguishes scientific enquiry from literary creation, Ch 3; cf n 7 above.
12 Ibid, p 36. The passage continues: 'Postmodern science is admittedly an analogical science that knows what it knows less well through what it knows better ... Other important seminal categories of the emergent paradigm are, to my mind, the ludic, the dramatic and the biographical analogies. The world is today either natural or social; tomorrow it will be both, and shall be looked at as if it were the text of a play, a stage or an autobiography'. Cf Haack, Chs 3 and 4.
13 Ibid p 38; contrast Haack, Ch 6. Elsewhere, Haack has considered the 'hard and tangled' question of the relationship between natural and social sciences, but would reject the passage in the text as 'romantic twaddle' (communication to the author). See below, pp 216-217.
14 Ibid p 46. In the context, Santos suggests that there has been a sharp epistemological break between science and common sense, which are interpreted differently from each point of view. Elsewhere (see p 202 above), Santos is more sympathetic to common sense than many critics and argues for 'a new, enchanted common sense' which is not sharply distinguished from science. Haack might agree that the ontology of, eg modern physics, is rather unlike commonsense physical objects, but would reject the suggestion that science is not continuous with everyday empirical enquiry in respect of method. Of course, scientific findings have often shown 'common sense' beliefs to be false, but they have also shown the same in respect of what have passed for warranted scientific truths. (see the 'Passes for Fallacy', below at p 217 n 8). On background beliefs see *Evidence and Inquiry* at pp 110-112 (see below, p 218).

8.   'All knowledge is self-knowledge';[15] ie the collapse of the traditional
      distinction between subject and object.

Taken at face value, these statements seem like a litany of post-modern
mantras which Susan Haack could be expected to detonate, not with a
whisper, but rather with a resounding 'bosh'. A preliminary complaint is
lack of clarity. Of course, some of these quotations require elucidation
in context. With charitable interpretation, some might even be found to
have grains of truth that could be accommodated within Haack's
position.[16] But nearly all of these statements, taken at face value, would
be rejected.

In this essay I adopt Haack's distinction between metaphysics and
epistemology, her 'innocent realism' (metaphysics), 'foundherentism'
(epistemology), the traditional scholarly values that she passionately
defends, and her main arguments in support of these views. I do this in
order to outline a philosophical position that is significantly different
from Santos's, but compatible with Calvino's (as I interpret him), without
getting embroiled in complex philosophical arguments about the reasons
for such differences as we have. The main point is to clarify my own
position regarding two significant strands in post-modernism and to
justify a significant convergence between Santos's and my views on
globalisation, legal pluralism etc, despite differences in our starting-
points and central concerns. I believe that some of Santos's theses, shorn
of unnecessary philosophical baggage, make a lot of sense. For this
purpose it is not necessary to enter into a detailed discussion of whether
Santos can be defended against the kind of philosophical criticism that
one might expect from Susan Haack.[17]

15   Santos, p 27, Contrast Haack, Ch 5.
16   *Manifesto*, Ch 9, 'Reflections on Relativism: From Momentous Tautology to
     Seductive Contradiction'. This essay contains a brief, but very illuminating,
     topography of different kinds of relativism. It deals with greater philosophical
     sophistication ideas that I tried to outline in 'Some scepticism about some
     scepticisms' (*RE*, Ch 4). On 'innocence', see above, p 205 n 18.
17   In an unpublished paper on *Manifesto*, entitled 'Rushing to Bosh?', I suggest that
     the trajectory of some of Haack's debunking, while philosophically sound, has
     unnecessarily conservative intellectual tendencies at a more applied level. *Manifesto*
     is sometimes too dismissive of the higher dismissiveness. For example, in an
     essay on multiculturalism (Ch 8) her main targets are (a) the idea that students
     should be educated exclusively in their own culture and (b) the idea that the
     'opinions, practices, institutions, traditions' of other cultures are equally deserving
     of respect because all criteria of evidence and evaluation are culture specific. I
     reject such views, but these seem to me to be soft targets. When Haack concedes
     some value in exposure to or the study of other cultures she mentions tolerance
     (p 140), mutual respect (pp 140-141) and better and more critical understanding
     of one's own culture (p 139). She adds: 'And, yes, knowledge of the customs of
     minority communities within a multicultural society surely can contribute to
     the accomplishment of a mutually tolerable, or with good luck and good will, a
     mutually enriching, modus vivendi' (pp 139-140). This seems to me to understate,

I shall explore some of these issues in more detail in relation to multiple descriptions and perspectives. Here, it may help to clarify my position by giving a few brief examples. First, if the idea of 'feminist epistemology' suggests that what constitutes evidence and truth for women is different from what it is for men, then I agree with Haack that the idea should be rejected. If, on the other hand, it is an emphatic way of saying that very many women, by virtue of their experience, vantage points and position as women, have different perspectives, points of view, and beliefs about important aspects of life/the world/social phenomena and that these views, voices, narratives and so on have been suppressed or marginalised in male-dominated cultures, then such claims need to be taken very seriously indeed.[18]

When Raymond Williams or Edward Said challenges literary or scholarly 'canons' for excluding vast ranges of experience and points of view – typically, but not necessarily, those of the underprivileged or the colonised – their argument is mainly about exclusion.[19] Radical changes to a canon or to our perceptions of particular institutions or practices, may not only lead us to be more inclusive, but as our understandings are changed, so too may the standards underpinning the canon be challenged and be shown to be in need of adjustment.[20]

Similar considerations apply within the discipline of law. Legal pluralists can point out that many significant forms of 'non-state law' have been marginalised or ignored by legal theorists and mainstream legal scholars alike – they are treated as invisible or as not really being 'law'. In most Western countries Islamic, Hindu, Chinese, and Jewish legal ideas and traditions are not treated as 'Jurisprudence', in that they rarely feature in the canons of schools, texts and individual jurists that are considered as belonging to the mainstream. Similarly, I have argued elsewhere that the dominant 'Country and Western Tradition' of Western Comparative Law has focused, in respect of micro-comparison, almost exclusively on the municipal law of industrialised capitalist societies, typically emphasising what are referred to increasingly inappropriately as 'parent legal systems'.

---

if not to miss, the most important reason why engagement with other cultures is important, viz enlarging and possibly significantly changing both one's understandings, in respect of ideas and perceptions, as well and our experience of life regarding such matters as cuisine, art and the handling of conflict. See, however, the more positive formulation in Haack (1999) (*TLS*).

18 Cf Haack, 'Knowledge and Propaganda: Reflections of an Old Feminist', *Manifesto*, Ch 7.

19 Raymond Williams, *Culture and Society* (1958); Edward Said, *Orientalism* (1985).

20 The point about standards is illustrated by problems surrounding notions of 'merit' in university admissions and hiring, see *LIC*, Ch 13 (in which different meanings of 'affirmative action' are explored and arguing that preferential treatment may sometimes be justified, despite the costs, especially where there are no defensible criteria of merit).

One reason why Santos's work is important is because it presents a much broader and more complex view of legal phenomena than are to be found in orthodox Western legal theory and scholarship. His work opens up new perspectives, and fresh lines of enquiry. This vision seems to be directly related to his rejection of orthodoxies that have dominated 'modernist' treatments of law. However, to subvert an orthodoxy or to provide a fresh perspective does not necessarily need a change of metaphysics or epistemology or a new 'paradigm'. One can hold firmly to the simple truths of innocent realism and empiricism, while welcoming challenges to what has passed for knowledge in our dominant intellectual, including jurisprudential, traditions.

(b) Calvino and Innocent Realism

How can I reconcile my endorsement of Haack with my agreement with many of Santos's ideas and my attraction to Calvino, when the former looks like a direct attack on some of the philosophical positions adopted by Santos? My central argument is that Santos' juristic ideas and Calvino's visions of complexity make sense at a less abstract level than Haack's lean metaphysics and that, on my interpretation, some important ideas and perspectives of both Santos and Calvino are quite compatible with innocent realism.

There may indeed be a seeming tension between the robust simplicity of innocent realism and an emphasis on multiple perspectives, complex phenomena, and a generally anti-reductionist stance. I do not believe that these are incompatible. One clue to this is suggested by the imaginative post-modernism of Italo Calvino.

In earlier essays I have drawn on two of Calvino's later books, *Invisible Cities* and *Mr Palomar*, which have attracted me both personally and as a jurist.[1] The sense of affinity was initially intuitive, but it has grown, and it can, to some extent, be rationalised.[2] Both works are concerned with a

1   *IC* and *MP*, op cit, n 1. My interest in Calvino and 'realism' began with *If on a Winter's Night a Traveler*, See *RE* at pp 366-368. In addition to the themes discussed in the text, I like Calvino's antipathy to consumerism, his questioning of settled assumptions, his ambivalence towards technology, his linking of complexity and historical continuity, his lightness of touch, and his capacity to maintain a sense of humour despite a pessimistic vision of the human condition.

2   This section draws heavily on two works by Katherine Hume, 'Grains of Sand in a Sea of Objects: Italo Calvino as Essayist', (1992a) 87 Modern Languages Review 72 and *Calvino's Fictions: Cogito and Cosmos* (1992b), especially the Introduction and Ch 6. I have also learned from Sara M Adler, *Calvino: The Writer as Fable-maker* (1979); Albert H Carter, *Italo Calvino: Metamorphoses of Fantasy* (1987); and Beno Weiss, *Understanding Italo Calvino* (1993).

search for understanding and meaning in a universe that seems endlessly complex. As Sara Adler puts it, Calvino's central concern is to 'portray the diversity and at the same time the universality of human experience'.[3]

Calvino, while emphasising complexity, paradox, elusiveness, uses models, geometrical designs, and even Tarot cards to construct patterns of understanding. The central problem is that 'reality is granular',[4] like a sea consisting of ever more minute, isolated particles in constant flux.[5] When Mr Palomar, seeking the key to mastering the world's complexity, begins by trying to describe a single wave, he is defeated. When he attempts to subject one small part of his lawn to statistical analysis, his efforts prove absurd. In some ways, it is easier to see the moon, or his lawn, or an ocean as a whole from a distance than to describe one small part. Understanding requires both small scale and large scale enquiries.

In *Invisible Cities* Kublai Khan claims to have constructed in his mind a model city based on principles from which all possible cities can be deduced[6] – a conceit reminiscent of common law caricatures of the civilian mentality. Marco Polo replies that he has thought of an alternative model city 'made only of exceptions, exclusions, incongruities, contradictions' – a sort of urban hearsay rule – but if he proceeds to describe a particular city by subtracting exceptions and abnormalities from the ideal type, beyond a certain limit, 'I would achieve cities too probable to be real'.[7] Yet Marco Polo's accounts allow Kublai Khan to discern 'the tracery of a pattern so subtle it could escape the termites' gnawing'.[8]

Ironically, *Invisible Cities* is itself highly schematic, organised on a formal geometric structure. It both embraces patterns and undermines them. Calvino recognised both the value of models and their limitations in capturing complexity. Katherine Hume suggests that the exchanges between Marco Polo and Kublai Khan can be interpreted as a dialogue within a single, composite mind.[9] The reader is expected to embrace multiplicity and different levels of understanding reality, as is required of any 'intelligent human being facing the social world'.[10]

3   Adler at p 49.
4   Hume (1992a) op cit, p 72.
5   *The Literature Machine: Essays* (1987) at p 268, quoted by Hume (1992a) at pp 72-73.
6   *IC*, p 69.
7   Ibid.
8   *IC*, pp 5-6. Cf Ch 6.6 above.
9   Hume (1992b) at p 149.
10   Hume (1992a), p 75. Haack in a recent essay, discusses the added difficulties of description arising from the fact that 'human beings intervene in the world in various ways, and they, and their physical and mental activities are themselves part of the world'. Haack (2000) op cit, p 205 n 19.

In 'Mapping Law' I explored both geographical and metaphorical mapping of the variety of legal orders in the world and what is involved in giving an account of one legal order.[11] The first part was similar in content, but different in style, to Santos's map of the transnational legal field. In the second part I suggested that describing a legal order is rather like describing a city in that both are highly complex phenomena that can be depicted in many different ways from a great variety of vantage points and perspectives. I drew on Italo Calvino's *Invisible Cities*, in which Marco Polo gives 55 highly imaginative evocations of cities – all couched in metaphorical language – and all significantly different. These might be read as accounts of 55 different cities, or 55 accounts of one city, Venice, or, more plausibly, 55 accounts all of which implicitly use Venice as the reference point of comparison.[12]

At first sight, 55 accounts of one city sound rather a lot. However, Calvino's number seems modest when set against the report that there are approximately 25,000 works dealing with the history of London.[13] For even if one discounts repetition and overlap, the obviously inaccurate, and the tendentious, it should not be difficult to find well over one hundred substantially different accounts of the history of London which prima facie have the potential to add to our understanding of the city. One could in fact find a hundred different maps of Central London that would satisfy this test, and maps are one of the most abstract and thin forms of depiction.[14] Most or all of the differences between 100 accounts of a city or its history might be explained in terms of different vantage points, perspectives and concerns. For example, 50 kinds of specialist, from drainage engineer to mythologist, could each give an account from two or more vantage points in time or space. A further 100 inhabitants or tourists or other visitors could describe different experiences and impressions of the same city … and so on. One of the central themes of post-modernism, but not exclusive to it, is its insistence on the value of looking at things from multiple points of view.

In a well-known passage about causation, R G Collingwood wrote:

'A car skids while cornering at a certain point, turns turtle, and bursts into flame. From the car-driver's point of view, the cause of the accident was cornering too fast and the lesson is that one must drive more carefully. From the county surveyor's point of view, the cause was a defective road surface, and the lesson is that one must

11 Above, Ch 6.
12 When Kublai Khan observes that there is one city of which Marco Polo never speaks, the response is: 'To distinguish other cities' qualities, I must speak of a first city that remains implicit. For me it is Venice'. *IC*, p 86.
13 Peter Ackroyd, London *Times*, 13 August 1998, at p 35.
14 Albert Carter, *Italo Calvino: Metamorphoses of Fantasy* (1987), pp 120-121.

make skid-proof roads. From the motor-manufacturer's point of view, the cause was defective design, and the lesson is that one must place the centre of gravity lower.'[15]

This a graphic way of saying that different perspectives are appropriate for different kinds of enquiries. Here each person draws practical lessons relevant to their respective spheres of action. Someone trying to explain the crash might combine these answers to provide a multi-factored explanation. On the other hand, someone concerned to attribute responsibility, might select one element as 'the cause' for this purpose. For example, a court might hold the driver responsible because his act of cornering fast was a voluntary human act, subsequent in time to the other conditions and, if he was not exercising reasonable care, he might be held liable in negligence. Here the court selects one condition from a set of jointly sufficient conditions as 'the cause' in order to determine an issue of responsibility.[16]

It would not be difficult to multiply the standpoints from which this event might be viewed. The question that concerns us here is whether cumulating multiple perspectives on an event of this kind can generally add to or deepen our understanding. I believe that it can, though it will not always do so. Merely cumulating descriptions may be tedious and laborious, with a prospect of diminishing returns.[17] Obviously with a very complex phenomenon, such as a city, reading 20 different accounts could add to one's knowledge simply by adding new facts, but that is not the point. Metaphors, such as 'multiple lenses', convey the idea that one can understand better by looking at the same object in different ways. This is, of course, almost an article of faith for those who favour multi-disciplinary studies.

In addressing problems of depicting the cosmos, the human condition, or a single object, Calvino adopts three main strategies: narrative, the construction of models or systems, and literary mimesis (including metaphors).[18] These are treated as complementary rather than rival ways of trying to grapple with the complexities, multiplicity and fluidity of reality. Calvino had a strong sense of the limitations of language. At key

15 R G Collingwood, 'On the So-called idea of Causation', (1937-38) *Proceedings of the Aristotelian Society*, pp 85, 96.

16 H L A Hart and A Honoré, *Causation in the Law* (2nd edn, 1985). The authors rightly criticise Collingwood for over-emphasising pragmatic concerns with causation to the exclusion of other kinds of enquiry: 'Collingwood ... was prepared heroically to accept the conclusion that it is logically impossible to speak of discovering the cause of a disease unless we can use our knowledge to cure it' (at p 300).

17 On 'descriptivism', see below at p 237.

18 Ibid, p 73. On Calvino's complex treatment of models and mirrors in Palomar, see Hume (1992b), pp 143-144.

moments, in evoking cities, words fail Marco Polo and he resorts to gestures, emblems, images, silences and other indirections. When Kublai Khan asks him to describe Venice, Polo replies:

'Memory's images, once they are fixed in words, are erased. Perhaps I am afraid of losing Venice all at once, if I speak of it. Or perhaps, speaking of other cities, I have already lost it little by little.'[19]

Emphasis on the uses and limitations of language as a tool of description or depiction, and the value of narrative, fables, models, metaphor, images and silence as complementary ways of capturing aspects of reality fit comfortably with the idea of multiple perspectives. But what has this to do with jurisprudence? And can Calvino's approach to description be accommodated by innocent realism?

I have suggested that depicting a legal order is analogous in important respects to depicting a city.[20] One similarity is that the objects are extremely complex. Another is that their particularity tends to be rooted in history. A third is that cities and legal orders are experienced differently by different types of people. The standpoint of an urban planner, a mayor, a tycoon, a travel writer, a photographer, a poet, a tourist, a vagrant, a burglar, a historian, an ethnographer, and all the other kinds of visitor, inhabitant, or functionary tend to be significantly different. And, of course, there is not just one kind of tourist, poet, or planner. Similarly in law the standpoints of rule-maker, adjudicator, enforcement officer, bureaucrat, disputant, advocate, deviant, good citizen, bad man, professional adviser, expositor, and jurist in respect of a given legal order will all be different. There are many kinds of participants and many kinds of observers with different vantage points, concerns, perspectives, and particular experiences. For limited enquiries, limited perspectives may be adequate. A broader understanding of a city or a legal system involves taking account of multiple standpoints. The main purpose of the discipline of law is to advance knowledge and understanding of law; my primary objective as a scholar is to gain a better general understanding of my chosen specialism as well as to pursue particular lines of enquiry.

It might be objected that cities are extremely complex phenomena, especially when considered historically as well as spatially. Millions of people, relations, events, physical objects, and other phenomena may be suggested by the idea of 'London' or 'Venice'. Any account of such complexity must inevitably be selective and it is hardly surprising that different accounts select different aspects for different purposes. But do

---

19 *IC*, p 87.
20 On the the application of standard metaphors in urban sociology (bazaar, jungle, machine and organism) see above, Ch 6.6.

the same considerations apply to smaller, more specific or 'manageable' objects of study?

Of course, any city is immeasurably complex, but so is a legal order, let alone all law in the world, the subject-matter of a global discipline of law. A granular conception of reality, such as Calvino's, suggests that it consists of smaller and smaller particles in flux. Mr Palomar can move from considering the cosmos to his lawn, to one small part of it, to a blade of grass, and so on down to 'collections of collections'.[1] Marco Polo uses the wood of a chessboard as the jumping-off point for a potentially endless enquiry. This is like 'seeing a world in a grain of sand', except that a grain of sand is not an ultimate unit, as atoms were once thought to be.

I think that the general enterprise of trying to study and understand law is rather like that. One can move from trying to map law in the world, an exercise that has its uses, through profiling or giving some other account of a legal family or a single legal order, to more and more particular studies of legal phenomena and relations. Most of these phenomena are social and invisible, two features that complicate the task of depicting and interpreting them.

I do not see these points as causing difficulties for 'innocent realism'. Calvino's concern is with the complexity and the elusiveness of reality and with problems of description. As I read him, he accepts that there is a reality independent of our knowledge of it, but emphasises the difficulty of describing it. Conversely, Haack's epistemology is fallibilist and she explicitly allows for multiple descriptions, all of which can be true.[2]

I have already suggested that one of the tendencies of post-modernist thought is to conflate epistemology and metaphysics. A standard example is the claim that there are 'multiple realities'. This can be interpreted as a denial of the idea that there is one real world which is largely independent of anyone's knowledge of it.[3] In innocent realism the concept of reality belongs to what is (ontology), while the concept of knowledge refers to our apprehension of what is (epistemology). However, the term 'multiple realities' is sometimes used loosely to refer to different experiences or descriptions of reality or different perspectives or vantage points or subjectivities. Innocent realism acknowledges that there can be many different descriptions of an object, event or phenomenon, all of which may be true, provided that they are compatible.[4] It accepts that

1   *MP*, 'The Infinite Lawn'.
2   *Manifesto*, pp 146-147.
3   The phrase can be interpreted as a loose way of talking about multiple impressions or pictures of reality, but some post-modernists (including Santos, it seems) insist that reality is subjective.
4   Haack at p 157; 'incompatible descriptions, however, cannot be jointly true'. Compatibility is, of course, a necessary but not a sufficient condition.

one can look at an object from different points of view, but it is the points of view not the object that are different. Here, I think that Santos' philosophical views are generally incompatible with innocent realism, but, on my interpretation, Calvino's are not. For me, post-modernism is better treated as being more like a mood than a philosophy.

In legal contexts there is a particular danger of confusing three different meanings of 'pluralism': 'plural' – meaning diverse; 'pluralism' – meaning a plurality of perspectives or standpoints – and 'legal pluralism', which refers either to the co-existence of multiple legal orders in the same context of time and space or the recognition of different legal traditions and sources of law within a single legal system.[5] Confusing these terms can lead to trouble, for example, conflating the ideas of multiple legal orders and multiple descriptions of a single legal order. A further source of confusion arises from the fact that 'legal pluralist' is used sometimes to apply to those who advocate legal pluralism as against state centralism and sometimes to refer to those who study the phenomenon with relative detachment. In legal contexts such confusions can be avoided by using 'legal pluralism' in a neutral sense and by substituting for 'pluralism' in the general sense some other term such as 'multiple perspectives'.

How does innocent realism cope with the idea of 'multiple perspectives'? It denies that 'multiple realities' exist, but it accepts that there are many different true descriptions of reality all, of course, compatible. The innocent realist can accommodate notions of describing from different points of view, using different vocabularies, multiple perspectives, and – moving into metaphor – multiple lenses.

Susan Haack's main examples of multiple descriptions relate to simple physical objects such as rocks (natural) and paper-clips (human artefacts). The post-modern thrust towards multiple perspectives and pluralist descriptions is more closely related to studying social institutions, practices, and discourses, including law. Haack acknowledges that enquiry in the social sciences can be harder than in the physical sciences, partly because it involves enquiry into mental states. In a recent essay, she discusses the added difficulties of description arising from the fact that 'human beings intervene in the world in various ways, and they, and their physical and mental activities are themselves part of the world'. She concludes:

'There are many different truths about the world. All these many different truths must, somehow, fit together; there can't be rival, incompatible truths or "knowledges". But this doesn't mean that

5   On different conceptions of 'legal pluralism' see above, Ch 3.5 and below, section 4(b).

all the truths about the world must fit together by being reducible to a privileged class of truths expressed in a privileged vocabulary (that they must be "unified" in the logical positivists' strong sense of that term). A better analogy would be the way a road map can be superimposed upon a contour map of the same territory.'[6]

A popular theme in post-modernism, but not confined to it, is that certain ways of looking at things, certain perspectives, standpoints, discourses, views etc, tend to be 'privileged' (in a socio-political sense), while others get marginalised or suppressed. For example, sociologists are fond of debunking 'official views' and what passes for 'common sense';[7] feminists complain about the repression of women's points of view; critical scholars talk of 'unheard voices', 'suppressed narratives' and so on. I personally have a great deal of sympathy with some such complaints, provided that they are not expressed in terms of a new epistemology or metaphysics. I agree that what passes for knowledge or common sense in a given society may be shown to be partial, biased, or just plain false.[8] But such ideas presuppose rather than reject an ontology and some conceptions of evidence, inference and warranted conclusions.

Post-modern enthusiasm for 'the ludic' has often occasioned comment.[9] A hard-nosed empiricist may be inclined to disdain metaphor and be suspicious of playful treatments of serious issues. For her, Santos's enthusiasm for the Baroque or Calvino's humorous fantasies may be too fanciful, if not frivolous, for the responsible enquirer. However, respected traditionalist philosophers, including Susan Haack, have acknowledged an important role for metaphor in enquiry, especially in its early stages:

'Both the friends and enemies of metaphor, it seems to me, exaggerate. Metaphors are sometimes cognitively vital; not seldom

6   Haack (2000) op cit, above, p 205 n 19. 'Privileged' here refers to a vocabulary to which other vocabularies can be reduced, but which cannot be reduced to others. This usage should be distinguished from the socio-political usage that is now rather more common.

7   RE at pp 92-93 and references there.

8   One of Haack's targets is what she calls 'the passes for fallacy': '... the New Cynics disdain the notions of evidence and warrant, because, as they are at pains to point out, what has passed for warranted theory, relevant evidence, known fact, objective truth, has often turned out to be no such thing. This is true; but the conclusion that the notions of warrant, evidence, truth, fact, reality, knowledge, are ideological humbug manifestly doesn't follow' (at p 93). See now Haack, 'Staying for an Answer', TLS, 9 July, 1999. I agree with Haack that this is a fallacy; it is not clear whether it can be attributed to Santos.

9   Eg Santos at p 504. On the issue of post-modernist contributions to politics, see the debate in the Law and Society Review (1992) No 4 on Joel Handler's Presidential address to the Law and Society Association, 'Postmodernism, Protest, and the New Social Movements', (p 697). See also above, Ch 3.3.

illuminating; perhaps more often than not harmless. Metaphors can also be feeble; can be exploited to the purpose of persuading by emotional appeal rather than strong evidence or good argument; can serve as lazy substitutes for adequate theoretical articulation; can lead inquiry into what turns out to be quite the wrong direction. Metaphor is neither a Good Thing nor a Bad Thing in itself; it is, rather, a linguistic device, capable of being put to good or bad use.'[10]

One can find metaphors cognitively useful, but still suspect that they may often be being used self-indulgently or as a cloak for laziness, lack of clarity, or even dishonesty. It is reasonable to ask of particular examples: Is your metaphor really necessary? Why don't you say what you mean? In what way exactly is the legal order of Xanadu like a city or a bazaar? Such questions can serve as a useful 'reality check' and help to differentiate the ludic from the ludicrous.

Furthermore, enquiry requires both imagination and checking out evidence. Haack's principal objection to the idea of 'studying {philosophy} in a literary spirit', is the suggested implication that imagination is not only necessary, but sufficient for serious enquiry and that checking out the truth by reference to evidence falls by the way.[11]

Haack's principal concern is to defend such values as intellectual integrity, disinterestedness, intellectual tolerance, respect for facts, and honest, open-minded enquiry. She sees these values as being under threat from 'the Higher Dismissiveness' and from tendencies that I have associated with irrationalist post-modernism. However, both Santos and Calvino purport to subscribe to such values, though less emphatically.[12] Conversely, Peirce's 'scientific attitude' can be viewed as being in much

10 *Manifesto*, p 72. One of Haack's most important ideas is that the structure of evidence is analogous to a crossword puzzle: '[A]n empirical proposition is more or less warranted depending on how well it is supported by experiential evidence and background beliefs (analogue: how well a crossword entry is supported by its clue and other completed entries); how secure the relevant background beliefs are, independently of the proposition in question (analogue: how reasonable those other entries are, independent of this one); and how much of the relevant evidence the evidence includes (analogue: how much of the crossword has been completed). How well evidence supports a proposition depends on how much the addition of the proposition in question improves its explanatory investigation' (*Manifesto* at p 106; cf pp 85-86). A fuller account is given in Haack's *Evidence and Inquiry* (1993), op cit. See also, 'staying for an Answer' (1999), op cit.
11 Haack, 'As for that phrase "studying in a literary spirit"', *Manifesto*, Ch 3.
12 Calvino's most eloquent statement is to be found in his posthumously published Charles Eliot Norton Lectures, *Six Memos for the Next Millennium* (tr Patrick Creagh, 1988). There may be a tension between some of Santos's rash philosophical claims and his commitment to scholarship, but I have no reason to believe that he rejects basic values of scholarly integrity.

the same spirit as post-modern resistance to 'closure'. There is nothing in Peirce or Haack that suggests that enquiry is easy or simple.[13] Nevertheless, seeking a complete rapprochement would be too glib. For Santos does appear to subscribe to some anti-rationalist views — such as the denial that objective truth is meaningful — that threaten central scholarly values.[14]

While Haack's defence of her views is passionate and robust, on some of the points that differentiate what I have called anti-rationalist and imaginative post-modernism she is clearly a moderate in relation to the latter, as the following statement illustrates:

> 'It is perfectly possible to acknowledge the short-comings of foundationalism and coherentism, human enquirers' pervasive epistemic dependence on one another, the social character of scientific inquiry, the complexity and fallibility of all human cognitive activity, the corruption of some claims to truth, without being obliged to grant either that epistemic standards are community- or culture-relative, or that inquiry is invariably political.'[15]

I have suggested that Calvino has no commitment to anti-rationalist post-modernism. But, it may be objected, is he not really a full-blooded post-modernist, especially in his later works? He was an admirer of Borges and Barthes. He indulged in baroque fantasy and fable. He emphasised the complexity and elusiveness of a cosmos in flux. Is not Marco Polo a paradigm case of post-modernism? And do not most commentators treat him as such? To me this illustrates the uselessness of such labels. The innocent realist starts with a simple premise and sticks with it: there is one world that is largely independent of our knowledge of it. Calvino stresses the complexity and elusiveness of reality and the difficulties in the way of knowing. I see no incompatibility here. In a lecture on multiplicity, published after his death, Calvino emphasised the continuity of our intellectual traditions. Writing of Flaubert, but also of Garda and Musil and Thomas Mann, he said:

> 'Flaubert's skepticism and his endless curiosity about the human knowledge accumulated over the centuries are the very qualities that are destined to be claimed for their own by the greatest writers of the twentieth century. But theirs I would tend to call active

13 See *Manifesto*, Ch 3.
14 See Haack's robust recent attack on 'the Higher Dismissiveness', see 'Staying for an Answer', op cit.
15 *Manifesto*, p 146.

skepticism, a kind of gambling and betting in a tireless effort to
establish relationships between discourse, methods, and levels of
meaning. Knowledge as multiplicity is the thread that binds
together the major works both of what is called modernism and of
what goes by the name of the *postmodern*, a thread – over and above
all labels attached to it – that I hope will continue into the next
millennium.'[16]

Why is emphasis on multiple standpoints and perspectives important?
For me, law is an infinitely complex subject and understanding law is an
endless and inevitably collective enterprise, a quest that will know no
closure. In an essay written in 1967, Calvino asked 'Whom do we write
a novel for? Whom do we write a poem for?'[17] He suggests that each new
book is written so that it can be placed on a hypothetical bookshelf
beside books that precede it and books that will inevitably succeed it.
His answer applies as much to a jurist as to a poet or novelist. As Katherine
Hume puts it:

> 'He weighs books and looks at the problems of the world and
> admits that the political weight of any book is extremely modest,
> and often not what the author intended. A book is only "un granello
> di sabbia", a grain of sand. However, an important book, literary
> or scientific, can raise consciousness to a new level by augmenting
> our instruments of understanding and imagining. Many books,
> many essays, are many grains of sand, and can be gathered in
> collections of sand. The claims made for any one must be minimal,
> but the number of potential grains is limitless and they may become
> significant.'[18]

On my interpretation, imaginative postmodernism, exemplified by
Calvino and some strands in Santos' work, is quite compatible with
innocent realism and Haack's critique of some fashionable fallacies
associated with anti-rational post-modernism. Against this background,
let us consider Santos's treatment of globalisation and law.

16 Italo Calvino, 'Multiplicity', in *Six Memos for the Next Millennium* (tr Patrick
    Creagh, 1993).
17 'Whom do we Write For? or The Hypothetical Bookshelf' (1967) in *The Uses of
    Literature* (tr Patrick Creagh, 1986).
18 Hume (1992a) at p 85.

4 SANTOS ON GLOBALISATION AND LAW

(a) Globalisation

'Far from being linear or unambiguous, the process of globalization is highly contradictory and uneven. It takes place through an apparently dialectical process, whereby new forms of globalization occur together with new or renewed forms of localization. Indeed, as global interaction and interdependence intensify, social relations in general seem to be increasingly deterritorialized, opening the way to new *rights to options*, crossing borders up until recently policed by customs, nationalism, language and ideology, oftentimes by all of them together. But, on the other hand, and in apparent contradiction with this trend, new regional, national and local identities are emerging that are built around a new prominence of *rights to roots*.

The process of globalization is, thus, selective, uneven, and fraught with tensions and contradictions. But it is not anarchic. It reproduces the hierarchies of the world system and the asymmetries among core, peripheral and semi-peripheral societies. There is, therefore, no genuine globalism. Under the conditions of the modern world system, globalism is the successful globalization of a given localism. The English language, as *lingua franca*, is one such example.'[19]

Santos's interpretation of globalisation is quite close to mine. Indeed, I have found his analysis helpful in trying to make sense of these bewildering phenomena. We agree, for example, that the processes of globalisation have a long history, that they are not unilinear (but the flow is more from North to South), and that they are rapidly changing the significance of national boundaries. So far as the legal landscape is concerned, we also agree that no one can understand their local law by focusing solely on municipal domestic law of a single jurisdiction or nation state; that the range of significant actors and processes has been extended; and that the phenomena of legal pluralism are central to understanding law in today's world.

Santos distinguishes between four forms of globalisation as process: globalised localism (eg Coca Cola, the English language); localised globalism (eg structural adjustment programmes, and luxurious tourist facilities in poor countries); cosmopolitanism (defined as 'the networking of local progressive struggles with the objective of maximizing their

19 Santos at p 262 (italics in the original). See also, David Crystal, *English as a Global Language* (1997).

emancipatory potential *in loco* through translocal/local connections');[20] and the common heritage of mankind (struggles to cope with issues of genuine global significance such as nuclear proliferation, global warming, exploration and appropriation of other planets, and the protection of the environment). Santos interprets the first two categories as mainly involving impositions and flows from centre to periphery or, using a different taxonomy, from North to South. He explicitly confines the other two categories to 'counter-hegemonic forces' resisting the domination of the industrialised West/North and other capitalist centres of power.

This explicitly ideological categorisation is suggestive, but it is, perhaps, a bit too neatly schematic. For example, while there are clear instances of globalised localisms (eg CNN, Coca Cola), it is not clear why structural adjustment programmes and luxurious tourist facilities belong to localised globalism rather than *vice versa*. For example, structural adjustment typically involves the imposition of relatively uniform Western ideas on other countries – a form of cultural export. Similarly, while the idea of 'a common heritage of mankind' emanated largely from sources representing Third World interests,[1] it is strange to suggest that debates about such global issues are framed, let alone dominated, by 'counter-hegemonic' forces. Santos recognises that resistance to genuinely global solutions has come from Western powers, especially the United States. It is surely unduly optimistic to equate transformative practices with 'counter-hegemonic forces' and adaptive practices with hegemonic countries – the reverse is often the case. Similarly, it is unclear where international drug syndicates or the Mafia fit into this scheme, unless they are treated as 'progressive'. Again, the Internet, which originated in the United States, has the potential to be an instrument of cultural domination or a locus of transnational counterculture or, more likely a mixture of both, in ways in which it is impossible to foretell, especially in Santos's long and indefinite time-frame. Santos's neat scheme may fit his broad thesis, but for most other purposes it is important to recognise the complexity of interactions at all levels from the global to the local, including many intermediate ones.

Interpretations of globalisation range from the apocalyptic (both utopian and pessimistic) to the sceptical, exemplified by Immanuel Wallerstein and Kenichi Omae, on the one hand, and Paul Hirst and

---

20 At p 264.
1   The history of the idea of *ius humanitatis* is outlined in Mary Victoria White, 'The Common Heritage of Mankind: An Assessment', (1982) 14 Case W. Res. J. Int. L. 509. For recent discussions, see *Annale de Droit Aérien et Spatial* (Montreal).

Grahame Thompson, on the other.[2] Not surprisingly, as a prophet of paradigmatic change, Santos follows Wallerstein quite closely. Hirst and Thompson argue that 'rhetorical globalists' exaggerate the unity of the world economy, the importance of multi-national corporations, and the decline in importance of the nation-state as the key actor in transnational ordering. As a relatively short-term interpreter of the current scene, I find much of this cautionary argument persuasive, except that I think that it tends to underplay the qualitative significance of recent changes, especially in respect of communications and financial markets.[3]

The main difference between Santos's and my interpretations of globalisation seems to be largely one of time-scale. He readily concedes that in the medium- and short-term the nation state is likely to remain by far the most significant actor at nearly all levels and what he calls 'counter-hegemonic forces' are currently underdeveloped and weak.[4] Conversely, given the rapidity of change and the complexity of the processes, I do not feel capable of making confident predictions about the longer term. Where he is utopian and optimistic, I am agnostic and rather more pessimistic.

Traditional legal theory has focused almost exclusively on two levels of law: the municipal law of nation states and public international law. Santos recognises the multiplicity of levels of law, but largely focuses on three: the global, the national and the sub-national. These are adequate for his purposes. In a different context I have suggested that normative ordering reflects all levels of human relations (including legal persons, groups etc) and that, for general purposes, it may be useful to differentiate between global, international, regional, transnational, inter-communal, territorial state, sub-state, and non-state local.[5] This, essentially geographical, characterisation is just one rough and ready taxonomy among many. It has the advantage of drawing attention to various levels

2   Immanuel Wallerstein's writings are extensive; see especially, *The Capitalist World Economy* (1979); 'the Withering Away of States', (1980) 8 International Journal of Sociology of Law 369; *Unthinking Social Science* (1991). Wallerstein has been one of the most persistent critics of the tendency to treat societies and nation-states as self-contained: 'It is the world-scale structure and the processes of its development that provide the true subject of our collective enquiry' (at p 77). Kenichi Omae, *The Borderless World: Power and Strategy in the Interlinked Economy* (1990). Hirst and Thompson, op cit, pp 6-7.

3   Like Santos, Hirst and Thompson have an explicitly political agenda, in their case to attack the idea that the nation-state has lost the capacity to regulate most aspects of economic relations. John Gray, while conceding some of their points, dismisses their political prescriptions, such as European social democracy, as outdated and no longer viable (J Gray, *False Dawn* (revised edn, 1998), at p 64).

4   Eg pp 345-347.

5   Ch 6. 2.

of non-state ordering and emphasising the point that these different levels are not neatly nested in a single vertical hierarchy. Here, despite the different taxonomies, Santos and I are in broad agreement, especially on the point that the cross-cutting of normative orders puts the phenomena of legal pluralism at the centre of understanding law. This is the subject of the next section.

(b)   Legal and Normative Pluralism[6]

Leading commentators, such as Merry and Griffiths, maintain that legal pluralism is a concept and a phenomenon rather than a 'school'. or perspective.[7] For them, as for me, the co-existence of multiple legal orders and multiple systems or bodies of rules are social facts. Their chief complaint is that these important phenomena are ignored or marginalised by orthodox legal theory and scholarship.

The concept has a long history and is often contested. Perhaps the conception that has been longest established refers to national or state legal systems that are 'pluralistic' in that they recognise as official sources of law bodies of personal or religious law belonging to different groups. This phenomenon is best-documented in relation to national legal systems in the colonial and immediate post-colonial periods.[8] For example, in Tanzania at the time of independence Muslim, Hindu and customary law were officially recognised as sources of state law, along with local legislation, supplemented by 'the substance of the common law, the doctrines of equity and 'statutes of general application so far as local circumstances admit'.[9] Anthropologists were quick to realise that there were often differences in scope, content and form between what was recognised as customary law by the courts and what was treated as

6   This section is an extension of the observations on pluralism made in Ch 3.5.
7   For references, see Ch 3.5.
8   For a general survey see Barry Hooker, *Legal Pluralism* (1975). 'Legal pluralism' in this sense has a long history, including the story of 'capitulations' (when colonists and other expatriate groups were allowed to be governed by their personal laws, often administered in special courts); the co-existence of alternative, sometimes competing, jurisdictions (as in England up to the nineteenth century); various kinds of involuntary receptions (see Sandra Burman and Barbara Harrell-Bond (eds), *The Imposition of Law* (1979)). Much of the history of law before the rise of the nation-state involved legal pluralism in a broader sense (see, for example, H J Berman, *Law and Revolution: The Formation of the Western Legal Tradition* (1983)).
9   The pre-Independence law was governed by the Tanganyika Order in Council 1920 (as amended) and continued, subject to local modifications, by the Interim Constitution (1965). On Sudan, see above, Ch 6.4. On immediate post-independence anglophone Africa, see A N Allott, *New Essays in African Law* (1970).

obligatory custom by the people subject to them.[10] In the period after World War II, academic lawyers who adopted a top-down perspective were concerned about practical problems facing the courts in ascertaining the content of customary law and in problems of choice of law or internal conflicts of laws.[11] These concerns led to proposals to codify, unify or 'restate' customary law at national level in order to assist the courts and other officials in ascertaining, interpreting, applying and enforcing the law as state law. Such proposals provoked quite sharp debates, for example in East Africa, the critics arguing that 'decontextualising' custom would lead to substantial changes in process, form and substance, while the proponents maintained that this was the only practicable way of incorporating and preserving traditional ideas and values within the official legal system.[12]

As jurists have become more conscious of 'multi-culturalism' and as societies have in fact become more plural, there has been increased recognition that all modern societies have to wrestle with the extent to which the state should recognise, make concessions to, or even enforce norms and values embedded in different religions, cultures, or traditions. Such recognition is exemplified by Federal Indian Law in the United States, the recent attention given to the position and rights of indigenous peoples in Australia, New Zealand and Canada, and the belated acknowledgement that there are issues relating to Muslim Law and that of other minorities within the United Kingdom.[13] Today, *state legal pluralism* is recognised as a fact in nearly all countries.[14] Some writers on the subject tend to be dismissive of state legal pluralism. In the context of a reaction against statist centralising interpretations this was perhaps

10 Eg Sally Falk Moore, *Law as Process: An Anthropological Approach* (1978).
11 Eg Allott (1970), op cit, Chs 4-7.
12 William Twining, *The Place of Customary Law in the National Legal Systems of East Africa* (1963); Eugene Cotran, 'The Place and Future of Customary Law in East Africa' in *East African Law Today* (1966); J Comaroff and S Roberts, *Rules and Processes* (1981); A N Allott, 'Hunting of the Snark or The Quest for the Holy Grail?: The search for customary law', in Ian Edge (ed) (SOAS Jubilee Lectures, forthcoming).
13 Eg David Pearl and Werner Menski, *Muslim Family Law* (3rd edn, 1998); Sebastian Poulter, *Ethnicity, Law and Rights: The English Experience* (1998) reviewed critically by Menski in (1999) 115 LQR 139.
14 John Griffiths in an important essay distinguishes between 'weak' and 'strong' concepts of legal pluralism, 'What is Legal Pluralism?' (1986) 24 Journal of Legal Pluralism 1. State legal pluralism is of increasing importance in the context of developing legal regimes, such as the EU, and the increased penetration of international human rights norms into municipal law (eg the Pinochet affair) and a possibly greater sensitivity to multiculturalism by legislatures and courts (for England see Poulter, and Menski and Pearl, op cit). Of course, cross-level interlegality involves not only interaction between different levels of 'official law' but also between state and non-state law.

justified. However, state legal pluralism has a continuing vitality, as was dramatically illustrated by the Otieno case in Kenya, in which litigation between the widow and the clan of a leading Nairobi lawyer about burial rights, dramatised, amid a blaze of publicity, issues about gender and culture, tradition and modernity, imported law and custom, tribalism, city and country, and a great deal else besides.[15]

However, 'legal pluralism' is more regularly associated with 'non-state law', a concept that is more problematic. Following Santos, one can distinguish between three main phases in the history of these concepts.[16] First, pioneers of the sociology of law, most notably Ehrlich, argued that a realistic depiction of the law in action had to take account of 'the living law' of sub-groups as well as 'the official law' of the state. They saw that these could diverge significantly and that sometimes one, sometimes the other would prevail. This was an important step not only in the direction of 'realism', but also away from the idea that the state has a monopoly of law-creation.

These ideas were developed in a number of directions. For example, Karl Llewellyn saw clearly that within a major group such as a nation-state, society or tribe, the basic functions or jobs of law, such as conflict prevention and dispute-resolution, could be performed at different levels by a variety of mechanisms in addition to rules – eg by education or the threat or use of brute force – and that different bodies of rules could co-exist without necessarily being ranked in a clear hierarchical order.[17] Kadish and Kadish developed the idea of legitimated interposition which in practice allows for departures from official law, even by officials.[18] For example, tax officials, health and safety inspectors, and environmental enforcement agencies typically develop more or less articulated norms that not only guide how formally authorised discretion is exercised, but sometimes go further to provide for waiving, ignoring, or even modifying

---

15 There is an extensive literature on the case. The best sources are S M Otieno, *Kenya's Unique Burial Saga* (Nation Newspapers, Nairobi, 1987) and J B Ojwang and J N K Mugambi (eds), *The S M Otieno Case* (Nairobi, 1989). More accessible are David William Cohen and E S Atieno Odhiambo, *Burying SM: The Politics of Knowledge and the Sociology of Power in Africa* (1992) and John W van Doren, 'Death African Style: The Case of S M Otieno' (1988) 36 American Journal of Comparative Law 329.

16 A different perspective with a longer time-frame is interestingly sketched by Massimo Corsale, 'Legal Pluralism and the Corporatist Model in the Welfare State', (1994) 7 Ratio Juris 95, linking pluralism to M Hauriou, Carl Schmitt and Santi Romano, among others.

17 The *locus classicus* is Karl Llewellyn, 'The Normative, The Legal and the Law-jobs' (1940) 49 Yale Law Journal 1355; see above, Ch 3.4(d).

18 M R Kadish and S H Kadish, *Discretion to Disobey: A Study of Lawful Departures from Rules* (1973). The concept is a complex one and arguably includes legal fictions, plea bargaining, refusal to prosecute even where there is a duty to do so, and 'perverse' jury verdicts.

official rules. These insights have been fruitfully applied and developed in empirical studies of regulation, among others.[19]

A second conception of legal pluralism was developed, mainly by legal anthropologists, in the late colonial and post-independence period. As anthropology began to escape from the idea that 'tribes' were self-contained units situated in a vacuum, there was increasing recognition that traditional norms, institutions and processes interacted with outside forces in complex ways. An early example, is Lloyd Fallers' classic account of Busoga law in Uganda, which brought out very clearly how traditional Soga ways of dispute-processing were linked to the colonial courts in a hierarchy. While the official legal system only recognised two or three levels of jurisdiction, disputants were generally required to move through two or more additional levels before reaching institutions that were recognised as courts of first instance.[20]

More recently, Sally Falk Moore, Martin Chanock and others have further glossed the idea of pluralism by showing that what passed for 'customary law' was often in large part an artificial creation of the colonial state, sometimes produced by negotiation between colonial officials and 'representatives' of the colonised – the result being a hybrid often bearing only a tenuous relation to traditional concepts, processes and norms, which might continue to survive and develop in different ways.[1] Chanock goes so far as to suggest that what has passed for 'customary law' in the discourse of both colonial administrators and post-Independence nationalist elites was 'a colonial myth based on need not knowledge' and 'an idealisation of the past developed in an attempt to cope with social dislocation'.[2] Indeed, what passed for customary law

---

19 Eg Keith Hawkins, *Environment and Enforcement* (1984); R Baldwin and J C McCrudden (eds), *Regulation and Public Law* (1987); and Julia Black, *Rules and Regulators* (1997).

20 'The "courts" held by parish chiefs, by village and sub-village headmen, and by lineage heads have never received legislative recognition, but the official courts have recognized their usefulness and have acted to maintain them ... From the point of view of the average villager, all these tribunals are a part of a single judicial system; all are nkiiko, with the authority "to cut cases",' Lloyd Fallers, *Law Without Precedent: Legal Ideas in Action in the Colonial Courts of Busoga* (1969) at p 59. Of course, such a phenomenon is not confined to traditional societies. In civil disputes in modern societies there are more or less formal, more or less voluntary, more or less institutionalised stages involving negotiation or mediation or some other 'alternative' means before a disputant gets anywhere near a court.

1 Sally Falk Moore, *Social Facts and Fabrications* (1986); Martin Chanock, *Law, Custom and Social Order* (1989).

2 At p 8 (citing Bloch); cf pp 236-237. The sceptical thesis about customary law being largely a product of colonial encounters can be over-generalised: in some places, eg today's Malaysia, there are well-documented examples of custom pre-dating colonisation and, of course, there were institutions and orderings in pre-colonial Africa.

was often a response to colonial rule, more modern than the imported law.

A third stage of development of the concept of 'legal pluralism' has evolved as the focus of attention moved back to 'non-state law' in modern or Western societies. Under this increasingly vague rubric, many empirical studies by socio-legal scholars, sociologists and others have been published, *The Journal of Legal Pluralism* has become established, and there have been some recent theoretical contributions – so that the field has become sufficiently diverse that it is dangerous to generalise.[3] There have been some stimulating contributions, but one is nevertheless left with a feeling of frustration about the literature: on the one hand the phenomena are important, on the other hand there is a worrying vagueness and lack of clear sense of direction about where this all leads. At this point, Santos appears to me to have made a very significant contribution.

Santos shares this sense of dissatisfaction. His own treatment of the topic advances the discussion in several important respects. First, until very recently nearly all discussions of 'legal pluralism' have focused on societies or sub-groups within them. Santos rightly emphasises the ways in which legal orders interact at all levels from the global to the very local. From a global perspective, the coexistence and interaction of legal orders at different levels is one reason why the phenomenon of legal pluralism must become central to general jurisprudence.

Secondly, the term 'legal pluralism' has some normative associations. Historically the term was often used rhetorically in political contexts as part of arguments against the centralisation of state power, its claims to having a monopoly of law, and the bogey of 'legal centralism'. So 'pluralism' has tended to be treated as a 'pro-word'. Santos identifies in the literature a tendency to nostalgia and romanticism. He is emphatic that 'To my mind there is nothing inherently good, progressive, or emancipatory about legal pluralism. Indeed, there are instances of legal pluralism that are quite reactionary.'[4] I agree with him that the term is more usefully treated as an analytical concept, without any necessary

---

3   A further development has been the introduction of the idea of 'legal polycentricity', but I agree with Gordon Woodman that, while some useful work has been done under this rubric, the concept is ambiguous and is of little or no analytical value (G Woodman, review of Hanne Petersen and Henrik Zahle (eds), *Legal Polycentricity: Consequences of Pluralism in Law* (1995) in (1997) 39 Journal of Legal Pluralism 155). See also Woodman (1998), op cit; cf Brian Tamanaha, 'The Folly of the Concept of Scientific Pluralism' (1993) 20 Journal of Law and Society 192. As was suggested above (Ch 3.5), most puzzles about normative pluralism are attributable to the complexity of the phenomenon; cf L Shelley, 'Transnational Organized Crime: The New Authoritarianism' in R Friman and P Andreas (eds) *The Illicit Global Economy* (1999).

4   At pp 114-115. For example, Santos describes the situation of pluralism in feudal society as 'complex, cumbersome, chaotic and arbitrary' (at p 58).

progressive connotations, that designates the co-existence of multiple orders, generally in a single time-space context.[5]

Thirdly, and probably most importantly, Santos develops the notion of 'interlegality' to refer to interactions between co-existing legal orders. It is a mistake to assume that because multiple legal orders co-exist they are necessarily self-contained, or in conflict with each other, or substantially different. Santos's case studies of squatter settlements in Brazil provide vivid illustrations of these points. For example, Pasagarda law – the internal legal order governing some social relations within a squatter settlement outside Rio[6] – borrowed some of its forms and rhetoric and concepts from 'asphalt law', ie state municipal law.[7] To some extent this regime was in conflict with the state, to some extent it was recognised as being an instrument of social ordering, so it served both as a brake on and an instrument of state control.

Santos's study of a series of disputes in Recife illustrates different aspects of legal pluralism in action: in a series of disputes between squatters and developers, both sides made use of the state legal system in different ways, but in two cases partial or total success was obtained by deploying other political and legal resources, including international human rights norms, constitutional law and natural law, as well as the media and the political influence of the Church. In both studies class conflict was central to the situation and the less privileged protagonists invoked a plurality of legal, political and ideological resources at a number of levels. In the case of Recife these ranged from the very local to the global.[8]

To capture the complexity of the relationships among legal orders and semi-autonomous legal fields, Santos introduces the concept of 'interlegality'. Using cartographic metaphors, he gives an ebullient account of his view in a passage quoted at the start of this essay. He claims to be presenting:

'... not the legal pluralism of traditional legal anthropology, in which the different legal orders are conceived as separate entities coexisting in the same political space, but rather, the conception of different legal spaces superimposed, interpenetrated, and mixed in our minds, as much as in our actions, either on occasions of

5   Some legal orders apply to 'imagined communities' that are dispersed and whose members do not know each other – eg gypsy law, some versions of Islamic or Jewish law. See Benedict Anderson, *Imagined Communities* (rev ed 1991).

6   The Pasagarda study was done in 1970, that of Recife in 1980.

7   Ironically this 'illegal legal system' was primarily concerned with property relations – leasing, inheritance, disputes between landlord and tenant – notwithstanding that the basic norm is illegal from the point of view of state law.

8   Santos, Ch 5.

qualitative leaps or sweeping crises in our life trajectories, or in the dull routine of eventless everyday life.'[9]

This passage is dismissed somewhat mockingly by Gunther Teubner: 'We are left with ambiguity and confusion'.[10] Teubner's concern here is to find a basis for distinguishing the social and the legal; his remedy is autopoiesis. Here I am more convinced by Santos's picture, despite the ebullience, than Teubner's version of systems theory.[11]

The concept of interlegality could usefully be developed, especially at transnational and global levels to provide fresh analyses of such phenomena as legal transplants, imposed law, and regional legal regimes. One way of proceeding might be along the following lines. As a preliminary to systematic analysis of examples or to further empirical work, it would be useful to develop a conceptual framework, including the following:

(a) typology or typologies of norms;[12]
(b) a typology of agglomerations of norms (eg systems, orders, codes, collections, digests, muddles, melees);
(c) a typology of relations and of interactions between, among, and within agglomerations of norms (eg symbiosis, competition, conflict, prioritisation, imposition, imitation, convergence, subsumption, integration).

There is, of course, a massive, but diffuse, literature on (a) within jurisprudence and other disciplines (eg game theory, the emergence of norms). One suspects that (b) is less well developed (but see Sampford, Teubner and his critics, and Bentham's *Of Laws in General*). It is my impression that the literature on (c) is fragmented and uneven. There is relative sophistication in the legal literature on conflicts of laws and private international law, on legal pluralism, and on such topics as subsidiarity in the European Union and reception. But, so far as I am aware, there is little systematic analysis about different kinds of relation between normative orders (and other kinds of agglomeration). How far existing categories and differentiations developed in other contexts would be helpful in providing a more systematic framework for the study of

---

9   At pp 472-473. This passage is quoted at greater length at the start of this essay.
10 Gunther Teubner, 'The Two faces of Janus: Rethinking Legal Pluralism', (1992) 13 Cardozo Law Review 1443.
11 See above Ch. 3.5. On the futility of sharply distinguishing 'legal' and 'non-legal' orders, see Griffiths, op cit, at pp 29-39 and below, p 231.
12 'Norm' is used here in the broad sense of the generic term for prescriptions, of which categorical precepts, principles, guidelines, standards, and perhaps maxims (eg the maxims of equity) are sub-sets.

normative and legal pluralism is a large question.[13] Such preliminary, mainly conceptual, analysis is a task for analytical jurisprudence.

Santos rightly emphasises the increase of significance of legal pluralism as part of the process of uncoupling notions of state, nation, and law. Nevertheless, like Teubner, he feels the need to identify the defining characteristics of law.[14] Here, I side with Griffiths and Llewellyn, who reject general definitions of law as unnecessary and misleading, because the indicia of 'the legal' are more like a continuum or more complex mix of attributes, which it is not necessary to set off artificially from closely related phenomena except for pragmatic reasons in quite specific contexts.[15]

Strangely, Santos does not set his discussion of legal pluralism or legal plurality in the broader context of normative pluralism. There seem to me to be at least two advantages in doing this. First, everyone experiences normative pluralism as a fact every day of their lives. Lawyers' scepticism of the importance of legal pluralism, or even of its existence[16] is most easily countered by starting with this undeniable fact of the co-existence of normative orders or agglomerations which, from an individual point of view, are not necessarily linked hierarchically. Secondly, it is easier to deal with problems of defining the borders of legal/non-legal phenomena for different specific purposes, if one sees legal pluralism as a rather fluid sub-species of normative pluralism.

This justifies a digression into the broader topic. One of the puzzling features of legal pluralism is that everybody lives under and experiences normative pluralism in their daily lives, yet when lawyers or law students are presented with examples of legal pluralism they tend to find it surprising, or puzzling, or 'not really law'. To take a homely example: An outsider doing an ethnographic study of my law school, the Faculty of Laws of University College London, might ask: 'What norms apply to members of this community?' In order to answer this question, one would first need to distinguish between norms applicable to the community (and its constituent individuals qua members of the community) and the sum total of norms applying to each of the individuals who are members of the community.

To start with the former: a preliminary list would include international treaties relating to copyright, European Union Law, the European

---

13   Eg within jurisprudence, familiar distinctions between primary and secondary rules (Hart), rules and principles (Dworkin), rules expressed in fixed verbal form and rules not so expressed (Twining and Miers) and so on.
14   At p112. His general definition is reminiscent of Hoebel's attempt that Karl Llewellyn refused to include in *The Cheyenne Way*, see *KLRM* at pp 177-179.
15   Griffiths, op cit; Llewellyn, *Jurisprudence, Realism in Theory and Practice* (1960) at p 3ff.
16   See Woodman (1997) op cit (commenting on J Vansina).

Convention on Human Rights, the Constitution of the United Kingdom (if such exists), United Kingdom law, English law, the bye-laws and regulations of the Borough of Camden, Internet Law, the Charter and Statutes of the University of London, the statutes, rules, regulations and policies of University College, Faculty Regulations and rules, the ethical norms of the Law Society and the Bar and their rules relating to admission, the marking schemes and Examination Regulations and conventions of the University of London, rules created by the Faculty, the students' Law Society, and a host of unwritten norms of courtesy, university custom and practice, UCL tradition, and the customs and conventions of the Faculty of Laws. Other bodies of rules, regulations and other norms would impact on significant sub-groups within the law school, such as the norms of the Universities' Funding Council, the Association of University Teachers, and the National Union of Students. Members of Faculty spasmodically enforce English rules of grammar and spelling and principles of logic. Almost any behaviour within this community can be guided, appraised, or sanctioned by invoking one or more sets or systems of these and other rules.

Yet the norms operating within Bentham House (the Law School building) are much more complex than that. I sometimes ask my students to write down what bodies of norms they have been subject to or have invoked during the previous 48 hours. Naturally their answers are very varied. Our students come from different ethnic backgrounds, belong to different religions, play different sports and games, live in hostels or at home, join clubs, societies and political parties, watch television,[17] engage in sexual relations, queue,[18] travel abroad or indulge in other transnational relations, make rash promises, invoke proverbs, mantras and maxims, and visit night clubs, prisons, schools and other institutions.

Lawyers and law students encounter normative pluralism every day of their lives, in legal and non-legal contexts. Yet legal pluralism is generally marginalised and viewed with scepticism in legal discourse. Perhaps the main reason for this is that for over 200 years Western legal theory has been dominated by conceptions of law that tend to be monist (one internally coherent legal system),[19] statist (the state has a monopoly of law within its territory), and positivist (what is not created or recognised as law by the state is not law).

---

17 About half of them deny being subject to rules of television watching, the other half are not sure what theirs are (*HTDTWR* at pp 12, 143-144).
18 On queuing rules see Neil MacCormick, 'Norms, Institutions, and Institutional Facts', (1998) *Law and Philosophy*, pp 1, 3ff.
19 Though not necessarily as comprehensively monist as Kelsen who subsumed all national legal systems under international law (above, Ch 3.3).

A second reason is that law is conceived of as what lawyers think it is rather than what those subject to it think it is; but lawyers' conceptions of law are derived from their training and socialisation, from their claims to having a monopoly of certain kinds of knowledge and expertise, and these in turn are derived from or bolstered by underlying – largely statist – conceptions of law. Concepts such as 'non-state law', 'folk law', and 'customary law' are generally associated with anthropology and sociology, even though academic lawyers have contributed to their study as much as scholars from other disciplines. One of the pioneers of the study of the responsiveness of English law to customs and values of minority cultures, the late Sebastian Poulter, has been criticised for claiming that he was the only lawyer taking a legal approach to legal pluralism.[20] In my view, the criticism was just, for many of the pioneers of the study of legal pluralism have been academic lawyers. However, Poulter had a point. For few people practice or write manuals or train people to be skilled in the use of non-state law. On the whole, non-state law and the strong version of legal pluralism have been mainly thought and written about by scholars adopting the standpoint of observers rather than participants.

I have tried to show how Santos and I have slightly different 'takes' on legal and normative pluralism, but our differences are not great. Much more important is the point that we both treat pluralism as a central phenomenon of law, especially when it is viewed from a global perspective.

(c) Mapping

'Just like maps, laws are ruled distortions or misreadings of social territories. They share these characteristics with poems ... Though for different reasons, maps, poems and laws all distort social realities, traditions or territories, and all according to certain rules. Maps distort reality in order to establish orientation; poems distort reality to establish originality; and laws distort reality in order to establish exclusivity.' (Santos)[1]

Maps and mapping provide some of the most popular metaphors and analogies in many disciplines. One maps a field to provide an overview, to establish its contours, to chart relations between topoi, to set a context, or to serve as a guide to the terrain or the landscape for particular purposes. It has even been suggested that maps are *the* fundamental

---

20 Poulter, (1998), and the review by Werner Menski (1999), op cit, p 225n.
1   At p 458.

analogy.[2] Whether or not this is so, mapping as a metaphor is commonplace in law: Leibniz, Blackstone, Austin, and Wigmore, as well as many contemporaries, provide well-known examples.[3] In recent years, others have used geographical mapping as aids to giving accounts of the distribution of legal services, access to rural courts, patterns of crime and other spatial relations of legal phenomena.[4] There is even a nascent law-and-geography movement.[5]

Both Santos and I have long been interested in legal cartography. We have been concerned with both geographical and mental mapping *of* law. Santos has gone one step further to develop the idea of laws *as* maps. His main point is that laws, like maps, systematically distort reality rather than merely reflect it.[6] Chapter 7 of *Toward a New Common Sense* embodies a revised version of his well-known essay of the same title from which I, among others, have learned a great deal.[7] It is dense, richly suggestive and full of tantalising, sometimes obscure, aperçus that need clarification and further development.

I have dealt with legal cartography at length in Chapter 6. Here I shall deal with it quite briefly, without fully doing justice to Santos's

2   Santos, at p 351, citing A Robinson and B Petchnik, *The Nature of Maps* (1976). Susan Haack uses mapping analogies, including in relation to multiple descriptions: 'A heterogeneous true description of the world is no less true for its heterogeneity; any more than a map which superimposes a depiction of the roads on a depiction of the contours of the relevant terrain, or a map which inserts a large-scale depiction of a major city in a corner of a small-scale depiction of a state, is less accurate for its heterogeneity' (*Manifesto* at p 160; cf Peirce op cit, at p 35).

3   For references see above, Ch 6.3 at p 141n.

4   Eg Paul Wiles, 'A Future Research Agenda for Analyzing Crime in Cities' (1997) 31 Comparative Law Review 24; Keith D Harries, *The Geography of Laws and Justice* (1978); and *Serious Violence: Patterns of Homicide and Assault in America* (1990).

5   Kim Economides, 'Law and Geography: New Frontiers', in Philip Thomas (ed) *Legal Frontiers* (1996). See above, Ch 6.3 and 6.4.

6   Santos is attracted to cartography especially because he sees it as 'disproving' epistemological foundationalism and correspondence theories. This is unconvincing. Ironically, one of the most popular examples of ideological mapping, Peters's Projection, claims to provide 'the map which represents countries accurately according to their surface areas' in contrast to the Eurocentric maps based on Mercator's projection, which incorrectly showed the colonial powers as being larger than they really were, 'while the Southern continents Africa, South America, are shown as far too small' (New Internationalist edition, 1999). The argument is that Peters's map corresponds more closely to reality. Santos himself talks of maps as distortions of 'reality' – which seems to presuppose rather than refute a correspondence theory of truth. The fact that Santos makes some insightful points about cartography and law reinforces my argument that his sociology of law owes little or nothing to his dubious epistemology.

7   The full title was: 'Law: A Map of Misreading. Toward a Postmodern Conception of Law', (1987) 14 Journal of Law and Society 279.

ideas. My essay on 'Mapping Law' was stimulated by dissatisfaction with the Grands Systèmes tradition of comparative law. The issues seemed significant, but simplistic Cook's Tours and confused debates about taxonomy seemed inadequate. I used the idea of geographical mapping to suggest why developing total pictures of law in the world and particular legal orders is difficult. The main reason is the complexity of the phenomena involved and their inter-relationships. Constructing 'whole views' of law in the world is difficult because there are many kinds of normative ordering, with different histories, that coincide, overlap, and interact in complex ways in the same geographical spaces. Hence the centrality of the ideas of normative and legal pluralism in understanding legal phenomena.

A second theme was that maps presuppose reliable and comparable data, but such data in respect of law are sparse, uneven, and in many respects underdeveloped. This is illustrated by the relative scarcity of global and national statistics for law compared to such fields as economics, trade, health, and education. How far this is attributable to the cultural specificity of most legal phenomena or to the underdevelopment of our discipline, especially its empirical aspects, are issues for a revived general jurisprudence. Some legal phenomena, like Mr Palomar's lawn or waves, are not easy to describe empirically, let alone to subject to statistical analysis. Others may be amenable to this kind of treatment, but localised legal studies and the unempirical tradition of comparative legal studies have not produced much data or adequate concepts for data collection.

A third theme, introduced in relation to Calvino's *Invisible Cities*, is that understanding a legal order, like understanding a city, requires multiple viewpoints and perspectives.

In *Toward a New Common Sense* Santos uses the idea of mapping law to develop a number of points in relation to levels of law, legal pluralism, and globalisation. As we have seen, though our enterprises are rather different, our conclusions are remarkably similar. Santos provides one chart which neatly pictures his research agenda for the study of 'the Transnationalization of the Legal Field' (see p 236). This chart is useful, though a bit too schematic for my taste: the division into three levels (global, national, local) only begins to catch the complexity of types of relation and their ordering and, if it suggests that significant levels of relations are neatly stratified in a single geographical hierarchy, it is misleading.[8]

---

8   Above, Ch 7.2. Santos is well aware of such complexities, but, like other writers on globalisation, he is inclined to jump straight from the national to the global level without dwelling on other important intermediate and cross-cutting relations (eg regional, alliances, non-state networking in the Commonwealth or the Hispanic-speaking world).

Table 3 Structure–Agency Map of Capitalist Societies in the World System

Dimensions	Social Agency	Institutions	Developmental Dynamics	Power Form	Legal Form	Epistemological Form
Structural Places						
Householdplace	gender, generation	marriage, family, kinship	affection maximizing	patriarchy	domestic law	fatalism, familial culture
Workplace	class, nature as 'capitalist nature'	factory, corporation	profit maximizing, maximizing the degradation of nature	exploitation of 'capitalist nature'	production law	productivisim, technologism, professional training, corporate culture
Marketplace	consumership	market	utility maixizing, maximizing the commodification of needs	fetishism of commodities	exchange law	consumerism, mass culture
Communityplace	ethnicity, race, nation, people, religion	community, neighborhood, region, grassroots, organization, church	identity maximizing	unequal differentiation	community law	local knowledge, community culture, tradition
Citizenplace	citizenship	state	loyalty maximizing	domination	territorial (state) law	educational and cultural nationalism, civic culture
Worldplace	nation-state	interstate system, international agencies and associations, international treaties	effectivity maximizing	unequal exchange	systemic law	science, universalistic progress, global culture

Source: B Santos, *Toward a New Common Sense* p 417.

One particularly valuable insight is the idea that viewing law from multiple perspectives requires focusing not solely or mainly on the citizenplace (state-citizen relations) but also on five other fields of social relations: the household, the workplace, the marketplace, the community, and the global setting ('the worldplace'). These are not just different fields of state law (suggested by terms such as 'family law', 'labour law' etc), but rather are themselves domains of power, knowledge and ordering that may be more or less independent of the state. Under 'modernity', attention has been focused almost entirely on 'the citizenplace', obscuring the significance of these other loci:

> 'As there is a literary canon that establishes what is and what is not literature, there is also a legal canon that establishes what is and what is not law.'[9]

The idea of pluralism applies also to knowledge and power and there are important connections affecting how law, knowledge and power are in fact distributed at a given time.

Santos warns that it is not enough to redraw the map of law, or more broadly of social relations, solely by adding to the list of loci, actors and enclaves of ordering, or by cumulating descriptions, any more than it is useful to give purely chronological accounts of historical development:

> '[M]erely to recognize the existence of a plurality of legal orders, without grounding it theoretically, implies a triple fallacy: the fallacy of descriptivism (as far as it goes, the list of pluralities is complete; but it could be added on to indefinitely without any loss of coherence); the fallacy of triviality (the more complete the list, the greater the probability that it will defeat itself as a description of reality; if law, power and knowledge are everywhere, they are nowhere); and finally, if I may borrow Sartre's term, the fallacy of seriality (the list is practico-inert, the relationship among its elements – irrespective of their number – is never more complex than the relationship between people in a queue waiting for the bus).'[10]

Santos is emphatic that the plurality of law, knowledge and power 'far from being chaotic or infinite, is structured and relational'.[11] Theory needs to give some account of the structures and relations that affect

---

9   At p 473.
10 At p 403 (citing Sartre, *Critique of Dialectical Reason* (1976)). Queuing is not as simple as Santos suggests, see above, p 232 n 18.
11 At pp 403-404.

these distributions. For example, in assessing the relative importance of the power of the nation state and of other actors and enclaves of power in the global context, it is not enough to list the variety of actors or catalogue changes in the distribution of knowledge, law and power. One has to go further and offer some explanation of these matters, as Santos attempts to do in his account of modernity, capitalism and the emergence of a new 'paradigm'. One may not be persuaded by Santos's answers – I suspect that the nation-state has more staying power than he suggests – but the questions are worth asking.

Perhaps the most original part of this chapter relates to the idea of laws *as* maps. Santos' main thesis can be summarised as follows: Maps distort reality with three specific, related mechanisms: *scale*, *projection*, and *symbolisation*.[12] Laws are like maps because each presents ordered distortions of reality, the physical world for geographical maps, social relations for laws. In both cases there is a tension between representation (image maps) and orientation (instrumental maps). Laws not only represent reality, but also create it – 'the different forms of law create different legal objects upon the same social objects'.[13] For example:

> 'Large-scale legality is rich in details and features; describes behavior and attitudes vividly; contextualizes them in their immediate surroundings; is sensitive to distinctions (and complex relations) between inside and outside, high and low, just and unjust. … On the contrary, small-scale legality is poor in detail and features. It skeletonizes behavior and attitudes, and reduces them to types of action. But, on the other hand, it determines with accuracy the relativity of positions (the angles between persons and things), provides sense of direction and schemes for shortcuts and, finally, is sensitive to distinctions between part and whole, past and present, functional and non-functional. In sum, this form of legality favors a pattern of regulation based on (and geared to) orientation and movement.'[14]

Santos gives convincing illustrations of large-scale and small-scale legality from his case studies in Brazil and from different levels of labour relations. For example, an industrial dispute will be perceived differently and will involve different distributions of power and knowledge on the shop-floor, in the local community, in national headquarters (of company

12 At pp 463–473.
13 Ar p 464. This may seem like a slide into dubious metaphysics; but that is not a necessary interpretation. For example, it is commonplace that murder, marriage and wills are in an important sense legal constructs. On law as institutional fact, see Neil MacCormick and Ota Weinberger, *An Institutional Theory of Law* (1986).
14 At p 465.

and union), at governmental level, and in the boardroom of a multi-national company.

Finally, Santos reiterates the point that maps inevitably involve selection and distortion based on value judgements. The choice of scale, projection and symbolisation similarly depend on the purpose of the map and the values of the map-maker. Maps in this sense are 'ideological distortions of reality'. These considerations apply to maps of laws and laws as maps. All of this is intriguing and potentially important, but in Santos's highly compressed presentation is no more than suggestive. These are themes that deserve more detailed development.

(d) Santos's research agenda

In a magisterial survey of what is involved in rethinking law from a global perspective, Santos identifies seven types of legal transnationalisation that particularly warrant attention. These are:

(1) *'The transnationalization of nation state law'*. for example movements to harmonise or unify branches of municipal law and programmes of structural adjustment, spearheaded by the World Bank, IMF, and Western donors, which use 'conditionality' as the lever for introducing 'modern', typically capitalist, ideas of commercial law, 'good governance, human rights and democracy'.

(2) The development of *legal regimes of regional integration*. European Union law is to date by far the most developed.

(3) *Transnational commercial regulation*, much of it involving non-state law, which Santos calls 'Global capital's own law'. Santos focuses on the contested topic of the development or 'revival' of a new *lex mercatoria* as a form of non-state law, but this important field of largely private justice also includes international commercial arbitration, the World Trade Organisation, and other more or less arcane institutions and processes through which transnational commercial relations are conducted.[15]

(4) *'The Law of People on the Move'*, that is the regulation and rights of migrants, refugees, and displaced persons. This usefully links together the problems of three categories of people whom conventional legal categories tend to treat as separate specialist areas of concern. Under this heading one might usefully add the situation of gypsies, pastoralists and other nomads.[16]

15 See, for example, Yves Dezalay and Bryant Garth, *Dealing in Virtue* (1996).
16 There is, of course, an extensive inter-disciplinary literature on migration and immigration, nomads, and so on. The legal literature seems rather uneven and tends to be confined within orthodox conceptions of municipal and public international law. However, that is changing. For example, the traditional

(5) Under the rubric 'Ancient Grievances and New Solidarities', Santos refers to *the Law of Indigenous Peoples*, an old issue that has gained a new prominence in the last two decades.[17] He rightly points to the beginnings of transnational linkages and coalitions between groups concerned with the collective rights of indigenous peoples such as Maories, Aborigines and native Americans. Informal networking and academic writings have begun to develop the potential for mutual learning and support on a South-South axis.[18]

(6) The topic of cosmopolitanism and *human rights* raises not only traditional issues about the development of international protection of human rights, but also fundamental issues about universalism, cultural relativism, self-determination, trade-offs between 'development' and human rights, and the emancipatory possibilities of a whole new post-modern portfolio or 'generation' of human rights.[19]

(7) Finally, Santos focuses on genuinely global law, so far only embodied in the vague and largely aspirational idea of a *common heritage of mankind (ius humanitatis)*. This refers in first instance to the possible allocation of territories and resources on this and other planets that have not to date been appropriated by nation states or capitalist entrepreneurs. These issues surfaced most visibly in relation to the Law of the Sea, and to a lesser extent in relation to Antarctica, and the Moon Treaty of 1979.[20] So far they have tended to be viewed from the outside as relatively arcane and undeveloped aspects of public international law. But as Santos points out, there is enormous potential in the long-term for an expanded application of the principle of the common heritage of mankind, stretching beyond territory and mineral rights to a range of other issues. This relatively undeveloped area provides the clearest example of what he calls cosmopolitan law.

Santos sees the first three lines of enquiry as relating to global capitalism and the last four as providing key foci of attention for cosmopolitan, anti-hegemonic, and utopian legalities.[1] This agenda fits Santos's

---

distinction between refugees and displaced persons has been over-ridden in a UN-sponsored study: Francis M Deng, *Protecting the Dispossessed: A Challenge to the International Community* (1993).

17 *TNC*, p at 313.

18 Ibid, pp 313-327.

19 Ibid, p 358.

20 For a 'Southern' view on the Law of the Sea Conference, see N Rembe, *Africa and the International Law of the Sea* (1980). On Antarctica see Olav S Stokke and Davor Vidas (eds) *Governing the Antarctic* (1997). On the Moon Treaty see Stephen Garove, *Developments in Space Law* (1991) and Carl Q Christol, 'The Moon Treaty and Allocation of Resources', (1997) 22 Annals of Air and Space Law 31.

1   Santos, at pp 373-377.

particular ideological standpoint. It does not claim to be comprehensive: within his own framework, one might, for example, add communications and media (including copyright and the Internet),[2] nuclear proliferation, the arms trade, transnational crime, the internationalisation of legal practice, the regulation of financial markets, and transnational democracy as similarly deserving attention. Each of the areas he identifies is already or has the potential to become a distinct field of legal specialisation. What Santos does is to bring these together within a single framework of social theory and to suggest lines of enquiry about each as part of the sociology of law. He surveys this vast series of landscapes in a mere 120 pages. In the process he may have stepped on some specialists' toes, but he is surely right in suggesting that all of these areas need theorising both within a broad contextual framework and more locally. Some of these fields are under-researched and almost all are under-theorised. Mainstream legal theory hardly addresses any of the issues that they raise – a partial exception being human rights.[3]

Santos's specific agenda is less interesting than his use of theory. During the past year I have attended two conferences concerned with globalisation and law and heard of many others. Each has differed in emphasis and orientation, though not surprisingly there has been considerable overlap. It would be foolish to try to predict in detail what specific areas of concern will be on such agendas in ten years' time. Nearly all of the lines of enquiry identified by Santos and others have developed in response to perceived problems and other stimuli rather than being led by theory. This is likely to continue. My own preliminary forays into the literature of several transnational fields (comparative law, international law, the jurisprudence of the World Bank) suggest that the level of theoretical sophistication is at best uneven, in some cases non-existent. They have evolved with little regard to developments in legal theory, which in turn has paid them scant attention.

Comparative law is a good example of a field in which practice has outrun theory.[4] In practice comparative legal studies are no longer confined within the boundaries of the Country and Western model,

2   See, eg P. Bernt Hugenholtz (ed), *The Future of Copyright Law in a Digital Environment* (1996).

3   A reasonable conspectus of the massive literature on the philosophy of human rights, including issues of cultural relativism, can be obtained from, eg Jeremy Waldron, *Nonsense Upon Stilts* (1987); Abdullahi A An-Na'im and Francis M Deng (eds), *Human Rights in Africa: Cross-cultural Perspectives* (1990); Stephen Shute and Susan Hurley (eds), *On Human Rights* (1993); Martha Nussbaum, *Women, Culture and Development* (1995). Useful readers include, Henry J Steiner and Philip Alston (eds), *International Human Rights in the Context of Law, Politics, and Morals* (1996), Richard A Wilson (ed), *Human Rights, Culture and Context* (1997).

4   Above, Ch 7.

focusing largely on private law doctrine of 'advanced' or 'parent' common law and civil law systems of modern Western states. There has been a rich proliferation of subject-matters, perspectives and approaches. But there are still striking disjunctures between talk about 'comparative law' and best practice. The methodological problems of comparative work have been neglected; in many respects the focus has continued to be narrow, and departures from the Country and Western model have been ad hoc, fragmented, and uneven. There is an intellectual lag of about fifty years between the more reflective literature on comparative law and contemporary legal theory, which itself still focuses almost exclusively on the municipal law of nation states and typically outdated pictures of public international law.

What then can legal theory offer? My answer is all the standard services of theorising.[5] First a coherent 'total picture', or series of such overviews, of law-in-the-world (the synthesising function). Secondly, as a necessary element at this and other levels, the construction and clarification of important general concepts, including exploration of the extent to which it is feasible and desirable to develop cross-cultural meta-languages for legal discourse (a revived general analytical jurisprudence). Thirdly, the development of general normative principles, the clarification of values, and addressing questions about their universalisability. Fourthly, the generation of middle order empirical hypotheses and general working theories for participants, for example in such areas as constitution-making and dispute-processing and the methodology of various kinds of transnational enquiry. Fifthly, intellectual history of law as a discipline and of its specialised sub-disciplines, such as public international law and comparative law. Sixthly and perhaps most important, critical examination of assumptions underlying legal discourse in both general and quite specific contexts. In short, if one looks on legal theorising as the general part of law as a discipline, it can perform a number of functions concerned with the health of that enterprise. Occasionally, it may provide leadership with inspiring visions and grand designs or hypotheses, but more often it is reactive, setting contexts, sharpening tools, suggesting refinements, questioning assumptions, and generally tidying up.

5   CONCLUSION

Toward a New Common Sense is, in my view, the most important work to date to view law from a global perspective. One purpose of this essay has

5   Above, Ch 1.

been to make this difficult, sometimes infuriating, book more accessible to students of jurisprudence and others who are concerned with law and globalisation. For this purpose, my suggestion is that one should by-pass the first and last chapters, concentrate on the centre, and forgive the unevenness and aberrations of style. For there is a lot in the book that deserves attention.

My second purpose has been to clarify my own views in relation to those of Santos. Like many commentators, I find the more general parts of *Toward a New Common Sense* obscure, jargon-ridden and, in some instances, wrong. I resisted the temptation simply to dismiss Santos's philosophy as 'bosh', because this kind of 'post-modern' writing is now both fashionable in academic law and too important to be ignored. Santos can be treated as reasonably representative of one important version of this fashion. In this essay, I have tried to steer a path between two strands in post-modernism: on the one hand, an anti-rationalist stream that involves, or appears to involve, strong versions of epistemological scepticism and cultural relativism that I reject. On these issues I am prepared to side with the moderate, but passionate, empiricism of Haack and Peirce. On the other hand, there are aspects of imaginative post-modernism that I find attractive, stimulating, and quite compatible with innocent realism. This strand, exemplified by Calvino, emphasises the complexities and elusiveness of reality, the difficulties of grasping it, and the value of imagination and multiple perspectives in facing these difficulties. Here, it is not necessary for me to agree with Susan Haack on particular issues, for her thin metaphysics can accommodate a variety of views at lower levels of abstraction. Santos, it seems to me, embodies the vices of anti-rationalist and the virtues of imaginative post-modernism, but on a number of philosophical issues I just find him obscure.

Despite significant differences in our enterprises there is a strong convergence in our views on law. Santos presents a utopian sociological theory of law as part of a grand politico-social theory. I am a more orthodox jurist, an insider, concerned with the health of my discipline in the next 10 to 20 years. The point of convergence is a shared interest in viewing law from a global perspective. We both interpret the complex processes of globalisation along similar lines, except that I am more of an agnostic than Santos about the likely long-term implications. Santos and I both agree that legal pluralism is central to understanding law from a global perspective, that the phenomenon cuts across different geographical levels, that the existing literature on the subject is not very satisfactory and that 'interlegality' is a key concept in need of development. Santos tries at a quite abstract level to differentiate law, broadly conceived, from other forms of ordering, whereas, following Karl Llewellyn, I hold that precise general definitions of law tend to obscure the continuities between law and different kinds of ordering. There is too much fluidity for precise boundary-drawing to be appropriate in the abstract. For this reason, I prefer to treat legal pluralism as a species of normative pluralism, postponing the setting of criteria for differentiating between species (and sub-species) until a specific context and standpoint have been identified.

On mapping, Santos and I have long had a shared interest and my own views owe a good deal to his early classic essay on the subject. One of the strengths of *Toward a New Common Sense* is that it depicts in a single landscape a wide range of issues and topics that need attention in a period of rapid globalisation. Santos's specific agenda for research is not, and could not be, definitive, but it provides an admirable starting-point for mapping significant lines of enquiry and how they interconnect. In the Epilogue I shall outline a possible agenda for a new general jurisprudence.

The case for a revival of general jurisprudence is essentially a response to the challenges and opportunities presented to the enterprise of studying law as it inevitably becomes more cosmopolitan. The main difference between Santos and myself is that he is concerned with the aspirational development of all law over a long, and indefinite, time-frame, according to a particular utopian vision, while I am concerned with the healthy development of the study of law over the next decade or so, according to a traditional liberal conception of what is involved in the advancement and dissemination of learning.

Chapter 9

Epilogue

1 PALOMAR IN PALO ALTO

'Afghan and Persian Cuisine, American, Barbeque and More!, Burmese, Cafes, Cajun Confusion, Caribbean, Chinese, French, Healthy Choice, Indian, International, Italian, Japanese and Sushi, Mediterranean, Mexican, Pizza, Seafood, Salvadorean, Swiss, Strict Vegetarian, Thai.'

What is this? Another list from Borges and Foucault? A post-modern romp? A Grands Systèmes approach to culinary families? In fact it is the headings of an advertisement in the latest *Palo Alto Weekly* for 'Good Places to Eat' within a fifteen mile radius. Last week under 'Goings On: Dance' after a notice about a visiting Chicago Dance company, the headings for 'Classes and Parties' are Vintage Dance, Argentine Tango, Art for Peace International Dance and Music Group, Basic Dance for Teens with Special Needs, Beginning Folk Dance (which folk unspecified), Belly Dance, Mystic Sun Studio of Mid-Eastern Dance, Brazilian Dance Class, Beginning Ballet for Adults, Big Band Swing, Beaudoin's School of Dance, Congolese African Dance class and so on for a total of 26 entries.

The audience and the focus of the *Palo Alto Weekly* are clearly local. It features past and future events, news stories, information, comment, and advertisements to meet the local interests and needs of the inhabitants living in a prosperous, semi-urban area. This week features Halloween parties, garage sales, private and commercial advertisements, the stock of locally based companies (including several MNCs), local elections (a whole page for the Sanitary District), vital statistics about minor crimes and fires, the trial of three youths for the killing of a NASA scientist. The week's events, especially films, lectures, and workshops are as cosmopolitan as those noted from an earlier edition in Chapter 1.

One interesting feature is how 'local' is interpreted – the word shifts smoothly from small neighbourhood ('What's up on your Block?'), through East Palo Alto, the City of Palo Alto, Silicon Valley, Central Peninsula, Peninsula, the Bay Area, to California, occasionally touching the national level. Another buzzword of the times, 'community', makes similar transitions, but two packed pages of lonely hearts advertisements ('Personal Connections') makes one ask what the idea of 'community' means to the advertisers.[1] As a short-term visitor to Palo Alto, I am more or less a member of at least eight different communities ranging from our condominium to a well-integrated research centre to Stanford University and greater Palo Alto. The fluidity of the ideas of 'local' and 'community' is summed up in the headline for a feature on a housing project in East Palo Alto: 'Peninsula Habitat for Humanity Builds Community'. The subject is a housing project in a poor section of Palo Alto; 'Peninsula' refers to an area of California that includes San Francisco; Peninsula Habitat, we are told, is one of over 1,400 affiliates in the United States, which in turn are linked to a world-wide organisation that is concerned with the housing needs of humanity.

Mr Palomar sits on a hill with views over a large part of the Bay Area, thinking about the last chapter of a book on globalisation and legal theory. The relativity of the 'local' and the vagueness of 'community' are only the start of the difficulties. If only his subject could be depicted simply in terms of expanding, concentric circles that spread out neatly from one's apartment, condominium, or block, through neighbourhood, area, state, nation, region, to the whole globe and beyond. But human relations and their ordering are not like that. They are infinitely complex at the microscopic level – consider, for example, the spoken and tacit rules governing the furniture in your living-room, if you have one, including the television set, if there is one.[2] Norms are elusive and of many different kinds. Different levels of normative ordering are not neatly nested in hierarchies; nor are they impervious; nor are they static. They interact in complex ways. Moreover, to understand law and legal ordering, the study of norms is almost never enough. One also has to take account of values, facts, meanings, processes, structures, power relations, personnel, and technologies. And then there is the matter of multiple standpoints and perspectives.

1   A poignant entry under 'Missed Connections' reads: 'Seka of Bulgaria: I came to your restaurant 3 times, first with my mother, second with friend, third alone, then you were gone. I hope I can find you', *Palo Alto Weekly* (Home and Real Estate section), October 29, 1999, p 25.
2   Denis Wood and Robert Beck, *Home Rules* (1994); *HTDTWR* at pp 12-16 and 143-144.

One thing is clear: closure is not an option. This book is a highly selective study of one part of a vast intellectual heritage and a rapidly burgeoning discipline. It is no more than a slim addition to Calvino's Hypothetical Bookshelf.[3] The central message is one of complexity. It is intended to challenge simplistic assumptions and narrow reductionist perspectives rather than to present a neatly packaged theory.

Perhaps one way to move ahead is to go back to the start of the project and take stock of where we have got to. The project for which this is an interim report began to be crystallised in the early 1990s. At first it was called 'Understanding Law' – a phrase which at least designates the primary role and aspiration of a jurist. However, the label drew mixed reactions from colleagues. Some said in effect: 'Aha! At last we are going to get a definitive statement of your position – Twining's theory of law'. But I am estopped from such a conceit, in that I have criticised the assumption that the main task of the theorist is to produce neatly packaged reified 'theories', as if they are mud pies.[4] The jurist as licensed subversive is as much concerned with questioning assumptions and opening up lines of enquiry – more or less gently stirring – as with defining and defending entrenched positions or striking artificially rigid postures.

Other colleagues were nearer the mark. They asked: 'Understanding law from what standpoint to what end?' As I pondered the point of the enterprise in various places – including Oxford, Nairobi, Hong Kong, Kampala, Wasenaar (near Leiden), Bangalore, Miami, and Boston – three points became crystallised. First, my primary concern was with the health of my discipline at a particular time – that is the institutionalised study of law – from the point of view of a scholar, educator, occasional activist, and mild agent provocateur. Secondly, although I jet-setted and networked in a number of countries, my home and my main professional base are in England, my working language – even in Kampala, Beijing, Miami, and the Netherlands – is English, and my expertise is largely Anglo-American.[5] Thirdly, words like 'global', 'globalisation', and 'globalism' were a growing part of the barrage of messages from the media and they had begun to become part of the daily vocabulary of neighbouring disciplines. So questions began to arise about the relevance of these new developments, if such they were, for my own subject.

By renaming my project 'Globalisation and Legal Theory' I significantly narrowed its focus. Although the literature on the global is large, it is highly repetitious and in a strange way deals with a quite

---

3   Italo Calvino, *The Literature Machine* (1987), see above, Ch 8.3(b).
4   *LIC*, pp 129-130.
5   It is, of course, parochial and misleading to treat places like Hong Kong, Kenya, and Uganda as 'anglophone', when a smaller percentage of the population reads or speaks or thinks in English than in the Netherlands!

narrow range of issues, not always helpfully. Furthermore, I decided to start from the familiar intellectual territory of Anglo-American legal theory from 1750 to the present day considered both historically and analytically. Since this is a vast heritage, I concentrated on a few texts of selected mainstream jurists, Bentham, Austin, Hart, Holmes, Llewellyn, Rawls, and Dworkin, to which were added over time some less obvious names, including Buckland, Eckhoff, Calvino, Santos, and Haack. This selection puts my project almost exactly in mid-Atlantic: Bentham, Austin, Hart, Eckhoff, and Calvino are European; Holmes, Llewellyn, and Rawls are clearly American, while Dworkin, Santos, and Haack, like myself, hover between Europe and North America.

As the project developed, it became obvious that it was important to move down one level of generality to engage with the underlying assumptions of mainstream work in sub-disciplines with a strong transnational element, such as public and private international law, European law, human rights law, and comparative law. I decided to start for various reasons with the last, mainly because it seems to me that this is a crucial basis for exploring how far the study of law can and should become 'cosmopolitan'.[6]

I began with a limited range of texts in English by leading figures about their conception of comparative law. Here, too, I found a strong trans-Atlantic flavour. This is largely because so many of the pioneers of modern comparative law came, mostly as refugees, from Germany and settled in the United Kingdom or the United States or both. While there have been important 'home grown' figures, such as Lawson, Nicholas, and Merryman, the field was defined and developed, largely after World War II, by a diaspora of extraordinarily talented Jewish émigrés – of whom Rabel, Rheinstein, Friedmann, Kahn-Freund, Mann, Kessler, Reisenfeld, Ehrenzweig, and Schlesinger are among the most prominent

After some time, I began to find the term 'globalisation' something of a liability. To some it seemed grandiose; for others it carried the suggestion that one was making assumptions about the unity of the world economy, or the 'victory' of capitalism or the decline of the nation state or the newness of the processes. For me these are largely open questions, on which I tend to be sceptical or agnostic. Over time the label was also constricting, as it suggested commitment to operating only at the global level. There is a tendency in the literature to jump

6   The term 'cosmopolitan' is sometimes used in a normative sense to refer to an ethic that contrasts with strong nationalism (eg Martha Nussbaum) or as 'counter-hegemonic' (Santos). As with 'globalisation' and 'pluralism', I intend it in a relatively detached descriptive sense. See further David Harvey's excellent paper 'Cosmopolitanism and the Banality of Geographical Evils' (*Public Culture*, forthcoming).

from the relatively local to the global without adequate consideration of a variety of intermediate stages. CNN and the Internet may circle the world, but they have not 'penetrated' very far in Uganda or India. Furthermore, there is an implicit bias towards belief in the possibility and validity of generalisations across cultures, traditions and local histories that just should not be taken for granted. One of the clearer lessons of these preliminary explorations is that there is a need for a strong revival of general jurisprudence, in which issues about generalisation, (normative, conceptual, empirical, interpretive) will be an important part of the agenda. They should be investigated and discussed rather than assumed. So my project has broadened and been renamed 'General Jurisprudence', and these essays are presented for what they are, preliminary explorations preparatory to developing an agenda for general jurisprudence more systematically.

2 TAKING STOCK OF THE HERITAGE

I suggested in the Introduction that one way of looking on jurisprudence is as a heritage of texts and ideas that are not only of historical interest, but can also be used as a resource in dealing with theoretical issues of contemporary significance.

In Chapter 2 the history of the distinction between general and particular jurisprudence was explored. For most of the nineteenth-century jurisprudence was assumed to be general, but as law schools sought to establish their credentials, there was a trend towards particular jurisprudence as being both more practical and more directly relevant to other subjects in the curriculum. Hart revived general jurisprudence in England in the 1950s, but he did not lay much store by the distinction until, in his posthumously published Postscript to *The Concept of Law*, he sought to use it as a basis for reducing his differences with Ronald Dworkin. I concluded that this attempt did not succeed. The distinction cannot bear much weight because generality and particularity are relative matters. However, the distinction is useful just because much of twentieth century Anglo-American jurisprudence has been either quite local or else indeterminate in respect of its geographical reach. The flexibility of 'general' in this context is a positive advantage compared to the more rigid 'global'. Thus the distinction between general and particular jurisprudence has a function, but it has been and is likely to be of limited value in setting an agenda for the discipline of law and for jurisprudence as its theoretical part.

In Chapters 3 to 5 I deliberately started with the familiar – a selection of individual jurists who have been treated as canonical in England and some other parts of the common law world in the early 1990s. These essays both set a historical context and explore how responsive this aspect of our heritage might be to the challenges of globalisation.

On the whole the conclusion is that they are more relevant than might at first be apparent. As we have seen, Hart's attempt to confine Dworkin to particular jurisprudence failed, for Dworkin's central ideas cannot be sensibly restricted to a single jurisdiction, or probably even to a liberal democratic state, but their geographical reach needs to be explored further.

There are unanswered questions as to whether Rawls's, or any other theory of justice based on the idea of societies as closed units, can be adjusted to guide and evaluate the design of institutions at global, regional and other levels.

Hart and Kelsen provide basic concepts for giving accounts of the form and structure of municipal legal systems, and possibly for a slightly wider range of legal orders. Both have provided useful concepts, distinctions, and insights, but they do not offer much in the way of tools for 'thick description'. Kelsen's monism provides a challenge to ideas about legal pluralism and non-state law. Hart's methods and style of conceptual clarification could be applied to a wider range of concepts than has been done hitherto.

Holmes's 'bad man' can be interpreted as representing a neglected standpoint, those subject to the law, when it is viewed as the product of other people's power. Such bottom-up views have often been neglected in jurisprudence. But even as subject, the bad man only represents one standpoint among many.

Llewellyn's law-jobs theory is a flexible and suggestive tool for investigating the institutionalised ordering of any human group, but to realise its potential it requires both refinement and development.

Of the individuals studied, Bentham was the one who was most consistently committed to the viewpoint of 'the citizen of the world'. But even he was ambivalent about the scope of 'community'. Although he did not develop his ideas very far in this respect, he was more sensitive than most of his successors to the limitations of 'black box' theories of national or municipal legal systems.[7] Although I personally dissent from many of his views, his grand vision of the range of questions that need to be addressed by a general theory concerned with the design of institutions, procedures and laws at all levels from the very local to the global deserves much more attention than it has so far received.

7   *RB*, pp 134-136.

These essays have not attempted to do justice to many other important strands in our juristic heritage such as the Natural Law tradition, macro-theoretical sociology of law, critical legal studies, feminist jurisprudence, or autopoiesis. It may be that our heritage contains other thinkers, or different texts by the same thinkers, that deserve more attention or even to be 'canonised'. And, of course, the Anglo-American tradition is only one among many.

This examination of the heritage of our canonical jurists suggested that most of them are more relevant to a global perspective on law and a revived general jurisprudence than might be expected. Jurists, as the generalists of legal scholarship, and legal specialists need each other. And, I suspect, the most fruitful way forward in developing a general jurisprudence will be to subject to critical scrutiny the discourses, concepts and agendas of different specialisms within law, both scholarly and activist, as a joint enterprise. The next step was to look more closely at the prevailing assumptions underpinning work in specialised sub-disciplines that contain a strong transnational element, such as public international law, European Union law, and comparative law.

Chapters 6 and 7 report on some first steps in this direction in relation to comparative law. 'Mapping Law' identifies some of the difficulties in constructing broad overviews of law in the world or of single legal orders. Some problems are attributable to the complexities of pluralism as a fact and to the multiplicity of standpoints and perspectives. Maps, both geographical and mental, presuppose usable data, which in turn presuppose meaningful categories. But in respect of legal phenomena these are remarkably undeveloped at global and transnational levels. Chapter 7 extends this theme through a preliminary stock-taking of two main strands in modern comparative law, notably the Grands Systèmes approach, which is most fully developed in Continental Europe, and micro-comparative studies in the Anglo-American tradition. The main conclusion in respect of each is that there is need for more theoretical sophistication in response to the challenges of globalisation.

Chapter 8 is a detailed assessment of Santos's *Toward a New Common Sense*, probably the most important theoretical work to date on globalisation and law. Santos's ideas also serve a useful sounding-board for trying to sort out what is attractive and what is unacceptable about some kinds of post-modernism. In this chapter I have tried to probe my ambivalence about Santos's ideas and to reconcile my acceptance of some of the basic ideas of such different writers as Susan Haack and Italo Calvino. The essay stakes out a position between two different strands in post-modernism – the anti-rational and the imaginative – as well as trying to make *Toward a New Common Sense* more accessible to non-specialists.

3   COSMOPOLITAN LEGAL STUDIES: SOME PROVOCATIVE PROPOSITIONS[8]

These essays report the explorations of one English jurist into selected aspects of one juristic tradition and its relevance to challenges of globalisation. This is quite a narrow base. But it provides a starting-point for further enquiries into what might be involved in developing a revived general jurisprudence and rethinking comparative law in the early years of the next millennium in order to construct a basis for a discipline that is more consistently cosmopolitan

I conclude by presenting as a basis for discussion some provocative propositions that extend a bit beyond what has gone before.

(a)   The Challenges of Globalisation

1.   Whatever one's interpretation of the significance of 'globalisation' – strong, weak, or agnostic – these complex processes clearly have important implications for the study of law.
2.   Globalisation does not minimise the importance of the local, but it does mandate setting the study of local issues and phenomena in broad geographical and historical contexts. For most legal scholars the maxim should be: 'Think global, focus local'.
3.   Globalisation presents three main challenges to traditional legal theory:
     a.   it challenges 'black box theories' that treat nation states, societies, legal systems, and legal orders as closed, impervious entities that can be studied in isolation;
     b.   it challenges the idea that the study of law and legal theory can be restricted to two types of legal ordering: municipal state law and public international law, conceived as dealing with relations between sovereign states; and
     c.   it challenges the adequacy of much of the present conceptual framework and vocabulary of legal discourse (both law talk and talk about law) for discussing legal phenomena across jurisdictions, traditions, and cultures.
4.   From a global perspective legal phenomena need to be viewed both geographically and historically. In terms of space these levels include the global, international, transnational, regional, inter-communal, municipal (or nation-state), sub-state and non-state local. In respect

8   Passages in the text discussing these propositions can be identified by reference to the index.

of time, they have complex histories of change, inertia, imposition, diffusion, interaction, and so on.

5. Different geographical levels of legal phenomena are not neatly nested in a single hierarchy of larger and smaller spaces. Rather they cut across each other, overlap, and interact in many complex ways. That is why normative pluralism as a fact is central to understanding law.

6. It is sometimes useful to distinguish between normative pluralism, legal pluralism as a species of normative pluralism, and pluralistic state legal systems and non-state legal orders as sub-species of legal pluralism.

7. However, when and where it is appropriate to draw sharp distinctions between legal and non-legal orders and other phenomena, or between state and non-state law, or between legal orders, systems, traditions, cultures and muddles, is context-dependent: that is it depends on one's vantage-point, perspectives and goals. Here, it is often unhelpful to seek for precise general definitions.

8. Law is a participant-oriented discipline.[9] This has led to a bias towards immediate practicalities and to emphasis on some distinctions, internal/external, participant/observer, general/particular that cannot bear much weight. This does not mean that these distinctions are meaningless or useless, but they can be overworked unless careful attention is paid to differentiation of standpoints and perspectives.

9. Legal phenomena can be viewed from a variety of standpoints. There is, not surprisingly, a top-down bias in much legal scholarship and legal discourse generally. For example, images of legal orders as machine (social engineering) or organism (functionalism) are more common than bottom up images, such as jungle (potentially hostile environment, a product of other people's power) and bazaar (user and consumer perspectives).

10. The word 'pluralism' is commonly used in three different senses in legal contexts: first, pluralism as a synonym for diversity, as in the statement 'Legal theory in London is characterised by a bewildering pluralism'; 'pluralism' applied to multiple perspectives; and normative and legal pluralism connoting the co-existence of multiple orders or collections of norms in the same context of time and space. None of these usages involved commitment to the idea of 'multiple realities' if that involves a denial of the idea that there is one real world that exists independently of our knowledge of it.

---

9   *BT*, pp 128-130.

(b) General Jurisprudence

1. One implication of globalisation is that the time is ripe both for exploring what is involved in looking at law from a global perspective and for a revival of general jurisprudence.

2. Ironically, general jurisprudence is broader and more intellectually ambitious than global jurisprudence because the former includes all the intermediate stages between considering two or more legal orders, traditions, or cultures and viewing law in the whole world and beyond. 'General' is relative in a way that 'global' is not.

3. The idea of general jurisprudence does not involve any necessary commitment to particular positions on universalisability, cultural or legal relativism, or the scope for developing a global meta-language, or empirical generalisations about legal phenomena. Such issues are all contested. Rather, a central question for general jurisprudence today is: how far is it feasible and desirable to generalise about law, conceptually, normatively, historically, empirically etc across jurisdictions, national boundaries, traditions, and cultures?

4. One of the functions of theory is to provide overviews or maps of the terrain to be studied. Constructing total pictures of law in the world is one task of general jurisprudence. Mapping law in the world is difficult (a) because of the multiplicity and complexity of levels of relations and ordering and (b) because maps presuppose data and data presuppose usable concepts, both of which are underdeveloped in respect of law at the global and transnational levels.

5. In so far as there are fruitful analogies between giving accounts of cities and of legal orders from multiple perspectives, Italo Calvino's *Invisible Cities* deserves to be added to our juristic canon.

6. The 'legal families' debate in comparative law has been bedevilled by a tendency to ignore different levels of ordering, an inadequate conceptual framework, and lack of genuinely comparable data.

7. For a variety of reasons (such as suspicion of 'grand theory', the relative parochialism of the sociology of law in its main home the United States, and the decline of the law and development movement) there is no contemporary equivalent to nineteenth-century historical jurisprudence and hence a relative dearth of bold hypotheses of the kind floated by Maine in the nineteenth century. There is a need for more hypotheses analogous to Alan Watson's provocative 'transplants thesis'. These in turn need to be refined and tested by rigorous empirical research. Again, adequate concepts for characterising phenomena cross-culturally and transnationally are a necessary part of developing such hypotheses.[10]

---

10 This proposition should not be taken as an endorsement of Donald Black's strongly positivistic approach to the sociology of law, although it is fair to say

8. This suggests a high priority for general analytical jurisprudence with a broad agenda that includes not only fundamental legal concepts such as rule, obligation, rights, and sanction, but also the much wider range of concepts that might form a cross-cultural meta-language for inter-disciplinary 'talk about law', such as the concepts of historical, anthropological, sociological, or political jurisprudence.

9. Analytical jurisprudence is not confined to conceptual elucidation: for example, it encompasses issues concerning form and structure, reasoning and rationality, and many other issues shared with analytical philosophy.

10. Normative jurisprudence is generally better developed than other aspects of general jurisprudence because of the richness of the Natural Law, utilitarian, Kantian and modern liberal democratic traditions. However, as is illustrated by the criticisms of Rawls's treatment of international relations and debates about cultural relativism in respect of human rights, there is a broad agenda of issues that deserve attention in respect of international ethics, transnational and cross-cultural morality, and universalisability in an interdependent world.

(c) Comparative Law and Cosmopolitan Legal Studies

1. Within the institutionalised discipline of law it can be useful to draw a broad distinction between more or less parochial and more or less cosmopolitan legal studies – that is to say studies that involve a substantial cross-jurisdictional or foreign dimension. Here one needs to distinguish between provenance, audience, focus, sources, perspectives, and significance. Few legal scholars today can afford to be strongly parochial in respect of focus or sources.

2. Because almost no society, community, or nation is completely autonomous or self-contained, most legal scholars have to deal with the phenomena of legal pluralism, multiple levels of ordering, and interlegality. Furthermore, nearly all description and interpretation involves at least implicit comparison.[11] In a loose sense, we are all comparatists now.

3. Nearly all legal studies are cosmopolitan in that legal scholars, law students, and many professional actors regularly have to use sources, materials and ideas developed in more than one jurisdiction and in more than one legal culture. They need to be equipped with at least

that much of the literature is too simply dismissive of his bold hypotheses, which at least deserve to be tested empirically. See especially, D Black, *The Behavior of Law* (1976).

11 Above, p 187.

the rudiments of coping with such material. So comparative method needs to be treated as a central element of 'legal method'.

4. How far primary legal education and training should become fully cosmopolitan is an open question involving complex issues. For the time being the best strategy may again be: 'Think global; focus local'.

5. Because comparatists can no longer (if they ever could) claim a near monopoly on comparative legal studies, it does not follow that there is no room for specialist scholars, associations, journals, courses, projects etc. On the contrary our discipline will more than ever need the insights, knowledge and skills that such specialised forms of learning can bring.

6. The practice of comparative law has diversified and increased in sophistication in recent years. But the conceptualisation of the field has not kept pace with the practice as is evidenced by the confusions plaguing the Grands Systèmes tradition, the narrowness of the Country and Western model of micro-comparative studies, and the tendency to shy away from addressing difficult theoretical questions concerning comparability, comparative method, the construction of usable cross-cultural concepts, generalisation, and so on.

7. For comparative law, a more pluralistic conception of legal relations and legal orders mandates a correspondingly plural range of phenomena to be compared at both macro and micro levels.

8. Few sophisticated comparatists indulge in sustained 'molecular' comparison *stricto sensu* and for good reason – they are aware of the difficulties.

9. Institutionalised comparative law has tended to be more or less marginalised within most traditions and cultures of academic law. Within the Anglo-American tradition it has also tended to be quite isolated from mainstream legal theory.

10. Comparative law and legal theory are interdependent. Foreign and comparative legal studies provide much of the essential raw material for developing a new general jurisprudence. Comparison is a crucial step on the way to generalisation. Conversely, rethinking comparative law from a global perspective will involve all the standard tasks of legal theorising.

Teaching about globalisation and law

INTRODUCTION

This note makes some pedagogical suggestions about using this book. It is based on experience of teaching about Globalisation and Law in seminars in Boston and Miami over three years and in parts of other courses and shorter workshops over a longer period. The main objective in each case has been to make law students aware of a wider world and of broader perspectives on law and to engage with issues raised by the processes of, and debates about, 'globalisation'. There are many ways of going about this. The approach adopted here works best if one uses a combination of readings, exercises, case studies, and individual projects.

For a semester-long seminar I have prescribed Santos's *Toward a New Common Sense* along with most of these essays (or their predecessors), supplemented by some shorter readings. We have focused almost exclusively on Chapters 3-7 of Santos's book, because many law students are put off by the more abstract chapters and even the substantial minority who become interested find them easier to understand after they have worked through the middle sections.[1] Most early sessions concentrate on exercises and case studies, examples of which are given below. We begin by considering competing views of globalisation, 'paradigmatic' or 'rhetorical' globalisers, such as Santos, and sceptics, represented by Paul Hirst and Grahame Thompson. The mapping and newspaper exercises help to set a broad context. Case studies of pluralism and non-state law provide some concrete material which can be helpful in discussing more abstract ideas.

---

1   See above, Ch 8.2.

As a sub-option in a course on Jurisprudence or in an advanced seminar on legal theory at undergraduate or post-graduate level, it is possible to build on students' prior exposure to some of the ideas and jurists involved. This is a desirable, but not a necessary, prerequisite and it makes it easier to deal with a broader range of issues.

The essays in this book have been arranged so that they can be read in conjunction with short original texts by the jurists discussed in them, though not necessarily strictly in the order they are presented here. For Austin, Bentham, Holmes, Llewellyn, and even Rawls the essays provide sufficient background for pairing with directly relevant texts to be quite straightforward (see below). For students who have not encountered Hart or Dworkin before, introducing their central ideas, let alone doing justice to them, in short compass is not easy. For both *The Concept of Law* and *Law's Empire* deserve longer engagement than can be given to them in a course of this kind. One option is to provide short general introductions to their ideas through lectures and secondary readings.[2] My preferred strategy is to ask each student to concentrate on two jurists and to make presentations about these in class, with one or two short texts treated as read by the rest of the class. This has the advantage of including thinkers and texts not represented in these essays, while preserving some common ground for the class as a whole.

Other courses on globalisation, with which I am familiar, focus mainly on the world economy and commercial and financial relations. While the focus of my teaching has been explicitly theoretical, I have found it important to use case studies and concrete illustrative material in order to engage the students' interest and to bring the subject alive. The range of possible material is almost limitless and what follows is merely illustrative, a selection of a selection, drawn from my own teaching.

A COURSE DESCRIPTION

Globalisation and Law[3]

This seminar will explore issues of legal theory from a global perspective. We shall consider the implications of globalisation and interdependence for the ideas of mainstream Anglo-American jurists (such as Bentham,

---

2   A convenient source of short introductions to older Anglo-American jurists (all dead), including Bentham, Austin, Holmes, Kelsen, and Llewellyn, is A W B Simpson, *Biographical Dictionary of the Common Law* (1983). Neil MacCormick, *H L A Hart* (1981) and Stephen Guest, *Ronald Dworkin* (2nd edn, 1997) are useful for reference.

3   Although the course is explicitly theoretical, the title is a concession to many law students' aversion to courses with 'theory' in the title.

Hart, Llewellyn, Dworkin, and Rawls) and for recent writings on legal pluralism, human rights, and feminist jurisprudence. We shall also consider critically some of the basic assumptions underlying selected writings about some transnational fields, such as comparative law, European Union Law, public international law, and human rights. Assessment will be by one substantial paper (or two shorter ones) on a topic approved by the instructor.

Exercises

(i)   The Newspaper Exercise

Buy a weekday edition of a leading national newspaper, eg *The Times*, *The Independent*, *The Guardian*, *Financial Times*, or The *Daily Telegraph* (or in USA, *The New York Times* or *the Herald Tribune* or *Newsweek*). Read the *whole* paper and mark any item that involves Global (G, including space), Transnational (T), International (I), Regional (R), non-state local (L), or foreign domestic (F) relations that might have legal implications involving some legal order(s) other than United Kingdom/ American state or federal municipal law. Before starting define what you mean by 'legal order' for the purpose of this exercise.

(ii)   Mapping

a.   draw a map of the main legal orders in the world in [2000];
b.   draw an historical chart of the rise (and fall) of the main legal cultures in the world;
c.   what is the basis for a and b and what is the relationship between them?
d.   what difficulties have you encountered in doing this exercise?

(iii)   Normative and Legal Pluralism and Non-state Law

Write a list of *all* of the main normative and legal orders that you have encountered in the past 24 hours (eg rules of football, conventions of English spelling, international human rights law, home rules on TV watching, Road Traffic Law, the law of contract).

or

Write down in chronological order the 20 main transactions and relations in which you were involved during the past week (eg bought a newspaper, violated 'fair copying' restrictions, roller bladed in the park, advised on a petition for political asylum, attended a tutorial on renvoi and a lecture on European Union Law, e-mailed boyfriend in Hong Kong). Identify the main legal and other normative orders relevant to each of these transactions and events.

(iv)   What Counts as a 'Legal Order'?

Consider critically the theoretical basis of claims for and against treating the following as viable and distinctive legal orders or regimes:
(i)   European Union Law;
(ii)   lex mercatoria;
(iii)   ius humanitatis;
(iv)   the social control system of an outlawed guerrilla organisation or an 'illegal' squatter settlement or a pirate ship;
(v)   the internal regime of a large multinational corporation;
(vi)   the common law;
(vii)   Islamic law;
(viii) Classical Roman Law;
(ix)   Canon Law.

(v)   Restructuring Nusquamia[4]

You are a member of an international team charged with assessing the extent to which the national legal system of Nusquamia conforms to orthodox standards of 'human rights, good governance, and the rule of law' as part of a programme of 'restructuring' backed by an international consortium of donors. To what extent does this remit involve commitment to a particular theory of law? To what extent can local historical, cultural, economic, and ideological factors be treated as relevant in making this assessment? Who is qualified to advise?

For further exercises See Ch 6.4(b) and (d).

---

4   For this exercise a special set of materials and readings on 'The Jurisprudence of the World Bank' is provided.

SUGGESTED READINGS[5]

Chapter I

Globalisation (Ch. 1.2)

Santos, Ch 4 (esp pp 250-281)

Paul Hirst and Grahame Thompson, 'Globalization – A Necessary Myth?' from *Globalization in Question*, (1996) Ch 1, 17 or Paul Hirst and Grahame Thompson, 'Globalisation: Ten Frequently Asked Questions and Some Surprising Answers' (1996) 4 Soundings 47 (Issue on The Public Good).

David Trubek et al, 'Global Restructuring and the Law' in symposium on the Future of the Legal Profession, (1994) 44 Case Western Law Review 407.

The Scope and Functions of Legal Theory (Ch 1.3 and Ch 2)

H L A Hart, 'Definition and Theory in Jurisprudence' (1953) 70 LQR 37.

Lon Fuller, 'The Case of the Speluncean Explorers', (1949) 62 Harvard Law Review 616.[6]

William Twining, 'The Great Juristic Bazaar', (1978) 14 JSPTL (NS) 185.

LIC, Ch 7.

Non-state Law and Normative and Legal Pluralism (Chs 3.5 and 8.4(b))

General

Santos, pp 111-122, 234-243.

John Griffiths, 'What is Legal Pluralism?' (1986) Journal of Legal Pluralism 24(M).

Sally M Merry, 'Legal Pluralism' (1988) 22 Law and Society Review 869-896.

G Teubner 'Two Faces of Janus; Rethinking Legal Pluralism' (1992) 13 Cardozo Law Review 1443.

H Kelsen, 'The Pure Theory of Law and Analytical Jurisprudence', (1941) 55 Harvard Law Review 44-70 or 'Law, State, and Justice in

---

5   For additions and alternatives see the footnotes to each chapter. More detailed information about the course may be obtained from the author.

6   Also in many anthologies. This is a good vehicle for discussing different conceptions of jurisprudence (see *LIC*, pp 213-217) and it links nicely with Seidman's 'The Inarticulate Premiss' (below) which is still useful for discussing state legal pluralism, even though it is dated. Both are included in James Allan's anthology, *The Speluncean Case* (1999).

the Pure Theory of Law' (1947-8) 57 Yale Law Journal 377, both reprinted in H Kelsen, *What is Justice?* (1957).

Case Studies[7]

Pasagarda, Santos, pp 124-249.
Recife, Santos, Ch 5 and pp 471-472.
The Otieno Burial Case, see Ch 8, n 000.
Cf R Seidman, 'The Inarticulate Premiss' (1965) 3 Journal Modern African Studies 567-87.
The Common Law Movement, Susan Koniak, 'When Law Risks Madness' (1996) 8 Cardozo Studies in Law and Literature 65; cf S Koniak (1997) 95 Michigan Law Review 1761 (and references there).
Gypsies, W Weyrauch and J Bell, 'Autonomous Lawmaking: The Case of the Gypsies' (1993) 103 Yale Law Journal 323 and Symposium on Gypsy Law (Romaniya) American Journal of Comparative Law 2.
The Pinochet Case, R v Bow Street Metropolitan Stipendiary Magistrate and others, ex p Pinochet Ugarte (No 3) [1999] 2 All. E R 97 (cf [1998] 4 All E R 897 (vacated) and commentaries on the case).

The Anglo-American canon: classic texts (Chapters 2-5)

Ch 2.2(a) and Ch 4.   J Bentham, extracts from *Fragment on Government* (various eds) and *Principles of International Law* (Bowring ed, 1838-43).[8]
Ch 2(b).   J Austin, *The Province of Jurisprudence Determined* Lecture 1 (1832) or 'The Uses of the Study of Jurisprudence' (1863, ed Hart, 1954).
Ch 2.4 and Ch 3.4(a).   H L A Hart, Postscript to *The Concept of Law* (1994). R Dworkin, 'The Model of Rules', (1967) 35 University Chicago Law Review 14 and/or *Law's Empire*, Chs 6 and 7.
Ch 3.4(b).   *Extent and International Ethics.* C Beitz, M Cohen, T Scanlon, and A J Simmons (eds) *International ethics: A Philosophy and Public*

---

7   There is a vast number of possible case studies to choose from. See, for example, Alison D Rentelm and Alan Dundes (eds), *Folk Law* (1994), (2 vols) and the *Journal of Legal Pluralism*. In addition to specific case studies, I usually arrange for short oral presentations on *lex mercatoria, ius humanitatis* (the common heritage of mankind), European Union Law, Mafia law, and 'Is the common law "law"?'.
8   Other possibles are 'Pannomial Fragments' and/or 'Of Time and Place in Legislation' (both in the Bowring edition of the *Works*) and/or Chs 1-6 of *Introduction to the Principles of Morals and Legislation* (various editions, the paperback version from the *Collected Works* with Introductions by F Rosen and H L A Hart is especially recommended).

Affairs Reader (1985) (Part V, articles by Singer, O'Neill, and Beitz. In addition, Part IV, Walzer and Luban).[9]

Ch 3.4(c).   J Rawls, *A Theory of Justice* (1971) (sections on international relations); 'The Law of Peoples', in Stephen Shute and Susan Hurley (eds), *On Human Rights* (1993). See also *Political Liberalism* (1993).[10]

Ch 3.3(d).   K N Llewellyn, 'The Normative, the Legal and the Law-Jobs' (1940-41) 49 Yale Law Journal 1355-1400 (or 'My Philosophy of Law' (from *My Philosophy of Law* (1941)).

Ch 5.   O W Holmes Jr 'The Path of the Law' (1897). Laura Nader, 'A User Theory of Law' (1984) 38 Southwestern Law Journal 951.

Ch 6.   (To be read *after* Exercise 1 and 2). Santos, Ch 7.

Ch 7 *Comparative Law*.[11]   Zweigert and Kotz, *Introduction to Comparative Law* (2nd ed, 1998) Ch 5; Basil Markesenis, *Foreign Law and Comparative Methodology* Ch 2 (1997); John Bell, 'English Law and French Law – Not So Different?' (1995) 48 CLP 63 or 'Comparative Law and Legal Theory' in W Krawietz et al, *Prescriptive Formality and Normative Rationality in Modern Legal Systems* (1994) p 19ff.

Law firms (for larger classes)

In order to distribute the load and to bring a variety of expertise and perspectives to bear on our discussions, you are asked to form law firms of not less than two and not more than four partners by the time of the third meeting. Each law firm is based in London or a major city in the United States, but has recently opened two branch offices, one in a core or semi-peripheral country and one in a 'South' country. In addition each firm has as clients one canonical jurist and one other theorist of your choice, whom you will be prepared to defend against charges of parochialism, irrelevance, incoherence, narrowness etc. We need to have a reasonable spread of countries and of jurists, but within that constraint you are encouraged to be guided by your own interests.

---

9   Further readings include Peter Singer, *Practical Ethics* (2nd edn 1993) Chs 8 and 9; Onora O'Neill, *The Faces of Hunger* (1986).

10   John Rawls, *The Law of Peoples* (1999) was published after this book went to press.

11   For references to 'internal critics' such as Legrand, Ewald, and Watson, see notes to Ch 7.

Index